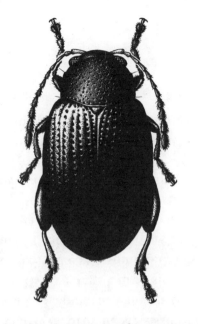

Common Names of Insects & Related Organisms 1989

Manya B. Stoetzel, Chairman
Committee on Common Names of Insects

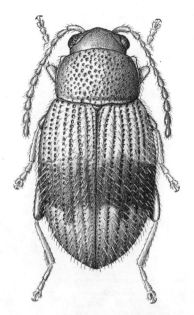

corn flea beetle
Chaetocnema pulicaria Melsheimer
COLEOPTERA: Chrysomelidae

tobacco flea beetle
Epitrix hirtipennis (Melsheimer)
COLEOPTERA: Chrysomelidae

ISBN 0-938522-34-5

D0904697

ESA Standing Committee on Common Names of Insects, 1988–1989

John W. Beardsley, University of Hawaii, Honolulu, Hawaii

Richard L. Brown, Mississippi State University, Mississippi State, Miss.

John L. Capinera, University of Florida, Gainesville, Fla.

Paul H. Freytag, University of Kentucky, Lexington, Ky.

Keith S. Pike, Washington State University, Prosser, Wash.

Carl W. Schaefer, University of Connecticut, Storrs, Conn.

Manya B. Stoetzel (chairman), Systematic Entomology Laboratory, PSI, ARS, USDA, Beltsville, Md.

Richard E. White (3 months), Systematic Entomology Laboratory, PSI, ARS, USDA, Washington, D.C.

Robert E. Woodruff (9 months), Florida Department of Agriculture, Gainesville, Fla.

Thomas R. Yonke, University of Missouri, Columbia, Mo.

Contents

Common Names of Insects
& Related Organisms
1989

Approved by the Entomological Society of America
Manya B. Stoetzel, *Chairman, Committee on Common Names of Insects*

Introduction

The American Association of Economic Entomologists (AAEE) was founded in 1889, and in 1903 AAEE established a Committee on Nomenclature. The first compilation of previously approved common names was published by AAEE in 1908 and contained 142 common names. Subsequently, 13 more lists have been published at irregular intervals. The Entomological Society of America (ESA) was founded in 1906 and established a Standing Committee on Nomenclature in 1907. The two organizations merged in 1953 under the name Entomological Society of America, and the duties and methods of electing the ESA Standing Committee on Common Names of Insects are outlined in Article V, Sections 1, 2, 3, and 6 of the Bylaws of the ESA Constitution. As the society celebrates the 100th anniversary of the founding of AAEE, it is fitting and timely that this updated 15th list be published as part of the centennial activities.

Standardized common names are useful when communicating with the public and with other entomologists. Of the 2,018 common names of insects in this list, the order Lepidoptera (butterflies and moths) has the most entries with 495, Coleoptera (beetles) has 478, and Homoptera (aphids, scale insects, hoppers, and allies) has 320. Among the various families of insects, the family Curculionidae (weevils) has the most entries with 121, and the Aphididae (aphids) is second with 103. In addition to insects, there are common names for 131 mites and ticks, 12 snails and slugs, 9 spiders, and 7 other noninsects.

Authors of papers submitted to ESA may use only ESA-approved common names of insects in their manuscripts. The committee has developed a proposal form, which is included at the end of this book and is published once a year (May or June) in the *ESA Newsletter*.

Individuals and committees have contributed to the establishment of basic rules and suggestions for the formation of common names. Informative articles have been written by Metcalf (1942. Common names of insects. J. Econ. Entomol. 35: 795–797), Gurney (1953. An appeal for a clearer understanding of principles concerning the use of common names. J. Econ. Entomol. 46: 207–211), and Chapin (1989. Common names of insects. Bull. Entomol. Soc. Am. 35(3): 177–180).

Rules and Regulations

1. Included species, in most cases, will inhabit the United States, Canada, or their possessions and territories. In special cases, other species may be added.

2. The list is intended to include those insects and other invertebrates commonly of concern to entomologists because of their economic or medical importance, striking appearance, abundant occurrence, or endangered status, or for any other sufficient reason.

3. A common name should consist of three words or fewer, but four are permissible if reasons are sufficient.

4. Most names have two parts, one indicating the family or group, and the other a modifier. In the case of names having two parts with one of them being a group name as given in Section IV, the group name will be a separate word when used in a sense that is systematically correct, as in "house fly" and "bed bug." If the group name used is not systematically correct, it must be combined in a single word with a modifier as in "citrus whitefly" and "citrus mealybug." The modifying part of the name should be based on some outstanding characteristic of the insect itself, its damage, host, or distribu-

tion. Hyphens between modifying words should be used only if the meaning is otherwise obscure.   .

5. The use of parts of the scientific name in the common name is undesirable unless the words involved are well established by usage as a common name.

6. Nongeographic, proper names will be in the nominative.

7. Only in special cases should a species have more than one common name.

8. In cases of insects warranting special concern in both larval and adult stages, the preferable name should be one suggested by the appearance or habits of the more important or better known stage or the one for which usage has become more established.

9. In all cases involving the adoption of new common names or changes in those previously established, the fullest consideration should be given to past usage and probable future usage. When practical, the opinions of entomologists experienced with the insects concerned should be obtained before names are proposed. Members who wish to recommend new names or changes in existing names should accept the responsibility for making the necessary investigation. All available evidence, both for and against, concerning the need for each proposed name should accompany the proposal when it is submitted to the committe chairman.

Committee Procedures

The committee has developed a proposal form, which is included at the back of this book and published once a year (May or June) in the *ESA Newsletter*. Proposal forms should be sent to ESA headquarters or to the committee chairman, whose responsibility it is to prepare proposals and ballots for committee consideration. Currently, proposals are sent to the committee during the first week of each month. Proposed common names receiving committee approval (at least seven of the nine members of the committee must approve a proposal for it to pass) are published in the *ESA Newsletter*. Any ESA member disapproving a proposed common name is requested to submit objections and evidence opposing the proposal to the committee in the 30-day period after publication. If substantial objections to a proposed common name are received, the committee reconsiders the case and makes a final decision (at least seven of the nine members of the committee must vote to override the objection). Notice of final adoption or rejection of the proposed common name is published in the *ESA Newsletter*. A summary of adopted common names is published yearly in the *Bulletin* and in the *ESA Newsletter*. The essential features of the foregoing procedures are provided for by the ESA Bylaws, Article V, Section 6.

Arrangement of Names

Section I.	common name	scientific name	order: family
Section II.	scientific name	common name	order: family
Section III.	order: family	scientific name	common name
Section IV.	phyllum, class, order, and family names		

Acknowledgments

The cover illustration of the boxelder bug, *Boisea trivittata* (Say), was drawn by F. Eugene Wood, Department of Entomology, University of Maryland, College Park, Md. The title page illustrations of the corn flea beetle, *Chaetocnema pulicaria* Melsheimer, and the tobacco flea beetle, *Epitrix hirtipennis* (Melsheimer), were drawn by committee member Richard E. White.

The scientific names in this list have been checked by systematists in various institutions. The committee gratefully appreciates the help of the following systematists in the Systematic Entomology Laboratory, Agriculture Research Service, U.S. Department of Agriculture and located in the U.S National Museum of Natural History, Washington, D.C. (SEL-ARS-USDA-NMNH) or at the Beltsville Agricultural Research Center, Beltsville, Md. (SEL-ARS-USDA-BARC) and in the Department of Entomology, U.S. National Museum of Natural History, Washington, D.C. (NMNH-SI): Donald M. Anderson (Coleoptera) SEL-ARS-USDA-NMNH, Edward W. Baker (Acari) SEL-ARS-USDA-BARC retired, John M. Burns (Lepidoptera) NMNH-SI, Jonathan Coddington (Myriapods and Arachnids) NMNH-SI, Donald R. Davis (Lepidoptera) NMNH-SI, Terry L. Erwin (Coleoptera)

NMNH-SI, Douglas C. Ferguson (Lepidoptera) SEL-ARS-USDA-NMNH, Oliver S. Flint, Jr. (neuropteroids) NMNH-SI, Raymond J. Gagne (Diptera) SEL-ARS-USDA-NMNH, Robert D. Gordon (Coleoptera) SEL-ARS-USDA-NMNH, E. Eric Grissell (Hymenoptera) SEL-ARS-USDA-NMNH, Thomas J. Henry (Heteroptera) SEL-ARS-USDA-NMNH, Ronald W. Hodges (Lepidoptera) SEL-ARS-USDA-NMNH, John M. Kingsolver (Coleoptera) SEL-ARS-USDA-BARC, Paul M. Marsh (Hymenoptera) SEL-ARS-USDA-NMNH, Wayne N. Mathis (Diptera) NMNH-SI, Ronald J. McGinley (Hymenoptera) SEL-ARS-USDA-NMNH, Arnold S. Menke (Hymenoptera) SEL-ARS-USDA-NMNH, Sueo Nakahara (Thysanoptera) SEL-ARS-USDA-BARC, David A. Nickle (orthopteroids) SEL-ARS-USDA-NMNH, Allen L. Norrbom (Diptera) SEL-ARS-USDA-NMNH, Robert V. Peterson (Diptera) SEL-ARS-USDA-NMNH, Robert W. Poole (Lepidoptera) SEL-ARS-USDA-NMNH, Louise M. Russell (Homoptera) SEL-ARS-USDA-BARC, Michael E. Schauff (Hymenoptera) SEL-ARS-USDA-NMNH, Robert L. Smiley (Acari) SEL-ARS-USDA-BARC, David R. Smith (Hymenoptera), SEL-ARS-USDA-NMNH, Theodore J. Spilman (Coleoptera) SEL-ARS-USDA-NMNH, Manya B. Stoetzel (Homoptera) SEL-ARS-USDA-BARC, F. Christian Thompson (Diptera) SEL-ARS-USDA-NMNH, Richard E. White (Coleoptera) SEL-ARS-USDA-NMNH, Donald R. Whitehead (Coleoptera) SEL-ARS-NMNH, Norman E. Woodley (Diptera) SEL-ARS-USDA-NMNH.

The committee appreciates the help of the following additional systematists: Victor L. Blackburn (Homoptera) Plant Protection and Quarantine, USDA, Beltsville, Md.; Lewis Deitz (Homoptera) Department of Entomology, North Carolina State University, Raleigh, N.C.; K. C. Emerson (Anoplura & Mallophaga) 560 Bolder Drive, Sanibel, Fla.; Andy Hamilton (Homoptera) Biosystematics Research Institute, Agriculture Canada, Ottawa, Ont., Canada; Edward L. Mockford (Psocoptera) Department of Biological Sciences, Illinois State University, Normal, Ill.; Lois B. O'Brien (Homoptera) Florida Agricultural and Mechanical University, Tallahassee, Fla.; Paul W. Oman (Homoptera) Department of Entomology, Oregon State University, Corvallis, Oreg.; Robert Traub (Siphonaptera) Museum Support Center, Smithsonian Institution, Suitland, Md.; and Robert D. Waltz (Collembola) Division of Entomology, Indiana Department of Natural Resources, Indianapolis, Ind.

The committee also thanks the members of the staff at ESA headquarters for their help in producing this publication.

Section I. Insects and Related Organisms Listed by Common Name

A

abbreviated wireworm	*Hypolithus abbreviatus* (Say)	COLEOPTERA: Elateridae
acacia psyllid	*Acizzia uncatoides* (Ferris & Klyver)	HOMOPTERA: Psyllidae
achemon sphinx	*Eumorpha achemon* (Drury)	LEPIDOPTERA: Sphingidae
acuminate scale	*Kilifia acuminata* (Signoret)	HOMOPTERA: Coccidae
acute-angled fungus beetle	*Cryptophagus acutangulus* Gyllenhal	COLEOPTERA: Cryptophagidae
aerial yellowjacket	*Dolichovespula arenaria* (Fabricius)	HYMENOPTERA: Vespidae
African mole cricket	*Gryllotalpa africana* Palisot de Beauvois	ORTHOPTERA: Gryllotalpidae
ailanthus webworm	*Atteva punctella* (Cramer)	LEPIDOPTERA: Yponomeutidae
alder bark beetle	*Alniphagus aspericollis* (LeConte)	COLEOPTERA: Scolytidae
alder flea beetle	*Macrohaltica ambiens* (LeConte)	COLEOPTERA: Chrysomelidae
alder spittlebug	*Clastoptera obtusa* (Say)	HOMOPTERA: Cercopidae
alfalfa blotch leafminer	*Agromyza frontella* (Rondani)	DIPTERA: Agromyzidae
alfalfa caterpillar	*Colias eurytheme* Boisduval	LEPIDOPTERA: Pieridae
alfalfa gall midge	*Asphondylia websteri* Felt	DIPTERA: Cecidomyiidae
alfalfa leafcutting bee	*Megachile rotundata* (Fabricius)	HYMENOPTERA: Megachilidae
alfalfa leaftier	*Dichomeris acuminata* (Standinger)	LEPIDOPTERA: Gelechiidae
alfalfa looper	*Autographa californica* (Speyer)	LEPIDOPTERA: Noctuidae
alfalfa plant bug	*Adelphocoris lineolatus* (Goeze)	HETEROPTERA: Miridae
alfalfa seed chalcid	*Bruchophagus roddi* (Gussakovsky)	HYMENOPTERA: Eurytomidae
alfalfa snout beetle	*Otiorhynchus ligustici* (Linnaeus)	COLEOPTERA: Curculionidae
alfalfa webworm	*Loxostege cereralis* (Zeller)	LEPIDOPTERA: Pyralidae
alfalfa weevil	*Hypera postica* (Gyllenhal)	COLEOPTERA: Curculionidae
alkali bee	*Nomia melanderi* Cockerell	HYMENOPTERA: Halictidae
Allegheny mound ant	*Formica exsectoides* Forel	HYMENOPTERA: Formicidae
Allegheny spruce beetle	*Dendroctonus punctatus* LeConte	COLEOPTERA: Scolytidae
almond moth	*Cadra cautella* (Walker)	LEPIDOPTERA: Pyralidae
aloe mite	*Eriophyes aloinis* Keifer	ACARI: Eriophyidae
American aspen beetle	*Gonioctena americana* (Schaeffer)	COLEOPTERA: Chrysomelidae
American black flour beetle	*Tribolium audax* Halstead	COLEOPTERA: Tenebrionidae
American cockroach	*Periplaneta americana* (Linnaeus)	BLATTODEA: Blattidae
American dagger moth	*Acronicta americana* (Harris)	LEPIDOPTERA: Noctuidae

Common name	Scientific name	Order: Family
American dog tick	Dermacentor variabilis (Say)	ACARI: Ixodidae
American grasshopper	Schistocerca americana (Drury)	ORTHOPTERA: Acrididae
American hornet moth	Sesia tibialis (Harris)	LEPIDOPTERA: Sesiidae
American house dust mite	Dermatophagoides farinae Hughes	ACARI: Epidermoptidae
American palm cixiid	Myndus crudus Van Duzee	HOMOPTERA: Cixiidae
American plum borer	Euzophera semifuneralis (Walker)	LEPIDOPTERA: Pyralidae
American spider beetle	Mezium americanum (Laporte)	COLEOPTERA: Ptinidae
Angora goat biting louse	Bovicola crassipes (Rudow)	MALLOPHAGA: Trichodectidae
Angoumois grain moth	Sitotroga cerealella (Olivier)	LEPIDOPTERA: Gelechiidae
angularwinged katydid	Microcentrum retinerve (Burmeister)	ORTHOPTERA: Tettigoniidae
angulate leafhopper	Acinopterus angulatus Lawson	HOMOPTERA: Cicadellidae
apple-and-thorn skeletonizer	Choreutis pariana (Clerck)	LEPIDOPTERA: Choreutidae
apple aphid	Aphis pomi De Geer	HOMOPTERA: Aphididae
apple bark borer	Synanthedon pyri (Harris)	LEPIDOPTERA: Sesiidae
apple barkminer	Marmara elotella (Busck)	LEPIDOPTERA: Gracillariidae
apple blotch leafminer	Phyllonorycter crataegella (Clemens)	LEPIDOPTERA: Gracillariidae
apple curculio	Tachypterellus quadrigibbus (Say)	COLEOPTERA: Curculionidae
apple flea weevil	Rhynchaenus pallicornis (Say)	COLEOPTERA: Curculionidae
apple fruit moth	Argyresthia conjugella Zeller	LEPIDOPTERA: Argyresthiidae
apple fruitminer	Marmara pomonella Busck	LEPIDOPTERA: Gracillariidae
apple grain aphid	Rhopalosiphum fitchii (Sanderson)	HOMOPTERA: Aphididae
apple leafhopper	Empoasca maligna (Walsh)	HOMOPTERA: Cicadellidae
apple maggot	Rhagoletis pomonella (Walsh)	DIPTERA: Tephritidae
apple mealybug	Phenacoccus aceris (Signoret)	HOMOPTERA: Pseudococcidae
apple red bug	Lygidea mendax Reuter	HETEROPTERA: Miridae
apple rust mite	Aculus schlechtendali (Nalepa)	ACARI: Eriophyidae
apple seed chalcid	Torymus varians (Walker)	HYMENOPTERA: Torymidae
apple sucker	Cacopsylla mali (Schmidberger)	HOMOPTERA: Psyllidae
apple twig beetle	Hypothenemus obscurus (Fabricius)	COLEOPTERA: Scolytidae
apple twig borer	Amphicerus bicaudatus (Say)	COLEOPTERA: Bostrichidae
appleleaf skeletonizer	Psorosina hammondi (Riley)	LEPIDOPTERA: Pyralidae
appleleaf trumpet miner	Tischeria malifoliella Clemens	LEPIDOPTERA: Tischeriidae
araucaria aphid	Neophyllaphis araucariae Takahashi	HOMOPTERA: Aphididae
arborvitae leafminer	Argyresthia thuiella (Packard)	LEPIDOPTERA: Argyresthiidae
arborvitae weevil	Phyllobius intrusus Kôno	COLEOPTERA: Curculionidae
Argentine ant	Iridomyrmex humilis (Mayr)	HYMENOPTERA: Formicidae
argus tortoise beetle	Chelymorpha cassidea (Fabricius)	COLEOPTERA: Chrysomelidae
army cutworm	Euxoa auxiliaris (Grote)	LEPIDOPTERA: Noctuidae

armyworm	*Pseudaletia unipuncta* (Haworth)	LEPIDOPTERA: Noctuidae
artichoke plume moth	*Platyptilia carduidactyla* (Riley)	LEPIDOPTERA: Pterophoridae
ash borer[1]	*Podosesia syringae* (Harris)	LEPIDOPTERA: Sesiidae
ash plant bug	*Tropidosteptes amoenus* Reuter	HETEROPTERA: Miridae
ashgray blister beetle	*Epicauta fabricii* (LeConte)	COLEOPTERA: Meloidae
Asian cockroach	*Blattella asahinai* Mizukubo	BLATTODEA: Blattellidae
Asiatic garden beetle	*Maladera castanea* (Arrow)	COLEOPTERA: Scarabaeidae
Asiatic oak weevil	*Cyrtepistomus castaneus* (Roelofs)	COLEOPTERA: Curculionidae
Asiatic rice borer	*Chilo suppressalis* (Walker)	LEPIDOPTERA: Pyralidae
Asiatic rose scale	*Aulacaspis rosarum* Borchsenius	HOMOPTERA: Diaspididae
asparagus aphid	*Brachycorynella asparagi* (Mordvilko)	HOMOPTERA: Aphididae
asparagus beetle	*Crioceris asparagi* (Linnaeus)	COLEOPTERA: Chrysomelidae
asparagus miner	*Ophiomyia simplex* (Loew)	DIPTERA: Agromyzidae
asparagus spider mite	*Schizotetranychus asparagi* (Oudemans)	ACARI: Tetranychidae
aspen blotchminer	*Phyllonorycter tremuloidiella* (Braun)	LEPIDOPTERA: Gracillariidae
aspen leaf beetle	*Chrysomela crotchi* Brown	COLEOPTERA: Chrysomelidae
aster leafhopper	*Macrosteles quadrilineatus* Forbes	HOMOPTERA: Cicadellidae
aster leafminer	*Calycomyza humeralis* (Roser)	DIPTERA: Agromyzidae
Australian cockroach	*Periplaneta australasiae* (Fabricius)	BLATTODEA: Blattidae
Australian fern weevil	*Syagrius fulvitarsis* Pascoe	COLEOPTERA: Curculionidae
Australian mantid	*Tenodera australasiae* (Leach)	MANTODEA: Mantidae
Australian rat flea	*Xenopsylla vexabilis* (Jordan)	SIPHONAPTERA: Pulicidae
Australian spider beetle	*Ptinus ocellus* Brown	COLEOPTERA: Ptinidae
Australianpine borer	*Chrysobothris tranquebarica* (Gmelin)	COLEOPTERA: Buprestidae
avocado brown mite	*Oligonychus punicae* (Hirst)	ACARI: Tetranychidae
avocado red mite	*Oligonychus yothersi* (McGregor)	ACARI: Tetranychidae
avocado whitefly	*Trialeurodes floridensis* (Quaintance)	HOMOPTERA: Aleyrodidae
azalea bark scale	*Eriococcus azaleae* Comstock	HOMOPTERA: Eriococcidae
azalea caterpillar	*Datana major* Grote & Robinson	LEPIDOPTERA: Notodontidae
azalea lace bug	*Stephanitis pyrioides* (Scott)	HETEROPTERA: Tingidae
azalea leafminer	*Caloptilia azaleella* (Brants)	LEPIDOPTERA: Gracillariidae
azalea plant bug	*Rhinocapsus vanduzeei* Uhler	HETEROPTERA: Miridae
azalea white mite	*Eotetranychus clitus* Pritchard & Baker	ACARI: Tetranychidae
azalea whitefly	*Pealius azaleae* (Baker & Moles)	HOMOPTERA: Aleyrodidae

---

[1]Also called lilac borer.

bagworm	*Thyridopteryx ephemeraeformis* (Haworth)	LEPIDOPTERA: Psychidae
Bahaman swallowtail	*Papilio andraemon bonhotei* Sharpe	LEPIDOPTERA: Papilionidae
baldcypress coneworm	*Dioryctria pygmaeella* Ragonot	LEPIDOPTERA: Pyralidae
baldfaced hornet	*Dolichovespula maculata* (Linnaeus)	HYMENOPTERA: Vespidae
balsam fir sawfly	*Neodiprion abietis* (Harris)	HYMENOPTERA: Diprionidae
balsam fir sawyer	*Monochamus marmorator* Kirby	COLEOPTERA: Cerambycidae
balsam gall midge	*Paradiplosis tumifex* Gagné	DIPTERA: Cecidomyiidae
balsam shootboring sawfly	*Pleroneura brunneicornis* Rohwer	HYMENOPTERA: Xyelidae
balsam twig aphid	*Mindarus abietinus* Koch	HOMOPTERA: Aphididae
balsam woolly adelgid	*Adelges piceae* (Ratzeburg)	HOMOPTERA: Adelgidae
bamboo borer	*Chlorophorus annularis* (Fabricius)	COLEOPTERA: Cerambycidae
bamboo mealybug	*Chaetococcus bambusae* (Maskell)	HOMOPTERA: Pseudococcidae
bamboo powderpost beetle	*Dinoderus minutus* (Fabricius)	COLEOPTERA: Bostrichidae
bamboo spider mite	*Schizotetranychus celarius* (Banks)	ACARI: Tetranychidae
banana aphid	*Pentalonia nigronervosa* Coquerel	HOMOPTERA: Aphididae
banana root borer	*Cosmopolites sordidus* (Germar)	COLEOPTERA: Curculionidae
banana skipper	*Erionota thrax* (Linnaeus)	LEPIDOPTERA: Hesperiidae
banded alder borer	*Rosalia funebris* Motschulsky	COLEOPTERA: Cerambycidae
banded ash clearwing	*Podosesia aureocincta* Purrington & Nielsen	LEPIDOPTERA: Sesiidae
banded cucumber beetle	*Diabrotica balteata* LeConte	COLEOPTERA: Chrysomelidae
banded greenhouse thrips	*Hercinothrips femoralis* (O.M. Reuter)	THYSANOPTERA: Thripidae
banded hickory borer	*Knulliana cincta* (Drury)	COLEOPTERA: Cerambycidae
banded sunflower moth	*Cochylis hospes* Walsingham	LEPIDOPTERA: Cochylidae
banded wood snail	*Cepaea nemoralis* (Linnaeus)	STYLOMMATOPHORA: Helicidae
banded woollybear	*Pyrrharctia isabella* (J.E. Smith)	LEPIDOPTERA: Arctiidae
bandedwinged whitefly	*Trialeurodes abutilonea* (Haldeman)	HOMOPTERA: Aleyrodidae
Banks grass mite	*Oligonychus pratensis* (Banks)	ACARI: Tetranychidae
banyan aphid	*Thoracaphis fici* (Takahashi)	HOMOPTERA: Aphididae
Barber brown lacewing	*Sympherobius barberi* (Banks)	NEUROPTERA: Hemerobiidae
barberpole caterpillar	*Mimoschinia rufofascialis* (Stephens)	LEPIDOPTERA: Pyralidae
barley jointworm	*Tetramesa hordei* (Harris)	HYMENOPTERA: Eurytomidae
barnacle scale	*Ceroplastes cirripediformis* Comstock	HOMOPTERA: Coccidae
basswood lace bug	*Gargaphia tiliae* (Walsh)	HETEROPTERA: Tingidae
basswood leafminer	*Baliosus nervosus* (Panzer)	COLEOPTERA: Chrysomelidae
basswood leafroller	*Pantographa limata* Grote & Robinson	LEPIDOPTERA: Pyralidae

beachgrass scale	*Eriococcus carolinae* Williams	HOMOPTERA: Eriococcidae
bean aphid	*Aphis fabae* Scopoli	HOMOPTERA: Aphididae
bean butterfly	*Lampides boeticus* (Linnaeus)	LEPIDOPTERA: Lycaenidae
bean capsid	*Pycnoderes quadrimaculatus* Guérin-Méneville	HETEROPTERA: Miridae
bean fly	*Ophiomyia phaseoli* (Tryon)	DIPTERA: Agromyzidae
bean leaf beetle	*Cerotoma trifurcata* (Forster)	COLEOPTERA: Chrysomelidae
bean leafroller	*Urbanus proteus* (Linnaeus)	LEPIDOPTERA: Hesperiidae
bean leafskeletonizer	*Autoplusia egena* (Guenée)	LEPIDOPTERA: Noctuidae
bean pod borer	*Maruca testulalis* (Geyer)	LEPIDOPTERA: Pyralidae
bean seed maggot	*Delia florilega* (Zetterstedt)	DIPTERA: Anthomyiidae
bean stalk weevil	*Sternechus paludatus* (Casey)	COLEOPTERA: Curculionidae
bean thrips	*Caliothrips fasciatus* (Pergande)	THYSANOPTERA: Thripidae
bean weevil	*Acanthoscelides obtectus* (Say)	COLEOPTERA: Bruchidae
Beardsley leafhopper	*Balclutha saltuella* (Kirschbaum)	HOMOPTERA: Cicadellidae
bed bug	*Cimex lectularius* Linnaeus	HETEROPTERA: Cimicidae
beech blight aphid	*Fagiphagus imbricator* (Fitch)	HOMOPTERA: Aphididae
beech scale	*Cryptococcus fagisuga* Lindinger	HOMOPTERA: Eriococcidae
beet armyworm	*Spodoptera exigua* (Hübner)	LEPIDOPTERA: Noctuidae
beet leaf beetle	*Erynephala puncticollis* (Say)	COLEOPTERA: Chrysomelidae
beet leafhopper	*Circulifer tenellus* (Baker)	HOMOPTERA: Cicadellidae
beet leafminer	*Pegomya betae* Curtis	DIPTERA: Anthomyiidae
beet webworm	*Loxostege sticticalis* (Linnaeus)	LEPIDOPTERA: Pyralidae
bella moth	*Utetheisa bella* (Linnaeus)	LEPIDOPTERA: Arctiidae
Bermudagrass mite	*Eriophyes cynodoniensis* Sayed	ACARI: Eriophyidae
bertha armyworm	*Mamestra configurata* Walker	LEPIDOPTERA: Noctuidae
bidens borer	*Epiblema otiosana* (Clemens)	LEPIDOPTERA: Tortricidae
bigheaded ant	*Pheidole megacephala* (Fabricius)	HYMENOPTERA: Formicidae
bigheaded grasshopper	*Aulocara elliotti* (Thomas)	ORTHOPTERA: Acrididae
birch bark beetle	*Dryocoetes betulae* Hopkins	COLEOPTERA: Scolytidae
birch casebearer[2]	*Coleophora serratella* (Linnaeus)	LEPIDOPTERA: Coleophoridae
birch leafminer	*Fenusa pusilla* (Lepeletier)	HYMENOPTERA: Tenthredinidae
birch sawfly	*Arge pectoralis* (Leach)	HYMENOPTERA: Argidae
birch skeletonizer	*Bucculatrix canadensisella* Chambers	LEPIDOPTERA: Lyonetiidae
birch tubemaker	*Acrobasis betulella* Hulst	LEPIDOPTERA: Pyralidae
bird cherry-oat aphid	*Rhopalosiphum padi* (Linnaeus)	HOMOPTERA: Aphididae

[2]Also called cigar casebearer.

bird tick	*Haemaphysalis chordeilis* (Packard)	ACARI: Ixodidae
black army cutworm	*Actebia fennica* (Tauscher)	LEPIDOPTERA: Noctuidae
black blister beetle	*Epicauta pennsylvanica* (De Geer)	COLEOPTERA: Meloidae
black blow fly	*Phormia regina* (Meigen)	DIPTERA: Calliphoridae
black bug	*Corimelaena pulicaria* (Germar)	HETEROPTERA: Thyreocoridae
black carpenter ant	*Camponotus pennsylvanicus* (De Geer)	HYMENOPTERA: Formicidae
black carpet beetle	*Attagenus unicolor* (Brahm)	COLEOPTERA: Dermestidae
black cherry aphid	*Myzus cerasi* (Fabricius)	HOMOPTERA: Aphididae
black cherry fruit fly	*Rhagoletis fausta* (Osten Sacken)	DIPTERA: Tephritidae
black citrus aphid	*Toxoptera aurantii* (Boyer de Fonscolombe)	HOMOPTERA: Aphididae
black cockroach wasp	*Dolichurus stantoni* (Ashmead)	HYMENOPTERA: Sphecidae
black cutworm	*Agrotis ipsilon* (Hufnagel)	LEPIDOPTERA: Noctuidae
black dung beetle	*Copris incertus prociduus* (Say)	COLEOPTERA: Scarabaeidae
black earwig	*Chelisoches morio* (Fabricius)	DERMAPTERA: Chelisochidae
black elm bark weevil	*Magdalis barbita* (Say)	COLEOPTERA: Curculionidae
black flower thrips	*Haplothrips gowdeyi* (Franklin)	THYSANOPTERA: Phlaeothripidae
black fungus beetle	*Alphitobius laevigatus* (Fabricius)	COLEOPTERA: Tenebrionidae
black grain stem sawfly	*Trachelus tabidus* (Fabricius)	HYMENOPTERA: Cephidae
black horse fly	*Tabanus atratus* Fabricius	DIPTERA: Tabanidae
black hunter thrips	*Leptothrips mali* (Fitch)	THYSANOPTERA: Phlaeothripidae
black imported fire ant	*Solenopsis richteri* Forel	HYMENOPTERA: Formicidae
black lady beetle	*Rhyzobius ventralis* (Erichson)	COLEOPTERA: Coccinellidae
black larder beetle	*Dermestes ater* De Geer	COLEOPTERA: Dermestidae
black peach aphid	*Brachycaudus persicae* (Passerini)	HOMOPTERA: Aphididae
black pecan aphid	*Melanocallis caryaefoliae* (Davis)	HOMOPTERA: Aphididae
black pineleaf scale	*Nuculaspis californica* (Coleman)	HOMOPTERA: Diaspididae
black potter wasp	*Delta pyriformis philippinensis* (Bequaert)	HYMENOPTERA: Vespidae
black scale	*Saissetia oleae* (Olivier)	HOMOPTERA: Coccidae
black soldier fly	*Hermetia illucens* (Linnaeus)	DIPTERA: Stratiomyidae
black stink bug	*Coptosoma xanthogramma* (White)	HETEROPTERA: Plataspidae
black sunflower stem weevil	*Apion (Fallapion) occidentale* Fall	COLEOPTERA: Curculionidae
black swallowtail[3]	*Papilio polyxenes asterius* Stoll	LEPIDOPTERA: Papilionidae
black thread scale	*Ischnaspis longirostris* (Signoret)	HOMOPTERA: Diaspididae
black turfgrass ataenius	*Ataenius spretulus* (Haldeman)	COLEOPTERA: Scarabaeidae
black turpentine beetle	*Dendroctonus terebrans* (Olivier)	COLEOPTERA: Scolytidae

---

[3]Immature called parsleyworm.

black twig borer	*Xylosandrus compactus* (Eichhoff)	COLEOPTERA: Scolytidae
black vine weevil	*Otiorhynchus sulcatus* (Fabricius)	COLEOPTERA: Curculionidae
black walnut curculio	*Conotrachelus retentus* (Say)	COLEOPTERA: Curculionidae
black widow spider	*Latrodectus mactans* (Fabricius)	ARANEAE: Theridiidae
black witch	*Ascalapha odorata* (Linnaeus)	LEPIDOPTERA: Noctuidae
blackbellied clerid	*Enoclerus lecontei* (Wolcott)	COLEOPTERA: Cleridae
blackberry skeletonizer	*Schreckensteinia festaliella* (Hübner)	LEPIDOPTERA: Heliodinidae
Blackburn butterfly	*Vaga blackburni* (Tuely)	LEPIDOPTERA: Lycaenidae
Blackburn damsel bug	*Nabis blackburni* White	HETEROPTERA: Nabidae
Blackburn dragonfly	*Nesogonia blackburni* (McLachlan)	ODONATA: Libellulidae
blackfaced leafhopper	*Graminella nigrifrons* (Forbes)	HOMOPTERA: Cicadellidae
blackheaded ash sawfly	*Tethida barda* (Say)	HYMENOPTERA: Tenthredinidae
blackheaded fireworm	*Rhopobota naevana* (Hübner)	LEPIDOPTERA: Tortricidae
blackheaded pine sawfly	*Neodiprion excitans* Rohwer	HYMENOPTERA: Diprionidae
blackhorned pine borer	*Callidium antennatum hesperum* Casey	COLEOPTERA: Cerambycidae
blackhorned tree cricket	*Oecanthus nigricornis* Walker	ORTHOPTERA: Gryllidae
blackjacket	*Vespula consobrina* (Saussure)	HYMENOPTERA: Vespidae
blacklegged tick	*Ixodes scapularis* Say	ACARI: Ixodidae
blacklegged tortoise beetle	*Jonthonota nigripes* (Olivier)	COLEOPTERA: Chrysomelidae
blackmargined aphid	*Monellia caryella* (Fitch)	HOMOPTERA: Aphididae
blister coneworm	*Dioryctria clarioralis* (Walker)	LEPIDOPTERA: Pyralidae
bloodsucking conenose	*Triatoma sanguisuga* (LeConte)	HETEROPTERA: Reduviidae
blue cactus borer	*Melitara dentata* (Grote)	LEPIDOPTERA: Pyralidae
blue horntail	*Sirex cyaneus* Fabricius	HYMENOPTERA: Siricidae
blue soldier fly	*Exaireta spinigera* (Wiedemann)	DIPTERA: Stratiomyidae
blueberry bud mite	*Acalitus vaccinii* (Keifer)	ACARI: Eriophyidae
blueberry case beetle	*Neochlamisus cribripennis* (LeConte)	COLEOPTERA: Chrysomelidae
blueberry flea beetle	*Altica sylvia* Malloch	COLEOPTERA: Chrysomelidae
blueberry maggot	*Rhagoletis mendax* Curran	DIPTERA: Tephritidae
blueberry thrips	*Frankliniella vaccinii* Morgan	THYSANOPTERA: Thripidae
blueberry tip midge	*Prodiplosis vaccinii* (Felt)	DIPTERA: Cecidomyiidae
bluegrass billbug	*Sphenophorus parvulus* Gyllenhal	COLEOPTERA: Curculionidae
bluegrass webworm	*Parapediasia teterrella* (Zincken)	LEPIDOPTERA: Pyralidae
bluntnosed cranberry leafhopper	*Scleroracus vaccinii* (Van Duzee)	HOMOPTERA: Cicadellidae
body louse	*Pediculus humanus humanus* Linnaeus	ANOPLURA: Pediculidae

Boisduval scale	*Diaspis boisduvalii* Signoret	HOMOPTERA: Diaspididae
boll weevil	*Anthonomus grandis grandis* Boheman	COLEOPTERA: Curculionidae
bollworm[4]	*Helicoverpa zea* (Boddie)	LEPIDOPTERA: Noctuidae
booklouse	*Liposcelis corrodens* Heymons	PSOCOPTERA: Liposcelidae
boxelder aphid	*Periphyllus negundinis* (Thomas)	HOMOPTERA: Aphididae
boxelder bug	*Boisea trivittata* (Say)	HETEROPTERA: Rhopalidae
boxelder leafroller	*Caloptilia negundella* (Chambers)	LEPIDOPTERA: Gracillariidae
boxelder psyllid	*Cacopsylla negundinis* Mally	HOMOPTERA: Psyllidae
boxelder twig borer	*Proteoteras willingana* (Kearfott)	LEPIDOPTERA: Tortricidae
boxwood leafminer	*Monarthropalpus flavus* (Schrank)	DIPTERA: Cecidomyiidae
boxwood psyllid	*Cacopsylla buxi* (Linnaeus)	HOMOPTERA: Psyllidae
bramble leafhopper	*Ribautiana tenerrima* (Herrich-Schäffer)	HOMOPTERA: Cicadellidae
Brasilian leafhopper	*Protalebrella brasiliensis* (Baker)	HOMOPTERA: Cicadellidae
bristly cutworm	*Lacinipolia renigera* (Stephens)	LEPIDOPTERA: Noctuidae
bristly roseslug	*Cladius difformis* (Panzer)	HYMENOPTERA: Tenthredinidae
broad mite	*Polyphagotarsonemus latus* (Banks)	ACARI: Tarsonemidae
broadbean weevil	*Bruchus rufimanus* Boheman	COLEOPTERA: Bruchidae
broadhorned flour beetle	*Gnatocerus cornutus* (Fabricius)	COLEOPTERA: Tenebrionidae
broadnecked root borer	*Prionus laticollis* (Drury)	COLEOPTERA: Cerambycidae
broadnosed grain weevil	*Caulophilus oryzae* (Gyllenhal)	COLEOPTERA: Curculionidae
broadwinged katydid	*Microcentrum rhombifolium* (Saussure)	ORTHOPTERA: Tettigoniidae
bromegrass seed midge	*Contarinia bromicola* (Marikovskij & Agafonova)	DIPTERA: Cecidomyiidae
bronze appletree weevil	*Magdalis aenescens* LeConte	COLEOPTERA: Curculionidae
bronze birch borer	*Agrilus anxius* Gory	COLEOPTERA: Buprestidae
bronze leaf beetle	*Diachus auratus* (Fabricius)	COLEOPTERA: Chrysomelidae
bronze poplar borer	*Agrilus liragus* Barter & Brown	COLEOPTERA: Buprestidae
bronzed cutworm	*Nephelodes minians* Guenée	LEPIDOPTERA: Noctuidae
brown chicken louse	*Goniodes dissimilis* Denny	MALLOPHAGA: Philopteridae
brown citrus aphid	*Toxoptera citricida* (Kirkaldy)	HOMOPTERA: Aphididae
brown cockroach	*Periplaneta brunnea* Burmeister	BLATTODEA: Blattidae
brown cotton leafworm	*Acontia dacia* Druce	LEPIDOPTERA: Noctuidae
brown dog tick	*Rhipicephalus sanguineus* (Latreille)	ACARI: Ixodidae
brown dung beetle	*Onthophagus gazella* Fabricius	COLEOPTERA: Scarabaeidae
brown flour mite	*Gohieria fusca* (Oudemans)	ACARI: Glycyphagidae
brown garden snail	*Helix aspersa* Müller	STYLOMMATOPHORA: Helicidae

---

[4]Also called corn earworm and tomato fruitworm.

brown house moth	*Hofmannophila pseudospretella* (Stainton)	LEPIDOPTERA: Oecophoridae
brown mite	*Bryobia rubrioculus* (Scheuten)	ACARI: Tetranychidae
brown pineapple scale	*Melanaspis bromiliae* (Leonardi)	HOMOPTERA: Diaspididae
brown recluse spider	*Loxosceles reclusa* Gertsch & Mulaik	ARANEAE: Loxoscelidae
brown saltmarsh mosquito	*Aedes cantator* (Coquillett)	DIPTERA: Culicidae
brown soft scale	*Coccus hesperidum* Linnaeus	HOMOPTERA: Coccidae
brown speckled leafhopper	*Paraphlepsius irroratus* (Say)	HOMOPTERA: Cicadellidae
brown spider beetle	*Ptinus clavipes* Panzer	COLEOPTERA: Ptinidae
brown stink bug	*Euschistus servus* (Say)	HETEROPTERA: Pentatomidae
brown wheat mite	*Petrobia latens* (Müller)	ACARI: Tetranychidae
brown widow spider	*Latrodectus geometricus* (Fabricius)	ARANEAE: Theridiidae
brownbanded cockroach	*Supella longipalpa* (Fabricius)	BLATTODEA: Blattellidae
brownheaded ash sawfly	*Tomostethus multicinctus* (Rohwer)	HYMENOPTERA: Tenthredinidae
brownheaded jack pine sawfly	*Neodiprion dubiosus* Schedl	HYMENOPTERA: Diprionidae
brownlegged grain mite	*Aleuroglyphus ovatus* (Troupeau)	ACARI: Acaridae
browntail moth	*Euproctis chrysorrhoea* (Linnaeus)	LEPIDOPTERA: Lymantriidae
Bruce spanworm	*Operophtera bruceata* (Hulst)	LEPIDOPTERA: Geometridae
buck moth	*Hemileuca maia* (Drury)	LEPIDOPTERA: Saturniidae
buckthorn aphid	*Aphis nasturtii* Kaltenbach	HOMOPTERA: Aphididae
buffalo treehopper	*Stictocephala bisonia* Kopp & Yonke	HOMOPTERA: Membracidae
buffalograss webworm	*Surattha indentella* Kearfott	LEPIDOPTERA: Pyralidae
bulb mite	*Rhizoglyphus echinopus* (Fumouze & Robin)	ACARI: Acaridae
bulb scale mite	*Steneotarsonemus laticeps* (Halbert)	ACARI: Tarsonemidae
bumble flower beetle	*Euphoria inda* (Linnaeus)	COLEOPTERA: Scarabaeidae
bumelia fruit fly	*Anastrepha pallens* Coquillett	DIPTERA: Tephritidae
burdock borer	*Papaipema cataphracta* (Grote)	LEPIDOPTERA: Noctuidae
Burmeister mantid	*Orthodera burmeisteri* Wood-Mason	MANTODEA: Mantidae
butternut curculio	*Conotrachelus juglandis* LeConte	COLEOPTERA: Curculionidae

C

cabbage aphid	*Brevicoryne brassicae* (Linnaeus)	HOMOPTERA: Aphididae
cabbage curculio	*Ceutorhynchus rapae* Gyllenhal	COLEOPTERA: Curculionidae
cabbage looper	*Trichoplusia ni* (Hübner)	LEPIDOPTERA: Noctuidae
cabbage maggot	*Delia radicum* (Linnaeus)	DIPTERA: Anthomyiidae
cabbage seedpod weevil	*Ceutorhynchus assimilis* (Paykull)	COLEOPTERA: Curculionidae

cabbage seedstalk curculio	*Ceutorhynchus quadridens* (Panzer)	COLEOPTERA: Curculionidae
cabbage webworm	*Hellula rogatalis* (Hulst)	LEPIDOPTERA: Pyralidae
cactus moth	*Cactoblastis cactorum* (Berg)	LEPIDOPTERA: Pyralidae
cactus scale	*Diaspis echinocacti* (Bouché)	HOMOPTERA: Diaspididae
cadelle	*Tenebroides mauritanicus* (Linnaeus)	COLEOPTERA: Trogositidae
Caledonia seed bug	*Nysius caledoniae* Distant	HETEROPTERA: Lygaeidae
calico scale	*Eulecanium cerasorum* (Cockerell)	HOMOPTERA: Coccidae
California fivespined ips	*Ips paraconfusus* Lanier	COLEOPTERA: Scolytidae
California flatheaded borer	*Melanophila californica* Van Dyke	COLEOPTERA: Buprestidae
California harvester ant	*Pogonomyrmex californicus* (Buckley)	HYMENOPTERA: Formicidae
California oakworm	*Phryganidia californica* Packard	LEPIDOPTERA: Dioptidae
California pear sawfly	*Pristiphora abbreviata* (Hartig)	HYMENOPTERA: Tenthredinidae
California prionus	*Prionus californicus* Motschulsky	COLEOPTERA: Cerambycidae
California red scale	*Aonidiella aurantii* (Maskell)	HOMOPTERA: Diaspididae
California saltmarsh mosquito	*Aedes squamiger* (Coquillett)	DIPTERA: Culicidae
California tortoiseshell	*Nymphalis californica* (Boisduval)	LEPIDOPTERA: Nymphalidae
camellia scale	*Lepidosaphes camelliae* Hoke	HOMOPTERA: Diaspididae
camphor scale	*Pseudaonidia duplex* (Cockerell)	HOMOPTERA: Diaspididae
camphor thrips	*Liothrips floridensis* (Watson)	THYSANOPTERA: Phlaeothripidae
caragana aphid	*Acyrthosiphon caraganae* (Cholodkovsky)	HOMOPTERA: Aphididae
caragana blister beetle	*Epicauta subglabra* (Fall)	COLEOPTERA: Meloidae
caragana plant bug	*Lopidea dakota* Knight	HETEROPTERA: Miridae
Caribbean black scale	*Saissetia neglecta* De Lotto	HOMOPTERA: Coccidae
Caribbean fruit fly	*Anastrepha suspensa* (Loew)	DIPTERA: Tephritidae
Caribbean pod borer	*Fundella pellucens* Zeller	LEPIDOPTERA: Pyralidae
carmine spider mite	*Tetranychus cinnabarinus* (Boisduval)	ACARI: Tetranychidae
carnation maggot	*Delia brunnescens* (Zetterstedt)	DIPTERA: Anthomyiidae
carnation tip maggot	*Delia echinata* (Séguy)	DIPTERA: Anthomyiidae
Carolina conifer aphid	*Cinara atlantica* (Wilson)	HOMOPTERA: Aphididae
Carolina grasshopper	*Dissosteira carolina* (Linnaeus)	ORTHOPTERA: Acrididae
Carolina mantid	*Stagmomantis carolina* (Johannson)	MANTODEA: Mantidae
carpenter bee	*Xylocopa virginica* (Linnaeus)	HYMENOPTERA: Anthophoridae
carpenterworm	*Prionoxystus robiniae* (Peck)	LEPIDOPTERA: Cossidae
carpet beetle	*Anthrenus scrophulariae* (Linnaeus)	COLEOPTERA: Dermestidae
carpet moth	*Trichophaga tapetzella* (Linnaeus)	LEPIDOPTERA: Tineidae
carrot beetle	*Ligyrus gibbosus* (De Geer)	COLEOPTERA: Scarabaeidae
carrot rust fly	*Psila rosae* (Fabricius)	DIPTERA: Psilidae
carrot weevil	*Listronotus oregonensis* (LeConte)	COLEOPTERA: Curculionidae

Common name	Scientific name	Order: Family
casemaking clothes moth	*Tinea pellionella* Linnaeus	LEPIDOPTERA: Tineidae
cat flea	*Ctenocephalides felis* (Bouché)	SIPHONAPTERA: Pulicidae
cat follicle mite	*Demodex cati* Mégnin	ACARI: Demodicidae
cat louse	*Felicola subrostratus* (Burmeister)	MALLOPHAGA: Trichodectidae
catalpa midge	*Contarinia catalpae* (Comstock)	DIPTERA: Cecidomyiidae
catalpa sphinx	*Ceratomia catalpae* (Boisduval)	LEPIDOPTERA: Sphingidae
cattle biting louse	*Bovicola bovis* (Linnaeus)	MALLOPHAGA: Trichodectidae
cattle follicle mite	*Demodex bovis* Stiles	ACARI: Demodicidae
cattle itch mite	*Sarcoptes bovis* Robin	ACARI: Sarcoptidae
cattle tail louse	*Haematopinus quadripertusus* Fahrenholz	ANOPLURA: Haematopinidae
cattle tick	*Boophilus annulatus* (Say)	ACARI: Ixodidae
Cayenne tick	*Amblyomma cajennense* (Fabricius)	ACARI: Ixodidae
ceanothus silk moth	*Hyalophora euryalus* (Boisduval)	LEPIDOPTERA: Saturniidae
cecropia moth	*Hyalophora cecropia* (Linnaeus)	LEPIDOPTERA: Saturniidae
cedartree borer	*Semanotus ligneus* (Fabricius)	COLEOPTERA: Cerambycidae
celery aphid	*Brachycolus heraclei* Takahashi	HOMOPTERA: Aphididae
celery leaftier[5]	*Udea rubigalis* (Guenée)	LEPIDOPTERA: Pyralidae
celery looper	*Anagrapha falcifera* (Kirby)	LEPIDOPTERA: Noctuidae
cereal leaf beetle	*Oulema melanopus* (Linnaeus)	COLEOPTERA: Chrysomelidae
chaff scale	*Parlatoria pergandii* Comstock	HOMOPTERA: Diaspididae
chainspotted geometer	*Cingilia catenaria* (Drury)	LEPIDOPTERA: Geometridae
changa	*Scapteriscus didactylus* (Latreille)	ORTHOPTERA: Gryllotalpidae
charcoal beetle	*Melanophila consputa* LeConte	COLEOPTERA: Buprestidae
cheese mite	*Tyrolichus casei* Oudemans	ACARI: Acaridae
cheese skipper	*Piophila casei* (Linnaeus)	DIPTERA: Piophilidae
cherry casebearer	*Coleophora pruniella* Clemens	LEPIDOPTERA: Coleophoridae
cherry fruit fly[6]	*Rhagoletis cingulata* (Loew)	DIPTERA: Tephritidae
cherry fruit sawfly	*Hoplocampa cookei* (Clarke)	HYMENOPTERA: Tenthredinidae
cherry fruitworm	*Grapholita packardi* Zeller	LEPIDOPTERA: Tortricidae
cherry leaf beetle	*Pyrrhalta cavicollis* (LeConte)	COLEOPTERA: Chrysomelidae
cherry maggot[7]	*Rhagoletis cingulata* (Loew)	DIPTERA: Tephritidae
chestnut timberworm	*Melittomma sericeum* (Harris)	COLEOPTERA: Lymexylidae
chicken body louse	*Menacanthus stramineus* (Nitzsch)	MALLOPHAGA: Menoponidae
chicken dung fly	*Fannia pusio* (Wiedemann)	DIPTERA: Muscidae

[5]Also called greenhouse leaftier.
[6]Immature called cherry maggot.
[7]Adult called cherry fruit fly.

chicken head louse	*Cuclotogaster heterographus* (Nitzsch)	MALLOPHAGA: Philopteridae
chicken mite	*Dermanyssus gallinae* (De Geer)	ACARI: Dermanyssidae
chigoe	*Tunga penetrans* (Linnaeus)	SIPHONAPTERA: Tungidae
chinch bug	*Blissus leucopterus leucopterus* (Say)	HETEROPTERA: Lygaeidae
Chinese dryinid	*Pseudogonatopus hospes* Perkins	HYMENOPTERA: Dryinidae
Chinese mantid	*Tenodera aridifolia sinensis* Saussure	MANTODEA: Mantidae
Chinese obscure scale	*Parlatoreopsis chinensis* (Marlatt)	HOMOPTERA: Diaspididae
Chinese rose beetle	*Adoretus sinicus* Burmeister	COLEOPTERA: Scarabaeidae
chokecherry leafroller	*Sparganothis directana* (Walker)	LEPIDOPTERA: Tortricidae
Christmas berry webworm	*Cryptoblabes gnidiella* (Millière)	LEPIDOPTERA: Pyralidae
chrysanthemum aphid	*Macrosiphoniella sanborni* (Gillette)	HOMOPTERA: Aphididae
chrysanthemum flower borer	*Lorita abornana* Busck	LEPIDOPTERA: Cochylidae
chrysanthemum gall midge	*Rhopalomyia chrysanthemi* (Ahlberg)	DIPTERA: Cecidomyiidae
chrysanthemum lace bug	*Corythucha marmorata* (Uhler)	HETEROPTERA: Tingidae
chrysanthemum leafminer	*Chromatomyia syngenesiae* Hardy	DIPTERA: Agromyzidae
chrysanthemum thrips	*Thrips nigropilosus* Uzel	THYSANOPTERA: Thripidae
cicada killer	*Sphecius speciosus* (Drury)	HYMENOPTERA: Sphecidae
cigar casebearer[8]	*Coleophora serratella* (Linnaeus)	LEPIDOPTERA: Coleophoridae
cigarette beetle	*Lasioderma serricorne* (Fabricius)	COLEOPTERA: Anobiidae
cinereous cockroach	*Nauphoeta cinerea* (Olivier)	BLATTODEA: Blaberidae
cinnabar moth	*Tyria jacobaeae* (Linnaeus)	LEPIDOPTERA: Arctiidae
citricola scale	*Coccus pseudomagnoliarum* (Kuwana)	HOMOPTERA: Coccidae
citrophilus mealybug	*Pseudococcus calceolariae* (Maskell)	HOMOPTERA: Pseudococcidae
citrus blackfly	*Aleurocanthus woglumi* Ashby	HOMOPTERA: Aleyrodidae
citrus bud mite	*Eriophyes sheldoni* Ewing	ACARI: Eriophyidae
citrus flat mite	*Brevipalpus lewisi* McGregor	ACARI: Tenuipalpidae
citrus mealybug	*Planococcus citri* (Risso)	HOMOPTERA: Pseudococcidae
citrus red mite	*Panonychus citri* (McGregor)	ACARI: Tetranychidae
citrus root weevil	*Pachnaeus litus* (Germar)	COLEOPTERA: Curculionidae
citrus rust mite	*Phyllocoptruta oleivora* (Ashmead)	ACARI: Eriophyidae
citrus snow scale	*Unaspis citri* (Comstock)	HOMOPTERA: Diaspididae
citrus swallowtail	*Papilio xuthus* Linnaeus	LEPIDOPTERA: Papilionidae
citrus thrips	*Scirtothrips citri* (Moulton)	THYSANOPTERA: Thripidae
citrus whitefly	*Dialeurodes citri* (Ashmead)	HOMOPTERA: Aleyrodidae
claybacked cutworm	*Agrotis gladiaria* Morrison	LEPIDOPTERA: Noctuidae

---

[8]Also called birch casebearer.

claycolored billbug	*Sphenophorus aequalis aequalis* Gyllenhal	COLEOPTERA: Curculionidae
claycolored leaf beetle	*Anomoea laticlavia* (Forster)	COLEOPTERA: Chrysomelidae
Clear Lake gnat	*Chaoborus astictopus* Dyar & Shannon	DIPTERA: Chaoboridae
clearwinged grasshopper	*Camnula pellucida* (Scudder)	ORTHOPTERA: Acrididae
clematis blister beetle	*Epicauta cinerea* (Forster)	COLEOPTERA: Meloidae
clidemia leafroller	*Blepharomastix ebulealis* (Guenée)	LEPIDOPTERA: Pyralidae
clidemia thrips	*Liothrips urichi* Karny	THYSANOPTERA: Phlaeothripidae
clouded plant bug	*Neurocolpus nubilus* (Say)	HETEROPTERA: Miridae
clouded sulfur	*Colias philodice* Godart	LEPIDOPTERA: Pieridae
cloudywinged whitefly	*Dialeurodes citrifolii* (Morgan)	HOMOPTERA: Aleyrodidae
clover aphid	*Nearctaphis bakeri* (Cowen)	HOMOPTERA: Aphididae
clover aphid parasite	*Aphelinus lapisliqni* Howard	HYMENOPTERA: Encyrtidae
clover cutworm	*Discestra trifolii* (Hufnagel)	LEPIDOPTERA: Noctuidae
clover hayworm	*Hypsopygia costalis* (Fabricius)	LEPIDOPTERA: Pyralidae
clover head caterpillar	*Grapholita interstinctana* (Clemens)	LEPIDOPTERA: Tortricidae
clover head weevil	*Hypera meles* (Fabricius)	COLEOPTERA: Curculionidae
clover leaf midge	*Dasineura trifolii* (Loew)	DIPTERA: Cecidomyiidae
clover leaf weevil	*Hypera punctata* (Fabricius)	COLEOPTERA: Curculionidae
clover leafhopper	*Aceratagallia sanguinolenta* (Provancher)	HOMOPTERA: Cicadellidae
clover looper	*Caenurgina crassiuscula* (Haworth)	LEPIDOPTERA: Noctuidae
clover mite	*Bryobia praetiosa* Koch	ACARI: Tetranychidae
clover root borer	*Hylastinus obscurus* (Marsham)	COLEOPTERA: Scolytidae
clover root curculio	*Sitona hispidulus* (Fabricius)	COLEOPTERA: Curculionidae
clover seed chalcid	*Bruchophagus platyptera* (Walker)	HYMENOPTERA: Eurytomidae
clover seed midge	*Dasineura leguminicola* (Lintner)	DIPTERA: Cecidomyiidae
clover seed weevil	*Tychius picirostris* (Fabricius)	COLEOPTERA: Curculionidae
clover stem borer	*Languria mozardi* Latreille	COLEOPTERA: Languriidae
cluster fly	*Pollenia rudis* (Fabricius)	DIPTERA: Calliphoridae
cochineal insect	*Dactylopius coccus* Costa	HOMOPTERA: Dactylopiidae
cocklebur weevil	*Rhodobaenus quinquedecimpunctatus* (Say)	COLEOPTERA: Curculionidae
coconut leafminer	*Agonoxena argaula* Meyrick	LEPIDOPTERA: Agonoxenidae
coconut leafroller	*Hedylepta blackburni* (Butler)	LEPIDOPTERA: Pyralidae
coconut mealybug	*Nipaecoccus nipae* (Maskell)	HOMOPTERA: Pseudococcidae
coconut scale	*Aspidiotus destructor* Signoret	HOMOPTERA: Diaspididae
codling moth	*Cydia pomonella* (Linnaeus)	LEPIDOPTERA: Tortricidae
coffee bean weevil	*Araecerus fasciculatus* (De Geer)	COLEOPTERA: Anthribidae
Colorado potato beetle	*Leptinotarsa decemlineata* (Say)	COLEOPTERA: Chrysomelidae
Columbia Basin wireworm	*Limonius subauratus* LeConte	COLEOPTERA: Elateridae

Columbian timber beetle	*Corthylus columbianus* Hopkins	COLEOPTERA: Scolytidae
columbine borer	*Papaipema purpurifascia* (Grote & Robinson)	LEPIDOPTERA: Noctuidae
columbine leafminer complex[9]	*Phytomyza* spp.	DIPTERA: Agromyzidae
Comanche lacewing	*Chrysopa comanche* Banks	NEUROPTERA: Chrysopidae
common Australian lady beetle	*Coelophora inaequalis* (Fabricius)	COLEOPTERA: Coccinellidae
common cattle grub	*Hypoderma lineatum* (Villers)	DIPTERA: Oestridae
common damsel bug	*Nabis americoferus* Carayon	HETEROPTERA: Nabidae
common green darner	*Anax junius* (Drury)	ODONATA: Aeschnidae
common green lacewing	*Chrysopa carnea* Stephens	NEUROPTERA: Chrysopidae
common malaria mosquito	*Anopheles quadrimaculatus* Say	DIPTERA: Culicidae
composite thrips	*Microcephalothrips abdominalis* (D.L. Crawford)	THYSANOPTERA: Thripidae
Comstock mealybug	*Pseudococcus comstocki* (Kuwana)	HOMOPTERA: Pseudococcidae
conchuela	*Chlorochroa ligata* (Say)	HETEROPTERA: Pentatomidae
confused flour beetle	*Tribolium confusum* Jacquelin du Val	COLEOPTERA: Tenebrionidae
conifer spider mite	*Oligonychus coniferarum* (McGregor)	ACARI: Tetranychidae
convergent lady beetle	*Hippodamia convergens* Guérin-Méneville	COLEOPTERA: Coccinellidae
Cooley spruce gall adelgid	*Adelges cooleyi* (Gillette)	HOMOPTERA: Adelgidae
corn blotch leafminer	*Agromyza parvicornis* Loew	DIPTERA: Agromyzidae
corn delphacid	*Peregrinus maidis* (Ashmead)	HOMOPTERA: Delphacidae
corn earworm[10]	*Helicoverpa zea* (Boddie)	LEPIDOPTERA: Noctuidae
corn flea beetle	*Chaetocnema pulicaria* Melsheimer	COLEOPTERA: Chrysomelidae
corn leaf aphid	*Rhopalosiphum maidis* (Fitch)	HOMOPTERA: Aphididae
corn leafhopper	*Dalbulus maidis* (DeLong & Wolcott)	HOMOPTERA: Cicadellidae
corn root aphid	*Anuraphis maidiradicis* (Forbes)	HOMOPTERA: Aphididae
corn root webworm	*Crambus caliginosellus* Clemens	LEPIDOPTERA: Pyralidae
corn sap beetle	*Carpophilus dimidiatus* (Fabricius)	COLEOPTERA: Nitidulidae
corn silk beetle	*Metrioidea brunneus* (Crotch)	COLEOPTERA: Chrysomelidae
cornfield ant	*Lasius alienus* (Foerster)	HYMENOPTERA: Formicidae
cosmopolitan grain psocid	*Lachesilla pedicularia* (Linnaeus)	PSOCOPTERA: Lachesillidae
cotton aphid[11]	*Aphis gossypii* Glover	HOMOPTERA: Aphididae
cotton blister mite	*Acalitus gossypii* (Banks)	ACARI: Eriophyidae
cotton fleahopper	*Pseudatomoscelis seriatus* (Reuter)	HETEROPTERA: Miridae
cotton lace bug	*Corythucha gossypii* (Fabricius)	HETEROPTERA: Tingidae
cotton leafminer	*Stigmella gossypii* (Forbes & Leonard)	LEPIDOPTERA: Nepticulidae

---

[9]Includes *Phytomyza aquilegiana* Frost, *P aquilegivora* Spenser, and *P. columbinae* Sehgal.
[10]Also called bollworm and tomato fruitworm.
[11]Also called melon aphid.

cotton leafperforator	*Bucculatrix thurberiella* Busck	LEPIDOPTERA: Lyonetiidae
cotton leafworm	*Alabama argillacea* (Hübner)	LEPIDOPTERA: Noctuidae
cotton square borer	*Strymon melinus* Hübner	LEPIDOPTERA: Lycaenidae
cotton stainer	*Dysdercus suturellus* (Herrich-Schäffer)	HETEROPTERA: Pyrrhocoridae
cotton stem moth	*Platyedra subcinerea* (Haworth)	LEPIDOPTERA: Gelechiidae
cottonwood borer	*Plectrodera scalator* (Fabricius)	COLEOPTERA: Cerambycidae
cottonwood dagger moth	*Acronicta lepusculina* Guenée	LEPIDOPTERA: Noctuidae
cottonwood leaf beetle	*Chrysomela scripta* Fabricius	COLEOPTERA: Chrysomelidae
cottonwood twig borer	*Gypsonoma haimbachiana* (Kearfott)	LEPIDOPTERA: Tortricidae
cottony cushion scale	*Icerya purchasi* Maskell	HOMOPTERA: Margarodidae
cottony maple scale	*Pulvinaria innumerabilis* (Rathvon)	HOMOPTERA: Coccidae
cottony peach scale	*Pulvinaria amygdali* Cockerell	HOMOPTERA: Coccidae
coulee cricket	*Peranabrus scabricollis* (Thomas)	ORTHOPTERA: Tettigoniidae
cowpea aphid	*Aphis craccivora* Koch	HOMOPTERA: Aphididae
cowpea curculio	*Chalcodermus aeneus* Boheman	COLEOPTERA: Curculionidae
cowpea weevil	*Callosobruchus maculatus* (Fabricius)	COLEOPTERA: Bruchidae
crab louse	*Pthirus pubis* (Linnaeus)	ANOPLURA: Pediculidae
crabhole mosquito	*Deinocerites cancer* Theobald	DIPTERA: Culicidae
cranberry fruitworm	*Acrobasis vaccinii* Riley	LEPIDOPTERA: Pyralidae
cranberry girdler	*Chrysoteuchia topiaria* (Zeller)	LEPIDOPTERA: Pyralidae
cranberry rootworm	*Rhabdopterus picipes* (Olivier)	COLEOPTERA: Chrysomelidae
cranberry weevil	*Anthonomus musculus* Say	COLEOPTERA: Curculionidae
crapemyrtle aphid	*Tinocallis kahawaluokalani* (Kirkaldy)	HOMOPTERA: Aphididae
crazy ant	*Paratrechina longicornis* (Latreille)	HYMENOPTERA: Formicidae
creosotebush spider mite	*Psedobryobia drummondi* (Ewing)	ACARI: Tetranychidae
crescentmarked lily aphid	*Neomyzus circumflexus* (Buckton)	HOMOPTERA: Aphididae
cribrate weevil	*Otiorhynchus cribricollis* Gyllenhal	COLEOPTERA: Curculionidae
crinkled flannel moth	*Lagoa crispata* (Packard)	LEPIDOPTERA: Megalopygidae
cross-striped cabbageworm	*Evergestis rimosalis* (Guenée)	LEPIDOPTERA: Pyralidae
croton caterpillar	*Achaea janata* (Linnaeus)	LEPIDOPTERA: Noctuidae
croton mussel scale	*Lepidosaphes tokionis* (Kuwana)	HOMOPTERA: Diaspididae
Cuban cockroach	*Panchlora nivea* (Linnaeus)	BLATTODEA: Blaberidae
Cuban laurel thrips	*Gynaikothrips ficorum* (Marchal)	THYSANOPTERA: Phlaeothripidae
cucurbit longicorn	*Apomecyna saltator* (Fabricius)	COLEOPTERA: Cerambycidae
cucurbit midge	*Prodiplosis citrulli* (Felt)	DIPTERA: Cecidomyiidae
curled rose sawfly	*Allantus cinctus* (Linnaeus)	HYMENOPTERA: Tenthredinidae
currant aphid	*Cryptomyzus ribis* (Linnaeus)	HOMOPTERA: Aphididae
currant borer	*Synanthedon tipuliformis* (Clerck)	LEPIDOPTERA: Sesiidae

currant bud mite	*Cecidophyopsis ribis* (Westwood)	ACARI: Eriophyidae
currant fruit fly	*Epochra canadensis* (Loew)	DIPTERA: Tephritidae
currant fruit weevil	*Pseudanthonomus validus* Dietz	COLEOPTERA: Curculionidae
currant spanworm	*Itame ribearia* (Fitch)	LEPIDOPTERA: Geometridae
currant stem girdler	*Janus integer* (Norton)	HYMENOPTERA: Cephidae
cyclamen mite	*Phytonemus pallidus* (Banks)	ACARI: Tarsonemidae
cynthia moth	*Samia cynthia* (Drury)	LEPIDOPTERA: Saturniidae

D

dandelion gall wasp	*Phanacis taraxaci* (Ashmead)	HYMENOPTERA: Cynipidae
dark mealworm	*Tenebrio obscurus* Fabricius	COLEOPTERA: Tenebrionidae
darksided cutworm	*Euxoa messoria* (Harris)	LEPIDOPTERA: Noctuidae
datebug	*Asarcopus palmarum* Horvath	HOMOPTERA: Issidae
depluming mite	*Knemidokoptes gallinae* (Railliet)	ACARI: Sarcoptidae
depressed flour beetle	*Palorus subdepressus* (Wollaston)	COLEOPTERA: Tenebrionidae
desert corn flea beetle	*Chaetocnema ectypa* Horn	COLEOPTERA: Chrysomelidae
desert spider mite	*Tetranychus desertorum* Banks	ACARI: Tetranychidae
devastating grasshopper	*Melanoplus devastator* Scudder	ORTHOPTERA: Acrididae
diamondback moth	*Plutella xylostella* (Linnaeus)	LEPIDOPTERA: Plutellidae
diamondbacked spittlebug	*Lepyronia quadrangularis* (Say)	HOMOPTERA: Cercopidae
dictyospermum scale	*Chrysomphalus dictyospermi* (Morgan)	HOMOPTERA: Diaspididae
differential grasshopper	*Melanoplus differentialis* (Thomas)	ORTHOPTERA: Acrididae
dingy cutworm	*Feltia ducens* Walker	LEPIDOPTERA: Noctuidae
dobsonfly[12]	*Corydalus cornutus* (Linnaeus)	NEUROPTERA: Corydalidae
dock sawfly	*Ametastegia glabrata* (Fallén)	HYMENOPTERA: Tenthredinidae
dodder gall weevil	*Smicronyx sculpticollis* Casey	COLEOPTERA: Curculionidae
dog biting louse	*Trichodectes canis* (De Geer)	MALLOPHAGA: Trichodectidae
dog flea	*Ctenocephalides canis* (Curtis)	SIPHONAPTERA: Pulicidae
dog follicle mite	*Demodex canis* Leydig	ACARI: Demodicidae
dog sucking louse	*Linognathus setosus* (Olfers)	ANOPLURA: Linognathidae
dogwood borer	*Synanthedon scitula* (Harris)	LEPIDOPTERA: Sesiidae
dogwood clubgall midge	*Resseliella clavula* (Beutenmüller)	DIPTERA: Cecidomyiidae

---

[12]Immature called hellgrammite.

dogwood scale	*Chionaspis corni* Cooley	HOMOPTERA: Diaspididae
dogwood spittlebug	*Clastoptera proteus* Fitch	HOMOPTERA: Cercopidae
dogwood twig borer	*Oberea tripunctata* (Swederus)	COLEOPTERA: Cerambycidae
Douglas-fir beetle	*Dendroctonus pseudotsugae* Hopkins	COLEOPTERA: Scolytidae
Douglas-fir cone moth	*Barbara colfaxiana* (Kearfott)	LEPIDOPTERA: Tortricidae
Douglas-fir engraver	*Scolytus unispinosus* LeConte	COLEOPTERA: Scolytidae
Douglas-fir pitch moth	*Synanthedon novaroensis* (Hy. Edwards)	LEPIDOPTERA: Sesiidae
Douglas-fir tussock moth	*Orgyia pseudotsugata* (McDunnough)	LEPIDOPTERA: Lymantriidae
Douglas-fir twig weevil	*Cylindrocopturus furnissi* Buchanan	COLEOPTERA: Curculionidae
driedfruit beetle	*Carpophilus hemipterus* (Linnaeus)	COLEOPTERA: Nitidulidae
driedfruit mite	*Carpoglyphus lactis* (Linnaeus)	ACARI: Carpoglyphidae
driedfruit moth	*Vitula edmandsae serratilineella* Ragonot	LEPIDOPTERA: Pyralidae
drone fly	*Eristalis tenax* (Linnaeus)	DIPTERA: Syrphidae
drugstore beetle	*Stegobium paniceum* (Linnaeus)	COLEOPTERA: Anobiidae
dryberry mite	*Phyllocoptes gracilis* (Nalepa)	ACARI: Eriophyidae
dryland wireworm	*Ctenicera glauca* (Germar)	COLEOPTERA: Elateridae
dusky birch sawfly	*Croesus latitarsus* Norton	HYMENOPTERA: Tenthredinidae
dusky sap beetle	*Carpophilus lugubris* Murray	COLEOPTERA: Nitidulidae
dusky stink bug	*Euschistus tristigmus* (Say)	HETEROPTERA: Pentatomidae
duskyback leafroller	*Archips mortuana* Kearfott	LEPIDOPTERA: Tortricidae

E

ear tick	*Otobius megnini* (Dugès)	ACARI: Argasidae
eastern blackheaded budworm	*Acleris variana* (Fernald)	LEPIDOPTERA: Tortricidae
eastern field wireworm	*Limonius agonus* (Say)	COLEOPTERA: Elateridae
eastern fivespined ips	*Ips grandicollis* (Eichhoff)	COLEOPTERA: Scolytidae
eastern grape leafhopper	*Erythroneura comes* (Say)	HOMOPTERA: Cicadellidae
eastern Hercules beetle	*Dynastes tityus* (Linnaeus)	COLEOPTERA: Scarabaeidae
eastern larch beetle	*Dendroctonus simplex* LeConte	COLEOPTERA: Scolytidae
eastern lubber grasshopper	*Romalea guttata* (Houttuyn)	ORTHOPTERA: Acrididae
eastern pine looper	*Lambdina pellucidaria* (Grote & Robinson)	LEPIDOPTERA: Geometridae
eastern pine seedworm	*Cydia toreuta* (Grote)	LEPIDOPTERA: Tortricidae
eastern pine shoot borer	*Eucosma gloriola* Heinrich	LEPIDOPTERA: Tortricidae
eastern pine weevil	*Pissodes nemorensis* Germar	COLEOPTERA: Curculionidae
eastern spruce gall adelgid	*Adelges abietis* (Linnaeus)	HOMOPTERA: Adelgidae

eastern subterranean termite	*Reticulitermes flavipes* (Kollar)	ISOPTERA: Rhinotermitidae
eastern tent caterpillar	*Malacosoma americanum* (Fabricius)	LEPIDOPTERA: Lasiocampidae
eastern yellowjacket	*Vespula maculifrons* (Buysson)	HYMENOPTERA: Vespidae
eggplant flea beetle	*Epitrix fuscula* Crotch	COLEOPTERA: Chrysomelidae
eggplant lace bug	*Gargaphia solani* Heidemann	HETEROPTERA: Tingidae
eggplant leafminer	*Tildenia inconspicuella* (Murtfeldt)	LEPIDOPTERA: Gelechiidae
Egyptian alfalfa weevil	*Hypera brunnipennis* (Boheman)	COLEOPTERA: Curculionidae
eightspotted forester	*Alypia octomaculata* (Fabricius)	LEPIDOPTERA: Noctuidae
El Segundo blue	*Euphilotes battoides allyni* (Shields)	LEPIDOPTERA: Lycaenidae
elder shoot borer	*Achatodes zeae* (Harris)	LEPIDOPTERA: Noctuidae
elm borer	*Saperda tridentata* Olivier	COLEOPTERA: Cerambycidae
elm calligrapha	*Calligrapha scalaris* (LeConte)	COLEOPTERA: Chrysomelidae
elm casebearer	*Coleophora ulmifoliella* McDunnough	LEPIDOPTERA: Coleophoridae
elm cockscombgall aphid	*Colopha ulmicola* (Fitch)	HOMOPTERA: Aphididae
elm flea beetle	*Altica carinata* Germar	COLEOPTERA: Chrysomelidae
elm lace bug	*Corythucha ulmi* Osborn & Drake	HETEROPTERA: Tingidae
elm leaf aphid	*Tinocallis ulmifolii* (Monell)	HOMOPTERA: Aphididae
elm leaf beetle	*Pyrrhalta luteola* (Müller)	COLEOPTERA: Chrysomelidae
elm leafminer	*Fenusa ulmi* Sundevall	HYMENOPTERA: Tenthredinidae
elm sawfly	*Cimbex americana* Leach	HYMENOPTERA: Cimbicidae
elm scurfy scale	*Chionaspis americana* Johnson	HOMOPTERA: Diaspididae
elm spanworm	*Ennomos subsignaria* (Hübner)	LEPIDOPTERA: Geometridae
elm sphinx	*Ceratomia amyntor* (Geyer)	LEPIDOPTERA: Sphingidae
elongate flea beetle	*Systena elongata* (Fabricius)	COLEOPTERA: Chrysomelidae
elongate hemlock scale	*Fiorinia externa* Ferris	HOMOPTERA: Diaspididae
emerald cockroach wasp	*Ampulex compressa* (Fabricius)	HYMENOPTERA: Sphecidae
Engelmann spruce weevil[13]	*Pissodes strobi* (Peck)	COLEOPTERA: Curculionidae
English grain aphid	*Sitobion avenae* (Fabricius)	HOMOPTERA: Aphididae
erigeron root aphid	*Aphis middletonii* (Thomas)	HOMOPTERA: Aphididae
ermine moth	*Yponomeuta padella* (Linnaeus)	LEPIDOPTERA: Yponomeutidae
eucalyptus longhorned borer	*Phoracantha semipunctata* (Fabricius)	COLEOPTERA: Cerambycidae
eugenia caterpillar	*Targalla delatrix* Guenée	LEPIDOPTERA: Noctuidae
euonymus scale	*Unaspis euonymi* (Comstock)	HOMOPTERA: Diaspididae
eupatorium gall fly	*Procecidochares utilis* Stone	DIPTERA: Tephritidae
Eurasian pine adelgid	*Pineus pini* (Macquart)	HOMOPTERA: Adelgidae

---

[13]Also called Sitka spruce weevil and white pine weevil.

European alder leafminer	*Fenusa dohrnii* (Tischbein)	HYMENOPTERA: Tenthredinidae
European apple sawfly	*Hoplocampa testudinea* (Klug)	HYMENOPTERA: Tenthredinidae
European chafer	*Rhizotrogus (Amphimallon) majalis* (Razoumowsky)	COLEOPTERA: Scarabaeidae
European chicken flea	*Ceratophyllus gallinae* (Schrank)	SIPHONAPTERA: Ceratophyllidae
European corn borer	*Ostrinia nubilalis* (Hübner)	LEPIDOPTERA: Pyralidae
European crane fly	*Tipula paludosa* Meigen	DIPTERA: Tipulidae
European earwig	*Forficula auricularia* Linnaeus	DERMAPTERA: Forficulidae
European elm scale	*Gossyparia spuria* (Modeer)	HOMOPTERA: Eriococcidae
European fruit lecanium	*Parthenolecanium corni* (Bouché)	HOMOPTERA: Coccidae
European fruit scale	*Quadraspidiotus ostreaeformis* (Curtis)	HOMOPTERA: Diaspididae
European grain moth	*Nemapogon granella* (Linnaeus)	LEPIDOPTERA: Tineidae
European honeysuckle leafroller	*Ypsolophus dentella* (Fabricius)	LEPIDOPTERA: Plutellidae
European hornet	*Vespa crabro* Linnaeus	HYMENOPTERA: Vespidae
European house dust mite	*Dermatophagoides pteronyssinus* (Trouessart)	ACARI: Epidermoptidae
European mantid	*Mantis religiosa* Linnaeus	MANTODEA: Mantidae
European mouse flea	*Leptopsylla segnis* (Schnherr)	SIPHONAPTERA: Leptopsyllidae
European peach scale	*Parthenolecanium persicae* (Fabricius)	HOMOPTERA: Coccidae
European pine sawfly	*Neodiprion sertifer* (Geoffroy)	HYMENOPTERA: Diprionidae
European pine shoot moth	*Rhyacionia buoliana* (Denis & Schiffermüller)	LEPIDOPTERA: Tortricidae
European red mite	*Panonychus ulmi* (Koch)	ACARI: Tetranychidae
European spruce beetle	*Dendroctonus micans* (Kugelann)	COLEOPTERA: Scolytidae
European spruce sawfly	*Gilpinia hercyniae* (Hartig)	HYMENOPTERA: Diprionidae
European wheat stem sawfly	*Cephus pygmaeus* (Linnaeus)	HYMENOPTERA: Cephidae
eyed click beetle	*Alaus oculatus* (Linnaeus)	COLEOPTERA: Elateridae
eyespotted bud moth	*Spilonota ocellana* (Denis & Schiffermüller)	LEPIDOPTERA: Tortricidae

---

F

---

face fly	*Musca autumnalis* De Geer	DIPTERA: Muscidae
fall armyworm	*Spodoptera frugiperda* (J.E. Smith)	LEPIDOPTERA: Noctuidae
fall cankerworm	*Alsophila pometaria* (Harris)	LEPIDOPTERA: Geometridae
fall webworm	*Hyphantria cunea* (Drury)	LEPIDOPTERA: Arctiidae
false celery leaftier	*Udea profundalis* (Packard)	LEPIDOPTERA: Pyralidae
false chinch bug	*Nysius raphanus* Howard	HETEROPTERA: Lygaeidae
false German cockroach	*Blattella lituricollis* (Walker)	BLATTODEA: Blattellidae
false hemlock looper	*Nepytia canosaria* (Walker)	LEPIDOPTERA: Geometridae

false potato beetle	*Leptinotarsa juncta* (Germar)	COLEOPTERA: Chrysomelidae
false stable fly	*Muscina stabulans* (Fallén)	DIPTERA: Muscidae
feather mite	*Megninia cubitalis* (Mégnin)	ACARI: Analgidae
fern aphid	*Idiopterus nephrelepidis* Davis	HOMOPTERA: Aphididae
fern scale	*Pinnaspis aspidistrae* (Signoret)	HOMOPTERA: Diaspididae
fiery hunter	*Calosoma calidum* (Fabricius)	COLEOPTERA: Carabidae
fiery skipper	*Hylephila phyleus* (Drury)	LEPIDOPTERA: Hesperiidae
fig mite	*Eriophyes ficus* Cotte	ACARI: Eriophyidae
fig scale	*Lepidosaphes conchiformis* (Gmelin)	HOMOPTERA: Diaspididae
fig wasp	*Blastophaga psenes* (Linnaeus)	HYMENOPTERA: Agaonidae
Fijian ginger weevil	*Elytroteinus subtruncatus* (Fairmaire)	COLEOPTERA: Curculionidae
filament bearer	*Nematocampa limbata* (Haworth)	LEPIDOPTERA: Geometridae
filbert aphid	*Myzocallis coryli* (Goetze)	HOMOPTERA: Aphididae
filbert bud mite	*Phytocoptella avellanae* (Nalepa)	ACARI: Nalepellidae
filbert weevil	*Curculio occidentis* (Casey)	COLEOPTERA: Curculionidae
filbertworm	*Cydia latiferreana* (Walsingham)	LEPIDOPTERA: Tortricidae
fir cone looper	*Eupithecia spermaphaga* (Dyar)	LEPIDOPTERA: Geometridae
fir engraver	*Scolytus ventralis* LeConte	COLEOPTERA: Scolytidae
fir seed moth	*Cydia bracteatana* (Fernald)	LEPIDOPTERA: Tortricidae
fire ant	*Solenopsis geminata* (Fabricius)	HYMENOPTERA: Formicidae
firebrat	*Thermobia domestica* (Packard)	THYSANURA: Lepismatidae
firtree borer	*Semanotus litigiosus* (Casey)	COLEOPTERA: Cerambycidae
flat grain beetle	*Cryptolestes pusillus* (Schnherr)	COLEOPTERA: Cucujidae
flatheaded appletree borer	*Chrysobothris femorata* (Olivier)	COLEOPTERA: Buprestidae
flatheaded cone borer	*Chrysophana placida conicola* Van Dyke	COLEOPTERA: Buprestidae
flatheaded fir borer	*Melanophila drummondi* (Kirby)	COLEOPTERA: Buprestidae
flax bollworm	*Heliothis ononis* (Denis & Schiffermüller)	LEPIDOPTERA: Noctuidae
Fletcher scale	*Parthenolecanium fletcheri* (Cockerell)	HOMOPTERA: Coccidae
floodwater mosquito	*Aedes sticticus* (Meigen)	DIPTERA: Culicidae
Florida carpenter ant	*Camponotus abdominalis* (Fabricius)	HYMENOPTERA: Formicidae
Florida fern caterpillar	*Callopistria floridensis* (Guenée)	LEPIDOPTERA: Noctuidae
Florida harvester ant	*Pogonomyrmex badius* (Latreille)	HYMENOPTERA: Formicidae
Florida red scale	*Chrysomphalus aonidum* (Linnaeus)	HOMOPTERA: Diaspididae
Florida wax scale	*Ceroplastes floridensis* Comstock	HOMOPTERA: Coccidae
flower thrips	*Frankliniella tritici* (Fitch)	THYSANOPTERA: Thripidae
fluff louse	*Goniocotes gallinae* (De Geer)	MALLOPHAGA: Philopteridae
follicle mite	*Demodex folliculorum* (Simon)	ACARI: Demodicidae
forage looper	*Caenurgina erechtea* (Cramer)	LEPIDOPTERA: Noctuidae

Forbes scale	*Quadraspidiotus forbesi* (Johnson)	HOMOPTERA: Diaspididae
foreign grain beetle	*Ahasverus advena* (Waltl)	COLEOPTERA: Cucujidae
forest day mosquito	*Aedes albopictus* (Skuse)	DIPTERA: Culicidae
forest tent caterpillar	*Malacosoma disstria* Hübner	LEPIDOPTERA: Lasiocampidae
forest tree termite	*Neotermes connexus* Snyder	ISOPTERA: Kalotermitidae
forktailed bush katydid	*Scudderia furcata* Brunner von Wattenwyl	ORTHOPTERA: Tettigoniidae
Formosan subterranean termite	*Coptotermes formosanus* Shiraki	ISOPTERA: Rhinotermitidae
fourbanded leafroller	*Argyrotaenia quadrifasciana* (Fernald)	LEPIDOPTERA: Tortricidae
fourlined plant bug	*Poecilocapsus lineatus* (Fabricius)	HETEROPTERA: Miridae
fourspotted spider mite	*Tetranychus canadensis* (McGregor)	ACARI: Tetranychidae
fourspotted tree cricket	*Oecanthus quadripunctatus* Beutenmüller	ORTHOPTERA: Gryllidae
fowl tick	*Argas persicus* (Oken)	ACARI: Argasidae
foxglove aphid	*Aulacorthum solani* (Kaltenbach)	HOMOPTERA: Aphididae
frigate bird fly	*Olfersia spinifera* (Leach)	DIPTERA: Hippoboscidae
fringed orchid aphid	*Cerataphis orchidearum* (Westwood)	HOMOPTERA: Aphididae
frit fly	*Oscinella frit* (Linnaeus)	DIPTERA: Chloropidae
fruittree leafroller	*Archips argyrospila* (Walker)	LEPIDOPTERA: Tortricidae
Fuller rose beetle	*Asynonychus godmani* Crotch	COLEOPTERA: Curculionidae
furniture beetle	*Anobium punctatum* (De Geer)	COLEOPTERA: Anobiidae
furniture carpet beetle	*Anthrenus flavipes* LeConte	COLEOPTERA: Dermestidae

G

gallmaking maple borer	*Xylotrechus aceris* Fisher	COLEOPTERA: Cerambycidae
garden fleahopper	*Halticus bractatus* (Say)	HETEROPTERA: Miridae
garden millipede	*Oxidus gracilis* Koch	POLYDESMIDA: Paradoxoxomatidae
garden springtail	*Bourletiella hortensis* (Fitch)	COLLEMBOLA: Bourletiellidae
garden symphylan	*Scutigerella immaculata* (Newport)	SYMPHYLA: Scutigerellidae
garden webworm	*Achyra rantalis* (Guenée)	LEPIDOPTERA: Pyralidae
gardenia bud mite	*Colomerus gardeniella* (Keifer)	ACARI: Eriophyidae
genista caterpillar	*Uresiphita reversalis* (Guenée)	LEPIDOPTERA: Pyralidae
German cockroach	*Blattella germanica* (Linnaeus)	BLATTODEA: Blattellidae
German yellowjacket	*Paravespula germanica* (Linnaeus)	HYMENOPTERA: Vespidae
giant African snail	*Achatina fulica* Bowdich	STYLOMMATOPHORA: Achatinidae
giant bark aphid	*Longistigma caryae* (Harris)	HOMOPTERA: Aphididae
giant Hawaiian dragonfly	*Anax strenuus* Hagen	ODONATA: Aeschnidae

giant stag beetle	Lucanus elaphus Fabricius	COLEOPTERA: Lucanidae
giant water bug	Lethocerus americanus (Leidy)	HETEROPTERA: Belostomatidae
Giffard whitefly	Bemisia giffardi (Kotinsky)	HOMOPTERA: Aleyrodidae
ginger maggot	Eumerus figurans Walker	DIPTERA: Syrphidae
gladiolus thrips	Thrips simplex (Morison)	THYSANOPTERA: Thripidae
glassy cutworm	Apamea devastator (Brace)	LEPIDOPTERA: Noctuidae
globose scale	Sphaerolecanium prunastri (Boyer de Fonscolombe)	HOMOPTERA: Coccidae
globular spider beetle	Trigonogenius globulum Solier	COLEOPTERA: Ptinidae
gloomy scale	Melanaspis tenebricosa (Comstock)	HOMOPTERA: Diaspididae
Glover scale	Lepidosaphes gloveri (Packard)	HOMOPTERA: Diaspididae
goat biting louse	Bovicola caprae (Gurlt)	MALLOPHAGA: Trichodectidae
goat follicle mite	Demodex caprae Railliet	ACARI: Demodicidae
goat sucking louse	Linognathus stenopsis (Burmeister)	ANOPLURA: Linognathidae
golden buprestid	Buprestis aurulenta Linnaeus	COLEOPTERA: Buprestidae
golden cricket wasp	Liris aurulentus (Fabricius)	HYMENOPTERA: Sphecidae
golden oak scale	Asterolecanium variolosum (Ratzeburg)	HOMOPTERA: Asterolecaniidae
golden paper wasp	Polistes fuscatus aurifer Saussure	HYMENOPTERA: Vespidae
golden spider beetle	Niptus hololeucus (Faldermann)	COLEOPTERA: Ptinidae
golden tortoise beetle	Metriona bicolor (Fabricius)	COLEOPTERA: Chrysomelidae
goldeneyed lacewing	Chrysopa oculata Say	NEUROPTERA: Chrysopidae
goldenglow aphid	Dactynotus rudbeckiae (Fitch)	HOMOPTERA: Aphididae
goose body louse	Trinoton anserinum (Fabricius)	MALLOPHAGA: Menoponidae
gooseberry fruitworm	Zophodia convolutella (Hübner)	LEPIDOPTERA: Pyralidae
gooseberry witchbroom aphid	Kakimia houghtonensis (Troop)	HOMOPTERA: Aphididae
gophertortoise tick	Amblyomma tuberculatum Marx	ACARI: Ixodidae
gorse seed weevil	Apion ulicis (Frster)	COLEOPTERA: Curculionidae
grain mite	Acarus siro Linnaeus	ACARI: Acaridae
grain rust mite	Abacarus hystrix (Nalepa)	ACARI: Eriophyidae
grain thrips	Limothrips cerealium (Haliday)	THYSANOPTERA: Thripidae
granary weevil	Sitophilus granarius (Linnaeus)	COLEOPTERA: Curculionidae
granulate cutworm	Agrotis subterranea (Fabricius)	LEPIDOPTERA: Noctuidae
grape berry moth	Endopiza viteana Clemens	LEPIDOPTERA: Tortricidae
grape blossom midge	Contarinia johnsoni Felt	DIPTERA: Cecidomyiidae
grape cane gallmaker	Ampeloglypter sesostris (LeConte)	COLEOPTERA: Curculionidae
grape colaspis	Colaspis brunnea (Fabricius)	COLEOPTERA: Chrysomelidae
grape curculio	Craponius inaequalis (Say)	COLEOPTERA: Curculionidae
grape erineum mite	Colomerus vitis (Pagenstecher)	ACARI: Eriophyidae
grape flea beetle	Altica chalybea Illiger	COLEOPTERA: Chrysomelidae

grape leaffolder	*Desmia funeralis* (Hübner)	LEPIDOPTERA: Pyralidae
grape mealybug	*Pseudococcus maritimus* (Ehrhorn)	HOMOPTERA: Pseudococcidae
grape phylloxera	*Daktulosphaira vitifoliae* (Fitch)	HOMOPTERA: Phylloxeridae
grape plume moth	*Pterophorus periscelidactylus* Fitch	LEPIDOPTERA: Pterophoridae
grape root borer	*Vitacea polistiformis* (Harris)	LEPIDOPTERA: Sesiidae
grape rootworm	*Fidia viticida* Walsh	COLEOPTERA: Chrysomelidae
grape sawfly	*Erythraspides vitis* (Harris)	HYMENOPTERA: Tenthredinidae
grape scale	*Diaspidiotus uvae* (Comstock)	HOMOPTERA: Diaspididae
grape seed chalcid	*Evoxysoma vitis* (Saunders)	HYMENOPTERA: Eurytomidae
grape thrips	*Drepanothrips reuteri* Uzel	THYSANOPTERA: Thripidae
grape trunk borer	*Clytoleptus albofasciatus* (Laporte & Gory)	COLEOPTERA: Cerambycidae
grape whitefly	*Trialeurodes vittata* (Quaintance)	HOMOPTERA: Aleyrodidae
grapeleaf skeletonizer	*Harrisina americana* (Guérin)	LEPIDOPTERA: Zygaenidae
grapevine aphid	*Aphis illinoisensis* Shimer	HOMOPTERA: Aphididae
grapevine looper	*Eulithis diversilineata* (Hübner)	LEPIDOPTERA: Geometridae
grass fleahopper	*Halticus chrysolepis* Kirkaldy	HETEROPTERA: Miridae
grass mite	*Siteroptes graminum* (Reuter)	ACARI: Siteroptidae
grass sawfly	*Pachynematus extensicornis* (Norton)	HYMENOPTERA: Tenthredinidae
grass scolytid	*Hypothenemus pubescens* Hopkins	COLEOPTERA: Scolytidae
grass sharpshooter	*Draeculacephala minerva* Ball	HOMOPTERA: Cicadellidae
grass sheathminer	*Cerodontha dorsalis* (Loew)	DIPTERA: Agromyzidae
grass thrips	*Anaphothrips obscurus* (Müller)	THYSANOPTERA: Thripidae
grass webworm	*Herpetogramma licarsisalis* (Walker)	LEPIDOPTERA: Pyralidae
grasshopper bee fly	*Systoechus vulgaris* Loew	DIPTERA: Bombyliidae
grasshopper maggots	*Blaesoxipha* spp.	DIPTERA: Sarcophagidae
gray garden slug	*Agriolimax reticulatus* (Müller)	STYLOMMATOPHORA: Limacidae
gray lawn leafhopper	*Exitianus exitiosus* (Uhler)	HOMOPTERA: Cicadellidae
gray pineapple mealybug	*Dysmicoccus neobrevipes* Beardsley	HOMOPTERA: Pseudococcidae
gray sugarcane mealybug	*Dysmicoccus boninsis* (Kuwana)	HOMOPTERA: Pseudococcidae
gray sunflower seed weevil	*Smicronyx sordidus* LeConte	COLEOPTERA: Curculionidae
gray willow leaf beetle	*Pyrrhalta decora decora* (Say)	COLEOPTERA: Chrysomelidae
graybanded leafroller	*Argyrotaenia mariana* (Fernald)	LEPIDOPTERA: Tortricidae
great ash sphinx	*Sphinx chersis* (Hübner)	LEPIDOPTERA: Sphingidae
Great Basin wireworm	*Ctenicera pruinina* (Horn)	COLEOPTERA: Elateridae
greater wax moth	*Galleria mellonella* (Linnaeus)	LEPIDOPTERA: Pyralidae
greedy scale	*Hemiberlesia rapax* (Comstock)	HOMOPTERA: Diaspididae
green budworm	*Hedya nubiferana* (Haworth)	LEPIDOPTERA: Tortricidae
green cloverworm	*Plathypena scabra* (Fabricius)	LEPIDOPTERA: Noctuidae

green fruitworm	*Lithophane antennata* (Walker)	LEPIDOPTERA: Noctuidae
green garden looper	*Chrysodeixis eriosoma* (Doubleday)	LEPIDOPTERA: Noctuidae
green June beetle	*Cotinis nitida* (Linnaeus)	COLEOPTERA: Scarabaeidae
green peach aphid	*Myzus persicae* (Sulzer)	HOMOPTERA: Aphididae
green rose chafer	*Dichelonyx backi* (Kirby)	COLEOPTERA: Scarabaeidae
green scale	*Coccus viridis* (Green)	HOMOPTERA: Coccidae
green shield scale	*Pulvinaria psidii* Maskell	HOMOPTERA: Coccidae
green sphinx	*Tinostoma smaragditis* (Meyrick)	LEPIDOPTERA: Sphingidae
green spruce aphid	*Cinara fornacula* Hottes	HOMOPTERA: Aphididae
green stink bug	*Acrosternum hilare* (Say)	HETEROPTERA: Pentatomidae
greenbug	*Schizaphis graminum* (Rondani)	HOMOPTERA: Aphididae
greenheaded spruce sawfly	*Pikonema dimmockii* (Cresson)	HYMENOPTERA: Tenthredinidae
greenhouse leaftier[14]	*Udea rubigalis* (Guenée)	LEPIDOPTERA: Pyralidae
greenhouse orthezia	*Orthezia insignis* Browne	HOMOPTERA: Ortheziidae
greenhouse slug	*Milax gagates* (Draparnaud)	STYLOMMATOPHORA: Limacidae
greenhouse stone cricket	*Tachycines asynamorus* Adelung	ORTHOPTERA: Gryllacrididae
greenhouse thrips	*Heliothrips haemorrhoidalis* (Bouché)	THYSANOPTERA: Thripidae
greenhouse whitefly	*Trialeurodes vaporariorum* (Westwood)	HOMOPTERA: Aleyrodidae
greenstriped grasshopper	*Chortophaga viridifasciata* (De Geer)	ORTHOPTERA: Acrididae
greenstriped mapleworm	*Dryocampa rubicunda* (Fabricius)	LEPIDOPTERA: Saturniidae
gregarious oak leafminer	*Cameraria cincinnatiella* (Chambers)	LEPIDOPTERA: Gracillariidae
ground mealybug	*Rhizoecus falcifer* Künckel d'Herculais	HOMOPTERA: Pseudococcidae
guar midge	*Contarinia texana* (Felt)	DIPTERA: Cecidomyiidae
Guinea ant	*Tetramorium bicarinatum* (Nylander)	HYMENOPTERA: Formicidae
Guinea feather louse	*Goniodes numidae* Mjberg	MALLOPHAGA: Philopteridae
Gulf Coast tick	*Amblyomma maculatum* Koch	ACARI: Ixodidae
Gulf wireworm	*Conoderus amplicollis* (Gyllenhal)	COLEOPTERA: Elateridae
gypsy moth	*Lymantria dispar* (Linnaeus)	LEPIDOPTERA: Lymantriidae

---

H

---

hackberry engraver	*Scolytus muticus* Say	COLEOPTERA: Scolytidae
hackberry lace bug	*Corythucha celtidis* Osborn & Drake	HETEROPTERA: Tingidae

---

[14]Also called celery leaftier.

hackberry nipplegall maker	*Pachypsylla celtidismamma* (Fletcher)	HOMOPTERA: Psyllidae
hag moth	*Phobetron pithecium* (J.E. Smith)	LEPIDOPTERA: Limacodidae
hairy chinch bug	*Blissus leucopterus hirtus* Montandon	HETEROPTERA: Lygaeidae
hairy fungus beetle	*Typhaea stercorea* (Linnaeus)	COLEOPTERA: Mycetophagidae
hairy maggot blow fly	*Chrysomya rufifacies* (Macquart)	DIPTERA: Calliphoridae
hairy rove beetle	*Creophilus maxillosus* (Linnaeus)	COLEOPTERA: Staphylinidae
hairy spider beetle	*Ptinus villiger* (Reitter)	COLEOPTERA: Ptinidae
Hall scale	*Nilotaspis halli* (Green)	HOMOPTERA: Diaspididae
hard maple budminer	*Obrussa ochrefasciella* (Chambers)	LEPIDOPTERA: Nepticulidae
harlequin bug	*Murgantia histrionica* (Hahn)	HETEROPTERA: Pentatomidae
harlequin cockroach	*Neostylopyga rhombifolia* (Stoll)	BLATTODEA: Blattidae
hau leafminer	*Philodoria hauicola* (Swezey)	LEPIDOPTERA: Gracillariidae
Hawaiian antlion	*Eidoleon wilsoni* (McLachlan)	NEUROPTERA: Myrmeleontidae
Hawaiian beet webworm	*Spoladea recurvalis* (Fabricius)	LEPIDOPTERA: Pyralidae
Hawaiian bud moth	*Helicoverpa hawaiiensis* (Quaintance & Brues)	LEPIDOPTERA: Noctuidae
Hawaiian carpenter ant	*Camponotus variegatus* (F. Smith)	HYMENOPTERA: Formicidae
Hawaiian flower thrips	*Thrips hawaiiensis* (Morgan)	THYSANOPTERA: Thripidae
Hawaiian grass thrips	*Anaphothrips swezeyi* Moulton	THYSANOPTERA: Thripidae
Hawaiian pelagic water strider	*Halobates hawaiiensis* Usinger	HETEROPTERA: Gerridae
Hawaiian sphinx	*Hyles calida* (Butler)	LEPIDOPTERA: Sphingidae
hawthorn lace bug	*Corythucha cydoniae* (Fitch)	HETEROPTERA: Tingidae
hazelnut weevil	*Curculio obtusus* (Blanchard)	COLEOPTERA: Curculionidae
head louse	*Pediculus humanus capitis* De Geer	ANOPLURA: Pediculidae
heath spittlebug	*Clastoptera saintcyri* Provancher	HOMOPTERA: Cercopidae
hellgrammite[15]	*Corydalus cornutus* (Linnaeus)	NEUROPTERA: Corydalidae
hemispherical scale	*Saissetia coffeae* (Walker)	HOMOPTERA: Coccidae
hemlock borer	*Melanophila fulvoguttata* (Harris)	COLEOPTERA: Buprestidae
hemlock looper	*Lambdina fiscellaria fiscellaria* (Guenée)	LEPIDOPTERA: Geometridae
hemlock sawfly	*Neodiprion tsugae* Middleton	HYMENOPTERA: Diprionidae
hemlock scale	*Abgrallaspis ithacae* (Ferris)	HOMOPTERA: Diaspididae
hemlock woolly adelgid	*Adelges tsugae* Annand	HOMOPTERA: Adelgidae
Hessian fly	*Mayetiola destructor* (Say)	DIPTERA: Cecidomyiidae
hibiscus leafminer	*Philodoria hibiscella* (Swezey)	LEPIDOPTERA: Gracillariidae
hibiscus mealybug	*Nipaecoccus viridis* (Newstead)	HOMOPTERA: Pseudococcidae

---

[15]Adult called dobsonfly.

hibiscus whitefly	*Singhius hibisci* (Kotinsky)	HOMOPTERA: Aleyrodidae
hickory bark beetle	*Scolytus quadrispinosus* Say	COLEOPTERA: Scolytidae
hickory horned devil[16]	*Citheronia regalis* (Fabricius)	LEPIDOPTERA: Saturniidae
hickory leafroller	*Argyrotaenia juglandana* (Fernald)	LEPIDOPTERA: Tortricidae
hickory plant bug	*Lygocoris caryae* (Knight)	HETEROPTERA: Miridae
hickory shuckworm	*Cydia caryana* (Fitch)	LEPIDOPTERA: Tortricidae
hickory tussock moth	*Lophocampa caryae* (Harris)	LEPIDOPTERA: Arctiidae
hide beetle	*Dermestes maculatus* De Geer	COLEOPTERA: Dermestidae
High Plains grasshopper	*Dissosteira longipennis* (Thomas)	ORTHOPTERA: Acrididae
hog follicle mite	*Demodex phylloides* Csokor	ACARI: Demodicidae
hog louse	*Haematopinus suis* (Linnaeus)	ANOPLURA: Haematopinidae
holly leafminer	*Phytomyza ilicis* Curtis	DIPTERA: Agromyzidae
holly scale	*Dynaspidiotus britannicus* (Newstead)	HOMOPTERA: Diaspididae
hollyhock plant bug	*Brooksetta althaeae* (Hussey)	HETEROPTERA: Miridae
hollyhock weevil	*Apion longirostre* Olivier	COLEOPTERA: Curculionidae
honey bee	*Apis mellifera* Linnaeus	HYMENOPTERA: Apidae
honey bee mite	*Acarapis woodi* (Rennie)	ACARI: Tarsonemidae
honeylocust plant bug	*Diaphnocoris chlorionis* (Say)	HETEROPTERA: Miridae
honeylocust spider mite	*Platytetranychus multidigitali* (Ewing)	ACARI: Tetranychidae
honeysuckle leafminer	*Swezeyula lonicerae* Zimmerman & Bradley	LEPIDOPTERA: Elachistidae
honeysuckle sawfly	*Zaraea inflata* Norton	HYMENOPTERA: Cimbicidae
hop aphid	*Phorodon humuli* (Schrank)	HOMOPTERA: Aphididae
hop flea beetle	*Psylliodes punctulata* Melsheimer	COLEOPTERA: Chrysomelidae
hop looper	*Hypena humuli* (Harris)	LEPIDOPTERA: Noctuidae
hop plant bug	*Taedia hawleyi* (Knight)	HETEROPTERA: Miridae
horn fly	*Haematobia irritans* (Linnaeus)	DIPTERA: Muscidae
horned passalus	*Odontotaenius disjunctus* (Illiger)	COLEOPTERA: Passalidae
horned squash bug	*Anasa armigera* (Say)	HETEROPTERA: Coreidae
hornet moth	*Sesia apiformis* (Clerck)	LEPIDOPTERA: Sesiidae
horse biting louse	*Bovicola equi* (Denny)	MALLOPHAGA: Trichodectidae
horse bot fly	*Gasterophilus intestinalis* (De Geer)	DIPTERA: Oestridae
horse follicle mite	*Demodex equi* Railliet	ACARI: Demodicidae
horse sucking louse	*Haematopinus asini* (Linnaeus)	ANOPLURA: Haematopinidae
horseradish flea beetle	*Phyllotreta armoraciae* (Koch)	COLEOPTERA: Chrysomelidae
house centipede	*Scutigera coleoptrata* (Linnaeus)	SCUTIGEROMORPHA: Scutigeridae

---

[16]Adult called regal moth.

house cricket	*Acheta domesticus* (Linnaeus)	ORTHOPTERA: Gryllidae
house fly	*Musca domestica* Linnaeus	DIPTERA: Muscidae
house mite	*Glycyphagus domesticus* (De Geer)	ACARI: Glycyphagidae
house mouse mite	*Liponyssoides sanguineus* (Hirst)	ACARI: Macronyssidae
household casebearer	*Phereoeca uterella* Walsingham	LEPIDOPTERA: Tineidae
human flea	*Pulex irritans* (Linnaeus)	SIPHONAPTERA: Pulicidae
hunting billbug	*Sphenophorus venatus vestitus* Chittenden	COLEOPTERA: Curculionidae
hyaline grass bug	*Liorhyssus hyalinus* (Fabricius)	HETEROPTERA: Rhopalidae

I

ilima leafminer	*Philodoria marginestrigata* (Walsingham)	LEPIDOPTERA: Gracillariidae
ilima moth	*Amyna natalis* (Walker)	LEPIDOPTERA: Noctuidae
imbricated snout beetle	*Epicaerus imbricatus* (Say)	COLEOPTERA: Curculionidae
immigrant acacia weevil	*Orthorhinus klugi* Boheman	COLEOPTERA: Curculionidae
imperial moth	*Eacles imperialis* (Drury)	LEPIDOPTERA: Saturniidae
imported cabbageworm	*Pieris rapae* (Linnaeus)	LEPIDOPTERA: Pieridae
imported crucifer weevil	*Baris lepidii* Germar	COLEOPTERA: Curculionidae
imported currantworm	*Nematus ribesii* (Scopoli)	HYMENOPTERA: Tenthredinidae
imported longhorned weevil	*Calomycterus setarius* Roelofs	COLEOPTERA: Curculionidae
imported willow leaf beetle	*Plagiodera versicolora* (Laicharting)	COLEOPTERA: Chrysomelidae
incense-cedar wasp	*Syntexis libocedrii* Rohwer	HYMENOPTERA: Anaxyelidae
Indianmeal moth	*Plodia interpunctella* (Hübner)	LEPIDOPTERA: Pyralidae
inornate scale	*Aonidiella inornata* McKenzie	HOMOPTERA: Diaspididae
insidious flower bug	*Orius insidiosus* (Say)	HETEROPTERA: Anthocoridae
introduced pine sawfly	*Diprion similis* (Hartig)	HYMENOPTERA: Diprionidae
io moth	*Automeris io* (Fabricius)	LEPIDOPTERA: Saturniidae
iris borer	*Macronoctua onusta* Grote	LEPIDOPTERA: Noctuidae
iris thrips	*Iridothrips iridis* (Watson)	THYSANOPTERA: Thripidae
iris weevil	*Mononychus vulpeculus* (Fabricius)	COLEOPTERA: Curculionidae
Italian pear scale	*Epidiaspis leperii* (Signoret)	HOMOPTERA: Diaspididae
itch mite	*Sarcoptes scabiei* (De Geer)	ACARI: Sarcoptidae
ivy aphid	*Aphis hederae* Kaltenbach	HOMOPTERA: Aphididae

J

jack pine budworm	*Choristoneura pinus* Freeman	LEPIDOPTERA: Tortricidae
jack pine sawfly	*Neodiprion pratti banksianae* Rohwer	HYMENOPTERA: Diprionidae
jack pine tip beetle	*Conophthorus banksianae* McPherson	COLEOPTERA: Scolytidae
Japanese beetle	*Popillia japonica* Newman	COLEOPTERA: Scarabaeidae
Japanese broadwinged katydid	*Holochlora japonica* Brunner von Wattenwyl	ORTHOPTERA: Tettigoniidae
Japanese grasshopper	*Oxya japonica* (Thunberg)	ORTHOPTERA: Acrididae
Jeffrey pine beetle	*Dendroctonus jeffreyi* Hopkins	COLEOPTERA: Scolytidae
Jerusalem cricket	*Stenopelmatus fuscus* Haldeman	ORTHOPTERA: Stenopelmatidae
juniper midge	*Contarinia juniperina* Felt	DIPTERA: Cecidomyiidae
juniper scale	*Carulaspis juniperi* (Bouché)	HOMOPTERA: Diaspididae
juniper tip midge	*Oligotrophus betheli* Felt	DIPTERA: Cecidomyiidae
juniper webworm	*Dichomeris marginella* (Fabricius)	LEPIDOPTERA: Gelechiidae

K

Kamehameha butterfly	*Vanessa tameamea* Eschscholtz	LEPIDOPTERA: Nymphalidae
keyhole wasp	*Pachodynerus nasidens* (Latreille)	HYMENOPTERA: Vespidae
khapra beetle	*Trogoderma granarium* Everts	COLEOPTERA: Dermestidae
kiawe bean weevil	*Algarobius bottimeri* Kingsolver	COLEOPTERA: Bruchidae
kiawe flower moth	*Ithome concolorella* (Chambers)	LEPIDOPTERA: Cosmopterigidae
kiawe roundheaded borer	*Placosternus crinicornis* (Chevrolat)	COLEOPTERA: Cerambycidae
kiawe scolytid	*Hypothenemus birmanus* (Eichhoff)	COLEOPTERA: Scolytidae
Kirkaldy whitefly	*Dialeurodes kirkaldyi* (Kotinsky)	HOMOPTERA: Aleyrodidae
Klamathweed beetle	*Chrysolina quadrigemina* (Suffrian)	COLEOPTERA: Chrysomelidae
koa bug	*Coleotichus blackburniae* White	HETEROPTERA: Pentatomidae
koa haole seed weevil	*Araecerus levipennis* Jordan	COLEOPTERA: Anthribidae
koa moth	*Scotorythra paludicola* (Butler)	LEPIDOPTERA: Geometridae
koa seedworm	*Cryptophlebia illepida* (Butler)	LEPIDOPTERA: Tortricidae
kou leafworm	*Ethmia nigroapicella* (Saalmüller)	LEPIDOPTERA: Oecophoridae

L

Common name	Scientific name	Classification
Lange metalmark	*Apodemia mormo langei* Comstock	LEPIDOPTERA: Riodinidae
lantana cerambycid	*Plagiohammus spinipennis* Thomson	COLEOPTERA: Cerambycidae
lantana defoliator caterpillar	*Hypena strigata* (Fabricius)	LEPIDOPTERA: Noctuidae
lantana gall fly	*Eutreta xanthochaeta* Aldrich	DIPTERA: Tephritidae
lantana hispid	*Uroplata girardi* Pic	COLEOPTERA: Chrysomelidae
lantana lace bug	*Teleonemia scrupulosa* Stål	HETEROPTERA: Tingidae
lantana leaf beetle	*Octotoma scabripennis* Guérin-Méneville	COLEOPTERA: Chrysomelidae
lantana leafminer	*Cremastobombycia lantanella* (Schrank)	LEPIDOPTERA: Gracillariidae
lantana leaftier	*Salbia haemorrhoidalis* Guenée	LEPIDOPTERA: Pyralidae
lantana plume moth	*Lantanophaga pusillidactyla* (Walker)	LEPIDOPTERA: Pterophoridae
lantana seed fly	*Ophiomyia lantanae* (Froggatt)	DIPTERA: Agromyzidae
lantana stick caterpillar	*Neogalea sunia* (Guenée)	LEPIDOPTERA: Noctuidae
lappet moth	*Phyllodesma americana* (Harris)	LEPIDOPTERA: Lasiocampidae
larch aphid	*Cinara laricis* (Walker)	HOMOPTERA: Aphididae
larch casebearer	*Coleophora laricella* (Hübner)	LEPIDOPTERA: Coleophoridae
larch sawfly	*Pristiphora erichsonii* (Hartig)	HYMENOPTERA: Tenthredinidae
larder beetle	*Dermestes lardarius* Linnaeus	COLEOPTERA: Dermestidae
large aspen tortrix	*Choristoneura conflictana* (Walker)	LEPIDOPTERA: Tortricidae
large bigeyed bug	*Geocoris bullatus* (Say)	HETEROPTERA: Lygaeidae
large brown spider	*Heteropoda venatoria* (Linnaeus)	ARANEAE: Sparassidae
large chestnut weevil	*Curculio caryatrypes* (Boheman)	COLEOPTERA: Curculionidae
large chicken louse	*Goniodes gigas* (Taschenberg)	MALLOPHAGA: Philopteridae
large cottony scale	*Pulvinaria mammeae* Maskell	HOMOPTERA: Coccidae
large duck louse	*Trinoton querquedulae* (Linnaeus)	MALLOPHAGA: Menoponidae
large kissing bug	*Triatoma rubrofasciata* (De Geer)	HETEROPTERA: Reduviidae
large milkweed bug	*Oncopeltus fasciatus* (Dallas)	HETEROPTERA: Lygaeidae
large red slug	*Arion ater rufus* (Linnaeus)	STYLOMMATOPHORA: Arionidae
large turkey louse	*Chelopistes meleagridis* (Linnaeus)	MALLOPHAGA: Philopteridae
larger black flour beetle	*Cynaeus angustus* (LeConte)	COLEOPTERA: Tenebrionidae
larger canna leafroller	*Calpodes ethlius* (Stoll)	LEPIDOPTERA: Hesperiidae
larger elm leaf beetle	*Monocesta coryli* (Say)	COLEOPTERA: Chrysomelidae
larger grain borer	*Prostephanus truncatus* (Horn)	COLEOPTERA: Bostrichidae
larger Hawaiian cutworm	*Agrotis crinigera* (Butler)	LEPIDOPTERA: Noctuidae
larger lantana butterfly	*Strymon echion* (Linnaeus)	LEPIDOPTERA: Lycaenidae
larger pale trogiid	*Trogium pulsatorium* (Linnaeus)	PSOCOPTERA: Trogiidae

larger shothole borer	*Scolytus mali* (Bechstein)	COLEOPTERA: Scolytidae
larger yellow ant	*Acanthomyops interjectus* (Mayr)	HYMENOPTERA: Formicidae
larkspur leafminer complex[17]	*Phytomyza* spp.	DIPTERA: Agromyzidae
latania scale	*Hemiberlesia lataniae* (Signoret)	HOMOPTERA: Diaspididae
latrine fly	*Fannia scalaris* (Fabricius)	DIPTERA: Muscidae
lawn armyworm	*Spodoptera mauritia* (Boisduval)	LEPIDOPTERA: Noctuidae
lawn leafhopper	*Deltocephalus hospes* Kirkaldy	HOMOPTERA: Cicadellidae
leadcable borer	*Scobicia declivis* (LeConte)	COLEOPTERA: Bostrichidae
leaf crumpler	*Acrobasis indigenella* (Zeller)	LEPIDOPTERA: Pyralidae
leaffooted bug	*Leptoglossus phyllopus* (Linnaeus)	HETEROPTERA: Coreidae
leaffooted pine seed bug	*Leptoglossus corculus* (Say)	HETEROPTERA: Coreidae
leafhopper assassin bug	*Zelus renardii* Kolenati	HETEROPTERA: Reduviidae
leek moth	*Acrolepiopsis assectella* (Zeller)	LEPIDOPTERA: Acrolepiidae
leopard moth	*Zeuzera pyrina* (Linnaeus)	LEPIDOPTERA: Cossidae
lespedeza webworm	*Tetralopha scortealis* (Lederer)	LEPIDOPTERA: Pyralidae
lesser appleworm	*Grapholita prunivora* (Walsh)	LEPIDOPTERA: Tortricidae
lesser brown scorpion	*Isometrus maculatus* De Geer	SCORPIONES: Buthidae
lesser bud moth	*Recurvaria nanella* (Denis & Schiffermüller)	LEPIDOPTERA: Gelechiidae
lesser bulb fly	*Eumerus tuberculatus* Rondani	DIPTERA: Syrphidae
lesser canna leafroller	*Geshna cannalis* (Quaintance)	LEPIDOPTERA: Pyralidae
lesser clover leaf weevil	*Hypera nigrirostris* (Fabricius)	COLEOPTERA: Curculionidae
lesser cornstalk borer	*Elasmopalpus lignosellus* (Zeller)	LEPIDOPTERA: Pyralidae
lesser ensign wasp	*Szepligetella sericea* (Cameron)	HYMENOPTERA: Evaniidae
lesser follicle mite	*Demodex brevis* Bulanova	ACARI: Demodicidae
lesser grain borer	*Rhyzopertha dominica* (Fabricius)	COLEOPTERA: Bostrichidae
lesser lawn leafhopper	*Graminella sonora* (Ball)	HOMOPTERA: Cicadellidae
lesser mealworm	*Alphitobius diaperinus* (Panzer)	COLEOPTERA: Tenebrionidae
lesser orchid weevil	*Orchidophilus peregrinator* Buchanan	COLEOPTERA: Curculionidae
lesser peachtree borer	*Synanthedon pictipes* (Grote & Robinson)	LEPIDOPTERA: Sesiidae
lesser wax moth	*Achroia grisella* (Fabricius)	LEPIDOPTERA: Pyralidae
lettuce root aphid	*Pemphigus bursarius* (Linnaeus)	HOMOPTERA: Aphididae
light brown apple moth	*Epiphyas postvittana* (Walker)	LEPIDOPTERA: Tortricidae
lilac borer[18]	*Podosesia syringae* (Harris)	LEPIDOPTERA: Sesiidae
lilac leafminer	*Caloptilia syringella* (Fabricius)	LEPIDOPTERA: Gracillariidae

---

[17]Includes *Phytomyza aconti* Hendel, *P. delphiniae* Frost, and *P. delphinivora* Spenser.
[18]Also called ash borer.

Common name	Scientific name	Order: Family
lily bulb thrips	*Liothrips vaneeckei* Priesner	THYSANOPTERA: Phlaeothripidae
lily leaf beetle	*Lilioceris lilii* (Scopoli)	COLEOPTERA: Chrysomelidae
lily weevil	*Agasphaerops nigra* Horn	COLEOPTERA: Curculionidae
limabean pod borer	*Etiella zinckenella* (Treitschke)	LEPIDOPTERA: Pyralidae
limabean vine borer	*Monoptilota pergratialis* (Hulst)	LEPIDOPTERA: Pyralidae
linden borer	*Saperda vestita* Say	COLEOPTERA: Cerambycidae
linden looper	*Erannis tiliaria* (Harris)	LEPIDOPTERA: Geometridae
lined click beetle	*Agriotes lineatus* (Linnaeus)	COLEOPTERA: Elateridae
lined spittlebug	*Neophilaenus lineatus* (Linnaeus)	HOMOPTERA: Cercopidae
lined stalk borer	*Oligia fractilinea* (Grote)	LEPIDOPTERA: Noctuidae
lion beetle	*Ulochaetes leoninus* LeConte	COLEOPTERA: Cerambycidae
litchi fruit moth	*Cryptophlebia ombrodelta* (Lower)	LEPIDOPTERA: Tortricidae
litchi mite	*Eriophyes litchii* Keifer	ACARI: Eriophyidae
little black ant	*Monomorium minimum* (Buckley)	HYMENOPTERA: Formicidae
little carpenterworm	*Prionoxystus macmurtrei* (Guérin)	LEPIDOPTERA: Cossidae
little fire ant	*Ochetomyrmex auropunctatus* (Roger)	HYMENOPTERA: Formicidae
little green leafhopper	*Balclutha incisa hospes* (Kirkaldy)	HOMOPTERA: Cicadellidae
little house fly	*Fannia canicularis* (Linnaeus)	DIPTERA: Muscidae
little yellow ant	*Plagiolepis alluaudi* Emery	HYMENOPTERA: Formicidae
loblolly pine sawfly	*Neodiprion taedae linearis* Ross	HYMENOPTERA: Diprionidae
locust borer	*Megacyllene robiniae* (Forster)	COLEOPTERA: Cerambycidae
locust leafminer	*Odontota dorsalis* (Thunberg)	COLEOPTERA: Chrysomelidae
locust leafroller	*Nephopterix subcaesiella* (Clemens)	LEPIDOPTERA: Pyralidae
locust twig borer	*Ecdytolopha insiticiana* Zeller	LEPIDOPTERA: Tortricidae
lodgepole cone beetle[19]	*Conophthorus ponderosae* Hopkins	COLEOPTERA: Scolytidae
lodgepole needleminer	*Coleotechnites milleri* (Busck)	LEPIDOPTERA: Gelechiidae
lodgepole pine beetle	*Dendroctonus murrayanae* Hopkins	COLEOPTERA: Scolytidae
lodgepole sawfly	*Neodiprion burkei* Middleton	HYMENOPTERA: Diprionidae
lodgepole terminal weevil	*Pissodes terminalis* Hopping	COLEOPTERA: Curculionidae
lone star tick	*Amblyomma americanum* (Linnaeus)	ACARI: Ixodidae
long brown scale	*Coccus longulus* (Douglas)	HOMOPTERA: Coccidae
longheaded flour beetle	*Latheticus oryzae* Waterhouse	COLEOPTERA: Tenebrionidae
longleaf pine seedworm	*Cydia ingens* (Heinrich)	LEPIDOPTERA: Tortricidae
longlegged ant	*Anoplolepis longipes* (Jerdon)	HYMENOPTERA: Formicidae
longnosed cattle louse	*Linognathus vituli* (Linnaeus)	ANOPLURA: Linognathidae

[19]Also called poderosa pine cone beetle.

longtailed fruit fly parasite	*Opius longicaudatus* Ashmead	HYMENOPTERA: Braconidae
longtailed mealybug	*Pseudococcus longispinus* (Targioni-Tozzetti)	HOMOPTERA: Pseudococcidae
lotis blue	*Lycaeides argyrognomon lotis* (Lintner)	LEPIDOPTERA: Lycaenidae
Louisiana red crayfish	*Procambarus clarkii* (Girard)	DECAPODA: Cambaridae
lowland tree termite	*Incisitermes immigrans* (Snyder)	ISOPTERA: Kalotermitidae
lubber grasshopper	*Brachystola magna* (Girard)	ORTHOPTERA: Acrididae
luna moth	*Actias luna* (Linnaeus)	LEPIDOPTERA: Saturniidae

M

Macao paper wasp	*Polistes macaensis* (Fabricius)	HYMENOPTERA: Vespidae
Madeira cockroach	*Leucophaea maderae* (Fabricius)	BLATTODEA: Blaberidae
magnolia scale	*Neolecanium cornuparvum* (Thro)	HOMOPTERA: Coccidae
mahogany bark weevil	*Macrocopturus floridanus* (Fall)	COLEOPTERA: Curculionidae
mahogany leafminer	*Phyllocnistis meliacella* Becker	LEPIDOPTERA: Gracillariidae
mahogany webworm	*Macalla thyrsisalis* Walker	LEPIDOPTERA: Pyralidae
maize billbug	*Sphenophorus maidis* Chittenden	COLEOPTERA: Curculionidae
maize weevil	*Sitophilus zeamais* Motschulsky	COLEOPTERA: Curculionidae
mango bark beetle	*Hypocryphalus mangiferae* (Stebbing)	COLEOPTERA: Scolytidae
mango bud mite	*Eriophyes mangiferae* (Sayed)	ACARI: Eriophyidae
mango flower beetle	*Protaetia fusca* (Herbst)	COLEOPTERA: Scarabaeidae
mango shoot caterpillar	*Penicillaria jocosatrix* Guenée	LEPIDOPTERA: Noctuidae
mango spider mite	*Oligonychus mangiferus* (Rahman & Sapra)	ACARI: Tetranychidae
mango weevil	*Cryptorhynchus mangiferae* (Fabricius)	COLEOPTERA: Curculionidae
maple bladdergall mite	*Vasates quadripedes* Shimer	ACARI: Eriophyidae
maple callus borer	*Synanthedon acerni* (Clemens)	LEPIDOPTERA: Sesiidae
maple leafcutter	*Paraclemensia acerifoliella* (Fitch)	LEPIDOPTERA: Incurvariidae
maple petiole borer	*Caulocampus acericaulis* (MacGillivray)	HYMENOPTERA: Tenthredinidae
maple trumpet skeletonizer	*Epinotia aceriella* (Clemens)	LEPIDOPTERA: Tortricidae
margined blister beetle	*Epicauta pestifera* Werner	COLEOPTERA: Meloidae
Maricopa harvester ant	*Pogonomyrmex maricopa* Wheeler	HYMENOPTERA: Formicidae
marsh slug	*Agriolimax laevis* (Müller)	STYLOMMATOPHORA: Limacidae
masked hunter	*Reduvius personatus* (Linnaeus)	HETEROPTERA: Reduviidae
mauna loa bean beetle	*Araeocorynus cumingi* Jekel	COLEOPTERA: Anthribidae
McDaniel spider mite	*Tetranychus mcdanieli* McGregor	ACARI: Tetranychidae
meadow plant bug	*Leptopterna dolabrata* (Linnaeus)	HETEROPTERA: Miridae

meadow spittlebug	*Philaenus spumarius* (Linnaeus)	HOMOPTERA: Cercopidae
meal moth	*Pyralis farinalis* Linnaeus	LEPIDOPTERA: Pyralidae
mealy plum aphid	*Hyalopterus pruni* (Geoffroy)	HOMOPTERA: Aphididae
mealybug destroyer	*Cryptolaemus montrouzieri* Mulsant	COLEOPTERA: Coccinellidae
Mediterranean flour moth	*Anagasta kuehniella* (Zeller)	LEPIDOPTERA: Pyralidae
Mediterranean fruit fly	*Ceratitis capitata* (Wiedemann)	DIPTERA: Tephritidae
melastoma borer	*Selca brunella* (Hampson)	LEPIDOPTERA: Noctuidae
melon aphid[20]	*Aphis gossypii* Glover	HOMOPTERA: Aphididae
melon fly	*Dacus cucurbitae* Coquillett	DIPTERA: Tephritidae
melonworm	*Diaphania hyalinata* (Linnaeus)	LEPIDOPTERA: Pyralidae
merchant grain beetle	*Oryzaephilus mercator* (Fauvel)	COLEOPTERA: Cucujidae
Mexican bean beetle	*Epilachna varivestis* Mulsant	COLEOPTERA: Coccinellidae
Mexican bean weevil	*Zabrotes subfasciatus* (Boheman)	COLEOPTERA: Bruchidae
Mexican black scale	*Saissetia miranda* (Cockerell & Parrott)	HOMOPTERA: Coccidae
Mexican corn rootworm	*Diabrotica virgifera zeae* Krysan & Smith	COLEOPTERA: Chrysomelidae
Mexican fruit fly	*Anastrepha ludens* (Loew)	DIPTERA: Tephritidae
Mexican leafroller	*Amorbia emigratella* Busck	LEPIDOPTERA: Tortricidae
Mexican mealybug	*Phenacoccus gossypii* Townsend & Cockerell	HOMOPTERA: Pseudococcidae
Mexican pine beetle	*Dendroctonus approximatus* Dietz	COLEOPTERA: Scolytidae
Mexican rice borer	*Eoreuma loftini* (Dyar)	LEPIDOPTERA: Pyralidae
migratory grasshopper	*Melanoplus sanguinipes* (Fabricius)	ORTHOPTERA: Acrididae
mimosa webworm	*Homadaula anisocentra* Meyrick	LEPIDOPTERA: Plutellidae
mining scale	*Howardia biclavis* (Comstock)	HOMOPTERA: Diaspididae
mint aphid	*Ovatus crataegarius* (Walker)	HOMOPTERA: Aphididae
minute egg parasite	*Trichogramma minutum* Riley	HYMENOPTERA: Trichogrammatidae
minute pirate bug	*Orius tristicolor* (White)	HETEROPTERA: Anthocoridae
mission blue	*Icaricia icarioides missionensis* (Hovanitz)	LEPIDOPTERA: Lycaenidae
mold mite	*Tyrophagus putrescentiae* (Schrank)	ACARI: Acaridae
monarch butterfly	*Danaus plexippus* (Linnaeus)	LEPIDOPTERA: Danaidae
monkeypod moth	*Polydesma umbricola* Boisduval	LEPIDOPTERA: Noctuidae
monkeypod roundheaded borer	*Xystrocera globosa* (Olivier)	COLEOPTERA: Cerambycidae
Monterey pine cone beetle	*Conophthorus radiatae* Hopkins	COLEOPTERA: Scolytidae
Monterey pine resin midge	*Cecidomyia resinicoloides* Williams	DIPTERA: Cecidomyiidae
Monterey pine weevil	*Pissodes radiatae* Hopkins	COLEOPTERA: Curculionidae
Mormon cricket	*Anabrus simplex* Haldeman	ORTHOPTERA: Tettigoniidae

---

[20]Also called cotton aphid.

morningglory leafminer	*Bedellia somnulentella* (Zeller)	LEPIDOPTERA: Lyonetiidae
Morrill lace bug	*Corythucha morrilli* Osborn & Drake	HETEROPTERA: Tingidae
mossyrose gall wasp	*Diplolepis rosae* (Linnaeus)	HYMENOPTERA: Cynipidae
mottled tortoise beetle	*Deloyala guttata* (Olivier)	COLEOPTERA: Chrysomelidae
mountain-ash sawfly	*Pristiphora geniculata* (Hartig)	HYMENOPTERA: Tenthredinidae
mountain leafhopper	*Colladonus montanus* (Van Duzee)	HOMOPTERA: Cicadellidae
mountain pine beetle	*Dendroctonus ponderosae* Hopkins	COLEOPTERA: Scolytidae
mountain pine coneworm	*Dioryctria yatesi* Mutuura & Munroe	LEPIDOPTERA: Pyralidae
mourningcloak butterfly	*Nymphalis antiopa* (Linnaeus)	LEPIDOPTERA: Nymphalidae
mulberry whitefly	*Tetraleurodes mori* (Quaintance)	HOMOPTERA: Aleyrodidae
mullein thrips	*Haplothrips verbasci* (Osborn)	THYSANOPTERA: Phlaeothripidae

---

N

Nantucket pine tip moth	*Rhyacionia frustrana* (Comstock)	LEPIDOPTERA: Tortricidae
narcissus bulb fly	*Merodon equestris* (Fabricius)	DIPTERA: Syrphidae
narrownecked grain beetle	*Anthicus floralis* (Linnaeus)	COLEOPTERA: Anthicidae
narrowwinged mantid	*Tenodera augustipennis* Saussure	MANTODEA: Mantidae
native elm bark beetle	*Hylurgopinus rufipes* (Eichhoff)	COLEOPTERA: Scolytidae
native holly leafminer	*Phytomyza ilicicola* Loew	DIPTERA: Agromyzidae
navel orangeworm	*Amyelois transitella* (Walker)	LEPIDOPTERA: Pyralidae
Nevada sage grasshopper	*Melanoplus rugglesi* Gurney	ORTHOPTERA: Acrididae
New Guinea sugarcane weevil	*Rhabdoscelus obscurus* (Boisduval)	COLEOPTERA: Curculionidae
new house borer	*Arhopalus productus* (LeConte)	COLEOPTERA: Cerambycidae
New York weevil	*Ithycerus noveboracensis* (Forster)	COLEOPTERA: Curculionidae
nigra scale	*Parasaissetra nigra* (Nietner)	HOMOPTERA: Coccidae
northeastern sawyer	*Monochamus notatus* (Drury)	COLEOPTERA: Cerambycidae
northern cattle grub	*Hypoderma bovis* (Linnaeus)	DIPTERA: Oestridae
northern corn rootworm	*Diabrotica barberi* Smith & Lawrence	COLEOPTERA: Chrysomelidae
northern fowl mite	*Ornithonyssus sylviarum* (Canestrini & Fanzago)	ACARI: Macronyssidae
northern house mosquito	*Culex pipiens* Linnaeus	DIPTERA: Culicidae
northern masked chafer	*Cyclocephala borealis* Arrow	COLEOPTERA: Scarabaeidae
northern mole cricket	*Neocurtilla hexadactyla* (Perty)	ORTHOPTERA: Gryllotalpidae
northern pitch twig moth	*Petrova albicapitana* (Busck)	LEPIDOPTERA: Tortricidae
northern rat flea	*Nosopsyllus fasciatus* (Bosc)	SIPHONAPTERA: Ceratophyllidae
northwest coast mosquito	*Aedes aboriginis* Dyar	DIPTERA: Culicidae

42

Norway maple aphid	*Periphyllus lyropictus* (Kessler)	HOMOPTERA: Aphididae
nose bot fly	*Gasterophilus haemorrhoidalis* (Linnaeus)	DIPTERA: Oestridae
nutgrass armyworm	*Spodoptera exempta* (Walker)	LEPIDOPTERA: Noctuidae
nutgrass billbug	*Sphenophorus cariosus* (Olivier)	COLEOPTERA: Curculionidae
nutgrass borer moth	*Bactra venosana* (Zeller)	LEPIDOPTERA: Tortricidae
nutgrass weevil	*Athesapeuta cyperi* Marshall	COLEOPTERA: Curculionidae
Nuttall blister beetle	*Lytta nuttalli* Say	COLEOPTERA: Meloidae

O

oak clearwing moth	*Paranthrene asilipennis* (Boisduval)	LEPIDOPTERA: Sesiidae
oak lace bug	*Corythucha arcuata* (Say)	HETEROPTERA: Tingidae
oak leafroller	*Archips semiferana* (Walker)	LEPIDOPTERA: Tortricidae
oak leaftier	*Croesia semipurpurana* (Kearfott)	LEPIDOPTERA: Tortricidae
oak lecanium	*Parthenolecanium quercifex* (Fitch)	HOMOPTERA: Coccidae
oak sapling borer	*Goes tesselatus* (Haldeman)	COLEOPTERA: Cerambycidae
oak skeletonizer	*Bucculatrix ainsliella* Murtfeldt	LEPIDOPTERA: Lyonetiidae
oak timberworm	*Arrhenodes minutus* (Drury)	COLEOPTERA: Brentidae
oak webworm	*Archips fervidana* (Clemens)	LEPIDOPTERA: Tortricidae
obliquebanded leafroller	*Choristoneura rosaceana* (Harris)	LEPIDOPTERA: Tortricidae
obscure mealybug	*Pseudococcus affinis* (Maskell)	HOMOPTERA: Pseudococcidae
obscure root weevil	*Sciopithes obscurus* Horn	COLEOPTERA: Curculionidae
obscure scale	*Melanaspis obscura* (Comstock)	HOMOPTERA: Diaspididae
oceanic burrower bug	*Geotomus pygmaeus* (Dallas)	HETEROPTERA: Cydnidae
oceanic embiid	*Aposthonia oceania* (Ross)	EMBIIDINA: Oligotomidae
oceanic field cricket	*Teleogryllus oceanicus* (Le Guillou)	ORTHOPTERA: Gryllidae
odd beetle	*Thylodrias contractus* Motschulsky	COLEOPTERA: Dermestidae
odorous house ant	*Tapinoma sessile* (Say)	HYMENOPTERA: Formicidae
old house borer	*Hylotrupes bajulus* (Linnaeus)	COLEOPTERA: Cerambycidae
oleander aphid	*Aphis nerii* Boyer de Fonscolombe	HOMOPTERA: Aphididae
oleander hawk moth	*Daphnis nerii* (Linnaeus)	LEPIDOPTERA: Sphingidae
oleander pit scale	*Asterolecanium pustulans* (Cockerell)	HOMOPTERA: Asterolecaniidae
oleander scale	*Aspidiotus nerii* Bouché	HOMOPTERA: Diaspididae
olive fruit fly	*Dacus oleae* (Gmelin)	DIPTERA: Tephritidae
olive scale	*Parlatoria oleae* (Colvée)	HOMOPTERA: Diaspididae
omnivorous leaftier	*Cnephasia longana* (Haworth)	LEPIDOPTERA: Tortricidae

omnivorous looper	*Sabulodes aegrotata* (Guenée)	LEPIDOPTERA: Geometridae
onespotted stink bug	*Euschistus variolarius* (Palisot de Beauvois)	HETEROPTERA: Pentatomidae
onion aphid	*Neotoxoptera formosana* (Takahashi)	HOMOPTERA: Aphididae
onion bulb fly	*Eumerus strigatus* (Fallén)	DIPTERA: Syrphidae
onion maggot	*Delia antiqua* (Meigen)	DIPTERA: Anthomyiidae
onion plant bug	*Lindbergocapsus allii* (Knight)	HETEROPTERA: Miridae
onion thrips	*Thrips tabaci* Lindeman	THYSANOPTERA: Thripidae
orange spiny whitefly	*Aleurocanthus spiniferus* (Quaintance)	HOMOPTERA: Aleyrodidae
orange tortrix	*Argyrotaenia citrana* (Fernald)	LEPIDOPTERA: Tortricidae
orangedog	*Papilio cresphontes* Cramer	LEPIDOPTERA: Papilionidae
orangehumped mapleworm	*Symmerista leucitys* Franclemont	LEPIDOPTERA: Notodontidae
orangestriped oakworm	*Anisota senatoria* (J.E. Smith)	LEPIDOPTERA: Saturniidae
orangetailed potter wasp	*Delta latreillei petiolaris* (Schulz)	HYMENOPTERA: Vespidae
orchid aphid	*Macrosiphum luteum* (Buckton)	HOMOPTERA: Aphididae
orchidfly	*Eurytoma orchidearum* (Westwood)	HYMENOPTERA: Eurytomidae
Oregon fir sawyer	*Monochamus scutellatus oregonensis* (LeConte)	COLEOPTERA: Cerambycidae
Oregon wireworm	*Melanotus longulus oregonensis* (LeConte)	COLEOPTERA: Elateridae
oriental beetle	*Anomala orientalis* Waterhouse	COLEOPTERA: Scarabaeidae
oriental cockroach	*Blatta orientalis* Linnaeus	BLATTODEA: Blattidae
oriental fruit fly	*Dacus dorsalis* Hendel	DIPTERA: Tephritidae
oriental fruit moth	*Grapholita molesta* (Busck)	LEPIDOPTERA: Tortricidae
oriental house fly	*Musca domestica vicina* Macquart	DIPTERA: Muscidae
oriental moth	*Cnidocampa flavescens* (Walker)	LEPIDOPTERA: Limacodidae
oriental rat flea	*Xenopsylla cheopis* (Rothschild)	SIPHONAPTERA: Pulicidae
oriental stink bug	*Plautia stali* Scott	HETEROPTERA: Pentatomidae
ornate aphid	*Myzus ornatus* Laing	HOMOPTERA: Aphididae
orthezia lady beetle	*Hyperaspis jocosa* (Mulsant)	COLEOPTERA: Coccinellidae
oval guineapig louse	*Gyropus ovalis* Burmeister	MALLOPHAGA: Gyropidae
oxalis spider mite	*Tetranychina harti* (Ewing)	ACARI: Tetranychidae
oxalis whitefly	*Aleyrodes shizuokensis* Kuwana	HOMOPTERA: Aleyrodidae
oystershell scale	*Lepidosaphes ulmi* (Linnaeus)	HOMOPTERA: Diaspididae

P

| Pacific beetle cockroach | *Diploptera punctata* (Eschscholtz) | BLATTODEA: Blaberidae |
| Pacific Coast tick | *Dermacentor occidentalis* Marx | ACARI: Ixodidae |

Pacific Coast wireworm	*Limonius canus* LeConte	COLEOPTERA: Elateridae
Pacific cockroach	*Euthyrrhapha pacifica* (Coquebert)	BLATTODEA: Polyphagidae
Pacific dampwood termite	*Zootermopsis angusticollis* (Hagen)	ISOPTERA: Termopsidae
Pacific flatheaded borer	*Chrysobothris mali* Horn	COLEOPTERA: Buprestidae
Pacific kissing bug	*Oncocephalus pacificus* (Kirkaldy)	HETEROPTERA: Reduviidae
Pacific pelagic water strider	*Halobates sericeus* Eschscholtz	HETEROPTERA: Gerridae
Pacific spider mite	*Tetranychus pacificus* McGregor	ACARI: Tetranychidae
Pacific tent caterpillar	*Malacosoma constrictum* (Hy. Edwards)	LEPIDOPTERA: Lasiocampidae
Pacific willow leaf beetle	*Pyrrhalta decora carbo* (LeConte)	COLEOPTERA: Chrysomelidae
Packard grasshopper	*Melanoplus packardii* Scudder	ORTHOPTERA: Acrididae
painted beauty	*Vanessa virginiensis* (Drury)	LEPIDOPTERA: Nymphalidae
painted hickory borer	*Megacyllene caryae* (Gahan)	COLEOPTERA: Cerambycidae
painted lady	*Vanessa cardui* (Linnaeus)	LEPIDOPTERA: Nymphalidae
painted leafhopper	*Endria inimica* (Say)	HOMOPTERA: Cicadellidae
painted maple aphid	*Drepanaphis acerifoliae* (Thomas)	HOMOPTERA: Aphididae
pale apple leafroller	*Pseudexentera mali* Freeman	LEPIDOPTERA: Tortricidae
pale damsel bug	*Nabis capsiformis* Germar	HETEROPTERA: Nabidae
pale juniper webworm	*Aethes rutilana* (Hübner)	LEPIDOPTERA: Cochylidae
pale leaf spider	*Chiracanthium mordax* Koch	ARANEAE: Clubionidae
pale leafcutting bee	*Megachile concinna* Smith	HYMENOPTERA: Megachilidae
pale legume bug	*Lygus elisus* Van Duzee	HETEROPTERA: Miridae
pale tussock moth	*Halysidota tessellaris* (J.E. Smith)	LEPIDOPTERA: Arctiidae
pale western cutworm	*Agrotis orthogonia* Morrison	LEPIDOPTERA: Noctuidae
pales weevil	*Hylobius pales* (Herbst)	COLEOPTERA: Curculionidae
palesided cutworm	*Agrotis malefida* Guenée	LEPIDOPTERA: Noctuidae
palestriped flea beetle	*Systena blanda* Melsheimer	COLEOPTERA: Chrysomelidae
palm leafskeletonizer	*Homaledra sabalella* (Chambers)	LEPIDOPTERA: Coleophoridae
palm mealybug	*Palmicultor palmarum* (Ehrhorn)	HOMOPTERA: Pseudococcidae
palmerworm	*Dichomeris ligulella* Hübner	LEPIDOPTERA: Gelechiidae
pandanus mealybug	*Laminicoccus pandani* (Cockerell)	HOMOPTERA: Pseudococcidae
pandora moth	*Coloradia pandora* Blake	LEPIDOPTERA: Saturniidae
papaya fruit fly	*Toxotrypana curvicauda* Gerstaecker	DIPTERA: Tephritidae
parasitic grain wasp	*Cephalonomia waterstoni* Gahan	HYMENOPTERA: Bethylidae
parlatoria date scale	*Parlatoria blanchardi* (Targioni-Tozzetti)	HOMOPTERA: Diaspididae
parsleyworm[21]	*Papilio polyxenes asterius* Stoll	LEPIDOPTERA: Papilionidae

---

[21]Adult called black swallowtail.

parsnip webworm	*Depressaria pastinacella* (Duponchel)	LEPIDOPTERA: Oecophoridae
pavement ant	*Tetramorium caespitum* (Linnaeus)	HYMENOPTERA: Formicidae
pea aphid	*Acyrthosiphon pisum* (Harris)	HOMOPTERA: Aphididae
pea leaf weevil	*Sitona lineatus* (Linnaeus)	COLEOPTERA: Curculionidae
pea leafminer	*Liriomyza huidobrensis* (Blanchard)	DIPTERA: Agromyzidae
pea moth	*Cydia nigricana* (Fabricius)	LEPIDOPTERA: Tortricidae
pea weevil	*Bruchus pisorum* (Linnaeus)	COLEOPTERA: Bruchidae
peach bark beetle	*Phloeotribus liminaris* (Harris)	COLEOPTERA: Scolytidae
peach silver mite	*Aculus cornutus* (Banks)	ACARI: Eriophyidae
peach twig borer	*Anarsia lineatella* Zeller	LEPIDOPTERA: Gelechiidae
peachtree borer	*Synanthedon exitiosa* (Say)	LEPIDOPTERA: Sesiidae
pear midge	*Contarinia pyrivora* (Riley)	DIPTERA: Cecidomyiidae
pear plant bug	*Lygocoris communis* (Knight)	HETEROPTERA: Miridae
pear psylla	*Cacopsylla pyricola* Foerster	HOMOPTERA: Psyllidae
pear rust mite	*Epitrimerus pyri* (Nalepa)	ACARI: Eriophyidae
pear sawfly	*Caliroa cerasi* (Linnaeus)	HYMENOPTERA: Tenthredinidae
pear thrips	*Taeniothrips inconsequens* (Uzel)	THYSANOPTERA: Thripidae
pearleaf blister mite	*Phytoptus pyri* Pagenstecher	ACARI: Eriophyidae
pecan bud moth	*Gretchena bolliana* (Slingerland)	LEPIDOPTERA: Tortricidae
pecan carpenterworm	*Cossula magnifica* (Strecker)	LEPIDOPTERA: Cossidae
pecan cigar casebearer	*Coleophora laticornella* Clemens	LEPIDOPTERA: Coleophoridae
pecan leaf casebearer	*Acrobasis juglandis* (LeBaron)	LEPIDOPTERA: Pyralidae
pecan leaf phylloxera	*Phylloxera notabilis* Pergande	HOMOPTERA: Phylloxeridae
pecan leaf scorch mite	*Eotetranychus hicoriae* (McGregor)	ACARI: Tetranychidae
pecan leafroll mite	*Eriophyes caryae* Keifer	ACARI: Eriophyidae
pecan nut casebearer	*Acrobasis nuxvorella* Neunzig	LEPIDOPTERA: Pyralidae
pecan phylloxera	*Phylloxera devastatrix* Pergande	HOMOPTERA: Phylloxeridae
pecan serpentine leafminer	*Stigmella juglandifoliella* (Clemens)	LEPIDOPTERA: Nepticulidae
pecan spittlebug	*Clastoptera achatina* Germar	HOMOPTERA: Cercopidae
pecan weevil	*Curculio caryae* (Horn)	COLEOPTERA: Curculionidae
pepper-and-salt moth	*Biston betularia cognataria* (Guenée)	LEPIDOPTERA: Geometridae
pepper maggot	*Zonosemata electa* (Say)	DIPTERA: Tephritidae
pepper weevil	*Anthonomus eugenii* Cano	COLEOPTERA: Curculionidae
peppergrass beetle	*Galeruca browni* Blake	COLEOPTERA: Chrysomelidae
periodical cicada	*Magicicada septendecim* (Linnaeus)	HOMOPTERA: Cicadidae
persimmon borer	*Sannina uroceriformis* Walker	LEPIDOPTERA: Sesiidae
persimmon psylla	*Trioza diospyri* (Ashmead)	HOMOPTERA: Psyllidae
phantom hemlock looper	*Nepytia phantasmaria* (Strecker)	LEPIDOPTERA: Geometridae

Pharaoh ant	*Monomorium pharaonis* (Linnaeus)	HYMENOPTERA: Formicidae
Philippine katydid	*Phaneroptera furcifera* Stål	ORTHOPTERA: Tettigoniidae
phlox plant bug	*Lopidea davisi* Knight	HETEROPTERA: Miridae
pickerelweed borer	*Bellura densa* (Walker)	LEPIDOPTERA: Noctuidae
pickleworm	*Diaphania nitidalis* (Stoll)	LEPIDOPTERA: Pyralidae
pigeon fly	*Pseudolynchia canariensis* (Macquart)	DIPTERA: Hippoboscidae
pigeon tremex	*Tremex columba* (Linnaeus)	HYMENOPTERA: Siricidae
pine bark adelgid	*Pineus strobi* (Hartig)	HOMOPTERA: Adelgidae
pine bud mite	*Trisetacus pini* (Nalepa)	ACARI: Nalepellidae
pine butterfly	*Neophasia menapia* (Felder & Felder)	LEPIDOPTERA: Pieridae
pine candle moth	*Exoteleia nepheos* Freeman	LEPIDOPTERA: Gelechiidae
pine chafer	*Anomala oblivia* Horn	COLEOPTERA: Scarabaeidae
pine colaspis	*Colaspis pini* Barber	COLEOPTERA: Chrysomelidae
pine conelet bug	*Platylyus luridus* (Reuter)	HETEROPTERA: Miridae
pine conelet looper	*Nepytia semiclusaria* (Walker)	LEPIDOPTERA: Geometridae
pine engraver	*Ips pini* (Say)	COLEOPTERA: Scolytidae
pine false webworm	*Acantholyda erythrocephala* (Linnaeus)	HYMENOPTERA: Pamphiliidae
pine gall weevil	*Podapion gallicola* Riley	COLEOPTERA: Curculionidae
pine leaf adelgid	*Pineus pinifoliae* (Fitch)	HOMOPTERA: Adelgidae
pine needle scale	*Chionaspis pinifoliae* (Fitch)	HOMOPTERA: Diaspididae
pine needle sheathminer	*Zelleria haimbachi* Busck	LEPIDOPTERA: Yponomeutidae
pine needleminer	*Exoteleia pinifoliella* (Chambers)	LEPIDOPTERA: Gelechiidae
pine root collar weevil	*Hylobius radicis* Buchanan	COLEOPTERA: Curculionidae
pine root tip weevil	*Hylobius assimilis* Boheman	COLEOPTERA: Curculionidae
pine rosette mite	*Trisetacus gemmavitians* Styer	ACARI: Nalepellidae
pine spittlebug	*Aphrophora parallela* (Say)	HOMOPTERA: Cercopidae
pine tortoise scale	*Toumeyella parvicornis* (Cockerell)	HOMOPTERA: Coccidae
pine tube moth	*Argyrotaenia pinatubana* (Kearfott)	LEPIDOPTERA: Tortricidae
pine tussock moth	*Dasychira pinicola* (Dyar)	LEPIDOPTERA: Lymantriidae
pine webworm	*Tetralopha robustella* Zeller	LEPIDOPTERA: Pyralidae
pineapple false spider mite	*Dolichotetranychus floridanus* (Banks)	ACARI: Tenuipalpidae
pineapple mealybug	*Dysmicoccus brevipes* (Cockerell)	HOMOPTERA: Pseudococcidae
pineapple scale	*Diaspis bromeliae* (Kerner)	HOMOPTERA: Diaspididae
pineapple tarsonemid	*Steneotarsoneumu ananas* (Tryon)	ACARI: Tarsonemidae
pineapple weevil	*Metamasius ritchiei* Marshall	COLEOPTERA: Curculionidae
pink bollworm	*Pectinophora gossypiella* (Saunders)	LEPIDOPTERA: Gelechiidae
pink scavenger caterpillar	*Pyroderces rileyi* (Walsingham)	LEPIDOPTERA: Cosmopterigidae
pink sugarcane mealybug	*Saccharicoccus sacchari* (Cockerell)	HOMOPTERA: Pseudococcidae

pinkstriped oakworm	*Anisota virginiensis* (Drury)	LEPIDOPTERA: Saturniidae
pinkwinged grasshopper	*Atractomorpha sinensis* Bolivar	ORTHOPTERA: Pyrgomorphidae
pinon cone beetle	*Conophthorus edulis* Hopkins	COLEOPTERA: Scolytidae
pipevine swallowtail	*Battus philenor* (Linnaeus)	LEPIDOPTERA: Papilionidae
pistol casebearer	*Coleophora malivorella* Riley	LEPIDOPTERA: Coleophoridae
pitch-eating weevil	*Pachylobius picivorus* (Germar)	COLEOPTERA: Curculionidae
pitch mass borer	*Synanthedon pini* (Kellicott)	LEPIDOPTERA: Sesiidae
pitch pine tip moth	*Rhyacionia rigidana* (Fernald)	LEPIDOPTERA: Tortricidae
pitch twig moth	*Petrova comstockiana* (Fernald)	LEPIDOPTERA: Tortricidae
pitcherplant mosquito	*Wyeomyia smithii* (Coquillett)	DIPTERA: Culicidae
plains false wireworm	*Eleodes opacus* (Say)	COLEOPTERA: Tenebrionidae
plaster beetle	*Cartodere constricta* (Gyllenhal)	COLEOPTERA: Lathridiidae
plum curculio	*Conotrachelus nenuphar* (Herbst)	COLEOPTERA: Curculionidae
plum gouger	*Coccotorus scutellaris* (LeConte)	COLEOPTERA: Curculionidae
plum leafhopper	*Macropsis trimaculata* (Fitch)	HOMOPTERA: Cicadellidae
plum rust mite	*Aculus fockeui* (Nalepa & Trouessart)	ACARI: Eriophyidae
plum webspinning sawfly	*Neurotoma inconspicua* (Norton)	HYMENOPTERA: Pamphiliidae
plumeria borer	*Lagocheirus undatus* (Voet)	COLEOPTERA: Cerambycidae
plumeria whitefly	*Paraleyrodes perseae* (Quaintance)	HOMOPTERA: Aleyrodidae
poinciana looper	*Pericyma cruegeri* (Butler)	LEPIDOPTERA: Noctuidae
polyphemus moth	*Antheraea polyphemus* (Cramer)	LEPIDOPTERA: Saturniidae
ponderosa pine bark borer	*Canonura princeps* (Walker)	COLEOPTERA: Cerambycidae
ponderosa pine cone beetle[22]	*Conophthorus ponderosae* Hopkins	COLEOPTERA: Scolytidae
poplar-and-willow borer	*Cryptorhynchus lapathi* (Linnaeus)	COLEOPTERA: Curculionidae
poplar borer	*Saperda calcarata* Say	COLEOPTERA: Cerambycidae
poplar leaffolding sawfly	*Phyllocolpa bozemani* (Cooley)	HYMENOPTERA: Tenthredinidae
poplar petiolegall aphid	*Pemphigus populitransversus* Riley	HOMOPTERA: Aphididae
poplar tentmaker	*Ichthyura inclusa* (Hübner)	LEPIDOPTERA: Notodontidae
poplar twig gall aphid	*Pemphigus populiramulorum* Riley	HOMOPTERA: Aphididae
poplar vagabond apid	*Mordvilkoja vagabunda* (Walsh)	HOMOPTERA: Aphididae
portulaca leafmining weevil	*Hypurus bertrandi* Perris	COLEOPTERA: Curculionidae
potato aphid	*Macrosiphum euphorbiae* (Thomas)	HOMOPTERA: Aphididae
potato flea beetle	*Epitrix cucumeris* (Harris)	COLEOPTERA: Chrysomelidae
potato leafhopper	*Empoasca fabae* (Harris)	HOMOPTERA: Cicadellidae

---

[22]Also called lodgepole cone beetle.

48

potato psyllid[23]	*Paratrioza cockerelli* (Sulc)	HOMOPTERA: Psyllidae
potato scab gnat	*Pnyxia scabiei* (Hopkins)	DIPTERA: Sciaridae
potato stalk borer	*Trichobaris trinotata* (Say)	COLEOPTERA: Curculionidae
potato stem borer	*Hydraecia micacea* (Esper)	LEPIDOPTERA: Noctuidae
potato tuberworm	*Phthorimaea operculella* (Zeller)	LEPIDOPTERA: Gelechiidae
poultry bug	*Haematosiphon inodorus* (Dugès)	HETEROPTERA: Cimicidae
poultry house moth	*Niditinea spretella* (Dennis & Schiffermüller)	LEPIDOPTERA: Tineidae
powderpost bostrichid	*Amphicerus cornutus* (Pallas)	COLEOPTERA: Bostrichidae
prairie flea beetle	*Altica canadensis* Gentner	COLEOPTERA: Chrysomelidae
prairie grain wireworm	*Ctenicera aeripennis destructor* (Brown)	COLEOPTERA: Elateridae
privet aphid	*Myzus ligustri* (Mosley)	HOMOPTERA: Aphididae
privet leafminer	*Caloptilia cuculipennella* (Hübner)	LEPIDOPTERA: Gracillariidae
privet mite	*Brevipalpus obovatus* Donnadieu	ACARI: Tenuipalpidae
privet thrips	*Dendrothrips ornatus* (Jablonowski)	THYSANOPTERA: Thripidae
promethea moth	*Callosamia promethea* (Drury)	LEPIDOPTERA: Saturniidae
pruinose bean weevil	*Stator pruininus* (Horn)	COLEOPTERA: Bruchidae
prune leafhopper	*Edwardsiana prunicola* (Edwards)	HOMOPTERA: Cicadellidae
Puget Sound wireworm	*Ctenicera aeripennis aeripennis* (Kirby)	COLEOPTERA: Elateridae
puncturevine seed weevil	*Microlarinus lareynii* (Jacquelin du Val)	COLEOPTERA: Curculionidae
puncturevine stem weevil	*Microlarinus lypriformis* (Wollaston)	COLEOPTERA: Curculionidae
purple scale	*Lepidosaphes beckii* (Newman)	HOMOPTERA: Diaspididae
purplebacked cabbageworm	*Evergestis pallidata* (Hufnagel)	LEPIDOPTERA: Pyralidae
purplespotted lily aphid	*Macrosiphum lilii* (Monell)	HOMOPTERA: Aphididae
puss caterpillar	*Megalopyge opercularis* (J.E. Smith)	LEPIDOPTERA: Megalopygidae
Putnam scale	*Diaspidiotus ancylus* (Putnam)	HOMOPTERA: Diaspididae
pyramid ant	*Conomyrma insana* (Buckley)	HYMENOPTERA: Formicidae
pyriform scale	*Protopulvinaria pyriformis* (Cockerell)	HOMOPTERA: Coccidae

Q

quince curculio	*Conotrachelus crataegi* Walsh	COLEOPTERA: Curculionidae
quince treehopper	*Glossonotus crataegi* (Fitch)	HOMOPTERA: Membracidae

[23]Also called tomato psyllid.

rabbit louse	*Haemodipsus ventricosus* (Denny)	ANOPLURA: Hoplopleuridae
rabbit tick	*Haemaphysalis leporispalustris* (Packard)	ACARI: Ixodidae
ragweed borer	*Epiblema strenuana* (Walker)	LEPIDOPTERA: Tortricidae
ragweed plant bug	*Chlamydatus associatus* (Uhler)	HETEROPTERA: Miridae
rain beetles	*Pleocoma* spp.	COLEOPTERA: Scarabaeidae
raisin moth	*Cadra figulilella* (Gregson)	LEPIDOPTERA: Pyralidae
range caterpillar	*Hemileuca oliviae* Cockerell	LEPIDOPTERA: Saturniidae
range crane fly	*Tipula simplex* Doane	DIPTERA: Tipulidae
rapid plant bug	*Adelphocoris rapidus* (Say)	HETEROPTERA: Miridae
raspberry bud moth	*Lampronia rubiella* (Bjerkander)	LEPIDOPTERA: Incurvariidae
raspberry cane borer	*Oberea bimaculata* (Olivier)	COLEOPTERA: Cerambycidae
raspberry cane maggot	*Pegomya rubivora* (Coquillett)	DIPTERA: Anthomyiidae
raspberry crown borer	*Pennisetia marginata* (Harris)	LEPIDOPTERA: Sesiidae
raspberry fruitworm	*Byturus unicolor* Say	COLEOPTERA: Byturidae
raspberry leafroller	*Olethreutes permundana* (Clemens)	LEPIDOPTERA: Tortricidae
raspberry sawfly	*Monophadnoides geniculatus* (Hartig)	HYMENOPTERA: Tenthredinidae
red admiral	*Vanessa atalanta rubria* (Fruhstorfer)	LEPIDOPTERA: Nymphalidae
red and black flat mite	*Brevipalpus phoenicis* (Geijskes)	ACARI: Tenuipalpidae
red assassin bug	*Haematoloecha rubescens* Distant	HETEROPTERA: Reduviidae
red carpenter ant	*Camponotus ferrugineus* (Fabricius)	HYMENOPTERA: Formicidae
red clover seed weevil	*Tychius stephensi* Schnherr	COLEOPTERA: Curculionidae
red date scale	*Phoenicococcus marlatti* Cockerell	HOMOPTERA: Phoenicococcidae
red elm bark weevil	*Magdalis armicollis* (Say)	COLEOPTERA: Curculionidae
red flour beetle	*Tribolium castaneum* (Herbst)	COLEOPTERA: Tenebrionidae
red grasshopper mite	*Eutrombidium trigonum* (Hermann)	ACARI: Trombidiidae
red harvester ant	*Pogonomyrmex barbatus* (F. Smith)	HYMENOPTERA: Formicidae
red imported fire ant	*Solenopsis invicta* Buren	HYMENOPTERA: Formicidae
red milkweed beetle	*Tetraopes tetrophthalmus* (Forster)	COLEOPTERA: Cerambycidae
red oak borer	*Enaphalodes rufulus* (Haldeman)	COLEOPTERA: Cerambycidae
red orchid scale	*Furcaspis biformis* (Cockerell)	HOMOPTERA: Diaspididae
red pine cone beetle	*Conophthorus resinosae* Hopkins	COLEOPTERA: Scolytidae
red pine sawfly	*Neodiprion nanulus nanulus* Schedl	HYMENOPTERA: Diprionidae
red pine scale	*Matsucoccus resinosae* Bean & Godwin	HOMOPTERA: Margarodidae
red pine shoot moth	*Dioryctria resinosella* Mutuura	LEPIDOPTERA: Pyralidae
red sunflower seed weevil	*Smicronyx fulvus* LeConte	COLEOPTERA: Curculionidae

red turnip beetle	*Entomoscelis americana* Brown	COLEOPTERA: Chrysomelidae
red turpentine beetle	*Dendroctonus valens* LeConte	COLEOPTERA: Scolytidae
red wax scale	*Ceroplastes rubens* Maskell	HOMOPTERA: Coccidae
redbacked cutworm	*Euxoa ochrogaster* (Guenée)	LEPIDOPTERA: Noctuidae
redbanded leafroller	*Argyrotaenia velutinana* (Walker)	LEPIDOPTERA: Tortricidae
redbanded thrips	*Selenothrips rubrocinctus* (Giard)	THYSANOPTERA: Thripidae
redberry mite	*Acalitus essigi* (Hassan)	ACARI: Eriophyidae
redblack oedemerid	*Eobia bicolor* (Fairmaire)	COLEOPTERA: Oedemeridae
redbud leaffolder	*Fascista cercerisella* (Chambers)	LEPIDOPTERA: Gelechiidae
redheaded ash borer	*Neoclytus acuminatus* (Fabricius)	COLEOPTERA: Cerambycidae
redheaded jack pine sawfly	*Neodiprion rugifrons* Middleton	HYMENOPTERA: Diprionidae
redheaded pine sawfly	*Neodiprion lecontei* (Fitch)	HYMENOPTERA: Diprionidae
redhumped caterpillar	*Schizura concinna* (J.E. Smith)	LEPIDOPTERA: Notodontidae
redlegged flea beetle	*Derocrepis erythropus* (Melsheimer)	COLEOPTERA: Chrysomelidae
redlegged grasshopper	*Melanoplus femurrubrum* (De Geer)	ORTHOPTERA: Acrididae
redlegged ham beetle	*Necrobia rufipes* (De Geer)	COLEOPTERA: Cleridae
redmargined assassin bug	*Scadra rufidens* Stål	HETEROPTERA: Reduviidae
rednecked cane borer	*Agrilus ruficollis* (Fabricius)	COLEOPTERA: Buprestidae
rednecked peanutworm	*Stegasta bosqueella* (Chambers)	LEPIDOPTERA: Gelechiidae
redshouldered ham beetle	*Necrobia ruficollis* (Fabricius)	COLEOPTERA: Cleridae
redshouldered stink bug	*Thyanta accerra* McAtee	HETEROPTERA: Pentatomidae
redtailed spider wasp	*Tachypompilus analis* (Fabricius)	HYMENOPTERA: Pompilidae
redtailed tachina	*Winthemia quadripustulata* (Fabricius)	DIPTERA: Tachinidae
regal moth[24]	*Citheronia regalis* (Fabricius)	LEPIDOPTERA: Saturniidae
relapsing fever tick	*Ornithodoros turicata* (Dugès)	ACARI: Argasidae
resplendent shield bearer	*Coptodisca splendoriferella* (Clemens)	LEPIDOPTERA: Heliozelidae
reticulate mite	*Lorryia reticulata* (Oudemans)	ACARI: Tydeidae
reticulatewinged trogiid	*Lepinotus reticulatus* Enderlein	PSOCOPTERA: Trogiidae
rhinoceros beetle	*Xyloryctes jamaicensis* (Drury)	COLEOPTERA: Scarabaeidae
Rhodesgrass mealybug	*Antonina graminis* (Maskell)	HOMOPTERA: Pseudococcidae
rhododendron borer	*Synanthedon rhododendri* (Beutenmüller)	LEPIDOPTERA: Sesiidae
rhododendron gall midge	*Clinodiplosis rhododendri* (Felt)	DIPTERA: Cecidomyiidae
rhododendron lace bug	*Stephanitis rhododendri* Horvath	HETEROPTERA: Tingidae
rhododendron whitefly	*Dialeurodes chittendeni* Laing	HOMOPTERA: Aleyrodidae
rhubarb curculio	*Lixus concavus* Say	COLEOPTERA: Curculionidae

---

[24]Immature called hickory horned devil.

rice delphacid	*Sogatodes orizicola* (Muir)	HOMOPTERA: Delphacidae
rice leaffolder	*Lerodea eufala* (Edwards)	LEPIDOPTERA: Hesperiidae
rice leafhopper	*Nephotettix nigropictus* (Stål)	HOMOPTERA: Cicadellidae
rice moth	*Corcyra cephalonica* (Stainton)	LEPIDOPTERA: Pyralidae
rice root aphid	*Rhopalosiphum rufiabdominalis* (Sasaki)	HOMOPTERA: Aphididae
rice stalk borer	*Chilo plejadellus* Zincken	LEPIDOPTERA: Pyralidae
rice stink bug	*Oebalus pugnax* (Fabricius)	HETEROPTERA: Pentatomidae
rice water weevil	*Lissorhoptrus oryzophilus* Kuschel	COLEOPTERA: Curculionidae
rice weevil	*Sitophilus oryzae* (Linnaeus)	COLEOPTERA: Curculionidae
ridgewinged fungus beetle	*Thes bergrothi* (Reitter)	COLEOPTERA: Lathridiidae
ringlegged earwig	*Euborellia annulipes* (Lucas)	DERMAPTERA: Labiduridae
robust leafhopper	*Penestrangania robusta* (Uhler)	HOMOPTERA: Cicadellidae
Rocky Mountain grasshopper	*Melanoplus spretus* (Walsh)	ORTHOPTERA: Acrididae
Rocky Mountain wood tick	*Dermacentor andersoni* Stiles	ACARI: Ixodidae
rose aphid	*Macrosiphum rosae* (Linnaeus)	HOMOPTERA: Aphididae
rose chafer	*Macrodactylus subspinosus* (Fabricius)	COLEOPTERA: Scarabaeidae
rose curculio	*Merhynchites bicolor* (Fabricius)	COLEOPTERA: Curculionidae
rose leaf beetle	*Nodonota puncticollis* (Say)	COLEOPTERA: Chrysomelidae
rose leafhopper	*Edwardsiana rosae* (Linnaeus)	HOMOPTERA: Cicadellidae
rose midge	*Dasineura rhodophaga* (Coquillett)	DIPTERA: Cecidomyiidae
rose scale	*Aulacaspis rosae* (Bouché)	HOMOPTERA: Diaspididae
rose stem girdler	*Agrilus aurichalceus* Redtenbacher	COLEOPTERA: Buprestidae
roseroot gall wasp	*Diplolepis radicum* (Osten Sacken)	HYMENOPTERA: Cynipidae
roseslug	*Endelomyia aethiops* (Fabricius)	HYMENOPTERA: Tenthredinidae
rosy apple aphid	*Dysaphis plantaginea* (Passerini)	HOMOPTERA: Aphididae
rosy predator snail	*Euglandina rosea* (Férussac)	STYLOMMATOPHORA: Oleacinidae
rotund tick	*Ixodes kingi* Bishopp	ACARI: Ixodidae
rough harvester ant	*Pogonomyrmex rugosus* Emery	HYMENOPTERA: Formicidae
rough stink bug	*Brochymena quadripustulata* (Fabricius)	HETEROPTERA: Pentatomidae
roughskinned cutworm	*Athetis mindara* (Barnes & McDunnough)	LEPIDOPTERA: Noctuidae
roundheaded appletree borer	*Saperda candida* Fabricius	COLEOPTERA: Cerambycidae
roundheaded cone borer	*Paratimia conicola* Fisher	COLEOPTERA: Cerambycidae
roundheaded fir borer	*Tetropium abietis* Fall	COLEOPTERA: Cerambycidae
roundheaded pine beetle	*Dendroctonus adjunctus* Blandford	COLEOPTERA: Scolytidae
Russian wheat aphid	*Diuraphis noxia* (Mordvilko)	HOMOPTERA: Aphididae
rustic borer	*Xylotrechus colonus* (Fabricius)	COLEOPTERA: Cerambycidae
rusty banded aphid	*Dysaphis apiifolia* (Theobald)	HOMOPTERA: Aphididae
rusty grain beetle	*Cryptolestes ferrugineus* (Stephens)	COLEOPTERA: Cucujidae

rusty millipede	*Trigoniulus lumbricinus* (Gerst)	SPIROBOLIDA: Pachybolidae
rusty plum aphid	*Hysteroneura setariae* (Thomas)	HOMOPTERA: Aphididae
rusty tussock moth	*Orgyia antiqua* (Linnaeus)	LEPIDOPTERA: Lymantriidae

S

saddleback caterpillar	*Sibine stimulea* (Clemens)	LEPIDOPTERA: Limacodidae
saddled leafhopper	*Colladonus clitellarius* (Say)	HOMOPTERA: Cicadellidae
saddled prominent	*Heterocampa guttivitta* (Walker)	LEPIDOPTERA: Notodontidae
sagebrush defoliator	*Aroga websteri* Clarke	LEPIDOPTERA: Gelechiidae
saltmarsh caterpillar	*Estigmene acrea* (Drury)	LEPIDOPTERA: Arctiidae
saltmarsh mosquito	*Aedes sollicitans* (Walker)	DIPTERA: Culicidae
San Bruno elfin	*Incisalia fotis bayensis* (R.M. Brown)	LEPIDOPTERA: Lycaenidae
San Jose scale	*Quadraspidiotus perniciosus* (Comstock)	HOMOPTERA: Diaspididae
sand wireworm	*Horistonotus uhlerii* Horn	COLEOPTERA: Elateridae
sandcherry weevil	*Coccotorus hirsutus* Bruner	COLEOPTERA: Curculionidae
sapwood timberworm	*Hylecoetus lugubris* Say	COLEOPTERA: Lymexylidae
Saratoga spittlebug	*Aphrophora saratogensis* (Fitch)	HOMOPTERA: Cercopidae
Saskatoon borer	*Saperda candida bipunctata* Hopping	COLEOPTERA: Cerambycidae
satin moth	*Leucoma salicis* (Linnaeus)	LEPIDOPTERA: Lymantriidae
Saunders embiid	*Oligotoma saundersii* (Westwood)	EMBIIDINA: Oligotomidae
sawtoothed grain beetle	*Oryzaephilus surinamensis* (Linnaeus)	COLEOPTERA: Cucujidae
Say blister beetle	*Lytta (Pomphopoea) sayi* (LeConte)	COLEOPTERA: Meloidae
Say stink bug	*Chlorochroa sayi* (Stål)	HETEROPTERA: Pentatomidae
scab mite	*Psoroptes equi* (Raspail)	ACARI: Psoroptidae
scaly grain mite	*Suidasia nesbitti* Hughes	ACARI: Acaridae
scalyleg mite	*Knemidokoptes mutans* (Robin & Lanquetin)	ACARI: Sarcoptidae
scarlet oak sawfly	*Caliroa quercuscoccineae* (Dyar)	HYMENOPTERA: Tenthredinidae
Schaus swallowtail	*Papilio aristodemus ponceanus* Schaus	LEPIDOPTERA: Papilionidae
Schoene spider mite	*Tetranychus schoenei* McGregor	ACARI: Tetranychidae
screwworm	*Cochliomyia hominivorax* (Coquerel)	DIPTERA: Calliphoridae
sculptured pine borer	*Chalcophora angulicollis* (LeConte)	COLEOPTERA: Buprestidae
scurfy scale	*Chionaspis furfura* (Fitch)	HOMOPTERA: Diaspididae
secondary screwworm	*Cochliomyia macellaria* (Fabricius)	DIPTERA: Calliphoridae
seed bugs	*Nysius* spp.	HETEROPTERA: Lygaeidae
seedcorn beetle	*Stenolophus lecontei* (Chaudoir)	COLEOPTERA: Carabidae

seedcorn maggot	*Delia platura* (Meigen)	DIPTERA: Anthomyiidae
sequoia pitch moth	*Synanthedon sequoiae* (Hy. Edwards)	LEPIDOPTERA: Sesiidae
serpentine leafminer	*Liriomyza brassicae* (Riley)	DIPTERA: Agromyzidae
sevenspotted lady beetle	*Coccinella septempunctata* Linnaeus	COLEOPTERA: Coccinellidae
shaft louse	*Menopon gallinae* (Linnaeus)	MALLOPHAGA: Menoponidae
shallot aphid	*Myzus ascalonicus* Doncaster	HOMOPTERA: Aphididae
sheep biting louse	*Bovicola ovis* (Schrank)	MALLOPHAGA: Trichodectidae
sheep bot fly	*Oestrus ovis* Linnaeus	DIPTERA: Oestridae
sheep follicle mite	*Demodex ovis* Railliet	ACARI: Demodicidae
sheep ked	*Melophagus ovinus* (Linnaeus)	DIPTERA: Hippoboscidae
sheep scab mite	*Psoroptes ovis* (Hering)	ACARI: Psoroptidae
shieldbacked pine seed bug	*Tetyra bipunctata* (Herrich-Schäffer)	HETEROPTERA: Pentatomidae
shortleaf pine cone borer	*Eucosma cocana* Kearfott	LEPIDOPTERA: Tortricidae
shortnosed cattle louse	*Haematopinus eurysternus* (Nitzsch)	ANOPLURA: Haematopinidae
shortwinged mole cricket	*Scapteriscus abbreviatus* Scudder	ORTHOPTERA: Gryllotalpidae
shothole borer	*Scolytus rugulosus* (Müller)	COLEOPTERA: Scolytidae
Sigmoid fungus beetle	*Cryptophagus varus* Woodroffe & Coombs	COLEOPTERA: Cryptophagidae
silkworm	*Bombyx mori* (Linnaeus)	LEPIDOPTERA: Bombycidae
silky ant	*Formica fusca* Linnaeus	HYMENOPTERA: Formicidae
silky cane weevil	*Metamasius hemipterus sericeus* (Olivier)	COLEOPTERA: Curculionidae
silverfish	*Lepisma saccharina* Linnaeus	THYSANURA: Lepismatidae
silverspotted skipper	*Epargyreus clarus* (Cramer)	LEPIDOPTERA: Hesperiidae
silverspotted tiger moth	*Lophocampa argentata* (Packard)	LEPIDOPTERA: Arctiidae
sinuate lady beetle	*Hippodamia sinuata* Mulsant	COLEOPTERA: Coccinellidae
sinuate peartree borer	*Agrilus sinuatus* (Olivier)	COLEOPTERA: Buprestidae
Sitka spruce weevil[25]	*Pissodes strobi* (Peck)	COLEOPTERA: Curculionidae
sixspined ips	*Ips calligraphus* (Germar)	COLEOPTERA: Scolytidae
sixspotted mite	*Eotetranychus sexmaculatus* (Riley)	ACARI: Tetranychidae
sixspotted thrips	*Scolothrips sexmaculatus* (Pergande)	THYSANOPTERA: Thripidae
slash pine flower thrips	*Gnophothrips fuscus* (Morgan)	THYSANOPTERA: Phlaeothripidae
slash pine sawfly	*Neodiprion merkeli* Ross	HYMENOPTERA: Diprionidae
slash pine seedworm	*Cydia anaranjada* (Miller)	LEPIDOPTERA: Tortricidae
slender duck louse	*Anaticola crassicornis* (Scopoli)	MALLOPHAGA: Philopteridae
slender goose louse	*Anaticola anseris* (Linnaeus)	MALLOPHAGA: Philopteridae
slender guinea louse	*Lipeurus numidae* (Denny)	MALLOPHAGA: Philopteridae

---

[25]Also called Englemann spruce weevil and white pine weevil.

Common name	Scientific name	Order: Family
slender guineapig louse	*Gliricola porcelli* (Schrank)	MALLOPHAGA: Gyropidae
slender pigeon louse	*Columbicola columbae* (Linnaeus)	MALLOPHAGA: Philopteridae
slender seedcorn beetle	*Clivina impressifrons* LeConte	COLEOPTERA: Carabidae
slender turkey louse	*Oxylipeurus polytrapezius* (Burmeister)	MALLOPHAGA: Philopteridae
slenderhorned flour beetle	*Gnatocerus maxillosus* (Fabricius)	COLEOPTERA: Tenebrionidae
small chestnut weevil	*Curculio sayi* (Gyllenhal)	COLEOPTERA: Curculionidae
small milkweed bug	*Lygaeus kalmii* Stål	HETEROPTERA: Lygaeidae
small pigeon louse	*Campanulotes bidentatus compar* (Burmeister)	MALLOPHAGA: Philopteridae
small southern pine engraver	*Ips avulsus* (Eichhoff)	COLEOPTERA: Scolytidae
smaller European elm bark beetle	*Scolytus multistriatus* (Marsham)	COLEOPTERA: Scolytidae
smaller Hawaiian cutworm	*Agrotis dislocata* (Walker)	LEPIDOPTERA: Noctuidae
smaller lantana butterfly	*Strymon bazochii gundlachianus* (Bates)	LEPIDOPTERA: Lycaenidae
smaller yellow ant	*Acanthomyops claviger* (Roger)	HYMENOPTERA: Formicidae
smalleyed flour beetle	*Palorus ratzeburgi* (Wissmann)	COLEOPTERA: Tenebrionidae
smartweed borer	*Ostrinia obumbratalis* (Lederer)	LEPIDOPTERA: Pyralidae
smeared dagger moth	*Acronicta oblinita* (J.E. Smith)	LEPIDOPTERA: Noctuidae
Smith blue	*Euphilotes enoptes smithi* (Mattoni)	LEPIDOPTERA: Lycaenidae
smokybrown cockroach	*Periplaneta fuliginosa* (Serville)	BLATTODEA: Blattidae
smut beetle	*Phalacrus politus* Melsheimer	COLEOPTERA: Phalacridae
snowball aphid	*Neoceruraphis viburnicola* (Gillette)	HOMOPTERA: Aphididae
snowy tree cricket	*Oecanthus fultoni* Walker	ORTHOPTERA: Gryllidae
solanaceous treehopper	*Antianthe expansa* (Germar)	HOMOPTERA: Membracidae
solitary oak leafminer	*Cameraria hamadryadella* (Clemens)	LEPIDOPTERA: Gracillariidae
sonchus fly	*Ensina sonchi* (Linnaeus)	DIPTERA: Tephritidae
Sonoran tent caterpillar	*Malacosoma tigris* (Dyar)	LEPIDOPTERA: Lasiocampidae
sorghum midge	*Contarinia sorghicola* (Coquillett)	DIPTERA: Cecidomyiidae
sorghum webworm	*Nola sorghiella* Riley	LEPIDOPTERA: Noctuidae
sourbush seed fly	*Acinia picturata* (Snow)	DIPTERA: Tephritidae
South African emex weevil	*Apion antiquum* Gyllenhal	COLEOPTERA: Curculionidae
south coastal coneworm	*Dioryctria ebeli* Mutuura & Munroe	LEPIDOPTERA: Pyralidae
southeastern blueberry bee	*Habropoda laboriosa* (Fabricius)	HYMENOPTERA: Anthophoridae
southern armyworm	*Spodoptera eridania* (Cramer)	LEPIDOPTERA: Noctuidae
southern beet webworm	*Herpetogramma bipunctalis* (Fabricius)	LEPIDOPTERA: Pyralidae
southern buffalo gnat	*Cnephia pecuarum* (Riley)	DIPTERA: Simuliidae
southern cabbageworm	*Pontia protodice* (Boisduval & LeConte)	LEPIDOPTERA: Pieridae
southern cattle tick	*Boophilus microplus* (Canestrini)	ACARI: Ixodidae
southern chinch bug	*Blissus insularis* Barber	HETEROPTERA: Lygaeidae
southern corn billbug	*Sphenophorus callosus* (Olivier)	COLEOPTERA: Curculionidae

southern corn rootworm[26]	*Diabrotica undecimpunctata howardi* Barber	COLEOPTERA: Chrysomelidae
southern cornstalk borer	*Diatraea crambidoides* (Grote)	LEPIDOPTERA: Pyralidae
southern fire ant	*Solenopsis xyloni* McCook	HYMENOPTERA: Formicidae
southern garden leafhopper	*Empoasca solana* DeLong	HOMOPTERA: Cicadellidae
southern green stink bug	*Nezara viridula* (Linnaeus)	HETEROPTERA: Pentatomidae
southern house mosquito	*Culex quinquefasciatus* Say	DIPTERA: Culicidae
southern lyctus beetle	*Lyctus planicollis* LeConte	COLEOPTERA: Lyctidae
southern masked chafer	*Cyclocephala immaculata* (Olivier)	COLEOPTERA: Scarabaeidae
southern mole cricket	*Scapteriscus acletus* Rehn & Hebard	ORTHOPTERA: Gryllotalpidae
southern pine beetle	*Dendroctonus frontalis* Zimmermann	COLEOPTERA: Scolytidae
southern pine coneworm	*Dioryctria amatella* (Hulst)	LEPIDOPTERA: Pyralidae
southern pine root weevil	*Hylobius aliradicis* Warner	COLEOPTERA: Curculionidae
southern pine sawyer	*Monochamus titillator* (Fabricius)	COLEOPTERA: Cerambycidae
southern potato wireworm	*Conoderus falli* Lane	COLEOPTERA: Elateridae
southern red mite	*Oligonychus ilicis* (McGregor)	ACARI: Tetranychidae
southwestern corn borer	*Diatraea grandiosella* Dyar	LEPIDOPTERA: Pyralidae
southwestern Hercules beetle	*Dynastes granti* Horn	COLEOPTERA: Scarabaeidae
southwestern pine tip moth	*Rhyacionia neomexicana* (Dyar)	LEPIDOPTERA: Tortricidae
southwestern squash vine borer	*Melittia calabaza* Duckworth & Eichlin	LEPIDOPTERA: Sesiidae
southwestern tent caterpillar	*Malacosoma incurvum* (Hy. Edwards)	LEPIDOPTERA: Lasiocampidae
sow thistle aphid	*Nasonovia lactucae* (Linnaeus)	HOMOPTERA: Aphididae
soybean looper	*Pseudoplusia includens* (Walker)	LEPIDOPTERA: Noctuidae
soybean nodule fly	*Rivellia quadrifasciata* (Macquart)	DIPTERA: Platystomatidae
soybean thrips	*Sericothrips variabilis* (Beach)	THYSANOPTERA: Thripidae
Spanishfly	*Lytta vesicatoria* (Linnaeus)	COLEOPTERA: Meloidae
spicebush swallowtail	*Papilio troilus* Linnaeus	LEPIDOPTERA: Papilionidae
spider mite destroyer	*Stethorus picipes* Casey	COLEOPTERA: Coccinellidae
spinach flea beetle	*Disonycha xanthomelas* (Dalman)	COLEOPTERA: Chrysomelidae
spinach leafminer	*Pegomya hyoscyami* (Panzer)	DIPTERA: Anthomyiidae
spined assassin bug	*Sinea diadema* (Fabricius)	HETEROPTERA: Reduviidae
spined rat louse	*Polyplax spinulosa* (Burmeister)	ANOPLURA: Hoplopleuridae
spined soldier bug	*Podisus maculiventris* (Say)	HETEROPTERA: Pentatomidae
spined stilt bug	*Jalysus wickhami* Van Duzee	HETEROPTERA: Berytidae
spiny assassin bug	*Polididus armatissimus* Stål	HETEROPTERA: Reduviidae
spiny oakworm	*Anisota stigma* (Fabricius)	LEPIDOPTERA: Saturniidae

---

[26]Adult called spotted cucumber beetle.

spinybacked spider	*Gasteracantha cancriformis* (Linnaeus)	ARANEAE: Araneidae
spirea aphid	*Aphis spiraecola* Patch	HOMOPTERA: Aphididae
spotted alfalfa aphid	*Therioaphis maculata* (Buckton)	HOMOPTERA: Aphididae
spotted asparagus beetle	*Crioceris duodecimpunctata* (Linnaeus)	COLEOPTERA: Chrysomelidae
spotted beet webworm	*Hymenia perspectalis* (Hübner)	LEPIDOPTERA: Pyralidae
spotted blister beetle	*Epicauta maculata* (Say)	COLEOPTERA: Meloidae
spotted cucumber beetle[27]	*Diabrotica undecimpunctata howardi* Barber	COLEOPTERA: Chrysomelidae
spotted cutworm	*Xestia* spp.	LEPIDOPTERA: Noctuidae
spotted garden slug	*Limax maximus* Linnaeus	STYLOMMATOPHORA: Limacidae
spotted hairy fungus beetle	*Mycetophagus quadriguttatus* P. Müller	COLEOPTERA: Mycetophagidae
spotted loblolly pine sawfly	*Neodiprion taedae taedae* Ross	HYMENOPTERA: Diprionidae
spotted Mediterranean cockroach	*Ectobius pallidus* (Olivier)	BLATTODEA: Blattellidae
spotted pine sawyer	*Monochamus mutator* LeConte	COLEOPTERA: Cerambycidae
spotted tentiform leafminer	*Phyllonorycter blancardella* (Fabricius)	LEPIDOPTERA: Gracillariidae
spotted tussock moth	*Lophocampa maculata* Harris	LEPIDOPTERA: Arctiidae
spottedwinged antlion	*Dendroleon obsoletus* (Say)	NEUROPTERA: Myrmeleontidae
spring cankerworm	*Paleacrita vernata* (Peck)	LEPIDOPTERA: Geometridae
spruce aphid	*Elatobium abietinum* (Walker)	HOMOPTERA: Aphididae
spruce beetle	*Dendroctonus rufipennis* (Kirby)	COLEOPTERA: Scolytidae
spruce bud midge	*Dasineura swainei* (Felt)	DIPTERA: Cecidomyiidae
spruce bud moth	*Zeiraphera canadensis* Mutuura & Freeman	LEPIDOPTERA: Tortricidae
spruce bud scale	*Physokermes piceae* (Schrank)	HOMOPTERA: Coccidae
spruce budworm	*Choristoneura fumiferana* (Clemens)	LEPIDOPTERA: Tortricidae
spruce coneworm	*Dioryctria reniculelloides* Mutuura & Munroe	LEPIDOPTERA: Pyralidae
spruce mealybug	*Puto sandini* Washburn	HOMOPTERA: Pseudococcidae
spruce needleminer	*Endothenia albolineana* (Kearfott)	LEPIDOPTERA: Tortricidae
spruce seed moth	*Cydia strobilella* (Linnaeus)	LEPIDOPTERA: Tortricidae
spruce spider mite	*Oligonychus ununguis* (Jacobi)	ACARI: Tetranychidae
squarenecked grain beetle	*Cathartus quadricollis* (Guérin-Méneville)	COLEOPTERA: Cucujidae
squarenosed fungus beetle	*Lathridius minutus* (Linnaeus)	COLEOPTERA: Lathridiidae
squash beetle	*Epilachna borealis* (Fabricius)	COLEOPTERA: Coccinellidae
squash bug	*Anasa tristis* (De Geer)	HETEROPTERA: Coreidae
squash vine borer	*Melittia cucurbitae* (Harris)	LEPIDOPTERA: Sesiidae
stable fly	*Stomoxys calcitrans* (Linnaeus)	DIPTERA: Muscidae
stalk borer	*Papaipema nebris* (Guenée)	LEPIDOPTERA: Noctuidae

---

[27]Immature called southern corn rootworm.

star jasmine thrips	*Thrips orientalis* (Bagnall)	THYSANOPTERA: Thripidae
steelblue lady beetle	*Orcus chalybeus* (Boisduval)	COLEOPTERA: Coccinellidae
Stevens leafhopper	*Empoasca stevensi* Young	HOMOPTERA: Cicadellidae
sticktight flea	*Echicnophaga gallinacea* (Westwood)	SIPHONAPTERA: Pulicidae
stinging rose caterpillar	*Parasa indetermina* (Boisduval)	LEPIDOPTERA: Limacodidae
stink beetle	*Nomius pygameus* (Dejean)	COLEOPTERA: Carabidae
stored nut moth	*Aphomia gularis* (Zeller)	LEPIDOPTERA: Pyralidae
straw itch mite	*Pyemotes tritici* (Lagrèze-Fossat & Montané)	ACARI: Pyemotidae
strawberry aphid	*Chaetosiphon fragaefolii* (Cockerell)	HOMOPTERA: Aphididae
strawberry bud weevil	*Anthonomus signatus* Say	COLEOPTERA: Curculionidae
strawberry crown borer	*Tyloderma fragariae* (Riley)	COLEOPTERA: Curculionidae
strawberry crown moth	*Synanthedon bibionipennis* (Boisduval)	LEPIDOPTERA: Sesiidae
strawberry crownminer	*Monochroa fragariae* (Busck)	LEPIDOPTERA: Gelechiidae
strawberry leafroller	*Ancylis comptana* (Froelich)	LEPIDOPTERA: Tortricidae
strawberry root aphid	*Aphis forbesi* Weed	HOMOPTERA: Aphididae
strawberry root weevil	*Otiorhynchus ovatus* (Linnaeus)	COLEOPTERA: Curculionidae
strawberry rootworm	*Paria fragariae* Wilcox	COLEOPTERA: Chrysomelidae
strawberry sap beetle	*Stelidota geminata* (Say)	COLEOPTERA: Nitidulidae
strawberry spider mite	*Tetranychus turkestani* Ugarov & Nikolski	ACARI: Tetranychidae
strawberry whitefly	*Trialeurodes packardi* (Morrill)	HOMOPTERA: Aleyrodidae
striped alder sawfly	*Hemichroa crocea* (Geoffroy)	HYMENOPTERA: Tenthredinidae
striped ambrosia beetle	*Trypodendron lineatum* (Olivier)	COLEOPTERA: Scolytidae
striped blister beetle	*Epicauta vittata* (Fabricius)	COLEOPTERA: Meloidae
striped cucumber beetle	*Acalymma vittatum* (Fabricius)	COLEOPTERA: Chrysomelidae
striped cutworm	*Euxoa tessellata* (Harris)	LEPIDOPTERA: Noctuidae
striped earwig	*Labidura riparia* (Pallas)	DERMAPTERA: Labiduridae
striped flea beetle	*Phyllotreta striolata* (Fabricius)	COLEOPTERA: Chrysomelidae
striped garden caterpillar	*Trichordestra legitima* (Grote)	LEPIDOPTERA: Noctuidae
striped horse fly	*Tabanus lineola* Fabricius	DIPTERA: Tabanidae
striped lynx spider	*Oxyopes salticus* Hentz	ARANEAE: Oxyopidae
striped mealybug	*Ferrisia virgata* (Cockerell)	HOMOPTERA: Pseudococcidae
subtropical pine tip moth	*Rhyacionia subtropica* Miller	LEPIDOPTERA: Tortricidae
subulina snail	*Subulina octona* (Bruguiere)	STYLOMMATOPHORA: Subulinidae
suckfly	*Cyrtopeltis notata* (Distant)	HETEROPTERA: Miridae
sugar maple borer	*Glycobius speciosus* (Say)	COLEOPTERA: Cerambycidae
sugar pine cone beetle	*Conophthorus lambertianae* Hopkins	COLEOPTERA: Scolytidae
sugarbeet crown borer	*Hulstia undulatella* (Clemens)	LEPIDOPTERA: Pyralidae
sugarbeet root aphid	*Pemphigus populivenae* Fitch	HOMOPTERA: Aphididae

sugarbeet root maggot	*Tetanops myopaeformis* (Rder)	DIPTERA: Otitidae
sugarbeet wireworm	*Limonius californicus* (Mannerheim)	COLEOPTERA: Elateridae
sugarcane aphid	*Melanaphis sacchari* (Zehntner)	HOMOPTERA: Aphididae
sugarcane beetle	*Euetheola humilis rugiceps* (LeConte)	COLEOPTERA: Scarabaeidae
sugarcane borer	*Diatraea saccharalis* (Fabricius)	LEPIDOPTERA: Pyralidae
sugarcane bud moth	*Neodecadarachis flavistriata* (Walsingham)	LEPIDOPTERA: Tineidae
sugarcane delphacid	*Perkinsiella saccharicida* Kirkaldy	HOMOPTERA: Delphacidae
sugarcane leaf mite	*Oligonychus indicus* (Hirst)	ACARI: Tetranychidae
sugarcane leafroller	*Hedylepta accepta* (Butler)	LEPIDOPTERA: Pyralidae
sugarcane stalk mite	*Steneotarsonemus bancrofti* (Michael)	ACARI: Tarsonemidae
sugarcane thrips	*Baliothrips minutus* (van Deventer)	THYSANOPTERA: Thripidae
sunflower beetle	*Zygogramma exclamationis* (Fabricius)	COLEOPTERA: Chrysomelidae
sunflower bud moth	*Suleima helianthana* (Riley)	LEPIDOPTERA: Tortricidae
sunflower headclipping weevil	*Haplorhynchites aeneus* (Boheman)	COLEOPTERA: Curculionidae
sunflower maggot	*Strauzia longipennis* (Wiedemann)	DIPTERA: Tephritidae
sunflower midge	*Contarinia schulzi* Gagné	DIPTERA: Cecidomyiidae
sunflower moth	*Homoeosoma electellum* (Hulst)	LEPIDOPTERA: Pyralidae
sunflower root weevil	*Baris strenua* (LeConte)	COLEOPTERA: Curculionidae
sunflower seed midge	*Neolasioptera murtfeldtiana* (Felt)	DIPTERA: Cecidomyiidae
sunflower spittlebug	*Clastoptera xanthocephala* Germar	HOMOPTERA: Cercopidae
sunflower stem weevil	*Cylindrocopturus adspersus* (LeConte)	COLEOPTERA: Curculionidae
superb plant bug	*Adelphocoris superbus* (Uhler)	HETEROPTERA: Miridae
Surinam cockroach	*Pycnoscelus surinamensis* (Linnaeus)	BLATTODEA: Blaberidae
Swaine jack pine sawfly	*Neodiprion swainei* Middleton	HYMENOPTERA: Diprionidae
swallow bug	*Oeciacus vicarius* Horvath	HETEROPTERA: Cimicidae
sweetclover aphid	*Therioaphis riehmi* (Brner)	HOMOPTERA: Aphididae
sweetclover root borer	*Walshia miscecolorella* (Chambers)	LEPIDOPTERA: Cosmopterigidae
sweetclover weevil	*Sitona cylindricollis* Fåhraeus	COLEOPTERA: Curculionidae
sweetfern leaf casebearer	*Acrobasis comptoniella* Hulst	LEPIDOPTERA: Pyralidae
sweetpotato flea beetle	*Chaetocnema confinis* Crotch	COLEOPTERA: Chrysomelidae
sweetpotato hornworm	*Agrius cingulata* (Fabricius)	LEPIDOPTERA: Sphingidae
sweetpotato leaf beetle	*Typophorus nigritus viridicyaneus* (Crotch)	COLEOPTERA: Chrysomelidae
sweetpotato leafminer	*Bedellia orchilella* Walsingham	LEPIDOPTERA: Lyonetiidae
sweetpotato leafroller	*Pilocrocis tripunctata* (Fabricius)	LEPIDOPTERA: Pyralidae
sweetpotato vine borer	*Omphisa anastomosalis* (Guenée)	LEPIDOPTERA: Pyralidae
sweetpotato weevil	*Cylas formicarius elegantulus* (Summers)	COLEOPTERA: Curculionidae
sweetpotato whitefly	*Bemisia tabaci* (Gennadius)	HOMOPTERA: Aleyrodidae

| sycamore lace bug | *Corythucha ciliata* (Say) | HETEROPTERA: Tingidae |
| sycamore tussock moth | *Halysidota harrisii* Walsh | LEPIDOPTERA: Arctiidae |

T

Tahitian coconut weevil	*Diocalandra taitensis* (Guérin-Méneville)	COLEOPTERA: Curculionidae
tamarind weevil	*Sitophilus linearis* (Herbst)	COLEOPTERA: Curculionidae
tamarix leafhopper	*Opsius stactogalus* Fieber	HOMOPTERA: Cicadellidae
tarnished plant bug	*Lygus lineolaris* (Palisot de Beauvois)	HETEROPTERA: Miridae
tawny garden slug	*Limax flavus* Linnaeus	STYLOMMATOPHORA: Limacidae
tawny mole cricket	*Scapteriscus vicinus* Scudder	ORTHOPTERA: Gryllotalpidae
tea scale	*Fiorinia theae* Green	HOMOPTERA: Diaspididae
tenlined June beetle	*Polyphylla decemlineata* (Say)	COLEOPTERA: Scarabaeidae
tenspotted lady beetle	*Coelophora pupillata* (Swartz)	COLEOPTERA: Coccinellidae
terrapin scale	*Mesolecanium nigrofasciatum* (Pergande)	HOMOPTERA: Coccidae
tessellated scale	*Eucalymnatus tessellatus* (Signoret)	HOMOPTERA: Coccidae
Texas citrus mite	*Eutetranychus banksi* (McGregor)	ACARI: Tetranychidae
Texas leafcutting ant	*Atta texana* (Buckley)	HYMENOPTERA: Formicidae
thief ant	*Solenopsis molesta* (Say)	HYMENOPTERA: Formicidae
thirteenspotted lady beetle	*Hippodamia tredecimpunctata tibialis* (Say)	COLEOPTERA: Coccinellidae
thistle aphid	*Brachycaudus cardui* (Linnaeus)	HOMOPTERA: Aphididae
thread bug	*Empicoris rubromaculatus* (Blackburn)	HETEROPTERA: Reduviidae
threebanded leafhopper	*Erythroneura tricincta* Fitch	HOMOPTERA: Cicadellidae
threecornered alfalfa hopper	*Spissistilus festinus* (Say)	HOMOPTERA: Membracidae
threelined leafroller	*Pandemis limitata* (Robinson)	LEPIDOPTERA: Tortricidae
threelined potato beetle	*Lema trilinea* White	COLEOPTERA: Chrysomelidae
threespotted flea beetle	*Disonycha triangularis* (Say)	COLEOPTERA: Chrysomelidae
threestriped blister beetle	*Epicauta lemniscata* (Fabricius)	COLEOPTERA: Meloidae
threestriped lady beetle	*Brumoides suturalis* (Fabricius)	COLEOPTERA: Coccinellidae
throat bot fly	*Gasterophilus nasalis* (Linnaeus)	DIPTERA: Oestridae
thurberia weevil	*Anthonomus grandis thurberiae* Pierce	COLEOPTERA: Curculionidae
tiger swallowtail	*Papilio glaucus* Linnaeus	LEPIDOPTERA: Papilionidae
tilehorned prionus	*Prionus imbricornis* (Linnaeus)	COLEOPTERA: Cerambycidae
tipdwarf mite	*Calepiterimerus thujae* (Garman)	ACARI: Eriophyidae
toad bug	*Gelastocoris oculatus* (Fabricius)	HETEROPTERA: Gelastocoridae
tobacco aphid	*Myzus nicotianae* Blackman	HOMOPTERA: Aphididae

tobacco budworm	*Helicoverpa virescens* (Fabricius)	LEPIDOPTERA: Noctuidae
tobacco flea beetle	*Epitrix hirtipennis* (Melsheimer)	COLEOPTERA: Chrysomelidae
tobacco hornworm	*Manduca sexta* (Linnaeus)	LEPIDOPTERA: Sphingidae
tobacco moth	*Ephestia elutella* (Hübner)	LEPIDOPTERA: Pyralidae
tobacco stalk borer	*Trichobaris mucorea* (LeConte)	COLEOPTERA: Curculionidae
tobacco thrips	*Frankliniella fusca* (Hinds)	THYSANOPTERA: Thripidae
tobacco wireworm	*Conoderus vespertinus* (Fabricius)	COLEOPTERA: Elateridae
tomato bug	*Cyrtopeltis modesta* (Distant)	HETEROPTERA: Miridae
tomato fruitworm[28]	*Helicoverpa zea* (Boddie)	LEPIDOPTERA: Noctuidae
tomato hornworm	*Manduca quinquemaculata* (Haworth)	LEPIDOPTERA: Sphingidae
tomato pinworm	*Keiferia lycopersicella* (Walsingham)	LEPIDOPTERA: Gelechiidae
tomato psyllid[29]	*Paratrioza cockerelli* (Sulc)	HOMOPTERA: Psyllidae
tomato russet mite	*Aculops lycopersici* (Massee)	ACARI: Eriophyidae
toothed flea beetle	*Chaetocnema denticulata* (Illiger)	COLEOPTERA: Chrysomelidae
torsalo	*Dermatobia hominis* (Linnaeus, Jr.)	DIPTERA: Oestridae
transparentwinged plant bug	*Hyalopeplus pellucidus* (Stål)	HETEROPTERA: Miridae
transverse lady beetle	*Coccinella transversoguttata richardsoni* Brown	COLEOPTERA: Coccinellidae
tropical fowl mite	*Ornithonyssus bursa* (Berlese)	ACARI: Macronyssidae
tropical horse tick	*Anocentor nitens* (Neumann)	ACARI: Ixodidae
tropical rat louse	*Hoplopleura pacifica* Ewing	ANOPLURA: Hoplopleuridae
tropical rat mite	*Ornithonyssus bacoti* (Hirst)	ACARI: Macronyssidae
tropical sod webworm	*Herpetogramma phaeopteralis* Guenée	LEPIDOPTERA: Pyralidae
tuber flea beetle	*Epitrix tuberis* Gentner	COLEOPTERA: Chrysomelidae
tufted apple bud moth	*Platynota idaeusalis* (Walker)	LEPIDOPTERA: Tortricidae
tule beetle	*Tanystoma maculicolle* (Dejean)	COLEOPTERA: Carabidae
tulip bulb aphid	*Dysaphis tulipae* (Boyer de Fonscolombe)	HOMOPTERA: Aphididae
tuliptree aphid	*Macrosiphum liriodendri* (Monell)	HOMOPTERA: Aphididae
tuliptree scale	*Toumeyella liriodendri* (Gmelin)	HOMOPTERA: Coccidae
tumid spider mite	*Tetranychus tumidus* Banks	ACARI: Tetranychidae
tupelo leafminer	*Antispila nysaefoliella* Clemens	LEPIDOPTERA: Heliozelidae
Turkestan cockroach	*Blatta (Shelfordella) lateralis* (Walker)	BLATTODEA: Blattidae
turkey chigger	*Neoschoengastia americana* (Hirst)	ACARI: Trombiculidae
turkey gnat	*Simulium meridionale* Riley	DIPTERA: Simuliidae
turnip aphid	*Lipaphis erysimi* (Kaltenbach)	HOMOPTERA: Aphididae

---

[28]Also called bollworm and corn earworm.
[29]Also called potato psyllid.

turnip maggot	*Delia floralis* (Fallén)	DIPTERA: Anthomyiidae
turpentine borer	*Buprestis apricans* Herbst	COLEOPTERA: Buprestidae
twicestabbed lady beetle	*Chilocorus stigma* (Say)	COLEOPTERA: Coccinellidae
twig girdler	*Oncideres cingulata* (Say)	COLEOPTERA: Cerambycidae
twig pruner	*Elaphidionoides villosus* (Fabricius)	COLEOPTERA: Cerambycidae
twinspotted budworm	*Hedya chionosema* (Zeller)	LEPIDOPTERA: Tortricidae
twobanded fungus beetle	*Alphitophagus bifasciatus* (Say)	COLEOPTERA: Tenebrionidae
twobanded Japanese weevil	*Callirhopalus bifasciatus* (Roelofs)	COLEOPTERA: Curculionidae
twolined chestnut borer	*Agrilus bilineatus* (Weber)	COLEOPTERA: Buprestidae
twolined spittlebug	*Prosapia bicincta* (Say)	HOMOPTERA: Cercopidae
twomarked treehopper	*Enchenopa binotata* (Say)	HOMOPTERA: Membracidae
twospotted lady beetle	*Adalia bipunctata* (Linnaeus)	COLEOPTERA: Coccinellidae
twospotted spider mite	*Tetranychus urticae* Koch	ACARI: Tetranychidae
twospotted stink bug	*Perillus bioculatus* (Fabricius)	HETEROPTERA: Pentatomidae
twostriped grasshopper	*Melanoplus bivittatus* (Say)	ORTHOPTERA: Acrididae
twostriped walkingstick	*Anisomorpha buprestoides* (Stoll)	PHASMATODEA: Pseudophasmatidae

---

U

---

uglynest caterpillar	*Archips cerasivorana* (Fitch)	LEPIDOPTERA: Tortricidae
unicorn caterpillar	*Schizura unicornis* (J.E. Smith)	LEPIDOPTERA: Notodontidae

---

V

---

vagabond crambus	*Agriphila vulgivagella* (Clemens)	LEPIDOPTERA: Pyralidae
vagrant grasshopper	*Schistocerca nitens nitens* (Thunberg)	ORTHOPTERA: Acrididae
Van Duzee treehopper	*Vanduzea segmentata* (Fowler)	HOMOPTERA: Membracidae
vanda thrips	*Dichromothrips corbetti* (Priesner)	THYSANOPTERA: Thripidae
variable oakleaf caterpillar	*Heterocampa manteo* (Doubleday)	LEPIDOPTERA: Notodontidae
varied carpet beetle	*Anthrenus verbasci* (Linnaeus)	COLEOPTERA: Dermestidae
variegated cutworm	*Peridroma saucia* (Hübner)	LEPIDOPTERA: Noctuidae
vedalia	*Rodolia cardinalis* (Mulsant)	COLEOPTERA: Coccinellidae
vegetable leafminer	*Liriomyza sativae* Blanchard	DIPTERA: Agromyzidae

vegetable weevil	*Listroderes difficilis* Germar	COLEOPTERA: Curculionidae
velvetbean caterpillar	*Anticarsia gemmatalis* Hübner	LEPIDOPTERA: Noctuidae
verbena bud moth	*Endothenia hebesana* (Walker)	LEPIDOPTERA: Tortricidae
vespiform thrips	*Franklinothrips vespiformis* (D.L. Crawford)	THYSANOPTERA: Aeolothripidae
vetch bruchid	*Bruchus brachialis* Fåhraeus	COLEOPTERA: Bruchidae
vexans mosquito	*Aedes vexans* (Meigen)	DIPTERA: Culicidae
viburnum aphid	*Aphis viburniphila* Patch	HOMOPTERA: Aphididae
viceroy	*Basilarchia archippus* (Cramer)	LEPIDOPTERA: Nymphalidae
violet aphid	*Micromyzus violae* (Pergande)	HOMOPTERA: Aphididae
violet sawfly	*Ametastegia pallipes* (Spinola)	HYMENOPTERA: Tenthredinidae
Virginia pine sawfly	*Neodiprion pratti pratti* (Dyar)	HYMENOPTERA: Diprionidae
Virginiacreeper leafhopper	*Erythroneura ziczac* Walsh	HOMOPTERA: Cicadellidae
Virginiacreeper sphinx	*Darapsa myron* (Cramer)	LEPIDOPTERA: Sphingidae

W

w-marked cutworm	*Spaelotis clandestina* (Harris)	LEPIDOPTERA: Noctuidae
walkingstick	*Diapheromera femorata* (Say)	PHASMATODEA: Heteronemiidae
walnut aphid	*Chromaphis juglandicola* (Kaltenbach)	HOMOPTERA: Aphididae
walnut blister mite	*Eriophyes erinea* (Nalepa)	ACARI: Eriophyidae
walnut caterpillar	*Datana integerrima* Grote & Robinson	LEPIDOPTERA: Notodontidae
walnut husk fly	*Rhagoletis completa* Cresson	DIPTERA: Tephritidae
walnut scale	*Quadraspidiotus juglandsregiae* (Comstock)	HOMOPTERA: Diaspididae
walnut shoot moth	*Acrobasis demotella* Grote	LEPIDOPTERA: Pyralidae
walnut sphinx	*Laothoe juglandis* (J.E. Smith)	LEPIDOPTERA: Sphingidae
wardrobe beetle	*Attagenus fasciatus* (Thunberg)	COLEOPTERA: Dermestidae
warehouse beetle	*Trogoderma variabile* Ballion	COLEOPTERA: Dermestidae
warehouse pirate bug	*Xylocoris flavipes* (Reuter)	HETEROPTERA: Anthocoridae
warty grain mite	*Aeroglyphus robustus* (Banks)	ACARI: Glycyphagidae
watercress leaf beetle	*Phaedon viridus* (Melsheimer)	COLEOPTERA: Chrysomelidae
watercress sharpshooter	*Draeculacephala mollipes* (Say)	HOMOPTERA: Cicadellidae
watercress sowbug	*Lirceus brachyurus* (Harger)	ISOPODA: Asellidae
waterlily aphid	*Rhopalosiphum nymphaeae* (Linnaeus)	HOMOPTERA: Aphididae
waterlily leaf beetle	*Galerucella nymphaeae* (Linnaeus)	COLEOPTERA: Chrysomelidae
waterlily leafcutter	*Synclita obliteralis* (Walker)	LEPIDOPTERA: Pyralidae
webbing clothes moth	*Tineola bisselliella* (Hummel)	LEPIDOPTERA: Tineidae

webbing coneworm	*Dioryctria disclusa* Heinrich	LEPIDOPTERA: Pyralidae
West Indian cane weevil	*Metamasius hemipterus hemipterus* (Linnaeus)	COLEOPTERA: Curculionidae
West Indian flatid	*Anormenis antillarum* (Kirkaldy)	HOMOPTERA: Flatidae
West Indian fruit fly	*Anastrepha obliqua* (Macquart)	DIPTERA: Tephritidae
West Indian sweetpotato weevil	*Euscepes postfaciatus* (Fairmaire)	COLEOPTERA: Curculionidae
western balsam bark beetle	*Dryocoetes confusus* Swaine	COLEOPTERA: Scolytidae
western bean cutworm	*Loxagrotis albicosta* (Smith)	LEPIDOPTERA: Noctuidae
western bigeyed bug	*Geocoris pallens* Stål	HETEROPTERA: Lygaeidae
western black flea beetle	*Phyllotreta pusilla* Horn	COLEOPTERA: Chrysomelidae
western blackheaded budworm	*Acleris gloverana* (Walsingham)	LEPIDOPTERA: Tortricidae
western bloodsucking conenose	*Triatoma protracta* (Uhler)	HETEROPTERA: Reduviidae
western boxelder bug	*Boisea rubrolineata* Barber	HETEROPTERA: Rhopalidae
western cedar bark beetle	*Phloeosinus punctatus* LeConte	COLEOPTERA: Scolytidae
western cedar borer	*Trachykele blondeli* Marseul	COLEOPTERA: Buprestidae
western cherry fruit fly	*Rhagoletis indifferens* Curran	DIPTERA: Tephritidae
western chicken flea	*Ceratophyllus niger* (Fox)	SIPHONAPTERA: Ceratophyllidae
western chinch bug	*Blissus occiduus* Barber	HETEROPTERA: Lygaeidae
western corn rootworm	*Diabrotica virgifera virgifera* LeConte	COLEOPTERA: Chrysomelidae
western damsel bug	*Nabis alternatus* Parshley	HETEROPTERA: Nabidae
western drywood termite	*Incisitermes minor* (Hagen)	ISOPTERA: Kalotermitidae
western field wireworm	*Limonius infuscatus* Motschulsky	COLEOPTERA: Elateridae
western flower thrips	*Frankliniella occidentalis* (Pergande)	THYSANOPTERA: Thripidae
western grape leafhopper	*Erythroneura elegantula* Osborn	HOMOPTERA: Cicadellidae
western grape rootworm	*Bromius obscurus* (Linnaeus)	COLEOPTERA: Chrysomelidae
western grapeleaf skeletonizer	*Harrisina brillians* Barnes & McDunnough	LEPIDOPTERA: Zygaenidae
western harvester ant	*Pogonomyrmex occidentalis* (Cresson)	HYMENOPTERA: Formicidae
western hemlock looper	*Lambdina fiscellaria lugubrosa* (Hulst)	LEPIDOPTERA: Geometridae
western lawn moth	*Tehama bonifatella* (Hulst)	LEPIDOPTERA: Pyralidae
western lily aphid	*Macrosiphum scoliopi* Essig	HOMOPTERA: Aphididae
western oak looper	*Lambdina fiscellaria somniaria* (Hulst)	LEPIDOPTERA: Geometridae
western pine beetle	*Dendroctonus brevicomis* LeConte	COLEOPTERA: Scolytidae
western pine shoot borer	*Eucosma sonomana* Kearfott	LEPIDOPTERA: Tortricidae
western plant bug	*Rhinacloa forticornis* Reuter	HETEROPTERA: Miridae
western poplar clearwing	*Paranthrene robiniae* (Hy. Edwards)	LEPIDOPTERA: Sesiidae
western potato flea beetle	*Epitrix subcrinita* LeConte	COLEOPTERA: Chrysomelidae
western potato leafhopper	*Empoasca abrupta* DeLong	HOMOPTERA: Cicadellidae
western predatory mite	*Galandromus occidentalis* (Nesbitt)	ACARI: Phytoseiidae

western spotted cucumber beetle	*Diabrotica undecimpunctata undecimpunctata* Mannerheim	COLEOPTERA: Chrysomelidae
western spruce budworm	*Choristoneura occidentalis* Freeman	LEPIDOPTERA: Tortricidae
western striped cucumber beetle	*Acalymma trivittatum* (Mannerheim)	COLEOPTERA: Chrysomelidae
western striped flea beetle	*Phyllotreta ramosa* (Crotch)	COLEOPTERA: Chrysomelidae
western subterranean termite	*Reticulitermes hesperus* Banks	ISOPTERA: Rhinotermitidae
western tent caterpillar	*Malacosoma californicum* (Packard)	LEPIDOPTERA: Lasiocampidae
western thatching ant	*Formica obscuripes* Forel	HYMENOPTERA: Formicidae
western treehole mosquito	*Aedes sierrensis* (Ludlow)	DIPTERA: Culicidae
western tussock moth	*Orgyia vetusta* (Boisduval)	LEPIDOPTERA: Lymantriidae
western w-marked cutworm	*Spaelotis havilae* (Grote)	LEPIDOPTERA: Noctuidae
western wheat aphid	*Diuraphis (Holcaphis) tritici* (Gillette)	HOMOPTERA: Aphididae
western yellowjacket	*Vespula pensylvanica* (Saussure)	HYMENOPTERA: Vespidae
western yellowstriped armyworm	*Spodoptera praefica* (Grote)	LEPIDOPTERA: Noctuidae
wharf borer	*Nacerdes melanura* (Linnaeus)	COLEOPTERA: Oedemeridae
wheat curl mite	*Eriophyes tulipae* Keifer	ACARI: Eriophyidae
wheat head armyworm	*Faronta diffusa* (Walker)	LEPIDOPTERA: Noctuidae
wheat jointworm	*Tetramesa tritici* (Fitch)	HYMENOPTERA: Eurytomidae
wheat midge	*Sitodiplosis mosellana* (Géhin)	DIPTERA: Cecidomyiidae
wheat stem maggot	*Meromyza americana* Fitch	DIPTERA: Chloropidae
wheat stem sawfly	*Cephus cinctus* Norton	HYMENOPTERA: Cephidae
wheat strawworm	*Tetramesa grandis* (Riley)	HYMENOPTERA: Eurytomidae
wheat wireworm	*Agriotes mancus* (Say)	COLEOPTERA: Elateridae
wheel bug	*Arilus cristatus* (Linnaeus)	HETEROPTERA: Reduviidae
white apple leafhopper	*Typhlocyba pomaria* McAtee	HOMOPTERA: Cicadellidae
white cutworm	*Euxoa scandens* (Riley)	LEPIDOPTERA: Noctuidae
white fir needleminer	*Epinotia meritana* Heinrich	LEPIDOPTERA: Tortricidae
white garden snail	*Theba pisana* (Müller)	STYLOMMATOPHORA: Helicidae
white oak borer	*Goes tigrinus* (De Geer)	COLEOPTERA: Cerambycidae
white peach scale	*Pseudaulacaspis pentagona* (Targioni-Tozzetti)	HOMOPTERA: Diaspididae
white pine aphid	*Cinara strobi* (Fitch)	HOMOPTERA: Aphididae
white pine cone beetle	*Conophthorus coniperda* (Schwarz)	COLEOPTERA: Scolytidae
white pine cone borer	*Eucosma tocullionana* Heinrich	LEPIDOPTERA: Tortricidae
white pine sawfly	*Neodiprion pinetum* (Norton)	HYMENOPTERA: Diprionidae
white pine weevil[30]	*Pissodes strobi* (Peck)	COLEOPTERA: Curculionidae

[30]Also called Englemann spruce weevil and Sitka spruce weevil.

whitebacked garden spider	*Argiope trifasciata* (Forskal)	ARANEAE: Araneidae
whitebanded elm leafhopper	*Scaphoideus luteolus* Van Duzee	HOMOPTERA: Cicadellidae
whitecrossed seed bug	*Neacoryphus bicrucis* (Say)	HETEROPTERA: Lygaeidae
whitefringed beetles	*Graphognathus* spp.	COLEOPTERA: Curculionidae
whitelined sphinx	*Hyles lineata* (Fabricius)	LEPIDOPTERA: Sphingidae
whitemargined cockroach	*Melanozosteria soror* (Brunner)	BLATTODEA: Blattidae
whitemarked fleahopper	*Spanagonicus albofasciatus* (Reuter)	HETEROPTERA: Miridae
whitemarked spider beetle	*Ptinus fur* (Linnaeus)	COLEOPTERA: Ptinidae
whitemarked treehopper	*Tricentrus albomaculatus* Distant	HOMOPTERA: Membracidae
whitemarked tussock moth	*Orgyia leucostigma* (J.E. Smith)	LEPIDOPTERA: Lymantriidae
whiteshouldered house moth	*Endrosis sarcitrella* (Linnaeus)	LEPIDOPTERA: Oecophoridae
whitespotted sawyer	*Monochamus scutellatus* (Say)	COLEOPTERA: Cerambycidae
willow beaked-gall midge	*Rabdophaga rigidae* (Osten Sacken)	DIPTERA: Cecidomyiidae
willow flea weevil	*Rhynchaenus rufipes* (LeConte)	COLEOPTERA: Curculionidae
willow redgall sawfly	*Pontania promixa* (Lepeletier)	HYMENOPTERA: Tenthredinidae
willow sawfly	*Nematus ventralis* Say	HYMENOPTERA: Tenthredinidae
willow shoot sawfly	*Janus abbreviatus* (Say)	HYMENOPTERA: Cephidae
Wilson sphinx	*Hyles wilsoni* (Rothschild)	LEPIDOPTERA: Sphingidae
wing louse	*Liperus caponis* (Linnaeus)	MALLOPHAGA: Philopteridae
winter grain mite	*Penthaleus major* (Dugès)	ACARI: Eupodidae
winter moth	*Operophtera brumata* (Linnaeus)	LEPIDOPTERA: Geometridae
winter tick	*Dermacentor albipictus* (Packard)	ACARI: Ixodidae
woodrose bug	*Graptostethus manillensis* (Stål)	HETEROPTERA: Lygaeidae
woods weevil	*Nemocestes incomptus* (Horn)	COLEOPTERA: Curculionidae
woolly alder aphid	*Paraprociphilus tessellatus* (Fitch)	HOMOPTERA: Aphididae
woolly apple aphid	*Eriosoma lanigerum* (Hausmann)	HOMOPTERA: Aphididae
woolly elm aphid	*Eriosoma americanum* (Riley)	HOMOPTERA: Aphididae
woolly pear aphid	*Eriosoma pyricola* Baker & Davidson	HOMOPTERA: Aphididae
woolly whitefly	*Aleurothrixus floccosus* (Maskell)	HOMOPTERA: Aleyrodidae

---

Y

---

yellow and black potter wasp	*Delta campaniformis campaniformis* (Fabricius)	HYMENOPTERA: Vespidae
yellow clover aphid	*Therioaphis trifolii* (Monell)	HOMOPTERA: Aphididae
yellow garden spider	*Argiope aurantia* Lucas	ARANEAE: Araneidae
yellow mealworm	*Tenebrio molitor* Linnaeus	COLEOPTERA: Tenebrionidae

yellow pecan aphid	*Monelliopsis pecanis* Bissell	HOMOPTERA: Aphididae
yellow rose aphid	*Acyrthosiphon (Rhodobium) porosum* (Sanderson)	HOMOPTERA: Aphididae
yellow scale	*Aonidiella citrina* (Coquillett)	HOMOPTERA: Diaspididae
yellow spider mite	*Eotetranychus carpini borealis* (Ewing)	ACARI: Tetranychidae
yellow sugarcane aphid	*Sipha flava* (Forbes)	HOMOPTERA: Aphididae
yellow woollybear	*Spilosoma virginica* (Fabricius)	LEPIDOPTERA: Arctiidae
yellowfaced leafhopper	*Scaphytopius loricatus* (Van Duzee)	HOMOPTERA: Cicadellidae
yellowfever mosquito	*Aedes aegypti* (Linnaeus)	DIPTERA: Culicidae
yellowheaded cutworm	*Apamea amputatrix* (Fitch)	LEPIDOPTERA: Noctuidae
yellowheaded fireworm	*Acleris minuta* (Robinson)	LEPIDOPTERA: Tortricidae
yellowheaded leafhopper	*Xyphon flaviceps* (Riley)	HOMOPTERA: Cicadellidae
yellowheaded spruce sawfly	*Pikonema alaskensis* (Rohwer)	HYMENOPTERA: Tenthredinidae
yellowmargined leaf beetle	*Microtheca ochroloma* Stål	COLEOPTERA: Chrysomelidae
yellownecked caterpillar	*Datana ministra* (Drury)	LEPIDOPTERA: Notodontidae
yellowshouldered lady beetle	*Scymnodes lividigaster* (Mulsant)	COLEOPTERA: Coccinellidae
yellowstriped armyworm	*Spodoptera ornithogalli* (Guenée)	LEPIDOPTERA: Noctuidae
Yosemite bark weevil	*Pissodes schwarzi* Hopkins	COLEOPTERA: Curculionidae
yucca moth	*Tegeticula yuccasella* (Riley)	LEPIDOPTERA: Incurvariidae
yucca plant bug	*Halticotoma valida* Townsend	HETEROPTERA: Miridae
Yuma spider mite	*Eotetranychus yumensis* (McGregor)	ACARI: Tetranychidae

Z

zebra caterpillar	*Melanchra picta* (Harris)	LEPIDOPTERA: Noctuidae
Zimmerman pine moth	*Dioryctria zimmermani* (Grote)	LEPIDOPTERA: Pyralidae

Section II. Insects and Related Organisms Listed by Scientific Name

A

Abacarus hystrix (Nalepa)	grain rust mite	ACARI: Eriophyidae
Abgrallaspis ithacae (Ferris)	hemlock scale	HOMOPTERA: Diaspididae
Acalitus essigi (Hassan)	redberry mite	ACARI: Eriophyidae
Acalitus gossypii (Banks)	cotton blister mite	ACARI: Eriophyidae
Acalitus vaccinii (Keifer)	blueberry bud mite	ACARI: Eriophyidae
Acalymma trivittatum (Mannerheim)	western striped cucumber beetle	COLEOPTERA: Chrysomelidae
Acalymma vittatum (Fabricius)	striped cucumber beetle	COLEOPTERA: Chrysomelidae
Acantholyda erythrocephala (Linnaeus)	pine false webworm	HYMENOPTERA: Pamphiliidae
Acanthomyops claviger (Roger)	smaller yellow ant	HYMENOPTERA: Formicidae
Acanthomyops interjectus (Mayr)	larger yellow ant	HYMENOPTERA: Formicidae
Acanthoscelides obtectus (Say)	bean weevil	COLEOPTERA: Bruchidae
Acarapis woodi (Rennie)	honey bee mite	ACARI: Tarsonemidae
Acarus siro Linnaeus	grain mite	ACARI: Acaridae
Aceratagallia sanguinolenta (Provancher)	clover leafhopper	HOMOPTERA: Cicadellidae
Achaea janata (Linnaeus)	croton caterpillar	LEPIDOPTERA: Noctuidae
Achatina fulica Bowdich	giant African snail	STYLOMMATOPHORA: Achatinidae
Achatodes zeae (Harris)	elder shoot borer	LEPIDOPTERA: Noctuidae
Acheta domesticus (Linnaeus)	house cricket	ORTHOPTERA: Gryllidae
Achroia grisella (Fabricius)	lesser wax moth	LEPIDOPTERA: Pyralidae
Achyra rantalis (Guenée)	garden webworm	LEPIDOPTERA: Pyralidae
Acinia picturata (Snow)	sourbush seed fly	DIPTERA: Tephritidae
Acinopterus angulatus Lawson	angulate leafhopper	HOMOPTERA: Cicadellidae
Acizzia uncatoides (Ferris & Klyver)	acacia psyllid	HOMOPTERA: Psyllidae
Acleris gloverana (Walsingham)	western blackheaded budworm	LEPIDOPTERA: Tortricidae
Acleris minuta (Robinson)	yellowheaded fireworm	LEPIDOPTERA: Tortricidae
Acleris variana (Fernald)	eastern blackheaded budworm	LEPIDOPTERA: Tortricidae
Acontia dacia Druce	brown cotton leafworm	LEPIDOPTERA: Noctuidae
Acrobasis betulella Hulst	birch tubemaker	LEPIDOPTERA: Pyralidae
Acrobasis comptoniella Hulst	sweetfern leaf casebearer	LEPIDOPTERA: Pyralidae
Acrobasis demotella Grote	walnut shoot moth	LEPIDOPTERA: Pyralidae
Acrobasis indigenella (Zeller)	leaf crumpler	LEPIDOPTERA: Pyralidae

Acrobasis juglandis (LeBaron)	pecan leaf casebearer	LEPIDOPTERA: Pyralidae
Acrobasis nuxvorella Neunzig	pecan nut casebearer	LEPIDOPTERA: Pyralidae
Acrobasis vaccinii Riley	cranberry fruitworm	LEPIDOPTERA: Pyralidae
Acrolepiopsis assectella (Zeller)	leek moth	LEPIDOPTERA: Acrolepiidae
Acronicta americana (Harris)	American dagger moth	LEPIDOPTERA: Noctuidae
Acronicta lepusculina Guenée	cottonwood dagger moth	LEPIDOPTERA: Noctuidae
Acronicta oblinita (J.E. Smith)	smeared dagger moth	LEPIDOPTERA: Noctuidae
Acrosternum hilare (Say)	green stink bug	HETEROPTERA: Pentatomidae
Actebia fennica (Tauscher)	black army cutworm	LEPIDOPTERA: Noctuidae
Actias luna (Linnaeus)	luna moth	LEPIDOPTERA: Saturniidae
Aculops lycopersici (Massee)	tomato russet mite	ACARI: Eriophyidae
Aculus cornutus (Banks)	peach silver mite	ACARI: Eriophyidae
Aculus fockeui (Nalepa & Trouessart)	plum rust mite	ACARI: Eriophyidae
Aculus schlechtendali (Nalepa)	apple rust mite	ACARI: Eriophyidae
Acyrthosiphon (Rhodobium) porosum (Sanderson)	yellow rose aphid	HOMOPTERA: Aphididae
Acyrthosiphon caraganae (Cholodkovsky)	caragana aphid	HOMOPTERA: Aphididae
Acyrthosiphon pisum (Harris)	pea aphid	HOMOPTERA: Aphididae
Adalia bipunctata (Linnaeus)	twospotted lady beetle	COLEOPTERA: Coccinellidae
Adelges abietis (Linnaeus)	eastern spruce gall adelgid	HOMOPTERA: Adelgidae
Adelges cooleyi (Gillette)	Cooley spruce gall adelgid	HOMOPTERA: Adelgidae
Adelges piceae (Ratzeburg)	balsam woolly adelgid	HOMOPTERA: Adelgidae
Adelges tsugae Annand	hemlock woolly adelgid	HOMOPTERA: Adelgidae
Adelphocoris lineolatus (Goeze)	alfalfa plant bug	HETEROPTERA: Miridae
Adelphocoris rapidus (Say)	rapid plant bug	HETEROPTERA: Miridae
Adelphocoris superbus (Uhler)	superb plant bug	HETEROPTERA: Miridae
Adoretus sinicus Burmeister	Chinese rose beetle	COLEOPTERA: Scarabaeidae
Aedes aboriginis Dyar	northwest coast mosquito	DIPTERA: Culicidae
Aedes aegypti (Linnaeus)	yellowfever mosquito	DIPTERA: Culicidae
Aedes albopictus (Skuse)	forest day mosquito	DIPTERA: Culicidae
Aedes cantator (Coquillett)	brown saltmarsh mosquito	DIPTERA: Culicidae
Aedes sierrensis (Ludlow)	western treehole mosquito	DIPTERA: Culicidae
Aedes sollicitans (Walker)	saltmarsh mosquito	DIPTERA: Culicidae
Aedes squamiger (Coquillett)	California saltmarsh mosquito	DIPTERA: Culicidae
Aedes sticticus (Meigen)	floodwater mosquito	DIPTERA: Culicidae
Aedes vexans (Meigen)	vexans mosquito	DIPTERA: Culicidae
Aeroglyphus robustus (Banks)	warty grain mite	ACARI: Glycyphagidae
Aethes rutilana (Hübner)	pale juniper webworm	LEPIDOPTERA: Cochylidae
Agasphaerops nigra Horn	lily weevil	COLEOPTERA: Curculionidae

Agonoxena argaula Meyrick	coconut leafminer	LEPIDOPTERA: Agonoxenidae
Agrilus anxius Gory	bronze birch borer	COLEOPTERA: Buprestidae
Agrilus aurichalceus Redtenbacher	rose stem girdler	COLEOPTERA: Buprestidae
Agrilus bilineatus (Weber)	twolined chestnut borer	COLEOPTERA: Buprestidae
Agrilus liragus Barter & Brown	bronze poplar borer	COLEOPTERA: Buprestidae
Agrilus ruficollis (Fabricius)	rednecked cane borer	COLEOPTERA: Buprestidae
Agrilus sinuatus (Olivier)	sinuate peartree borer	COLEOPTERA: Buprestidae
Agriolimax laevis (Müller)	marsh slug	STYLOMMATOPHORA: Limacidae
Agriolimax reticulatus (Müller)	gray garden slug	STYLOMMATOPHORA: Limacidae
Agriotes lineatus (Linnaeus)	lined click beetle	COLEOPTERA: Elateridae
Agriotes mancus (Say)	wheat wireworm	COLEOPTERA: Elateridae
Agriphila vulgivagella (Clemens)	vagabond crambus	LEPIDOPTERA: Pyralidae
Agrius cingulata (Fabricius)	sweetpotato hornworm	LEPIDOPTERA: Sphingidae
Agromyza frontella (Rondani)	alfalfa blotch leafminer	DIPTERA: Agromyzidae
Agromyza parvicornis Loew	corn blotch leafminer	DIPTERA: Agromyzidae
Agrotis crinigera (Butler)	larger Hawaiian cutworm	LEPIDOPTERA: Noctuidae
Agrotis dislocata (Walker)	smaller Hawaiian cutworm	LEPIDOPTERA: Noctuidae
Agrotis gladiaria Morrison	claybacked cutworm	LEPIDOPTERA: Noctuidae
Agrotis ipsilon (Hufnagel)	black cutworm	LEPIDOPTERA: Noctuidae
Agrotis malefida Guenée	palesided cutworm	LEPIDOPTERA: Noctuidae
Agrotis orthogonia Morrison	pale western cutworm	LEPIDOPTERA: Noctuidae
Agrotis subterranea (Fabricius)	granulate cutworm	LEPIDOPTERA: Noctuidae
Ahasverus advena (Waltl)	foreign grain beetle	COLEOPTERA: Cucujidae
Alabama argillacea (Hübner)	cotton leafworm	LEPIDOPTERA: Noctuidae
Alaus oculatus (Linnaeus)	eyed click beetle	COLEOPTERA: Elateridae
Aleurocanthus spiniferus (Quaintance)	orange spiny whitefly	HOMOPTERA: Aleyrodidae
Aleurocanthus woglumi Ashby	citrus blackfly	HOMOPTERA: Aleyrodidae
Aleuroglyphus ovatus (Troupeau)	brownlegged grain mite	ACARI: Acaridae
Aleurothrixus floccosus (Maskell)	woolly whitefly	HOMOPTERA: Aleyrodidae
Aleyrodes shizuokensis Kuwana	oxalis whitefly	HOMOPTERA: Aleyrodidae
Algarobius bottimeri Kingsolver	kiawe bean weevil	COLEOPTERA: Bruchidae
Allantus cinctus (Linnaeus)	curled rose sawfly	HYMENOPTERA: Tenthredinidae
Alniphagus aspericollis (LeConte)	alder bark beetle	COLEOPTERA: Scolytidae
Alphitobius diaperinus (Panzer)	lesser mealworm	COLEOPTERA: Tenebrionidae
Alphitobius laevigatus (Fabricius)	black fungus beetle	COLEOPTERA: Tenebrionidae
Alphitophagus bifasciatus (Say)	twobanded fungus beetle	COLEOPTERA: Tenebrionidae
Alsophila pometaria (Harris)	fall cankerworm	LEPIDOPTERA: Geometridae
Altica canadensis Gentner	prairie flea beetle	COLEOPTERA: Chrysomelidae

Altica carinata Germar	elm flea beetle	COLEOPTERA: Chrysomelidae
Altica chalybea Illiger	grape flea beetle	COLEOPTERA: Chrysomelidae
Altica sylvia Malloch	blueberry flea beetle	COLEOPTERA: Chrysomelidae
Alypia octomaculata (Fabricius)	eightspotted forester	LEPIDOPTERA: Noctuidae
Amblyomma americanum (Linnaeus)	lone star tick	ACARI: Ixodidae
Amblyomma cajennense (Fabricius)	Cayenne tick	ACARI: Ixodidae
Amblyomma maculatum Koch	Gulf Coast tick	ACARI: Ixodidae
Amblyomma tuberculatum Marx	gophertortoise tick	ACARI: Ixodidae
Ametastegia glabrata (Fallén)	dock sawfly	HYMENOPTERA: Tenthredinidae
Ametastegia pallipes (Spinola)	violet sawfly	HYMENOPTERA: Tenthredinidae
Amorbia emigratella Busck	Mexican leafroller	LEPIDOPTERA: Tortricidae
Ampeloglypter sesostris (LeConte)	grape cane gallmaker	COLEOPTERA: Curculionidae
Amphicerus bicaudatus (Say)	apple twig borer	COLEOPTERA: Bostrichidae
Amphicerus cornutus (Pallas)	powderpost bostrichid	COLEOPTERA: Bostrichidae
Ampulex compressa (Fabricius)	emerald cockroach wasp	HYMENOPTERA: Sphecidae
Amyelois transitella (Walker)	navel orangeworm	LEPIDOPTERA: Pyralidae
Amyna natalis (Walker)	ilima moth	LEPIDOPTERA: Noctuidae
Anabrus simplex Haldeman	Mormon cricket	ORTHOPTERA: Tettigoniidae
Anagasta kuehniella (Zeller)	Mediterranean flour moth	LEPIDOPTERA: Pyralidae
Anagrapha falcifera (Kirby)	celery looper	LEPIDOPTERA: Noctuidae
Anaphothrips obscurus (Müller)	grass thrips	THYSANOPTERA: Thripidae
Anaphothrips swezeyi Moulton	Hawaiian grass thrips	THYSANOPTERA: Thripidae
Anarsia lineatella Zeller	peach twig borer	LEPIDOPTERA: Gelechiidae
Anasa armigera (Say)	horned squash bug	HETEROPTERA: Coreidae
Anasa tristis (De Geer)	squash bug	HETEROPTERA: Coreidae
Anastrepha ludens (Loew)	Mexican fruit fly	DIPTERA: Tephritidae
Anastrepha obliqua (Macquart)	West Indian fruit fly	DIPTERA: Tephritidae
Anastrepha pallens Coquillett	bumelia fruit fly	DIPTERA: Tephritidae
Anastrepha suspensa (Loew)	Caribbean fruit fly	DIPTERA: Tephritidae
Anaticola anseris (Linnaeus)	slender goose louse	MALLOPHAGA: Philopteridae
Anaticola crassicornis (Scopoli)	slender duck louse	MALLOPHAGA: Philopteridae
Anax junius (Drury)	common green darner	ODONATA: Aeschnidae
Anax strenuus Hagen	giant Hawaiian dragonfly	ODONATA: Aeschnidae
Ancylis comptana (Froelich)	strawberry leafroller	LEPIDOPTERA: Tortricidae
Anisomorpha buprestoides (Stoll)	twostriped walkingstick	PHASMATODEA: Pseudophasmatidae
Anisota senatoria (J.E. Smith)	orangestriped oakworm	LEPIDOPTERA: Saturniidae
Anisota stigma (Fabricius)	spiny oakworm	LEPIDOPTERA: Saturniidae
Anisota virginiensis (Drury)	pinkstriped oakworm	LEPIDOPTERA: Saturniidae

Anobium punctatum (De Geer)	furniture beetle	COLEOPTERA: Anobiidae
Anocentor nitens (Neumann)	tropical horse tick	ACARI: Ixodidae
Anomala oblivia Horn	pine chafer	COLEOPTERA: Scarabaeidae
Anomala orientalis Waterhouse	oriental beetle	COLEOPTERA: Scarabaeidae
Anomoea laticlavia (Forster)	claycolored leaf beetle	COLEOPTERA: Chrysomelidae
Anopheles quadrimaculatus Say	common malaria mosquito	DIPTERA: Culicidae
Anoplolepis longipes (Jerdon)	longlegged ant	HYMENOPTERA: Formicidae
Anormenis antillarum (Kirkaldy)	West Indian flatid	HOMOPTERA: Flatidae
Antheraea polyphemus (Cramer)	polyphemus moth	LEPIDOPTERA: Saturniidae
Anthicus floralis (Linnaeus)	narrownecked grain beetle	COLEOPTERA: Anthicidae
Anthonomus eugenii Cano	pepper weevil	COLEOPTERA: Curculionidae
Anthonomus grandis grandis Boheman	boll weevil	COLEOPTERA: Curculionidae
Anthonomus grandis thurberiae Pierce	thurberia weevil	COLEOPTERA: Curculionidae
Anthonomus musculus Say	cranberry weevil	COLEOPTERA: Curculionidae
Anthonomus signatus Say	strawberry bud weevil	COLEOPTERA: Curculionidae
Anthrenus flavipes LeConte	furniture carpet beetle	COLEOPTERA: Dermestidae
Anthrenus scrophulariae (Linnaeus)	carpet beetle	COLEOPTERA: Dermestidae
Anthrenus verbasci (Linnaeus)	varied carpet beetle	COLEOPTERA: Dermestidae
Antianthe expansa (Germar)	solanaceous treehopper	HOMOPTERA: Membracidae
Anticarsia gemmatalis Hübner	velvetbean caterpillar	LEPIDOPTERA: Noctuidae
Antispila nysaefoliella Clemens	tupelo leafminer	LEPIDOPTERA: Heliozelidae
Antonina graminis (Maskell)	Rhodesgrass mealybug	HOMOPTERA: Pseudococcidae
Anuraphis maidiradicis (Forbes)	corn root aphid	HOMOPTERA: Aphididae
Aonidiella aurantii (Maskell)	California red scale	HOMOPTERA: Diaspididae
Aonidiella citrina (Coquillett)	yellow scale	HOMOPTERA: Diaspididae
Aonidiella inornata McKenzie	inornate scale	HOMOPTERA: Diaspididae
Apamea amputatrix (Fitch)	yellowheaded cutworm	LEPIDOPTERA: Noctuidae
Apamea devastator (Brace)	glassy cutworm	LEPIDOPTERA: Noctuidae
Aphelinus lapisliqni Howard	clover aphid parasite	HYMENOPTERA: Encyrtidae
Aphis craccivora Koch	cowpea aphid	HOMOPTERA: Aphididae
Aphis fabae Scopoli	bean aphid	HOMOPTERA: Aphididae
Aphis forbesi Weed	strawberry root aphid	HOMOPTERA: Aphididae
Aphis gossypii Glover	cotton aphid[31]	HOMOPTERA: Aphididae
Aphis hederae Kaltenbach	ivy aphid	HOMOPTERA: Aphididae
Aphis illinoisensis Shimer	grapevine aphid	HOMOPTERA: Aphididae

[31]Also called melon aphid.

Aphis middletonii (Thomas)	erigeron root aphid	HOMOPTERA: Aphididae
Aphis nasturtii Kaltenbach	buckthorn aphid	HOMOPTERA: Aphididae
Aphis nerii Boyer de Fonscolombe	oleander aphid	HOMOPTERA: Aphididae
Aphis pomi De Geer	apple aphid	HOMOPTERA: Aphididae
Aphis spiraecola Patch	spirea aphid	HOMOPTERA: Aphididae
Aphis viburniphila Patch	viburnum aphid	HOMOPTERA: Aphididae
Aphomia gularis (Zeller)	stored nut moth	LEPIDOPTERA: Pyralidae
Aphrophora parallela (Say)	pine spittlebug	HOMOPTERA: Cercopidae
Aphrophora saratogensis (Fitch)	Saratoga spittlebug	HOMOPTERA: Cercopidae
Apion (Fallapion) occidentale Fall	black sunflower stem weevil	COLEOPTERA: Curculionidae
Apion antiquum Gyllenhal	South African emex weevil	COLEOPTERA: Curculionidae
Apion longirostre Olivier	hollyhock weevil	COLEOPTERA: Curculionidae
Apion ulicis (Furster)	gorse seed weevil	COLEOPTERA: Curculionidae
Apis mellifera Linnaeus	honey bee	HYMENOPTERA: Apidae
Apodemia mormo langei Comstock	Lange metalmark	LEPIDOPTERA: Riodinidae
Apomecyna saltator (Fabricius)	cucurbit longicorn	COLEOPTERA: Cerambycidae
Aposthonia oceania (Ross)	oceanic embiid	EMBIIDINA: Oligotomidae
Araecerus fasciculatus (De Geer)	coffee bean weevil	COLEOPTERA: Anthribidae
Araecerus levipennis Jordan	koa haole seed weevil	COLEOPTERA: Anthribidae
Araeocorynus cumingi Jekel	mauna loa bean beetle	COLEOPTERA: Anthribidae
Archips argyrospila (Walker)	fruittree leafroller	LEPIDOPTERA: Tortricidae
Archips cerasivorana (Fitch)	uglynest caterpillar	LEPIDOPTERA: Tortricidae
Archips fervidana (Clemens)	oak webworm	LEPIDOPTERA: Tortricidae
Archips mortuana Kearfott	duskyback leafroller	LEPIDOPTERA: Tortricidae
Archips semiferana (Walker)	oak leafroller	LEPIDOPTERA: Tortricidae
Argas persicus (Oken)	fowl tick	ACARI: Argasidae
Arge pectoralis (Leach)	birch sawfly	HYMENOPTERA: Argidae
Argiope aurantia Lucas	yellow garden spider	ARANEAE: Araneidae
Argiope trifasciata (Forskal)	whitebacked garden spider	ARANEAE: Araneidae
Argyresthia conjugella Zeller	apple fruit moth	LEPIDOPTERA: Argyresthiidae
Argyresthia thuiella (Packard)	arborvitae leafminer	LEPIDOPTERA: Argyresthiidae
Argyrotaenia citrana (Fernald)	orange tortrix	LEPIDOPTERA: Tortricidae
Argyrotaenia juglandana (Fernald)	hickory leafroller	LEPIDOPTERA: Tortricidae
Argyrotaenia mariana (Fernald)	graybanded leafroller	LEPIDOPTERA: Tortricidae
Argyrotaenia pinatubana (Kearfott)	pine tube moth	LEPIDOPTERA: Tortricidae
Argyrotaenia quadrifasciana (Fernald)	fourbanded leafroller	LEPIDOPTERA: Tortricidae
Argyrotaenia velutinana (Walker)	redbanded leafroller	LEPIDOPTERA: Tortricidae
Arhopalus productus (LeConte)	new house borer	COLEOPTERA: Cerambycidae

Arilus cristatus (Linnaeus)	wheel bug	HETEROPTERA: Reduviidae
Arion ater rufus (Linnaeus)	large red slug	STYLOMMATOPHORA: Arionidae
Aroga websteri Clarke	sagebrush defoliator	LEPIDOPTERA: Gelechiidae
Arrhenodes minutus (Drury)	oak timberworm	COLEOPTERA: Brentidae
Asarcopus palmarum Horvath	datebug	HOMOPTERA: Issidae
Ascalapha odorata (Linnaeus)	black witch	LEPIDOPTERA: Noctuidae
Asphondylia websteri Felt	alfalfa gall midge	DIPTERA: Cecidomyiidae
Aspidiotus destructor Signoret	coconut scale	HOMOPTERA: Diaspididae
Aspidiotus nerii Bouché	oleander scale	HOMOPTERA: Diaspididae
Asterolecanium pustulans (Cockerell)	oleander pit scale	HOMOPTERA: Asterolecaniidae
Asterolecanium variolosum (Ratzeburg)	golden oak scale	HOMOPTERA: Asterolecaniidae
Asynonychus godmani Crotch	Fuller rose beetle	COLEOPTERA: Curculionidae
Ataenius spretulus (Haldeman)	black turfgrass ataenius	COLEOPTERA: Scarabaeidae
Athesapeuta cyperi Marshall	nutgrass weevil	COLEOPTERA: Curculionidae
Athetis mindara (Barnes & McDunnough)	roughskinned cutworm	LEPIDOPTERA: Noctuidae
Atractomorpha sinensis Bolivar	pinkwinged grasshopper	ORTHOPTERA: Pyrgomorphidae
Atta texana (Buckley)	Texas leafcutting ant	HYMENOPTERA: Formicidae
Attagenus fasciatus (Thunberg)	wardrobe beetle	COLEOPTERA: Dermestidae
Attagenus unicolor (Brahm)	black carpet beetle	COLEOPTERA: Dermestidae
Atteva punctella (Cramer)	ailanthus webworm	LEPIDOPTERA: Yponomeutidae
Aulacaspis rosae (Bouché)	rose scale	HOMOPTERA: Diaspididae
Aulacaspis rosarum Borchsenius	Asiatic rose scale	HOMOPTERA: Diaspididae
Aulacorthum solani (Kaltenbach)	foxglove aphid	HOMOPTERA: Aphididae
Aulocara elliotti (Thomas)	bigheaded grasshopper	ORTHOPTERA: Acrididae
Autographa californica (Speyer)	alfalfa looper	LEPIDOPTERA: Noctuidae
Automeris io (Fabricius)	io moth	LEPIDOPTERA: Saturniidae
Autoplusia egena (Guenée)	bean leafskeletonizer	LEPIDOPTERA: Noctuidae

B

Bactra venosana (Zeller)	nutgrass borer moth	LEPIDOPTERA: Tortricidae
Balclutha incisa hospes (Kirkaldy)	little green leafhopper	HOMOPTERA: Cicadellidae
Balclutha saltuella (Kirschbaum)	Beardsley leafhopper	HOMOPTERA: Cicadellidae
Baliosus nervosus (Panzer)	basswood leafminer	COLEOPTERA: Chrysomelidae
Baliothrips minutus (van Deventer)	sugarcane thrips	THYSANOPTERA: Thripidae
Barbara colfaxiana (Kearfott)	Douglas-fir cone moth	LEPIDOPTERA: Tortricidae

Baris lepidii Germar	imported crucifer weevil	COLEOPTERA: Curculionidae
Baris strenua (LeConte)	sunflower root weevil	COLEOPTERA: Curculionidae
Basilarchia archippus (Cramer)	viceroy	LEPIDOPTERA: Nymphalidae
Battus philenor (Linnaeus)	pipevine swallowtail	LEPIDOPTERA: Papilionidae
Bedellia orchilella Walsingham	sweetpotato leafminer	LEPIDOPTERA: Lyonetiidae
Bedellia somnulentella (Zeller)	morningglory leafminer	LEPIDOPTERA: Lyonetiidae
Bellura densa (Walker)	pickerelweed borer	LEPIDOPTERA: Noctuidae
Bemisia giffardi (Kotinsky)	Giffard whitefly	HOMOPTERA: Aleyrodidae
Bemisia tabaci (Gennadius)	sweetpotato whitefly	HOMOPTERA: Aleyrodidae
Biston betularia cognataria (Guenée)	pepper-and-salt moth	LEPIDOPTERA: Geometridae
Blaesoxipha spp.	grasshopper maggots	DIPTERA: Sarcophagidae
Blastophaga psenes (Linnaeus)	fig wasp	HYMENOPTERA: Agaonidae
Blatta (Shelfordella) lateralis (Walker)	Turkestan cockroach	BLATTODEA: Blattidae
Blatta orientalis Linnaeus	oriental cockroach	BLATTODEA: Blattidae
Blattella asahinai Mizukubo	Asian cockroach	BLATTODEA: Blattellidae
Blattella germanica (Linnaeus)	German cockroach	BLATTODEA: Blattellidae
Blattella lituricollis (Walker)	false German cockroach	BLATTODEA: Blattellidae
Blepharomastix ebulealis (Guenée)	clidemia leafroller	LEPIDOPTERA: Pyralidae
Blissus insularis Barber	southern chinch bug	HETEROPTERA: Lygaeidae
Blissus leucopterus hirtus Montandon	hairy chinch bug	HETEROPTERA: Lygaeidae
Blissus leucopterus leucopterus (Say)	chinch bug	HETEROPTERA: Lygaeidae
Blissus occiduus Barber	western chinch bug	HETEROPTERA: Lygaeidae
Boisea rubrolineata Barber	western boxelder bug	HETEROPTERA: Rhopalidae
Boisea trivittata (Say)	boxelder bug	HETEROPTERA: Rhopalidae
Bombyx mori (Linnaeus)	silkworm	LEPIDOPTERA: Bombycidae
Boophilus annulatus (Say)	cattle tick	ACARI: Ixodidae
Boophilus microplus (Canestrini)	southern cattle tick	ACARI: Ixodidae
Bourletiella hortensis (Fitch)	garden springtail	COLLEMBOLA: Bourletiellidae
Bovicola bovis (Linnaeus)	cattle biting louse	MALLOPHAGA: Trichodectidae
Bovicola caprae (Gurlt)	goat biting louse	MALLOPHAGA: Trichodectidae
Bovicola crassipes (Rudow)	Angora goat biting louse	MALLOPHAGA: Trichodectidae
Bovicola equi (Denny)	horse biting louse	MALLOPHAGA: Trichodectidae
Bovicola ovis (Schrank)	sheep biting louse	MALLOPHAGA: Trichodectidae
Brachycaudus cardui (Linnaeus)	thistle aphid	HOMOPTERA: Aphididae
Brachycaudus persicae (Passerini)	black peach aphid	HOMOPTERA: Aphididae
Brachycolus heraclei Takahashi	celery aphid	HOMOPTERA: Aphididae
Brachycorynella asparagi (Mordvilko)	asparagus aphid	HOMOPTERA: Aphididae
Brachystola magna (Girard)	lubber grasshopper	ORTHOPTERA: Acrididae

Brevicoryne brassicae (Linnaeus)	cabbage aphid	HOMOPTERA: Aphididae
Brevipalpus lewisi McGregor	citrus flat mite	ACARI: Tenuipalpidae
Brevipalpus obovatus Donnadieu	privet mite	ACARI: Tenuipalpidae
Brevipalpus phoenicis (Geijskes)	red and black flat mite	ACARI: Tenuipalpidae
Brochymena quadripustulata (Fabricius)	rough stink bug	HETEROPTERA: Pentatomidae
Bromius obscurus (Linnaeus)	western grape rootworm	COLEOPTERA: Chrysomelidae
Brooksetta althaeae (Hussey)	hollyhock plant bug	HETEROPTERA: Miridae
Bruchophagus platyptera (Walker)	clover seed chalcid	HYMENOPTERA: Eurytomidae
Bruchophagus roddi (Gussakovsky)	alfalfa seed chalcid	HYMENOPTERA: Eurytomidae
Bruchus brachialis Fåhraeus	vetch bruchid	COLEOPTERA: Bruchidae
Bruchus pisorum (Linnaeus)	pea weevil	COLEOPTERA: Bruchidae
Bruchus rufimanus Boheman	broadbean weevil	COLEOPTERA: Bruchidae
Brumoides suturalis (Fabricius)	threestriped lady beetle	COLEOPTERA: Coccinellidae
Bryobia praetiosa Koch	clover mite	ACARI: Tetranychidae
Bryobia rubrioculus (Scheuten)	brown mite	ACARI: Tetranychidae
Bucculatrix ainsliella Murtfeldt	oak skeletonizer	LEPIDOPTERA: Lyonetiidae
Bucculatrix canadensisella Chambers	birch skeletonizer	LEPIDOPTERA: Lyonetiidae
Bucculatrix thurberiella Busck	cotton leafperforator	LEPIDOPTERA: Lyonetiidae
Buprestis apricans Herbst	turpentine borer	COLEOPTERA: Buprestidae
Buprestis aurulenta Linnaeus	golden buprestid	COLEOPTERA: Buprestidae
Byturus unicolor Say	raspberry fruitworm	COLEOPTERA: Byturidae

C

Cacopsylla buxi (Linnaeus)	boxwood psyllid	HOMOPTERA: Psyllidae
Cacopsylla mali (Schmidberger)	apple sucker	HOMOPTERA: Psyllidae
Cacopsylla negundinis Mally	boxelder psyllid	HOMOPTERA: Psyllidae
Cacopsylla pyricola Foerster	pear psylla	HOMOPTERA: Psyllidae
Cactoblastis cactorum (Berg)	cactus moth	LEPIDOPTERA: Pyralidae
Cadra cautella (Walker)	almond moth	LEPIDOPTERA: Pyralidae
Cadra figulilella (Gregson)	raisin moth	LEPIDOPTERA: Pyralidae
Caenurgina crassiuscula (Haworth)	clover looper	LEPIDOPTERA: Noctuidae
Caenurgina erechtea (Cramer)	forage looper	LEPIDOPTERA: Noctuidae
Calepiterimerus thujae (Garman)	tipdwarf mite	ACARI: Eriophyidae
Caliothrips fasciatus (Pergande)	bean thrips	THYSANOPTERA: Thripidae
Caliroa cerasi (Linnaeus)	pear sawfly	HYMENOPTERA: Tenthredinidae

Scientific name	Common name	Order: Family
Caliroa quercuscoccineae (Dyar)	scarlet oak sawfly	HYMENOPTERA: Tenthredinidae
Callidium antennatum hesperum Casey	blackhorned pine borer	COLEOPTERA: Cerambycidae
Calligrapha scalaris (LeConte)	elm calligrapha	COLEOPTERA: Chrysomelidae
Callirhopalus bifasciatus (Roelofs)	twobanded Japanese weevil	COLEOPTERA: Curculionidae
Callopistria floridensis (Guenée)	Florida fern caterpillar	LEPIDOPTERA: Noctuidae
Callosamia promethea (Drury)	promethea moth	LEPIDOPTERA: Saturniidae
Callosobruchus maculatus (Fabricius)	cowpea weevil	COLEOPTERA: Bruchidae
Calomycterus setarius Roelofs	imported longhorned weevil	COLEOPTERA: Curculionidae
Caloptilia azaleella (Brants)	azalea leafminer	LEPIDOPTERA: Gracillariidae
Caloptilia cuculipennella (Hübner)	privet leafminer	LEPIDOPTERA: Gracillariidae
Caloptilia negundella (Chambers)	boxelder leafroller	LEPIDOPTERA: Gracillariidae
Caloptilia syringella (Fabricius)	lilac leafminer	LEPIDOPTERA: Gracillariidae
Calosoma calidum (Fabricius)	fiery hunter	COLEOPTERA: Carabidae
Calpodes ethlius (Stoll)	larger canna leafroller	LEPIDOPTERA: Hesperiidae
Calycomyza humeralis (Roser)	aster leafminer	DIPTERA: Agromyzidae
Cameraria cincinnatiella (Chambers)	gregarious oak leafminer	LEPIDOPTERA: Gracillariidae
Cameraria hamadryadella (Clemens)	solitary oak leafminer	LEPIDOPTERA: Gracillariidae
Camnula pellucida (Scudder)	clearwinged grasshopper	ORTHOPTERA: Acrididae
Campanulotes bidentatus compar (Burmeister)	small pigeon louse	MALLOPHAGA: Philopteridae
Camponotus abdominalis (Fabricius)	Florida carpenter ant	HYMENOPTERA: Formicidae
Camponotus ferrugineus (Fabricius)	red carpenter ant	HYMENOPTERA: Formicidae
Camponotus pennsylvanicus (De Geer)	black carpenter ant	HYMENOPTERA: Formicidae
Camponotus variegatus (F. Smith)	Hawaiian carpenter ant	HYMENOPTERA: Formicidae
Canonura princeps (Walker)	ponderosa pine bark borer	COLEOPTERA: Cerambycidae
Carpoglyphus lactis (Linnaeus)	driedfruit mite	ACARI: Carpoglyphidae
Carpophilus dimidiatus (Fabricius)	corn sap beetle	COLEOPTERA: Nitidulidae
Carpophilus hemipterus (Linnaeus)	driedfruit beetle	COLEOPTERA: Nitidulidae
Carpophilus lugubris Murray	dusky sap beetle	COLEOPTERA: Nitidulidae
Cartodere constricta (Gyllenhal)	plaster beetle	COLEOPTERA: Lathridiidae
Carulaspis juniperi (Bouché)	juniper scale	HOMOPTERA: Diaspididae
Cathartus quadricollis (Guérin-Méneville)	squarenecked grain beetle	COLEOPTERA: Cucujidae
Caulocampus acericaulis (MacGillivray)	maple petiole borer	HYMENOPTERA: Tenthredinidae
Caulophilus oryzae (Gyllenhal)	broadnosed grain weevil	COLEOPTERA: Curculionidae
Cecidomyia resinicoloides Williams	Monterey pine resin midge	DIPTERA: Cecidomyiidae
Cecidophyopsis ribis (Westwood)	currant bud mite	ACARI: Eriophyidae
Cepaea nemoralis (Linnaeus)	banded wood snail	STYLOMMATOPHORA: Helicidae
Cephalonomia waterstoni Gahan	parasitic grain wasp	HYMENOPTERA: Bethylidae
Cephus cinctus Norton	wheat stem sawfly	HYMENOPTERA: Cephidae

Cephus pygmaeus (Linnaeus)	European wheat stem sawfly	HYMENOPTERA: Cephidae
Cerataphis orchidearum (Westwood)	fringed orchid aphid	HOMOPTERA: Aphididae
Ceratitis capitata (Wiedemann)	Mediterranean fruit fly	DIPTERA: Tephritidae
Ceratomia amyntor (Geyer)	elm sphinx	LEPIDOPTERA: Sphingidae
Ceratomia catalpae (Boisduval)	catalpa sphinx	LEPIDOPTERA: Sphingidae
Ceratophyllus gallinae (Schrank)	European chicken flea	SIPHONAPTERA: Ceratophyllidae
Ceratophyllus niger (Fox)	western chicken flea	SIPHONAPTERA: Ceratophyllidae
Cerodontha dorsalis (Loew)	grass sheathminer	DIPTERA: Agromyzidae
Ceroplastes cirripediformis Comstock	barnacle scale	HOMOPTERA: Coccidae
Ceroplastes floridensis Comstock	Florida wax scale	HOMOPTERA: Coccidae
Ceroplastes rubens Maskell	red wax scale	HOMOPTERA: Coccidae
Cerotoma trifurcata (Forster)	bean leaf beetle	COLEOPTERA: Chrysomelidae
Ceutorhynchus assimilis (Paykull)	cabbage seedpod weevil	COLEOPTERA: Curculionidae
Ceutorhynchus quadridens (Panzer)	cabbage seedstalk curculio	COLEOPTERA: Curculionidae
Ceutorhynchus rapae Gyllenhal	cabbage curculio	COLEOPTERA: Curculionidae
Chaetocnema confinis Crotch	sweetpotato flea beetle	COLEOPTERA: Chrysomelidae
Chaetocnema denticulata (Illiger)	toothed flea beetle	COLEOPTERA: Chrysomelidae
Chaetocnema ectypa Horn	desert corn flea beetle	COLEOPTERA: Chrysomelidae
Chaetocnema pulicaria Melsheimer	corn flea beetle	COLEOPTERA: Chrysomelidae
Chaetococcus bambusae (Maskell)	bamboo mealybug	HOMOPTERA: Pseudococcidae
Chaetosiphon fragaefolii (Cockerell)	strawberry aphid	HOMOPTERA: Aphididae
Chalcodermus aeneus Boheman	cowpea curculio	COLEOPTERA: Curculionidae
Chalcophora angulicollis (LeConte)	sculptured pine borer	COLEOPTERA: Buprestidae
Chaoborus astictopus Dyar & Shannon	Clear Lake gnat	DIPTERA: Chaoboridae
Chelisoches morio (Fabricius)	black earwig	DERMAPTERA: Chelisochidae
Chelopistes meleagridis (Linnaeus)	large turkey louse	MALLOPHAGA: Philopteridae
Chelymorpha cassidea (Fabricius)	argus tortoise beetle	COLEOPTERA: Chrysomelidae
Chilo plejadellus Zincken	rice stalk borer	LEPIDOPTERA: Pyralidae
Chilo suppressalis (Walker)	Asiatic rice borer	LEPIDOPTERA: Pyralidae
Chilocorus stigma (Say)	twicestabbed lady beetle	COLEOPTERA: Coccinellidae
Chionaspis americana Johnson	elm scurfy scale	HOMOPTERA: Diaspididae
Chionaspis corni Cooley	dogwood scale	HOMOPTERA: Diaspididae
Chionaspis furfura (Fitch)	scurfy scale	HOMOPTERA: Diaspididae
Chionaspis pinifoliae (Fitch)	pine needle scale	HOMOPTERA: Diaspididae
Chiracanthium mordax Koch	pale leaf spider	ARANEAE: Clubionidae
Chlamydatus associatus (Uhler)	ragweed plant bug	HETEROPTERA: Miridae
Chlorochroa ligata (Say)	conchuela	HETEROPTERA: Pentatomidae
Chlorochroa sayi (Stål)	Say stink bug	HETEROPTERA: Pentatomidae

Chlorophorus annularis (Fabricius)	bamboo borer	COLEOPTERA: Cerambycidae
Choreutis pariana (Clerck)	apple-and-thorn skeletonizer	LEPIDOPTERA: Choreutidae
Choristoneura conflictana (Walker)	large aspen tortrix	LEPIDOPTERA: Tortricidae
Choristoneura fumiferana (Clemens)	spruce budworm	LEPIDOPTERA: Tortricidae
Choristoneura occidentalis Freeman	western spruce budworm	LEPIDOPTERA: Tortricidae
Choristoneura pinus Freeman	jack pine budworm	LEPIDOPTERA: Tortricidae
Choristoneura rosaceana (Harris)	obliquebanded leafroller	LEPIDOPTERA: Tortricidae
Chortophaga viridifasciata (De Geer)	greenstriped grasshopper	ORTHOPTERA: Acrididae
Chromaphis juglandicola (Kaltenbach)	walnut aphid	HOMOPTERA: Aphididae
Chromatomyia syngenesiae Hardy	chrysanthemum leafminer	DIPTERA: Agromyzidae
Chrysobothris femorata (Olivier)	flatheaded appletree borer	COLEOPTERA: Buprestidae
Chrysobothris mali Horn	Pacific flatheaded borer	COLEOPTERA: Buprestidae
Chrysobothris tranquebarica (Gmelin)	Australianpine borer	COLEOPTERA: Buprestidae
Chrysodeixis eriosoma (Doubleday)	green garden looper	LEPIDOPTERA: Noctuidae
Chrysolina quadrigemina (Suffrian)	Klamathweed beetle	COLEOPTERA: Chrysomelidae
Chrysomela crotchi Brown	aspen leaf beetle	COLEOPTERA: Chrysomelidae
Chrysomela scripta Fabricius	cottonwood leaf beetle	COLEOPTERA: Chrysomelidae
Chrysomphalus aonidum (Linnaeus)	Florida red scale	HOMOPTERA: Diaspididae
Chrysomphalus dictyospermi (Morgan)	dictyospermum scale	HOMOPTERA: Diaspididae
Chrysomya rufifacies (Macquart)	hairy maggot blow fly	DIPTERA: Calliphoridae
Chrysopa carnea Stephens	common green lacewing	NEUROPTERA: Chrysopidae
Chrysopa comanche Banks	Comanche lacewing	NEUROPTERA: Chrysopidae
Chrysopa oculata Say	goldeneyed lacewing	NEUROPTERA: Chrysopidae
Chrysophana placida conicola Van Dyke	flatheaded cone borer	COLEOPTERA: Buprestidae
Chrysoteuchia topiaria (Zeller)	cranberry girdler	LEPIDOPTERA: Pyralidae
Cimbex americana Leach	elm sawfly	HYMENOPTERA: Cimbicidae
Cimex lectularius Linnaeus	bed bug	HETEROPTERA: Cimicidae
Cinara atlantica (Wilson)	Carolina conifer aphid	HOMOPTERA: Aphididae
Cinara fornacula Hottes	green spruce aphid	HOMOPTERA: Aphididae
Cinara laricis (Walker)	larch aphid	HOMOPTERA: Aphididae
Cinara strobi (Fitch)	white pine aphid	HOMOPTERA: Aphididae
Cingilia catenaria (Drury)	chainspotted geometer	LEPIDOPTERA: Geometridae
Circulifer tenellus (Baker)	beet leafhopper	HOMOPTERA: Cicadellidae
Citheronia regalis (Fabricius)	regal moth[32]	LEPIDOPTERA: Saturniidae
Cladius difformis (Panzer)	bristly roseslug	HYMENOPTERA: Tenthredinidae

---

[32]Immature called hickory horned devil.

Clastoptera achatina Germar	pecan spittlebug	HOMOPTERA: Cercopidae
Clastoptera obtusa (Say)	alder spittlebug	HOMOPTERA: Cercopidae
Clastoptera proteus Fitch	dogwood spittlebug	HOMOPTERA: Cercopidae
Clastoptera saintcyri Provancher	heath spittlebug	HOMOPTERA: Cercopidae
Clastoptera xanthocephala Germar	sunflower spittlebug	HOMOPTERA: Cercopidae
Clinodiplosis rhododendri (Felt)	rhododendron gall midge	DIPTERA: Cecidomyiidae
Clivina impressifrons LeConte	slender seedcorn beetle	COLEOPTERA: Carabidae
Clytoleptus albofasciatus (Laporte & Gory)	grape trunk borer	COLEOPTERA: Cerambycidae
Cnephasia longana (Haworth)	omnivorous leaftier	LEPIDOPTERA: Tortricidae
Cnephia pecuarum (Riley)	southern buffalo gnat	DIPTERA: Simuliidae
Cnidocampa flavescens (Walker)	oriental moth	LEPIDOPTERA: Limacodidae
Coccinella septempunctata Linnaeus	sevenspotted lady beetle	COLEOPTERA: Coccinellidae
Coccinella transversoguttata richardsoni Brown	transverse lady beetle	COLEOPTERA: Coccinellidae
Coccotorus hirsutus Bruner	sandcherry weevil	COLEOPTERA: Curculionidae
Coccotorus scutellaris (LeConte)	plum gouger	COLEOPTERA: Curculionidae
Coccus hesperidum Linnaeus	brown soft scale	HOMOPTERA: Coccidae
Coccus longulus (Douglas)	long brown scale	HOMOPTERA: Coccidae
Coccus pseudomagnoliarum (Kuwana)	citricola scale	HOMOPTERA: Coccidae
Coccus viridis (Green)	green scale	HOMOPTERA: Coccidae
Cochliomyia hominivorax (Coquerel)	screwworm	DIPTERA: Calliphoridae
Cochliomyia macellaria (Fabricius)	secondary screwworm	DIPTERA: Calliphoridae
Cochylis hospes Walsingham	banded sunflower moth	LEPIDOPTERA: Cochylidae
Coelophora inaequalis (Fabricius)	common Australian lady beetle	COLEOPTERA: Coccinellidae
Coelophora pupillata (Swartz)	tenspotted lady beetle	COLEOPTERA: Coccinellidae
Colaspis brunnea (Fabricius)	grape colaspis	COLEOPTERA: Chrysomelidae
Colaspis pini Barber	pine colaspis	COLEOPTERA: Chrysomelidae
Coleophora laricella (Hübner)	larch casebearer	LEPIDOPTERA: Coleophoridae
Coleophora laticornella Clemens	pecan cigar casebearer	LEPIDOPTERA: Coleophoridae
Coleophora malivorella Riley	pistol casebearer	LEPIDOPTERA: Coleophoridae
Coleophora pruniella Clemens	cherry casebearer	LEPIDOPTERA: Coleophoridae
Coleophora serratella (Linnaeus)	birch casebearer[33]	LEPIDOPTERA: Coleophoridae
Coleophora ulmifoliella McDunnough	elm casebearer	LEPIDOPTERA: Coleophoridae
Coleotechnites milleri (Busck)	lodgepole needleminer	LEPIDOPTERA: Gelechiidae
Coleotichus blackburniae White	koa bug	HETEROPTERA: Pentatomidae
Colias eurytheme Boisduval	alfalfa caterpillar	LEPIDOPTERA: Pieridae

---

[33]Also called cigar casebearer.

Colias philodice Godart	clouded sulfur	LEPIDOPTERA: Pieridae
Colladonus clitellarius (Say)	saddled leafhopper	HOMOPTERA: Cicadellidae
Colladonus montanus (Van Duzee)	mountain leafhopper	HOMOPTERA: Cicadellidae
Colomerus gardeniella (Keifer)	gardenia bud mite	ACARI: Eriophyidae
Colomerus vitis (Pagenstecher)	grape erineum mite	ACARI: Eriophyidae
Colopha ulmicola (Fitch)	elm cockscombgall aphid	HOMOPTERA: Aphididae
Coloradia pandora Blake	pandora moth	LEPIDOPTERA: Saturniidae
Columbicola columbae (Linnaeus)	slender pigeon louse	MALLOPHAGA: Philopteridae
Conoderus amplicollis (Gyllenhal)	Gulf wireworm	COLEOPTERA: Elateridae
Conoderus falli Lane	southern potato wireworm	COLEOPTERA: Elateridae
Conoderus vespertinus (Fabricius)	tobacco wireworm	COLEOPTERA: Elateridae
Conomyrma insana (Buckley)	pyramid ant	HYMENOPTERA: Formicidae
Conophthorus banksianae McPherson	jack pine tip beetle	COLEOPTERA: Scolytidae
Conophthorus coniperda (Schwarz)	white pine cone beetle	COLEOPTERA: Scolytidae
Conophthorus edulis Hopkins	pinon cone beetle	COLEOPTERA: Scolytidae
Conophthorus lambertianae Hopkins	sugar pine cone beetle	COLEOPTERA: Scolytidae
Conophthorus ponderosae Hopkins	ponderosa pine cone beetle[34]	COLEOPTERA: Scolytidae
Conophthorus radiatae Hopkins	Monterey pine cone beetle	COLEOPTERA: Scolytidae
Conophthorus resinosae Hopkins	red pine cone beetle	COLEOPTERA: Scolytidae
Conotrachelus crataegi Walsh	quince curculio	COLEOPTERA: Curculionidae
Conotrachelus juglandis LeConte	butternut curculio	COLEOPTERA: Curculionidae
Conotrachelus nenuphar (Herbst)	plum curculio	COLEOPTERA: Curculionidae
Conotrachelus retentus (Say)	black walnut curculio	COLEOPTERA: Curculionidae
Contarinia bromicola (Marikovskij & Agafonova)	bromegrass seed midge	DIPTERA: Cecidomyiidae
Contarinia catalpae (Comstock)	catalpa midge	DIPTERA: Cecidomyiidae
Contarinia johnsoni Felt	grape blossom midge	DIPTERA: Cecidomyiidae
Contarinia juniperina Felt	juniper midge	DIPTERA: Cecidomyiidae
Contarinia pyrivora (Riley)	pear midge	DIPTERA: Cecidomyiidae
Contarinia schulzi Gagné	sunflower midge	DIPTERA: Cecidomyiidae
Contarinia sorghicola (Coquillett)	sorghum midge	DIPTERA: Cecidomyiidae
Contarinia texana (Felt)	guar midge	DIPTERA: Cecidomyiidae
Copris incertus prociduus (Say)	black dung beetle	COLEOPTERA: Scarabaeidae
Coptodisca splendoriferella (Clemens)	resplendent shield bearer	LEPIDOPTERA: Heliozelidae
Coptosoma xanthogramma (White)	black stink bug	HETEROPTERA: Plataspidae

---

[34]Also called lodgepole cone beetle.

Coptotermes formosanus Shiraki	Formosan subterranean termite	ISOPTERA: Rhinotermitidae
Corcyra cephalonica (Stainton)	rice moth	LEPIDOPTERA: Pyralidae
Corimelaena pulicaria (Germar)	black bug	HETEROPTERA: Thyreocoridae
Corthylus columbianus Hopkins	Columbian timber beetle	COLEOPTERA: Scolytidae
Corydalus cornutus (Linnaeus)	dobsonfly[35]	NEUROPTERA: Corydalidae
Corythucha arcuata (Say)	oak lace bug	HETEROPTERA: Tingidae
Corythucha celtidis Osborn & Drake	hackberry lace bug	HETEROPTERA: Tingidae
Corythucha ciliata (Say)	sycamore lace bug	HETEROPTERA: Tingidae
Corythucha cydoniae (Fitch)	hawthorn lace bug	HETEROPTERA: Tingidae
Corythucha gossypii (Fabricius)	cotton lace bug	HETEROPTERA: Tingidae
Corythucha marmorata (Uhler)	chrysanthemum lace bug	HETEROPTERA: Tingidae
Corythucha morrilli Osborn & Drake	Morrill lace bug	HETEROPTERA: Tingidae
Corythucha ulmi Osborn & Drake	elm lace bug	HETEROPTERA: Tingidae
Cosmopolites sordidus (Germar)	banana root borer	COLEOPTERA: Curculionidae
Cossula magnifica (Strecker)	pecan carpenterworm	LEPIDOPTERA: Cossidae
Cotinis nitida (Linnaeus)	green June beetle	COLEOPTERA: Scarabaeidae
Crambus caliginosellus Clemens	corn root webworm	LEPIDOPTERA: Pyralidae
Craponius inaequalis (Say)	grape curculio	COLEOPTERA: Curculionidae
Cremastobombycia lantanella (Schrank)	lantana leafminer	LEPIDOPTERA: Gracillariidae
Creophilus maxillosus (Linnaeus)	hairy rove beetle	COLEOPTERA: Staphylinidae
Crioceris asparagi (Linnaeus)	asparagus beetle	COLEOPTERA: Chrysomelidae
Crioceris duodecimpunctata (Linnaeus)	spotted asparagus beetle	COLEOPTERA: Chrysomelidae
Croesia semipurpurana (Kearfott)	oak leaftier	LEPIDOPTERA: Tortricidae
Croesus latitarsus Norton	dusky birch sawfly	HYMENOPTERA: Tenthredinidae
Cryptoblabes gnidiella (Millière)	Christmas berry webworm	LEPIDOPTERA: Pyralidae
Cryptococcus fagisuga Lindinger	beech scale	HOMOPTERA: Eriococcidae
Cryptolaemus montrouzieri Mulsant	mealybug destroyer	COLEOPTERA: Coccinellidae
Cryptolestes ferrugineus (Stephens)	rusty grain beetle	COLEOPTERA: Cucujidae
Cryptolestes pusillus (Schnherr)	flat grain beetle	COLEOPTERA: Cucujidae
Cryptomyzus ribis (Linnaeus)	currant aphid	HOMOPTERA: Aphididae
Cryptophagus acutangulus Gyllenhal	acute-angled fungus beetle	COLEOPTERA: Cryptophagidae
Cryptophagus varus Woodroffe & Coombs	Sigmoid fungus beetle	COLEOPTERA: Cryptophagidae
Cryptophlebia illepida (Butler)	koa seedworm	LEPIDOPTERA: Tortricidae
Cryptophlebia ombrodelta (Lower)	litchi fruit moth	LEPIDOPTERA: Tortricidae
Cryptorhynchus lapathi (Linnaeus)	poplar-and-willow borer	COLEOPTERA: Curculionidae

---

[35]Immature called hellgrammite.

Cryptorhynchus mangiferae (Fabricius)	mango weevil	COLEOPTERA: Curculionidae
Ctenicera aeripennis aeripennis (Kirby)	Puget Sound wireworm	COLEOPTERA: Elateridae
Ctenicera aeripennis destructor (Brown)	prairie grain wireworm	COLEOPTERA: Elateridae
Ctenicera glauca (Germar)	dryland wireworm	COLEOPTERA: Elateridae
Ctenicera pruinina (Horn)	Great Basin wireworm	COLEOPTERA: Elateridae
Ctenocephalides canis (Curtis)	dog flea	SIPHONAPTERA: Pulicidae
Ctenocephalides felis (Bouché)	cat flea	SIPHONAPTERA: Pulicidae
Cuclotogaster heterographus (Nitzsch)	chicken head louse	MALLOPHAGA: Philopteridae
Culex pipiens Linnaeus	northern house mosquito	DIPTERA: Culicidae
Culex quinquefasciatus Say	southern house mosquito	DIPTERA: Culicidae
Curculio caryae (Horn)	pecan weevil	COLEOPTERA: Curculionidae
Curculio caryatrypes (Boheman)	large chestnut weevil	COLEOPTERA: Curculionidae
Curculio obtusus (Blanchard)	hazelnut weevil	COLEOPTERA: Curculionidae
Curculio occidentis (Casey)	filbert weevil	COLEOPTERA: Curculionidae
Curculio sayi (Gyllenhal)	small chestnut weevil	COLEOPTERA: Curculionidae
Cyclocephala borealis Arrow	northern masked chafer	COLEOPTERA: Scarabaeidae
Cyclocephala immaculata (Olivier)	southern masked chafer	COLEOPTERA: Scarabaeidae
Cydia anaranjada (Miller)	slash pine seedworm	LEPIDOPTERA: Tortricidae
Cydia bracteatana (Fernald)	fir seed moth	LEPIDOPTERA: Tortricidae
Cydia caryana (Fitch)	hickory shuckworm	LEPIDOPTERA: Tortricidae
Cydia ingens (Heinrich)	longleaf pine seedworm	LEPIDOPTERA: Tortricidae
Cydia latiferreana (Walsingham)	filbertworm	LEPIDOPTERA: Tortricidae
Cydia nigricana (Fabricius)	pea moth	LEPIDOPTERA: Tortricidae
Cydia pomonella (Linnaeus)	codling moth	LEPIDOPTERA: Tortricidae
Cydia strobilella (Linnaeus)	spruce seed moth	LEPIDOPTERA: Tortricidae
Cydia toreuta (Grote)	eastern pine seedworm	LEPIDOPTERA: Tortricidae
Cylas formicarius elegantulus (Summers)	sweetpotato weevil	COLEOPTERA: Curculionidae
Cylindrocopturus adspersus (LeConte)	sunflower stem weevil	COLEOPTERA: Curculionidae
Cylindrocopturus furnissi Buchanan	Douglas-fir twig weevil	COLEOPTERA: Curculionidae
Cynaeus angustus (LeConte)	larger black flour beetle	COLEOPTERA: Tenebrionidae
Cyrtepistomus castaneus (Roelofs)	Asiatic oak weevil	COLEOPTERA: Curculionidae
Cyrtopeltis modesta (Distant)	tomato bug	HETEROPTERA: Miridae
Cyrtopeltis notata (Distant)	suckfly	HETEROPTERA: Miridae

D

Dactylopius coccus Costa	cochineal insect	HOMOPTERA: Dactylopiidae
Dactynotus rudbeckiae (Fitch)	goldenglow aphid	HOMOPTERA: Aphididae
Dacus cucurbitae Coquillett	melon fly	DIPTERA: Tephritidae
Dacus dorsalis Hendel	oriental fruit fly	DIPTERA: Tephritidae
Dacus oleae (Gmelin)	olive fruit fly	DIPTERA: Tephritidae
Daktulosphaira vitifoliae (Fitch)	grape phylloxera	HOMOPTERA: Phylloxeridae
Dalbulus maidis (DeLong & Wolcott)	corn leafhopper	HOMOPTERA: Cicadellidae
Danaus plexippus (Linnaeus)	monarch butterfly	LEPIDOPTERA: Danaidae
Daphnis nerii (Linnaeus)	oleander hawk moth	LEPIDOPTERA: Sphingidae
Darapsa myron (Cramer)	Virginiacreeper sphinx	LEPIDOPTERA: Sphingidae
Dasineura leguminicola (Lintner)	clover seed midge	DIPTERA: Cecidomyiidae
Dasineura rhodophaga (Coquillett)	rose midge	DIPTERA: Cecidomyiidae
Dasineura swainei (Felt)	spruce bud midge	DIPTERA: Cecidomyiidae
Dasineura trifolii (Loew)	clover leaf midge	DIPTERA: Cecidomyiidae
Dasychira pinicola (Dyar)	pine tussock moth	LEPIDOPTERA: Lymantriidae
Datana integerrima Grote & Robinson	walnut caterpillar	LEPIDOPTERA: Notodontidae
Datana major Grote & Robinson	azalea caterpillar	LEPIDOPTERA: Notodontidae
Datana ministra (Drury)	yellownecked caterpillar	LEPIDOPTERA: Notodontidae
Deinocerites cancer Theobald	crabhole mosquito	DIPTERA: Culicidae
Delia antiqua (Meigen)	onion maggot	DIPTERA: Anthomyiidae
Delia brunnescens (Zetterstedt)	carnation maggot	DIPTERA: Anthomyiidae
Delia echinata (Séguy)	carnation tip maggot	DIPTERA: Anthomyiidae
Delia floralis (Fallén)	turnip maggot	DIPTERA: Anthomyiidae
Delia florilega (Zetterstedt)	bean seed maggot	DIPTERA: Anthomyiidae
Delia platura (Meigen)	seedcorn maggot	DIPTERA: Anthomyiidae
Delia radicum (Linnaeus)	cabbage maggot	DIPTERA: Anthomyiidae
Deloyala guttata (Olivier)	mottled tortoise beetle	COLEOPTERA: Chrysomelidae
Delta campaniformis campaniformis (Fabricius)	yellow and black potter wasp	HYMENOPTERA: Vespidae
Delta latreillei petiolaris (Schulz)	orangetailed potter wasp	HYMENOPTERA: Vespidae
Delta pyriformis philippinensis (Bequaert)	black potter wasp	HYMENOPTERA: Vespidae
Deltocephalus hospes Kirkaldy	lawn leafhopper	HOMOPTERA: Cicadellidae
Demodex bovis Stiles	cattle follicle mite	ACARI: Demodicidae
Demodex brevis Bulanova	lesser follicle mite	ACARI: Demodicidae
Demodex canis Leydig	dog follicle mite	ACARI: Demodicidae
Demodex caprae Railliet	goat follicle mite	ACARI: Demodicidae

Demodex cati Mégnin	cat follicle mite	ACARI: Demodicidae
Demodex equi Railliet	horse follicle mite	ACARI: Demodicidae
Demodex folliculorum (Simon)	follicle mite	ACARI: Demodicidae
Demodex ovis Railliet	sheep follicle mite	ACARI: Demodicidae
Demodex phylloides Csokor	hog follicle mite	ACARI: Demodicidae
Dendroctonus adjunctus Blandford	roundheaded pine beetle	COLEOPTERA: Scolytidae
Dendroctonus approximatus Dietz	Mexican pine beetle	COLEOPTERA: Scolytidae
Dendroctonus brevicomis LeConte	western pine beetle	COLEOPTERA: Scolytidae
Dendroctonus frontalis Zimmermann	southern pine beetle	COLEOPTERA: Scolytidae
Dendroctonus jeffreyi Hopkins	Jeffrey pine beetle	COLEOPTERA: Scolytidae
Dendroctonus micans (Kugelann)	European spruce beetle	COLEOPTERA: Scolytidae
Dendroctonus murrayanae Hopkins	lodgepole pine beetle	COLEOPTERA: Scolytidae
Dendroctonus ponderosae Hopkins	mountain pine beetle	COLEOPTERA: Scolytidae
Dendroctonus pseudotsugae Hopkins	Douglas-fir beetle	COLEOPTERA: Scolytidae
Dendroctonus punctatus LeConte	Allegheny spruce beetle	COLEOPTERA: Scolytidae
Dendroctonus rufipennis (Kirby)	spruce beetle	COLEOPTERA: Scolytidae
Dendroctonus simplex LeConte	eastern larch beetle	COLEOPTERA: Scolytidae
Dendroctonus terebrans (Olivier)	black turpentine beetle	COLEOPTERA: Scolytidae
Dendroctonus valens LeConte	red turpentine beetle	COLEOPTERA: Scolytidae
Dendroleon obsoletus (Say)	spottedwinged antlion	NEUROPTERA: Myrmeleontidae
Dendrothrips ornatus (Jablonowski)	privet thrips	THYSANOPTERA: Thripidae
Depressaria pastinacella (Duponchel)	parsnip webworm	LEPIDOPTERA: Oecophoridae
Dermacentor albipictus (Packard)	winter tick	ACARI: Ixodidae
Dermacentor andersoni Stiles	Rocky Mountain wood tick	ACARI: Ixodidae
Dermacentor occidentalis Marx	Pacific Coast tick	ACARI: Ixodidae
Dermacentor variabilis (Say)	American dog tick	ACARI: Ixodidae
Dermanyssus gallinae (De Geer)	chicken mite	ACARI: Dermanyssidae
Dermatobia hominis (Linnaeus, Jr.)	torsalo	DIPTERA: Oestridae
Dermatophagoides farinae Hughes	American house dust mite	ACARI: Epidermoptidae
Dermatophagoides pteronyssinus (Trouessart)	European house dust mite	ACARI: Epidermoptidae
Dermestes ater De Geer	black larder beetle	COLEOPTERA: Dermestidae
Dermestes lardarius Linnaeus	larder beetle	COLEOPTERA: Dermestidae
Dermestes maculatus De Geer	hide beetle	COLEOPTERA: Dermestidae
Derocrepis erythropus (Melsheimer)	redlegged flea beetle	COLEOPTERA: Chrysomelidae
Desmia funeralis (Hübner)	grape leaffolder	LEPIDOPTERA: Pyralidae

86

Diabrotica balteata LeConte	banded cucumber beetle	COLEOPTERA: Chrysomelidae
Diabrotica barberi Smith & Lawrence	northern corn rootworm	COLEOPTERA: Chrysomelidae
Diabrotica undecimpunctata howardi Barber	spotted cucumber beetle[36]	COLEOPTERA: Chrysomelidae
Diabrotica undecimpunctata undecimpunctata Mannerheim	western spotted cucumber beetle	COLEOPTERA: Chrysomelidae
Diabrotica virgifera virgifera LeConte	western corn rootworm	COLEOPTERA: Chrysomelidae
Diabrotica virgifera zeae Krysan & Smith	Mexican corn rootworm	COLEOPTERA: Chrysomelidae
Diachus auratus (Fabricius)	bronze leaf beetle	COLEOPTERA: Chrysomelidae
Dialeurodes chittendeni Laing	rhododendron whitefly	HOMOPTERA: Aleyrodidae
Dialeurodes citri (Ashmead)	citrus whitefly	HOMOPTERA: Aleyrodidae
Dialeurodes citrifolii (Morgan)	cloudywinged whitefly	HOMOPTERA: Aleyrodidae
Dialeurodes kirkaldyi (Kotinsky)	Kirkaldy whitefly	HOMOPTERA: Aleyrodidae
Diaphania hyalinata (Linnaeus)	melonworm	LEPIDOPTERA: Pyralidae
Diaphania nitidalis (Stoll)	pickleworm	LEPIDOPTERA: Pyralidae
Diapheromera femorata (Say)	walkingstick	PHASMATODEA: Heteronemiidae
Diaphnocoris chlorionis (Say)	honeylocust plant bug	HETEROPTERA: Miridae
Diaspidiotus ancylus (Putnam)	Putnam scale	HOMOPTERA: Diaspididae
Diaspidiotus uvae (Comstock)	grape scale	HOMOPTERA: Diaspididae
Diaspis boisduvalii Signoret	Boisduval scale	HOMOPTERA: Diaspididae
Diaspis bromeliae (Kerner)	pineapple scale	HOMOPTERA: Diaspididae
Diaspis echinocacti (Bouché)	cactus scale	HOMOPTERA: Diaspididae
Diatraea crambidoides (Grote)	southern cornstalk borer	LEPIDOPTERA: Pyralidae
Diatraea grandiosella Dyar	southwestern corn borer	LEPIDOPTERA: Pyralidae
Diatraea saccharalis (Fabricius)	sugarcane borer	LEPIDOPTERA: Pyralidae
Dichelonyx backi (Kirby)	green rose chafer	COLEOPTERA: Scarabaeidae
Dichomeris acuminata (Standinger)	alfalfa leaftier	LEPIDOPTERA: Gelechiidae
Dichomeris ligulella Hübner	palmerworm	LEPIDOPTERA: Gelechiidae
Dichomeris marginella (Fabricius)	juniper webworm	LEPIDOPTERA: Gelechiidae
Dichromothrips corbetti (Priesner)	vanda thrips	THYSANOPTERA: Thripidae
Dinoderus minutus (Fabricius)	bamboo powderpost beetle	COLEOPTERA: Bostrichidae
Diocalandra taitensis (Guérin-Méneville)	Tahitian coconut weevil	COLEOPTERA: Curculionidae
Dioryctria amatella (Hulst)	southern pine coneworm	LEPIDOPTERA: Pyralidae
Dioryctria clarioralis (Walker)	blister coneworm	LEPIDOPTERA: Pyralidae
Dioryctria disclusa Heinrich	webbing coneworm	LEPIDOPTERA: Pyralidae
Dioryctria ebeli Mutuura & Munroe	south coastal coneworm	LEPIDOPTERA: Pyralidae

[36]Immature called southern corn rootworm.

Dioryctria pygmaeella Ragonot	baldcypress coneworm	LEPIDOPTERA: Pyralidae
Dioryctria reniculelloides Mutuura & Munroe	spruce coneworm	LEPIDOPTERA: Pyralidae
Dioryctria resinosella Mutuura	red pine shoot moth	LEPIDOPTERA: Pyralidae
Dioryctria yatesi Mutuura & Munroe	mountain pine coneworm	LEPIDOPTERA: Pyralidae
Dioryctria zimmermani (Grote)	Zimmerman pine moth	LEPIDOPTERA: Pyralidae
Diplolepis radicum (Osten Sacken)	roseroot gall wasp	HYMENOPTERA: Cynipidae
Diplolepis rosae (Linnaeus)	mossyrose gall wasp	HYMENOPTERA: Cynipidae
Diploptera punctata (Eschscholtz)	Pacific beetle cockroach	BLATTODEA: Blaberidae
Diprion similis (Hartig)	introduced pine sawfly	HYMENOPTERA: Diprionidae
Discestra trifolii (Hufnagel)	clover cutworm	LEPIDOPTERA: Noctuidae
Disonycha triangularis (Say)	threespotted flea beetle	COLEOPTERA: Chrysomelidae
Disonycha xanthomelas (Dalman)	spinach flea beetle	COLEOPTERA: Chrysomelidae
Dissosteira carolina (Linnaeus)	Carolina grasshopper	ORTHOPTERA: Acrididae
Dissosteira longipennis (Thomas)	High Plains grasshopper	ORTHOPTERA: Acrididae
Diuraphis (Holcaphis) tritici (Gillette)	western wheat aphid	HOMOPTERA: Aphididae
Diuraphis noxia (Mordvilko)	Russian wheat aphid	HOMOPTERA: Aphididae
Dolichotetranychus floridanus (Banks)	pineapple false spider mite	ACARI: Tenuipalpidae
Dolichovespula arenaria (Fabricius)	aerial yellowjacket	HYMENOPTERA: Vespidae
Dolichovespula maculata (Linnaeus)	baldfaced hornet	HYMENOPTERA: Vespidae
Dolichurus stantoni (Ashmead)	black cockroach wasp	HYMENOPTERA: Sphecidae
Draeculacephala minerva Ball	grass sharpshooter	HOMOPTERA: Cicadellidae
Draeculacephala mollipes (Say)	watercress sharpshooter	HOMOPTERA: Cicadellidae
Drepanaphis acerifoliae (Thomas)	painted maple aphid	HOMOPTERA: Aphididae
Drepanothrips reuteri Uzel	grape thrips	THYSANOPTERA: Thripidae
Dryocampa rubicunda (Fabricius)	greenstriped mapleworm	LEPIDOPTERA: Saturniidae
Dryocoetes betulae Hopkins	birch bark beetle	COLEOPTERA: Scolytidae
Dryocoetes confusus Swaine	western balsam bark beetle	COLEOPTERA: Scolytidae
Dynaspidiotus britannicus (Newstead)	holly scale	HOMOPTERA: Diaspididae
Dynastes granti Horn	southwestern Hercules beetle	COLEOPTERA: Scarabaeidae
Dynastes tityus (Linnaeus)	eastern Hercules beetle	COLEOPTERA: Scarabaeidae
Dysaphis apiifolia (Theobald)	rusty banded aphid	HOMOPTERA: Aphididae
Dysaphis plantaginea (Passerini)	rosy apple aphid	HOMOPTERA: Aphididae
Dysaphis tulipae (Boyer de Fonscolombe)	tulip bulb aphid	HOMOPTERA: Aphididae
Dysdercus suturellus (Herrich-Schäffer)	cotton stainer	HETEROPTERA: Pyrrhocoridae
Dysmicoccus boninsis (Kuwana)	gray sugarcane mealybug	HOMOPTERA: Pseudococcidae
Dysmicoccus brevipes (Cockerell)	pineapple mealybug	HOMOPTERA: Pseudococcidae
Dysmicoccus neobrevipes Beardsley	gray pineapple mealybug	HOMOPTERA: Pseudococcidae

E

Scientific name	Common name	Order: Family
Eacles imperialis (Drury)	imperial moth	LEPIDOPTERA: Saturniidae
Ecdytolopha insiticiana Zeller	locust twig borer	LEPIDOPTERA: Tortricidae
Echicnophaga gallinacea (Westwood)	sticktight flea	SIPHONAPTERA: Pulicidae
Ectobius pallidus (Olivier)	spotted Mediterranean cockroach	BLATTODEA: Blattellidae
Edwardsiana prunicola (Edwards)	prune leafhopper	HOMOPTERA: Cicadellidae
Edwardsiana rosae (Linnaeus)	rose leafhopper	HOMOPTERA: Cicadellidae
Eidoleon wilsoni (McLachlan)	Hawaiian antlion	NEUROPTERA: Myrmeleontidae
Elaphidionoides villosus (Fabricius)	twig pruner	COLEOPTERA: Cerambycidae
Elasmopalpus lignosellus (Zeller)	lesser cornstalk borer	LEPIDOPTERA: Pyralidae
Elatobium abietinum (Walker)	spruce aphid	HOMOPTERA: Aphididae
Eleodes opacus (Say)	plains false wireworm	COLEOPTERA: Tenebrionidae
Elytroteinus subtruncatus (Fairmaire)	Fijian ginger weevil	COLEOPTERA: Curculionidae
Empicoris rubromaculatus (Blackburn)	thread bug	HETEROPTERA: Reduviidae
Empoasca abrupta DeLong	western potato leafhopper	HOMOPTERA: Cicadellidae
Empoasca fabae (Harris)	potato leafhopper	HOMOPTERA: Cicadellidae
Empoasca maligna (Walsh)	apple leafhopper	HOMOPTERA: Cicadellidae
Empoasca solana DeLong	southern garden leafhopper	HOMOPTERA: Cicadellidae
Empoasca stevensi Young	Stevens leafhopper	HOMOPTERA: Cicadellidae
Enaphalodes rufulus (Haldeman)	red oak borer	COLEOPTERA: Cerambycidae
Enchenopa binotata (Say)	twomarked treehopper	HOMOPTERA: Membracidae
Endelomyia aethiops (Fabricius)	roseslug	HYMENOPTERA: Tenthredinidae
Endopiza viteana Clemens	grape berry moth	LEPIDOPTERA: Tortricidae
Endothenia albolineana (Kearfott)	spruce needleminer	LEPIDOPTERA: Tortricidae
Endothenia hebesana (Walker)	verbena bud moth	LEPIDOPTERA: Tortricidae
Endria inimica (Say)	painted leafhopper	HOMOPTERA: Cicadellidae
Endrosis sarcitrella (Linnaeus)	whiteshouldered house moth	LEPIDOPTERA: Oecophoridae
Ennomos subsignaria (Hübner)	elm spanworm	LEPIDOPTERA: Geometridae
Enoclerus lecontei (Wolcott)	blackbellied clerid	COLEOPTERA: Cleridae
Ensina sonchi (Linnaeus)	sonchus fly	DIPTERA: Tephritidae
Entomoscelis americana Brown	red turnip beetle	COLEOPTERA: Chrysomelidae
Eobia bicolor (Fairmaire)	redblack oedemerid	COLEOPTERA: Oedemeridae
Eoreuma loftini (Dyar)	Mexican rice borer	LEPIDOPTERA: Pyralidae
Eotetranychus carpini borealis (Ewing)	yellow spider mite	ACARI: Tetranychidae
Eotetranychus clitus Pritchard & Baker	azalea white mite	ACARI: Tetranychidae
Eotetranychus hicoriae (McGregor)	pecan leaf scorch mite	ACARI: Tetranychidae

Eotetranychus sexmaculatus (Riley)	sixspotted mite	ACARI: Tetranychidae
Eotetranychus yumensis (McGregor)	Yuma spider mite	ACARI: Tetranychidae
Epargyreus clarus (Cramer)	silverspotted skipper	LEPIDOPTERA: Hesperiidae
Ephestia elutella (Hübner)	tobacco moth	LEPIDOPTERA: Pyralidae
Epiblema otiosana (Clemens)	bidens borer	LEPIDOPTERA: Tortricidae
Epiblema strenuana (Walker)	ragweed borer	LEPIDOPTERA: Tortricidae
Epicaerus imbricatus (Say)	imbricated snout beetle	COLEOPTERA: Curculionidae
Epicauta cinerea (Forster)	clematis blister beetle	COLEOPTERA: Meloidae
Epicauta fabricii (LeConte)	ashgray blister beetle	COLEOPTERA: Meloidae
Epicauta lemniscata (Fabricius)	threestriped blister beetle	COLEOPTERA: Meloidae
Epicauta maculata (Say)	spotted blister beetle	COLEOPTERA: Meloidae
Epicauta pennsylvanica (De Geer)	black blister beetle	COLEOPTERA: Meloidae
Epicauta pestifera Werner	margined blister beetle	COLEOPTERA: Meloidae
Epicauta subglabra (Fall)	caragana blister beetle	COLEOPTERA: Meloidae
Epicauta vittata (Fabricius)	striped blister beetle	COLEOPTERA: Meloidae
Epidiaspis leperii (Signoret)	Italian pear scale	HOMOPTERA: Diaspididae
Epilachna borealis (Fabricius)	squash beetle	COLEOPTERA: Coccinellidae
Epilachna varivestis Mulsant	Mexican bean beetle	COLEOPTERA: Coccinellidae
Epinotia aceriella (Clemens)	maple trumpet skeletonizer	LEPIDOPTERA: Tortricidae
Epinotia meritana Heinrich	white fir needleminer	LEPIDOPTERA: Tortricidae
Epiphyas postvittana (Walker)	light brown apple moth	LEPIDOPTERA: Tortricidae
Epitrimerus pyri (Nalepa)	pear rust mite	ACARI: Eriophyidae
Epitrix cucumeris (Harris)	potato flea beetle	COLEOPTERA: Chrysomelidae
Epitrix fuscula Crotch	eggplant flea beetle	COLEOPTERA: Chrysomelidae
Epitrix hirtipennis (Melsheimer)	tobacco flea beetle	COLEOPTERA: Chrysomelidae
Epitrix subcrinita LeConte	western potato flea beetle	COLEOPTERA: Chrysomelidae
Epitrix tuberis Gentner	tuber flea beetle	COLEOPTERA: Chrysomelidae
Epochra canadensis (Loew)	currant fruit fly	DIPTERA: Tephritidae
Erannis tiliaria (Harris)	linden looper	LEPIDOPTERA: Geometridae
Eriococcus azaleae Comstock	azalea bark scale	HOMOPTERA: Eriococcidae
Eriococcus carolinae Williams	beachgrass scale	HOMOPTERA: Eriococcidae
Erionota thrax (Linnaeus)	banana skipper	LEPIDOPTERA: Hesperiidae
Eriophyes aloinis Keifer	aloe mite	ACARI: Eriophyidae
Eriophyes caryae Keifer	pecan leafroll mite	ACARI: Eriophyidae
Eriophyes cynodoniensis Sayed	Bermudagrass mite	ACARI: Eriophyidae
Eriophyes erinea (Nalepa)	walnut blister mite	ACARI: Eriophyidae
Eriophyes ficus Cotte	fig mite	ACARI: Eriophyidae
Eriophyes litchii Keifer	litchi mite	ACARI: Eriophyidae

Eriophyes mangiferae (Sayed)	mango bud mite	ACARI: Eriophyidae
Eriophyes sheldoni Ewing	citrus bud mite	ACARI: Eriophyidae
Eriophyes tulipae Keifer	wheat curl mite	ACARI: Eriophyidae
Eriosoma americanum (Riley)	woolly elm aphid	HOMOPTERA: Aphididae
Eriosoma lanigerum (Hausmann)	woolly apple aphid	HOMOPTERA: Aphididae
Eriosoma pyricola Baker & Davidson	woolly pear aphid	HOMOPTERA: Aphididae
Eristalis tenax (Linnaeus)	drone fly	DIPTERA: Syrphidae
Erynephala puncticollis (Say)	beet leaf beetle	COLEOPTERA: Chrysomelidae
Erythraspides vitis (Harris)	grape sawfly	HYMENOPTERA: Tenthredinidae
Erythroneura comes (Say)	eastern grape leafhopper	HOMOPTERA: Cicadellidae
Erythroneura elegantula Osborn	western grape leafhopper	HOMOPTERA: Cicadellidae
Erythroneura tricincta Fitch	threebanded leafhopper	HOMOPTERA: Cicadellidae
Erythroneura ziczac Walsh	Virginiacreeper leafhopper	HOMOPTERA: Cicadellidae
Estigmene acrea (Drury)	saltmarsh caterpillar	LEPIDOPTERA: Arctiidae
Ethmia nigroapicella (Saalmüller)	kou leafworm	LEPIDOPTERA: Oecophoridae
Etiella zinckenella (Treitschke)	limabean pod borer	LEPIDOPTERA: Pyralidae
Euborellia annulipes (Lucas)	ringlegged earwig	DERMAPTERA: Labiduridae
Eucalymnatus tessellatus (Signoret)	tessellated scale	HOMOPTERA: Coccidae
Eucosma cocana Kearfott	shortleaf pine cone borer	LEPIDOPTERA: Tortricidae
Eucosma gloriola Heinrich	eastern pine shoot borer	LEPIDOPTERA: Tortricidae
Eucosma sonomana Kearfott	western pine shoot borer	LEPIDOPTERA: Tortricidae
Eucosma tocullionana Heinrich	white pine cone borer	LEPIDOPTERA: Tortricidae
Euetheola humilis rugiceps (LeConte)	sugarcane beetle	COLEOPTERA: Scarabaeidae
Euglandina rosea (Férussac)	rosy predator snail	STYLOMMATOPHORA: Oleacinidae
Eulecanium cerasorum (Cockerell)	calico scale	HOMOPTERA: Coccidae
Eulithis diversilineata (Hübner)	grapevine looper	LEPIDOPTERA: Geometridae
Eumerus figurans Walker	ginger maggot	DIPTERA: Syrphidae
Eumerus strigatus (Fallén)	onion bulb fly	DIPTERA: Syrphidae
Eumerus tuberculatus Rondani	lesser bulb fly	DIPTERA: Syrphidae
Eumorpha achemon (Drury)	achemon sphinx	LEPIDOPTERA: Sphingidae
Euphilotes battoides allyni (Shields)	El Segundo blue	LEPIDOPTERA: Lycaenidae
Euphilotes enoptes smithi (Mattoni)	Smith blue	LEPIDOPTERA: Lycaenidae
Euphoria inda (Linnaeus)	bumble flower beetle	COLEOPTERA: Scarabaeidae
Eupithecia spermaphaga (Dyar)	fir cone looper	LEPIDOPTERA: Geometridae
Euproctis chrysorrhoea (Linnaeus)	browntail moth	LEPIDOPTERA: Lymantriidae
Eurytoma orchidearum (Westwood)	orchidfly	HYMENOPTERA: Eurytomidae
Euscepes postfaciatus (Fairmaire)	West Indian sweetpotato weevil	COLEOPTERA: Curculionidae
Euschistus servus (Say)	brown stink bug	HETEROPTERA: Pentatomidae

Euschistus tristigmus (Say)	dusky stink bug	HETEROPTERA: Pentatomidae
Euschistus variolarius (Palisot de Beauvois)	onespotted stink bug	HETEROPTERA: Pentatomidae
Eutetranychus banksi (McGregor)	Texas citrus mite	ACARI: Tetranychidae
Euthyrrhapha pacifica (Coquebert)	Pacific cockroach	BLATTODEA: Polyphagidae
Eutreta xanthochaeta Aldrich	lantana gall fly	DIPTERA: Tephritidae
Eutrombidium trigonum (Hermann)	red grasshopper mite	ACARI: Trombidiidae
Euxoa auxiliaris (Grote)	army cutworm	LEPIDOPTERA: Noctuidae
Euxoa messoria (Harris)	darksided cutworm	LEPIDOPTERA: Noctuidae
Euxoa ochrogaster (Guenée)	redbacked cutworm	LEPIDOPTERA: Noctuidae
Euxoa scandens (Riley)	white cutworm	LEPIDOPTERA: Noctuidae
Euxoa tessellata (Harris)	striped cutworm	LEPIDOPTERA: Noctuidae
Euzophera semifuneralis (Walker)	American plum borer	LEPIDOPTERA: Pyralidae
Evergestis pallidata (Hufnagel)	purplebacked cabbageworm	LEPIDOPTERA: Pyralidae
Evergestis rimosalis (Guenée)	cross-striped cabbageworm	LEPIDOPTERA: Pyralidae
Evoxysoma vitis (Saunders)	grape seed chalcid	HYMENOPTERA: Eurytomidae
Exaireta spinigera (Wiedemann)	blue soldier fly	DIPTERA: Stratiomyidae
Exitianus exitiosus (Uhler)	gray lawn leafhopper	HOMOPTERA: Cicadellidae
Exoteleia nepheos Freeman	pine candle moth	LEPIDOPTERA: Gelechiidae
Exoteleia pinifoliella (Chambers)	pine needleminer	LEPIDOPTERA: Gelechiidae

---

F

Fagiphagus imbricator (Fitch)	beech blight aphid	HOMOPTERA: Aphididae
Fannia canicularis (Linnaeus)	little house fly	DIPTERA: Muscidae
Fannia pusio (Wiedemann)	chicken dung fly	DIPTERA: Muscidae
Fannia scalaris (Fabricius)	latrine fly	DIPTERA: Muscidae
Faronta diffusa (Walker)	wheat head armyworm	LEPIDOPTERA: Noctuidae
Fascista cerceriserella (Chambers)	redbud leaffolder	LEPIDOPTERA: Gelechiidae
Felicola subrostratus (Burmeister)	cat louse	MALLOPHAGA: Trichodectidae
Feltia ducens Walker	dingy cutworm	LEPIDOPTERA: Noctuidae
Fenusa dohrnii (Tischbein)	European alder leafminer	HYMENOPTERA: Tenthredinidae
Fenusa pusilla (Lepeletier)	birch leafminer	HYMENOPTERA: Tenthredinidae
Fenusa ulmi Sundevall	elm leafminer	HYMENOPTERA: Tenthredinidae
Ferrisia virgata (Cockerell)	striped mealybug	HOMOPTERA: Pseudococcidae
Fidia viticida Walsh	grape rootworm	COLEOPTERA: Chrysomelidae
Fiorinia externa Ferris	elongate hemlock scale	HOMOPTERA: Diaspididae

Fiorinia theae Green	tea scale	HOMOPTERA: Diaspididae
Forficula auricularia Linnaeus	European earwig	DERMAPTERA: Forficulidae
Formica exsectoides Forel	Allegheny mound ant	HYMENOPTERA: Formicidae
Formica fusca Linnaeus	silky ant	HYMENOPTERA: Formicidae
Formica obscuripes Forel	western thatching ant	HYMENOPTERA: Formicidae
Frankliniella fusca (Hinds)	tobacco thrips	THYSANOPTERA: Thripidae
Frankliniella occidentalis (Pergande)	western flower thrips	THYSANOPTERA: Thripidae
Frankliniella tritici (Fitch)	flower thrips	THYSANOPTERA: Thripidae
Frankliniella vaccinii Morgan	blueberry thrips	THYSANOPTERA: Thripidae
Franklinothrips vespiformis (D.L. Crawford)	vespiform thrips	THYSANOPTERA: Aeolothripidae
Fundella pellucens Zeller	Caribbean pod borer	LEPIDOPTERA: Pyralidae
Furcaspis biformis (Cockerell)	red orchid scale	HOMOPTERA: Diaspididae

G

Galandromus occidentalis (Nesbitt)	western predatory mite	ACARI: Phytoseiidae
Galeruca browni Blake	peppergrass beetle	COLEOPTERA: Chrysomelidae
Galerucella nymphaeae (Linnaeus)	waterlily leaf beetle	COLEOPTERA: Chrysomelidae
Galleria mellonella (Linnaeus)	greater wax moth	LEPIDOPTERA: Pyralidae
Gargaphia solani Heidemann	eggplant lace bug	HETEROPTERA: Tingidae
Gargaphia tiliae (Walsh)	basswood lace bug	HETEROPTERA: Tingidae
Gasteracantha cancriformis (Linnaeus)	spinybacked spider	ARANEAE: Araneidae
Gasterophilus haemorrhoidalis (Linnaeus)	nose bot fly	DIPTERA: Oestridae
Gasterophilus intestinalis (De Geer)	horse bot fly	DIPTERA: Oestridae
Gasterophilus nasalis (Linnaeus)	throat bot fly	DIPTERA: Oestridae
Gelastocoris oculatus (Fabricius)	toad bug	HETEROPTERA: Gelastocoridae
Geocoris bullatus (Say)	large bigeyed bug	HETEROPTERA: Lygaeidae
Geocoris pallens Stål	western bigeyed bug	HETEROPTERA: Lygaeidae
Geotomus pygmaeus (Dallas)	oceanic burrower bug	HETEROPTERA: Cydnidae
Geshna cannalis (Quaintance)	lesser canna leafroller	LEPIDOPTERA: Pyralidae
Gilpinia hercyniae (Hartig)	European spruce sawfly	HYMENOPTERA: Diprionidae
Gliricola porcelli (Schrank)	slender guineapig louse	MALLOPHAGA: Gyropidae
Glossonotus crataegi (Fitch)	quince treehopper	HOMOPTERA: Membracidae
Glycobius speciosus (Say)	sugar maple borer	COLEOPTERA: Cerambycidae
Glycyphagus domesticus (De Geer)	house mite	ACARI: Glycyphagidae
Gnatocerus cornutus (Fabricius)	broadhorned flour beetle	COLEOPTERA: Tenebrionidae

Gnatocerus maxillosus (Fabricius)	slenderhorned flour beetle	COLEOPTERA: Tenebrionidae
Gnophothrips fuscus (Morgan)	slash pine flower thrips	THYSANOPTERA: Phlaeothripidae
Goes tesselatus (Haldeman)	oak sapling borer	COLEOPTERA: Cerambycidae
Goes tigrinus (De Geer)	white oak borer	COLEOPTERA: Cerambycidae
Gohieria fusca (Oudemans)	brown flour mite	ACARI: Glycyphagidae
Goniocotes gallinae (De Geer)	fluff louse	MALLOPHAGA: Philopteridae
Gonioctena americana (Schaeffer)	American aspen beetle	COLEOPTERA: Chrysomelidae
Goniodes dissimilis Denny	brown chicken louse	MALLOPHAGA: Philopteridae
Goniodes gigas (Taschenberg)	large chicken louse	MALLOPHAGA: Philopteridae
Goniodes numidae Mjberg	Guinea feather louse	MALLOPHAGA: Philopteridae
Gossyparia spuria (Modeer)	European elm scale	HOMOPTERA: Eriococcidae
Graminella nigrifrons (Forbes)	blackfaced leafhopper	HOMOPTERA: Cicadellidae
Graminella sonora (Ball)	lesser lawn leafhopper	HOMOPTERA: Cicadellidae
Graphognathus spp.	whitefringed beetles	COLEOPTERA: Curculionidae
Grapholita interstinctana (Clemens)	clover head caterpillar	LEPIDOPTERA: Tortricidae
Grapholita molesta (Busck)	oriental fruit moth	LEPIDOPTERA: Tortricidae
Grapholita packardi Zeller	cherry fruitworm	LEPIDOPTERA: Tortricidae
Grapholita prunivora (Walsh)	lesser appleworm	LEPIDOPTERA: Tortricidae
Graptostethus manillensis (Stål)	woodrose bug	HETEROPTERA: Lygaeidae
Gretchena bolliana (Slingerland)	pecan bud moth	LEPIDOPTERA: Tortricidae
Gryllotalpa africana Palisot de Beauvois	African mole cricket	ORTHOPTERA: Gryllotalpidae
Gynaikothrips ficorum (Marchal)	Cuban laurel thrips	THYSANOPTERA: Phlaeothripidae
Gypsonoma haimbachiana (Kearfott)	cottonwood twig borer	LEPIDOPTERA: Tortricidae
Gyropus ovalis Burmeister	oval guineapig louse	MALLOPHAGA: Gyropidae

H

Habropoda laboriosa (Fabricius)	southeastern blueberry bee	HYMENOPTERA: Anthophoridae
Haemaphysalis chordeilis (Packard)	bird tick	ACARI: Ixodidae
Haemaphysalis leporispalustris (Packard)	rabbit tick	ACARI: Ixodidae
Haematobia irritans (Linnaeus)	horn fly	DIPTERA: Muscidae
Haematoloecha rubescens Distant	red assassin bug	HETEROPTERA: Reduviidae
Haematopinus asini (Linnaeus)	horse sucking louse	ANOPLURA: Haematopinidae
Haematopinus eurysternus (Nitzsch)	shortnosed cattle louse	ANOPLURA: Haematopinidae
Haematopinus quadripertusus Fahrenholz	cattle tail louse	ANOPLURA: Haematopinidae
Haematopinus suis (Linnaeus)	hog louse	ANOPLURA: Haematopinidae

Species	Common name	Order: Family
Haematosiphon inodorus (Dugès)	poultry bug	HETEROPTERA: Cimicidae
Haemodipsus ventricosus (Denny)	rabbit louse	ANOPLURA: Hoplopleuridae
Halobates hawaiiensis Usinger	Hawaiian pelagic water strider	HETEROPTERA: Gerridae
Halobates sericeus Eschscholtz	Pacific pelagic water strider	HETEROPTERA: Gerridae
Halticotoma valida Townsend	yucca plant bug	HETEROPTERA: Miridae
Halticus bractatus (Say)	garden fleahopper	HETEROPTERA: Miridae
Halticus chrysolepis Kirkaldy	grass fleahopper	HETEROPTERA: Miridae
Halysidota harrisii Walsh	sycamore tussock moth	LEPIDOPTERA: Arctiidae
Halysidota tessellaris (J.E. Smith)	pale tussock moth	LEPIDOPTERA: Arctiidae
Haplorhynchites aeneus (Boheman)	sunflower headclipping weevil	COLEOPTERA: Curculionidae
Haplothrips gowdeyi (Franklin)	black flower thrips	THYSANOPTERA: Phlaeothripidae
Haplothrips verbasci (Osborn)	mullein thrips	THYSANOPTERA: Phlaeothripidae
Harrisina americana (Guérin)	grapeleaf skeletonizer	LEPIDOPTERA: Zygaenidae
Harrisina brillians Barnes & McDunnough	western grapeleaf skeletonizer	LEPIDOPTERA: Zygaenidae
Hedya chionosema (Zeller)	twinspotted budworm	LEPIDOPTERA: Tortricidae
Hedya nubiferana (Haworth)	green budworm	LEPIDOPTERA: Tortricidae
Hedylepta accepta (Butler)	sugarcane leafroller	LEPIDOPTERA: Pyralidae
Hedylepta blackburni (Butler)	coconut leafroller	LEPIDOPTERA: Pyralidae
Helicoverpa hawaiiensis (Quaintance & Brues)	Hawaiian bud moth	LEPIDOPTERA: Noctuidae
Helicoverpa virescens (Fabricius)	tobacco budworm	LEPIDOPTERA: Noctuidae
Helicoverpa zea (Boddie)	bollworm[37]	LEPIDOPTERA: Noctuidae
Heliothis ononis (Denis & Schiffermüller)	flax bollworm	LEPIDOPTERA: Noctuidae
Heliothrips haemorrhoidalis (Bouché)	greenhouse thrips	THYSANOPTERA: Thripidae
Helix aspersa Müller	brown garden snail	STYLOMMATOPHORA: Helicidae
Hellula rogatalis (Hulst)	cabbage webworm	LEPIDOPTERA: Pyralidae
Hemiberlesia lataniae (Signoret)	latania scale	HOMOPTERA: Diaspididae
Hemiberlesia rapax (Comstock)	greedy scale	HOMOPTERA: Diaspididae
Hemichroa crocea (Geoffroy)	striped alder sawfly	HYMENOPTERA: Tenthredinidae
Hemileuca maia (Drury)	buck moth	LEPIDOPTERA: Saturniidae
Hemileuca oliviae Cockerell	range caterpillar	LEPIDOPTERA: Saturniidae
Hercinothrips femoralis (O.M. Reuter)	banded greenhouse thrips	THYSANOPTERA: Thripidae
Hermetia illucens (Linnaeus)	black soldier fly	DIPTERA: Stratiomyidae
Herpetogramma bipunctalis (Fabricius)	southern beet webworm	LEPIDOPTERA: Pyralidae
Herpetogramma licarsisalis (Walker)	grass webworm	LEPIDOPTERA: Pyralidae
Herpetogramma phaeopteralis Guenée	tropical sod webworm	LEPIDOPTERA: Pyralidae

[37]Also called corn earworm and tomato fruitworm.

Heterocampa guttivitta (Walker)	saddled prominent	LEPIDOPTERA: Notodontidae
Heterocampa manteo (Doubleday)	variable oakleaf caterpillar	LEPIDOPTERA: Notodontidae
Heteropoda venatoria (Linnaeus)	large brown spider	ARANEAE: Sparassidae
Hippodamia convergens Guérin-Méneville	convergent lady beetle	COLEOPTERA: Coccinellidae
Hippodamia sinuata Mulsant	sinuate lady beetle	COLEOPTERA: Coccinellidae
Hippodamia tredecimpunctata tibialis (Say)	thirteenspotted lady beetle	COLEOPTERA: Coccinellidae
Hofmannophila pseudospretella (Stainton)	brown house moth	LEPIDOPTERA: Oecophoridae
Holochlora japonica Brunner von Wattenwyl	Japanese broadwinged katydid	ORTHOPTERA: Tettigoniidae
Homadaula anisocentra Meyrick	mimosa webworm	LEPIDOPTERA: Plutellidae
Homaledra sabalella (Chambers)	palm leafskeletonizer	LEPIDOPTERA: Coleophoridae
Homoeosoma electellum (Hulst)	sunflower moth	LEPIDOPTERA: Pyralidae
Hoplocampa cookei (Clarke)	cherry fruit sawfly	HYMENOPTERA: Tenthredinidae
Hoplocampa testudinea (Klug)	European apple sawfly	HYMENOPTERA: Tenthredinidae
Hoplopleura pacifica Ewing	tropical rat louse	ANOPLURA: Hoplopleuridae
Horistonotus uhlerii Horn	sand wireworm	COLEOPTERA: Elateridae
Howardia biclavis (Comstock)	mining scale	HOMOPTERA: Diaspididae
Hulstia undulatella (Clemens)	sugarbeet crown borer	LEPIDOPTERA: Pyralidae
Hyalopeplus pellucidus (Stål)	transparentwinged plant bug	HETEROPTERA: Miridae
Hyalophora cecropia (Linnaeus)	cecropia moth	LEPIDOPTERA: Saturniidae
Hyalophora euryalus (Boisduval)	ceanothus silk moth	LEPIDOPTERA: Saturniidae
Hyalopterus pruni (Geoffroy)	mealy plum aphid	HOMOPTERA: Aphididae
Hydraecia micacea (Esper)	potato stem borer	LEPIDOPTERA: Noctuidae
Hylastinus obscurus (Marsham)	clover root borer	COLEOPTERA: Scolytidae
Hylecoetus lugubris Say	sapwood timberworm	COLEOPTERA: Lymexylidae
Hylephila phyleus (Drury)	fiery skipper	LEPIDOPTERA: Hesperiidae
Hyles calida (Butler)	Hawaiian sphinx	LEPIDOPTERA: Sphingidae
Hyles lineata (Fabricius)	whitelined sphinx	LEPIDOPTERA: Sphingidae
Hyles wilsoni (Rothschild)	Wilson sphinx	LEPIDOPTERA: Sphingidae
Hylobius aliradicis Warner	southern pine root weevil	COLEOPTERA: Curculionidae
Hylobius assimilis Boheman	pine root tip weevil	COLEOPTERA: Curculionidae
Hylobius pales (Herbst)	pales weevil	COLEOPTERA: Curculionidae
Hylobius radicis Buchanan	pine root collar weevil	COLEOPTERA: Curculionidae
Hylotrupes bajulus (Linnaeus)	old house borer	COLEOPTERA: Cerambycidae
Hylurgopinus rufipes (Eichhoff)	native elm bark beetle	COLEOPTERA: Scolytidae
Hymenia perspectalis (Hübner)	spotted beet webworm	LEPIDOPTERA: Pyralidae
Hypena humuli (Harris)	hop looper	LEPIDOPTERA: Noctuidae
Hypena strigata (Fabricius)	lantana defoliator caterpillar	LEPIDOPTERA: Noctuidae
Hypera brunnipennis (Boheman)	Egyptian alfalfa weevil	COLEOPTERA: Curculionidae

Hypera meles (Fabricius)	clover head weevil	COLEOPTERA: Curculionidae
Hypera nigrirostris (Fabricius)	lesser clover leaf weevil	COLEOPTERA: Curculionidae
Hypera postica (Gyllenhal)	alfalfa weevil	COLEOPTERA: Curculionidae
Hypera punctata (Fabricius)	clover leaf weevil	COLEOPTERA: Curculionidae
Hyperaspis jocosa (Mulsant)	orthezia lady beetle	COLEOPTERA: Coccinellidae
Hyphantria cunea (Drury)	fall webworm	LEPIDOPTERA: Arctiidae
Hypocryphalus mangiferae (Stebbing)	mango bark beetle	COLEOPTERA: Scolytidae
Hypoderma bovis (Linnaeus)	northern cattle grub	DIPTERA: Oestridae
Hypoderma lineatum (Villers)	common cattle grub	DIPTERA: Oestridae
Hypolithus abbreviatus (Say)	abbreviated wireworm	COLEOPTERA: Elateridae
Hypothenemus birmanus (Eichhoff)	kiawe scolytid	COLEOPTERA: Scolytidae
Hypothenemus obscurus (Fabricius)	apple twig beetle	COLEOPTERA: Scolytidae
Hypothenemus pubescens Hopkins	grass scolytid	COLEOPTERA: Scolytidae
Hypsopygia costalis (Fabricius)	clover hayworm	LEPIDOPTERA: Pyralidae
Hypurus bertrandi Perris	portulaca leafmining weevil	COLEOPTERA: Curculionidae
Hysteroneura setariae (Thomas)	rusty plum aphid	HOMOPTERA: Aphididae

---

I

Icaricia icarioides missionensis (Hovanitz)	mission blue	LEPIDOPTERA: Lycaenidae
Icerya purchasi Maskell	cottony cushion scale	HOMOPTERA: Margarodidae
Ichthyura inclusa (Hübner)	poplar tentmaker	LEPIDOPTERA: Notodontidae
Idiopterus nephrelepidis Davis	fern aphid	HOMOPTERA: Aphididae
Incisalia fotis bayensis (R.M. Brown)	San Bruno elfin	LEPIDOPTERA: Lycaenidae
Incisitermes immigrans (Snyder)	lowland tree termite	ISOPTERA: Kalotermitidae
Incisitermes minor (Hagen)	western drywood termite	ISOPTERA: Kalotermitidae
Ips avulsus (Eichhoff)	small southern pine engraver	COLEOPTERA: Scolytidae
Ips calligraphus (Germar)	sixspined ips	COLEOPTERA: Scolytidae
Ips grandicollis (Eichhoff)	eastern fivespined ips	COLEOPTERA: Scolytidae
Ips paraconfusus Lanier	California fivespined ips	COLEOPTERA: Scolytidae
Ips pini (Say)	pine engraver	COLEOPTERA: Scolytidae
Iridomyrmex humilis (Mayr)	Argentine ant	HYMENOPTERA: Formicidae
Iridothrips iridis (Watson)	iris thrips	THYSANOPTERA: Thripidae
Ischnaspis longirostris (Signoret)	black thread scale	HOMOPTERA: Diaspididae
Isometrus maculatus De Geer	lesser brown scorpion	SCORPIONES: Buthidae
Itame ribearia (Fitch)	currant spanworm	LEPIDOPTERA: Geometridae

Ithome concolorella (Chambers)	kiawe flower moth	LEPIDOPTERA: Cosmopterigidae
Ithycerus noveboracensis (Forster)	New York weevil	COLEOPTERA: Curculionidae
Ixodes kingi Bishopp	rotund tick	ACARI: Ixodidae
Ixodes scapularis Say	blacklegged tick	ACARI: Ixodidae

J

Jalysus wickhami Van Duzee	spined stilt bug	HETEROPTERA: Berytidae
Janus abbreviatus (Say)	willow shoot sawfly	HYMENOPTERA: Cephidae
Janus integer (Norton)	currant stem girdler	HYMENOPTERA: Cephidae
Jonthonota nigripes (Olivier)	blacklegged tortoise beetle	COLEOPTERA: Chrysomelidae

K

Kakimia houghtonensis (Troop)	gooseberry witchbroom aphid	HOMOPTERA: Aphididae
Keiferia lycopersicella (Walsingham)	tomato pinworm	LEPIDOPTERA: Gelechiidae
Kilifia acuminata (Signoret)	acuminate scale	HOMOPTERA: Coccidae
Knemidokoptes gallinae (Railliet)	depluming mite	ACARI: Sarcoptidae
Knemidokoptes mutans (Robin & Lanquetin)	scalyleg mite	ACARI: Sarcoptidae
Knulliana cincta (Drury)	banded hickory borer	COLEOPTERA: Cerambycidae

L

Labidura riparia (Pallas)	striped earwig	DERMAPTERA: Labiduridae
Lachesilla pedicularia (Linnaeus)	cosmopolitan grain psocid	PSOCOPTERA: Lachesillidae
Lacinipolia renigera (Stephens)	bristly cutworm	LEPIDOPTERA: Noctuidae
Lagoa crispata (Packard)	crinkled flannel moth	LEPIDOPTERA: Megalopygidae
Lagocheirus undatus (Voet)	plumeria borer	COLEOPTERA: Cerambycidae
Lambdina fiscellaria fiscellaria (Guenée)	hemlock looper	LEPIDOPTERA: Geometridae
Lambdina fiscellaria lugubrosa (Hulst)	western hemlock looper	LEPIDOPTERA: Geometridae

Lambdina fiscellaria somniaria (Hulst)	western oak looper	LEPIDOPTERA: Geometridae
Lambdina pellucidaria (Grote & Robinson)	eastern pine looper	LEPIDOPTERA: Geometridae
Laminicoccus pandani (Cockerell)	pandanus mealybug	HOMOPTERA: Pseudococcidae
Lampides boeticus (Linnaeus)	bean butterfly	LEPIDOPTERA: Lycaenidae
Lampronia rubiella (Bjerkander)	raspberry bud moth	LEPIDOPTERA: Incurvariidae
Languria mozardi Latreille	clover stem borer	COLEOPTERA: Languriidae
Lantanophaga pusillidactyla (Walker)	lantana plume moth	LEPIDOPTERA: Pterophoridae
Laothoe juglandis (J.E. Smith)	walnut sphinx	LEPIDOPTERA: Sphingidae
Lasioderma serricorne (Fabricius)	cigarette beetle	COLEOPTERA: Anobiidae
Lasius alienus (Foerster)	cornfield ant	HYMENOPTERA: Formicidae
Latheticus oryzae Waterhouse	longheaded flour beetle	COLEOPTERA: Tenebrionidae
Lathridius minutus (Linnaeus)	squarenosed fungus beetle	COLEOPTERA: Lathridiidae
Latrodectus geometricus (Fabricius)	brown widow spider	ARANEAE: Theridiidae
Latrodectus mactans (Fabricius)	black widow spider	ARANEAE: Theridiidae
Lema trilinea White	threelined potato beetle	COLEOPTERA: Chrysomelidae
Lepidosaphes beckii (Newman)	purple scale	HOMOPTERA: Diaspididae
Lepidosaphes camelliae Hoke	camellia scale	HOMOPTERA: Diaspididae
Lepidosaphes conchiformis (Gmelin)	fig scale	HOMOPTERA: Diaspididae
Lepidosaphes gloveri (Packard)	Glover scale	HOMOPTERA: Diaspididae
Lepidosaphes tokionis (Kuwana)	croton mussel scale	HOMOPTERA: Diaspididae
Lepidosaphes ulmi (Linnaeus)	oystershell scale	HOMOPTERA: Diaspididae
Lepinotus reticulatus Enderlein	reticulatewinged trogiid	PSOCOPTERA: Trogiidae
Lepisma saccharina Linnaeus	silverfish	THYSANURA: Lepismatidae
Leptinotarsa decemlineata (Say)	Colorado potato beetle	COLEOPTERA: Chrysomelidae
Leptinotarsa juncta (Germar)	false potato beetle	COLEOPTERA: Chrysomelidae
Leptoglossus corculus (Say)	leaffooted pine seed bug	HETEROPTERA: Coreidae
Leptoglossus phyllopus (Linnaeus)	leaffooted bug	HETEROPTERA: Coreidae
Leptopsylla segnis (Schnherr)	European mouse flea	SIPHONAPTERA: Leptopsyllidae
Leptopterna dolabrata (Linnaeus)	meadow plant bug	HETEROPTERA: Miridae
Leptothrips mali (Fitch)	black hunter thrips	THYSANOPTERA: Phlaeothripidae
Lepyronia quadrangularis (Say)	diamondbacked spittlebug	HOMOPTERA: Cercopidae
Lerodea eufala (Edwards)	rice leaffolder	LEPIDOPTERA: Hesperiidae
Lethocerus americanus (Leidy)	giant water bug	HETEROPTERA: Belostomatidae
Leucoma salicis (Linnaeus)	satin moth	LEPIDOPTERA: Lymantriidae
Leucophaea maderae (Fabricius)	Madeira cockroach	BLATTODEA: Blaberidae
Ligyrus gibbosus (De Geer)	carrot beetle	COLEOPTERA: Scarabaeidae
Lilioceris lilii (Scopoli)	lily leaf beetle	COLEOPTERA: Chrysomelidae
Limax flavus Linnaeus	tawny garden slug	STYLOMMATOPHORA: Limacidae

Limax maximus Linnaeus	spotted garden slug	STYLOMMATOPHORA: Limacidae
Limonius agonus (Say)	eastern field wireworm	COLEOPTERA: Elateridae
Limonius californicus (Mannerheim)	sugarbeet wireworm	COLEOPTERA: Elateridae
Limonius canus LeConte	Pacific Coast wireworm	COLEOPTERA: Elateridae
Limonius infuscatus Motschulsky	western field wireworm	COLEOPTERA: Elateridae
Limonius subauratus LeConte	Columbia Basin wireworm	COLEOPTERA: Elateridae
Limothrips cerealium (Haliday)	grain thrips	THYSANOPTERA: Thripidae
Lindbergocapsus allii (Knight)	onion plant bug	HETEROPTERA: Miridae
Linognathus setosus (Olfers)	dog sucking louse	ANOPLURA: Linognathidae
Linognathus stenopsis (Burmeister)	goat sucking louse	ANOPLURA: Linognathidae
Linognathus vituli (Linnaeus)	longnosed cattle louse	ANOPLURA: Linognathidae
Liorhyssus hyalinus (Fabricius)	hyaline grass bug	HETEROPTERA: Rhopalidae
Liothrips floridensis (Watson)	camphor thrips	THYSANOPTERA: Phlaeothripidae
Liothrips urichi Karny	clidemia thrips	THYSANOPTERA: Phlaeothripidae
Liothrips vaneeckei Priesner	lily bulb thrips	THYSANOPTERA: Phlaeothripidae
Lipaphis erysimi (Kaltenbach)	turnip aphid	HOMOPTERA: Aphididae
Liperus caponis (Linnaeus)	wing louse	MALLOPHAGA: Philopteridae
Lipeurus numidae (Denny)	slender guinea louse	MALLOPHAGA: Philopteridae
Liponyssoides sanguineus (Hirst)	house mouse mite	ACARI: Macronyssidae
Liposcelis corrodens Heymons	booklouse	PSOCOPTERA: Liposcelidae
Lirceus brachyurus (Harger)	watercress sowbug	ISOPODA: Asellidae
Liriomyza brassicae (Riley)	serpentine leafminer	DIPTERA: Agromyzidae
Liriomyza huidobrensis (Blanchard)	pea leafminer	DIPTERA: Agromyzidae
Liriomyza sativae Blanchard	vegetable leafminer	DIPTERA: Agromyzidae
Liris aurulentus (Fabricius)	golden cricket wasp	HYMENOPTERA: Sphecidae
Lissorhoptrus oryzophilus Kuschel	rice water weevil	COLEOPTERA: Curculionidae
Listroderes difficilis Germar	vegetable weevil	COLEOPTERA: Curculionidae
Listronotus oregonensis (LeConte)	carrot weevil	COLEOPTERA: Curculionidae
Lithophane antennata (Walker)	green fruitworm	LEPIDOPTERA: Noctuidae
Lixus concavus Say	rhubarb curculio	COLEOPTERA: Curculionidae
Longistigma caryae (Harris)	giant bark aphid	HOMOPTERA: Aphididae
Lophocampa argentata (Packard)	silverspotted tiger moth	LEPIDOPTERA: Arctiidae
Lophocampa caryae (Harris)	hickory tussock moth	LEPIDOPTERA: Arctiidae
Lophocampa maculata Harris	spotted tussock moth	LEPIDOPTERA: Arctiidae
Lopidea dakota Knight	caragana plant bug	HETEROPTERA: Miridae
Lopidea davisi Knight	phlox plant bug	HETEROPTERA: Miridae
Lorita abornana Busck	chrysanthemum flower borer	LEPIDOPTERA: Cochylidae
Lorryia reticulata (Oudemans)	reticulate mite	ACARI: Tydeidae

Loxagrotis albicosta (Smith)	western bean cutworm	LEPIDOPTERA: Noctuidae
Loxosceles reclusa Gertsch & Mulaik	brown recluse spider	ARANEAE: Loxoscelidae
Loxostege cereralis (Zeller)	alfalfa webworm	LEPIDOPTERA: Pyralidae
Loxostege sticticalis (Linnaeus)	beet webworm	LEPIDOPTERA: Pyralidae
Lucanus elaphus Fabricius	giant stag beetle	COLEOPTERA: Lucanidae
Lycaeides argyrognomon lotis (Lintner)	lotis blue	LEPIDOPTERA: Lycaenidae
Lyctus planicollis LeConte	southern lyctus beetle	COLEOPTERA: Lyctidae
Lygaeus kalmii Stål	small milkweed bug	HETEROPTERA: Lygaeidae
Lygidea mendax Reuter	apple red bug	HETEROPTERA: Miridae
Lygocoris caryae (Knight)	hickory plant bug	HETEROPTERA: Miridae
Lygocoris communis (Knight)	pear plant bug	HETEROPTERA: Miridae
Lygus elisus Van Duzee	pale legume bug	HETEROPTERA: Miridae
Lygus lineolaris (Palisot de Beauvois)	tarnished plant bug	HETEROPTERA: Miridae
Lymantria dispar (Linnaeus)	gypsy moth	LEPIDOPTERA: Lymantriidae
Lytta (Pomphopoea) sayi (LeConte)	Say blister beetle	COLEOPTERA: Meloidae
Lytta nuttalli Say	Nuttall blister beetle	COLEOPTERA: Meloidae
Lytta vesicatoria (Linnaeus)	Spanishfly	COLEOPTERA: Meloidae

M

Macalla thyrsisalis Walker	mahogany webworm	LEPIDOPTERA: Pyralidae
Macrocopturus floridanus (Fall)	mahogany bark weevil	COLEOPTERA: Curculionidae
Macrodactylus subspinosus (Fabricius)	rose chafer	COLEOPTERA: Scarabaeidae
Macrohaltica ambiens (LeConte)	alder flea beetle	COLEOPTERA: Chrysomelidae
Macronoctua onusta Grote	iris borer	LEPIDOPTERA: Noctuidae
Macropsis trimaculata (Fitch)	plum leafhopper	HOMOPTERA: Cicadellidae
Macrosiphoniella sanborni (Gillette)	chrysanthemum aphid	HOMOPTERA: Aphididae
Macrosiphum euphorbiae (Thomas)	potato aphid	HOMOPTERA: Aphididae
Macrosiphum lilii (Monell)	purplespotted lily aphid	HOMOPTERA: Aphididae
Macrosiphum liriodendri (Monell)	tuliptree aphid	HOMOPTERA: Aphididae
Macrosiphum luteum (Buckton)	orchid aphid	HOMOPTERA: Aphididae
Macrosiphum rosae (Linnaeus)	rose aphid	HOMOPTERA: Aphididae
Macrosiphum scoliopi Essig	western lily aphid	HOMOPTERA: Aphididae
Macrosteles quadrilineatus Forbes	aster leafhopper	HOMOPTERA: Cicadellidae
Magdalis aenescens LeConte	bronze appletree weevil	COLEOPTERA: Curculionidae
Magdalis armicollis (Say)	red elm bark weevil	COLEOPTERA: Curculionidae

Magdalis barbita (Say)	black elm bark weevil	COLEOPTERA: Curculionidae
Magicicada septendecim (Linnaeus)	periodical cicada	HOMOPTERA: Cicadidae
Malacosoma americanum (Fabricius)	eastern tent caterpillar	LEPIDOPTERA: Lasiocampidae
Malacosoma californicum (Packard)	western tent caterpillar	LEPIDOPTERA: Lasiocampidae
Malacosoma constrictum (Hy. Edwards)	Pacific tent caterpillar	LEPIDOPTERA: Lasiocampidae
Malacosoma disstria Hübner	forest tent caterpillar	LEPIDOPTERA: Lasiocampidae
Malacosoma incurvum (Hy. Edwards)	southwestern tent caterpillar	LEPIDOPTERA: Lasiocampidae
Malacosoma tigris (Dyar)	Sonoran tent caterpillar	LEPIDOPTERA: Lasiocampidae
Maladera castanea (Arrow)	Asiatic garden beetle	COLEOPTERA: Scarabaeidae
Mamestra configurata Walker	bertha armyworm	LEPIDOPTERA: Noctuidae
Manduca quinquemaculata (Haworth)	tomato hornworm	LEPIDOPTERA: Sphingidae
Manduca sexta (Linnaeus)	tobacco hornworm	LEPIDOPTERA: Sphingidae
Mantis religiosa Linnaeus	European mantid	MANTODEA: Mantidae
Marmara elotella (Busck)	apple barkminer	LEPIDOPTERA: Gracillariidae
Marmara pomonella Busck	apple fruitminer	LEPIDOPTERA: Gracillariidae
Maruca testulalis (Geyer)	bean pod borer	LEPIDOPTERA: Pyralidae
Matsucoccus resinosae Bean & Godwin	red pine scale	HOMOPTERA: Margarodidae
Mayetiola destructor (Say)	Hessian fly	DIPTERA: Cecidomyiidae
Megachile concinna Smith	pale leafcutting bee	HYMENOPTERA: Megachilidae
Megachile rotundata (Fabricius)	alfalfa leafcutting bee	HYMENOPTERA: Megachilidae
Megacyllene caryae (Gahan)	painted hickory borer	COLEOPTERA: Cerambycidae
Megacyllene robiniae (Forster)	locust borer	COLEOPTERA: Cerambycidae
Megalopyge opercularis (J.E. Smith)	puss caterpillar	LEPIDOPTERA: Megalopygidae
Megninia cubitalis (Mégnin)	feather mite	ACARI: Analgidae
Melanaphis sacchari (Zehntner)	sugarcane aphid	HOMOPTERA: Aphididae
Melanaspis bromiliae (Leonardi)	brown pineapple scale	HOMOPTERA: Diaspididae
Melanaspis obscura (Comstock)	obscure scale	HOMOPTERA: Diaspididae
Melanaspis tenebricosa (Comstock)	gloomy scale	HOMOPTERA: Diaspididae
Melanchra picta (Harris)	zebra caterpillar	LEPIDOPTERA: Noctuidae
Melanocallis caryaefoliae (Davis)	black pecan aphid	HOMOPTERA: Aphididae
Melanophila californica Van Dyke	California flatheaded borer	COLEOPTERA: Buprestidae
Melanophila consputa LeConte	charcoal beetle	COLEOPTERA: Buprestidae
Melanophila drummondi (Kirby)	flatheaded fir borer	COLEOPTERA: Buprestidae
Melanophila fulvoguttata (Harris)	hemlock borer	COLEOPTERA: Buprestidae
Melanoplus bivittatus (Say)	twostriped grasshopper	ORTHOPTERA: Acrididae
Melanoplus devastator Scudder	devastating grasshopper	ORTHOPTERA: Acrididae
Melanoplus differentialis (Thomas)	differential grasshopper	ORTHOPTERA: Acrididae
Melanoplus femurrubrum (De Geer)	redlegged grasshopper	ORTHOPTERA: Acrididae

Melanoplus packardii Scudder	Packard grasshopper	ORTHOPTERA: Acrididae
Melanoplus rugglesi Gurney	Nevada sage grasshopper	ORTHOPTERA: Acrididae
Melanoplus sanguinipes (Fabricius)	migratory grasshopper	ORTHOPTERA: Acrididae
Melanoplus spretus (Walsh)	Rocky Mountain grasshopper	ORTHOPTERA: Acrididae
Melanotus longulus oregonensis (LeConte)	Oregon wireworm	COLEOPTERA: Elateridae
Melanozosteria soror (Brunner)	whitemargined cockroach	BLATTODEA: Blattidae
Melitara dentata (Grote)	blue cactus borer	LEPIDOPTERA: Pyralidae
Melittia calabaza Duckworth & Eichlin	southwestern squash vine borer	LEPIDOPTERA: Sesiidae
Melittia cucurbitae (Harris)	squash vine borer	LEPIDOPTERA: Sesiidae
Melittomma sericeum (Harris)	chestnut timberworm	COLEOPTERA: Lymexylidae
Melophagus ovinus (Linnaeus)	sheep ked	DIPTERA: Hippoboscidae
Menacanthus stramineus (Nitzsch)	chicken body louse	MALLOPHAGA: Menoponidae
Menopon gallinae (Linnaeus)	shaft louse	MALLOPHAGA: Menoponidae
Merhynchites bicolor (Fabricius)	rose curculio	COLEOPTERA: Curculionidae
Merodon equestris (Fabricius)	narcissus bulb fly	DIPTERA: Syrphidae
Meromyza americana Fitch	wheat stem maggot	DIPTERA: Chloropidae
Mesolecanium nigrofasciatum (Pergande)	terrapin scale	HOMOPTERA: Coccidae
Metamasius hemipterus hemipterus (Linnaeus)	West Indian cane weevil	COLEOPTERA: Curculionidae
Metamasius hemipterus sericeus (Olivier)	silky cane weevil	COLEOPTERA: Curculionidae
Metamasius ritchiei Marshall	pineapple weevil	COLEOPTERA: Curculionidae
Metrioidea brunneus (Crotch)	corn silk beetle	COLEOPTERA: Chrysomelidae
Metriona bicolor (Fabricius)	golden tortoise beetle	COLEOPTERA: Chrysomelidae
Mezium americanum (Laporte)	American spider beetle	COLEOPTERA: Ptinidae
Microcentrum retinerve (Burmeister)	angularwinged katydid	ORTHOPTERA: Tettigoniidae
Microcentrum rhombifolium (Saussure)	broadwinged katydid	ORTHOPTERA: Tettigoniidae
Microcephalothrips abdominalis (D.L. Crawford)	composite thrips	THYSANOPTERA: Thripidae
Microlarinus lareynii (Jacquelin du Val)	puncturevine seed weevil	COLEOPTERA: Curculionidae
Microlarinus lypriformis (Wollaston)	puncturevine stem weevil	COLEOPTERA: Curculionidae
Micromyzus violae (Pergande)	violet aphid	HOMOPTERA: Aphididae
Microtheca ochroloma Stål	yellowmargined leaf beetle	COLEOPTERA: Chrysomelidae
Milax gagates (Draparnaud)	greenhouse slug	STYLOMMATOPHORA: Limacidae
Mimoschinia rufofascialis (Stephens)	barberpole caterpillar	LEPIDOPTERA: Pyralidae
Mindarus abietinus Koch	balsam twig aphid	HOMOPTERA: Aphididae
Monarthropalpus flavus (Schrank)	boxwood leafminer	DIPTERA: Cecidomyiidae
Monellia caryella (Fitch)	blackmargined aphid	HOMOPTERA: Aphididae
Monelliopsis pecanis Bissell	yellow pecan aphid	HOMOPTERA: Aphididae
Monocesta coryli (Say)	larger elm leaf beetle	COLEOPTERA: Chrysomelidae
Monochamus marmorator Kirby	balsam fir sawyer	COLEOPTERA: Cerambycidae

Monochamus mutator LeConte	spotted pine sawyer	COLEOPTERA: Cerambycidae
Monochamus notatus (Drury)	northeastern sawyer	COLEOPTERA: Cerambycidae
Monochamus scutellatus (Say)	whitespotted sawyer	COLEOPTERA: Cerambycidae
Monochamus scutellatus oregonensis (LeConte)	Oregon fir sawyer	COLEOPTERA: Cerambycidae
Monochamus titillator (Fabricius)	southern pine sawyer	COLEOPTERA: Cerambycidae
Monochroa fragariae (Busck)	strawberry crownminer	LEPIDOPTERA: Gelechiidae
Monomorium minimum (Buckley)	little black ant	HYMENOPTERA: Formicidae
Monomorium pharaonis (Linnaeus)	Pharaoh ant	HYMENOPTERA: Formicidae
Mononychus vulpeculus (Fabricius)	iris weevil	COLEOPTERA: Curculionidae
Monophadnoides geniculatus (Hartig)	raspberry sawfly	HYMENOPTERA: Tenthredinidae
Monoptilota pergratialis (Hulst)	limabean vine borer	LEPIDOPTERA: Pyralidae
Mordvilkoja vagabunda (Walsh)	poplar vagabond apid	HOMOPTERA: Aphididae
Murgantia histrionica (Hahn)	harlequin bug	HETEROPTERA: Pentatomidae
Musca autumnalis De Geer	face fly	DIPTERA: Muscidae
Musca domestica Linnaeus	house fly	DIPTERA: Muscidae
Musca domestica vicina Macquart	oriental house fly	DIPTERA: Muscidae
Muscina stabulans (Fallén)	false stable fly	DIPTERA: Muscidae
Mycetophagus quadriguttatus P. Müller	spotted hairy fungus beetle	COLEOPTERA: Mycetophagidae
Myndus crudus Van Duzee	American palm cixiid	HOMOPTERA: Cixiidae
Myzocallis coryli (Goetze)	filbert aphid	HOMOPTERA: Aphididae
Myzus ascalonicus Doncaster	shallot aphid	HOMOPTERA: Aphididae
Myzus cerasi (Fabricius)	black cherry aphid	HOMOPTERA: Aphididae
Myzus ligustri (Mosley)	privet aphid	HOMOPTERA: Aphididae
Myzus nicotianae Blackman	tobacco aphid	HOMOPTERA: Aphididae
Myzus ornatus Laing	ornate aphid	HOMOPTERA: Aphididae
Myzus persicae (Sulzer)	green peach aphid	HOMOPTERA: Aphididae

N

Nabis alternatus Parshley	western damsel bug	HETEROPTERA: Nabidae
Nabis americoferus Carayon	common damsel bug	HETEROPTERA: Nabidae
Nabis blackburni White	Blackburn damsel bug	HETEROPTERA: Nabidae
Nabis capsiformis Germar	pale damsel bug	HETEROPTERA: Nabidae
Nacerdes melanura (Linnaeus)	wharf borer	COLEOPTERA: Oedemeridae
Nasonovia lactucae (Linnaeus)	sow thistle aphid	HOMOPTERA: Aphididae
Nauphoeta cinerea (Olivier)	cinereous cockroach	BLATTODEA: Blaberidae

Neacoryphus bicrucis (Say)	whitecrossed seed bug	HETEROPTERA: Lygaeidae
Nearctaphis bakeri (Cowen)	clover aphid	HOMOPTERA: Aphididae
Necrobia ruficollis (Fabricius)	redshouldered ham beetle	COLEOPTERA: Cleridae
Necrobia rufipes (De Geer)	redlegged ham beetle	COLEOPTERA: Cleridae
Nemapogon granella (Linnaeus)	European grain moth	LEPIDOPTERA: Tineidae
Nematocampa limbata (Haworth)	filament bearer	LEPIDOPTERA: Geometridae
Nematus ribesii (Scopoli)	imported currantworm	HYMENOPTERA: Tenthredinidae
Nematus ventralis Say	willow sawfly	HYMENOPTERA: Tenthredinidae
Nemocestes incomptus (Horn)	woods weevil	COLEOPTERA: Curculionidae
Neoceruraphis viburnicola (Gillette)	snowball aphid	HOMOPTERA: Aphididae
Neochlamisus cribripennis (LeConte)	blueberry case beetle	COLEOPTERA: Chrysomelidae
Neoclytus acuminatus (Fabricius)	redheaded ash borer	COLEOPTERA: Cerambycidae
Neocurtilla hexadactyla (Perty)	northern mole cricket	ORTHOPTERA: Gryllotalpidae
Neodecadarachis flavistriata (Walsingham)	sugarcane bud moth	LEPIDOPTERA: Tineidae
Neodiprion abietis (Harris)	balsam fir sawfly	HYMENOPTERA: Diprionidae
Neodiprion burkei Middleton	lodgepole sawfly	HYMENOPTERA: Diprionidae
Neodiprion dubiosus Schedl	brownheaded jack pine sawfly	HYMENOPTERA: Diprionidae
Neodiprion excitans Rohwer	blackheaded pine sawfly	HYMENOPTERA: Diprionidae
Neodiprion lecontei (Fitch)	redheaded pine sawfly	HYMENOPTERA: Diprionidae
Neodiprion merkeli Ross	slash pine sawfly	HYMENOPTERA: Diprionidae
Neodiprion nanulus nanulus Schedl	red pine sawfly	HYMENOPTERA: Diprionidae
Neodiprion pinetum (Norton)	white pine sawfly	HYMENOPTERA: Diprionidae
Neodiprion pratti banksianae Rohwer	jack pine sawfly	HYMENOPTERA: Diprionidae
Neodiprion pratti pratti (Dyar)	Virginia pine sawfly	HYMENOPTERA: Diprionidae
Neodiprion rugifrons Middleton	redheaded jack pine sawfly	HYMENOPTERA: Diprionidae
Neodiprion sertifer (Geoffroy)	European pine sawfly	HYMENOPTERA: Diprionidae
Neodiprion swainei Middleton	Swaine jack pine sawfly	HYMENOPTERA: Diprionidae
Neodiprion taedae linearis Ross	loblolly pine sawfly	HYMENOPTERA: Diprionidae
Neodiprion taedae taedae Ross	spotted loblolly pine sawfly	HYMENOPTERA: Diprionidae
Neodiprion tsugae Middleton	hemlock sawfly	HYMENOPTERA: Diprionidae
Neogalea sunia (Guenée)	lantana stick caterpillar	LEPIDOPTERA: Noctuidae
Neolasioptera murtfeldtiana (Felt)	sunflower seed midge	DIPTERA: Cecidomyiidae
Neolecanium cornuparvum (Thro)	magnolia scale	HOMOPTERA: Coccidae
Neomyzus circumflexus (Buckton)	crescentmarked lily aphid	HOMOPTERA: Aphididae
Neophasia menapia (Felder & Felder)	pine butterfly	LEPIDOPTERA: Pieridae
Neophilaenus lineatus (Linnaeus)	lined spittlebug	HOMOPTERA: Cercopidae
Neophyllaphis araucariae Takahashi	araucaria aphid	HOMOPTERA: Aphididae
Neoschoengastia americana (Hirst)	turkey chigger	ACARI: Trombiculidae

Neostylopyga rhombifolia (Stoll)	harlequin cockroach	BLATTODEA: Blattidae
Neotermes connexus Snyder	forest tree termite	ISOPTERA: Kalotermitidae
Neotoxoptera formosana (Takahashi)	onion aphid	HOMOPTERA: Aphididae
Nephelodes minians Guenée	bronzed cutworm	LEPIDOPTERA: Noctuidae
Nephopterix subcaesiella (Clemens)	locust leafroller	LEPIDOPTERA: Pyralidae
Nephotettix nigropictus (Stål)	rice leafhopper	HOMOPTERA: Cicadellidae
Nepytia canosaria (Walker)	false hemlock looper	LEPIDOPTERA: Geometridae
Nepytia phantasmaria (Strecker)	phantom hemlock looper	LEPIDOPTERA: Geometridae
Nepytia semiclusaria (Walker)	pine conelet looper	LEPIDOPTERA: Geometridae
Nesogonia blackburni (McLachlan)	Blackburn dragonfly	ODONATA: Libellulidae
Neurocolpus nubilus (Say)	clouded plant bug	HETEROPTERA: Miridae
Neurotoma inconspicua (Norton)	plum webspinning sawfly	HYMENOPTERA: Pamphiliidae
Nezara viridula (Linnaeus)	southern green stink bug	HETEROPTERA: Pentatomidae
Niditinea spretella (Dennis & Schiffermüller)	poultry house moth	LEPIDOPTERA: Tineidae
Nilotaspis halli (Green)	Hall scale	HOMOPTERA: Diaspididae
Nipaecoccus nipae (Maskell)	coconut mealybug	HOMOPTERA: Pseudococcidae
Nipaecoccus viridis (Newstead)	hibiscus mealybug	HOMOPTERA: Pseudococcidae
Niptus hololeucus (Faldermann)	golden spider beetle	COLEOPTERA: Ptinidae
Nodonota puncticollis (Say)	rose leaf beetle	COLEOPTERA: Chrysomelidae
Nola sorghiella Riley	sorghum webworm	LEPIDOPTERA: Noctuidae
Nomia melanderi Cockerell	alkali bee	HYMENOPTERA: Halictidae
Nomius pygameus (Dejean)	stink beetle	COLEOPTERA: Carabidae
Nosopsyllus fasciatus (Bosc)	northern rat flea	SIPHONAPTERA: Ceratophyllidae
Nuculaspis californica (Coleman)	black pineleaf scale	HOMOPTERA: Diaspididae
Nymphalis antiopa (Linnaeus)	mourningcloak butterfly	LEPIDOPTERA: Nymphalidae
Nymphalis californica (Boisduval)	California tortoiseshell	LEPIDOPTERA: Nymphalidae
Nysius caledoniae Distant	Caledonia seed bug	HETEROPTERA: Lygaeidae
Nysius raphanus Howard	false chinch bug	HETEROPTERA: Lygaeidae
Nysius spp.	seed bugs	HETEROPTERA: Lygaeidae

O

Oberea bimaculata (Olivier)	raspberry cane borer	COLEOPTERA: Cerambycidae
Oberea tripunctata (Swederus)	dogwood twig borer	COLEOPTERA: Cerambycidae
Obrussa ochrefasciella (Chambers)	hard maple budminer	LEPIDOPTERA: Nepticulidae
Ochetomyrmex auropunctatus (Roger)	little fire ant	HYMENOPTERA: Formicidae

Octotoma scabripennis Guérin-Méneville	lantana leaf beetle	COLEOPTERA: Chrysomelidae
Odontota dorsalis (Thunberg)	locust leafminer	COLEOPTERA: Chrysomelidae
Odontotaenius disjunctus (Illiger)	horned passalus	COLEOPTERA: Passalidae
Oebalus pugnax (Fabricius)	rice stink bug	HETEROPTERA: Pentatomidae
Oecanthus fultoni Walker	snowy tree cricket	ORTHOPTERA: Gryllidae
Oecanthus nigricornis Walker	blackhorned tree cricket	ORTHOPTERA: Gryllidae
Oecanthus quadripunctatus Beutenmüller	fourspotted tree cricket	ORTHOPTERA: Gryllidae
Oeciacus vicarius Horvath	swallow bug	HETEROPTERA: Cimicidae
Oestrus ovis Linnaeus	sheep bot fly	DIPTERA: Oestridae
Olethreutes permundana (Clemens)	raspberry leafroller	LEPIDOPTERA: Tortricidae
Olfersia spinifera (Leach)	frigate bird fly	DIPTERA: Hippoboscidae
Oligia fractilinea (Grote)	lined stalk borer	LEPIDOPTERA: Noctuidae
Oligonychus coniferarum (McGregor)	conifer spider mite	ACARI: Tetranychidae
Oligonychus ilicis (McGregor)	southern red mite	ACARI: Tetranychidae
Oligonychus indicus (Hirst)	sugarcane leaf mite	ACARI: Tetranychidae
Oligonychus mangiferus (Rahman & Sapra)	mango spider mite	ACARI: Tetranychidae
Oligonychus pratensis (Banks)	Banks grass mite	ACARI: Tetranychidae
Oligonychus punicae (Hirst)	avocado brown mite	ACARI: Tetranychidae
Oligonychus ununguis (Jacobi)	spruce spider mite	ACARI: Tetranychidae
Oligonychus yothersi (McGregor)	avocado red mite	ACARI: Tetranychidae
Oligotoma saundersii (Westwood)	Saunders embiid	EMBIIDINA: Oligotomidae
Oligotrophus betheli Felt	juniper tip midge	DIPTERA: Cecidomyiidae
Omphisa anastomosalis (Guenée)	sweetpotato vine borer	LEPIDOPTERA: Pyralidae
Oncideres cingulata (Say)	twig girdler	COLEOPTERA: Cerambycidae
Oncocephalus pacificus (Kirkaldy)	Pacific kissing bug	HETEROPTERA: Reduviidae
Oncopeltus fasciatus (Dallas)	large milkweed bug	HETEROPTERA: Lygaeidae
Onthophagus gazella Fabricius	brown dung beetle	COLEOPTERA: Scarabaeidae
Operophtera bruceata (Hulst)	Bruce spanworm	LEPIDOPTERA: Geometridae
Operophtera brumata (Linnaeus)	winter moth	LEPIDOPTERA: Geometridae
Ophiomyia lantanae (Froggatt)	lantana seed fly	DIPTERA: Agromyzidae
Ophiomyia phaseoli (Tryon)	bean fly	DIPTERA: Agromyzidae
Ophiomyia simplex (Loew)	asparagus miner	DIPTERA: Agromyzidae
Opius longicaudatus Ashmead	longtailed fruit fly parasite	HYMENOPTERA: Braconidae
Opsius stactogalus Fieber	tamarix leafhopper	HOMOPTERA: Cicadellidae
Orchidophilus peregrinator Buchanan	lesser orchid weevil	COLEOPTERA: Curculionidae
Orcus chalybeus (Boisduval)	steelblue lady beetle	COLEOPTERA: Coccinellidae
Orgyia antiqua (Linnaeus)	rusty tussock moth	LEPIDOPTERA: Lymantriidae
Orgyia leucostigma (J.E. Smith)	whitemarked tussock moth	LEPIDOPTERA: Lymantriidae

Orgyia pseudotsugata (McDunnough)	Douglas-fir tussock moth	LEPIDOPTERA: Lymantriidae
Orgyia vetusta (Boisduval)	western tussock moth	LEPIDOPTERA: Lymantriidae
Orius insidiosus (Say)	insidious flower bug	HETEROPTERA: Anthocoridae
Orius tristicolor (White)	minute pirate bug	HETEROPTERA: Anthocoridae
Ornithodoros turicata (Dugès)	relapsing fever tick	ACARI: Argasidae
Ornithonyssus bacoti (Hirst)	tropical rat mite	ACARI: Macronyssidae
Ornithonyssus bursa (Berlese)	tropical fowl mite	ACARI: Macronyssidae
Ornithonyssus sylviarum (Canestrini & Fanzago)	northern fowl mite	ACARI: Macronyssidae
Orthezia insignis Browne	greenhouse orthezia	HOMOPTERA: Ortheziidae
Orthodera burmeisteri Wood-Mason	Burmeister mantid	MANTODEA: Mantidae
Orthorhinus klugi Boheman	immigrant acacia weevil	COLEOPTERA: Curculionidae
Oryzaephilus mercator (Fauvel)	merchant grain beetle	COLEOPTERA: Cucujidae
Oryzaephilus surinamensis (Linnaeus)	sawtoothed grain beetle	COLEOPTERA: Cucujidae
Oscinella frit (Linnaeus)	frit fly	DIPTERA: Chloropidae
Ostrinia nubilalis (Hübner)	European corn borer	LEPIDOPTERA: Pyralidae
Ostrinia obumbratalis (Lederer)	smartweed borer	LEPIDOPTERA: Pyralidae
Otiorhynchus cribricollis Gyllenhal	cribrate weevil	COLEOPTERA: Curculionidae
Otiorhynchus ligustici (Linnaeus)	alfalfa snout beetle	COLEOPTERA: Curculionidae
Otiorhynchus ovatus (Linnaeus)	strawberry root weevil	COLEOPTERA: Curculionidae
Otiorhynchus sulcatus (Fabricius)	black vine weevil	COLEOPTERA: Curculionidae
Otobius megnini (Dugès)	ear tick	ACARI: Argasidae
Oulema melanopus (Linnaeus)	cereal leaf beetle	COLEOPTERA: Chrysomelidae
Ovatus crataegarius (Walker)	mint aphid	HOMOPTERA: Aphididae
Oxidus gracilis Koch	garden millipede	POLYDESMIDA: Paradoxoxomatidae
Oxya japonica (Thunberg)	Japanese grasshopper	ORTHOPTERA: Acrididae
Oxylipeurus polytrapezius (Burmeister)	slender turkey louse	MALLOPHAGA: Philopteridae
Oxyopes salticus Hentz	striped lynx spider	ARANEAE: Oxyopidae

P

Pachnaeus litus (Germar)	citrus root weevil	COLEOPTERA: Curculionidae
Pachodynerus nasidens (Latreille)	keyhole wasp	HYMENOPTERA: Vespidae
Pachylobius picivorus (Germar)	pitch-eating weevil	COLEOPTERA: Curculionidae
Pachynematus extensicornis (Norton)	grass sawfly	HYMENOPTERA: Tenthredinidae
Pachypsylla celtidismamma (Fletcher)	hackberry nipplegall maker	HOMOPTERA: Psyllidae
Paleacrita vernata (Peck)	spring cankerworm	LEPIDOPTERA: Geometridae

Palmicultor palmarum (Ehrhorn)	palm mealybug	HOMOPTERA: Pseudococcidae
Palorus ratzeburgi (Wissmann)	smalleyed flour beetle	COLEOPTERA: Tenebrionidae
Palorus subdepressus (Wollaston)	depressed flour beetle	COLEOPTERA: Tenebrionidae
Panchlora nivea (Linnaeus)	Cuban cockroach	BLATTODEA: Blaberidae
Pandemis limitata (Robinson)	threelined leafroller	LEPIDOPTERA: Tortricidae
Panonychus citri (McGregor)	citrus red mite	ACARI: Tetranychidae
Panonychus ulmi (Koch)	European red mite	ACARI: Tetranychidae
Pantographa limata Grote & Robinson	basswood leafroller	LEPIDOPTERA: Pyralidae
Papaipema cataphracta (Grote)	burdock borer	LEPIDOPTERA: Noctuidae
Papaipema nebris (Guenée)	stalk borer	LEPIDOPTERA: Noctuidae
Papaipema purpurifascia (Grote & Robinson)	columbine borer	LEPIDOPTERA: Noctuidae
Papilio andraemon bonhotei Sharpe	Bahaman swallowtail	LEPIDOPTERA: Papilionidae
Papilio aristodemus ponceanus Schaus	Schaus swallowtail	LEPIDOPTERA: Papilionidae
Papilio cresphontes Cramer	orangedog	LEPIDOPTERA: Papilionidae
Papilio glaucus Linnaeus	tiger swallowtail	LEPIDOPTERA: Papilionidae
Papilio polyxenes asterius Stoll	black swallowtail[38]	LEPIDOPTERA: Papilionidae
Papilio troilus Linnaeus	spicebush swallowtail	LEPIDOPTERA: Papilionidae
Papilio xuthus Linnaeus	citrus swallowtail	LEPIDOPTERA: Papilionidae
Paraclemensia acerifoliella (Fitch)	maple leafcutter	LEPIDOPTERA: Incurvariidae
Paradiplosis tumifex Gagné	balsam gall midge	DIPTERA: Cecidomyiidae
Paraleyrodes perseae (Quaintance)	plumeria whitefly	HOMOPTERA: Aleyrodidae
Paranthrene asilipennis (Boisduval)	oak clearwing moth	LEPIDOPTERA: Sesiidae
Paranthrene robiniae (Hy. Edwards)	western poplar clearwing	LEPIDOPTERA: Sesiidae
Parapediasia teterrella (Zincken)	bluegrass webworm	LEPIDOPTERA: Pyralidae
Paraphlepsius irroratus (Say)	brown speckled leafhopper	HOMOPTERA: Cicadellidae
Paraprociphilus tessellatus (Fitch)	woolly alder aphid	HOMOPTERA: Aphididae
Parasa indetermina (Boisduval)	stinging rose caterpillar	LEPIDOPTERA: Limacodidae
Parasaissetra nigra (Nietner)	nigra scale	HOMOPTERA: Coccidae
Paratimia conicola Fisher	roundheaded cone borer	COLEOPTERA: Cerambycidae
Paratrechina longicornis (Latreille)	crazy ant	HYMENOPTERA: Formicidae
Paratrioza cockerelli (Sulc)	potato psyllid[39]	HOMOPTERA: Psyllidae
Paravespula germanica (Linnaeus)	German yellowjacket	HYMENOPTERA: Vespidae
Paria fragariae Wilcox	strawberry rootworm	COLEOPTERA: Chrysomelidae
Parlatoreopsis chinensis (Marlatt)	Chinese obscure scale	HOMOPTERA: Diaspididae

---

[38]Immature called parsleyworm.
[39]Also called tomato psyllid.

Parlatoria blanchardi (Targioni-Tozzetti)	parlatoria date scale	HOMOPTERA: Diaspididae
Parlatoria oleae (Colvée)	olive scale	HOMOPTERA: Diaspididae
Parlatoria pergandii Comstock	chaff scale	HOMOPTERA: Diaspididae
Parthenolecanium corni (Bouché)	European fruit lecanium	HOMOPTERA: Coccidae
Parthenolecanium fletcheri (Cockerell)	Fletcher scale	HOMOPTERA: Coccidae
Parthenolecanium persicae (Fabricius)	European peach scale	HOMOPTERA: Coccidae
Parthenolecanium quercifex (Fitch)	oak lecanium	HOMOPTERA: Coccidae
Pealius azaleae (Baker & Moles)	azalea whitefly	HOMOPTERA: Aleyrodidae
Pectinophora gossypiella (Saunders)	pink bollworm	LEPIDOPTERA: Gelechiidae
Pediculus humanus capitis De Geer	head louse	ANOPLURA: Pediculidae
Pediculus humanus humanus Linnaeus	body louse	ANOPLURA: Pediculidae
Pegomya betae Curtis	beet leafminer	DIPTERA: Anthomyiidae
Pegomya hyoscyami (Panzer)	spinach leafminer	DIPTERA: Anthomyiidae
Pegomya rubivora (Coquillett)	raspberry cane maggot	DIPTERA: Anthomyiidae
Pemphigus bursarius (Linnaeus)	lettuce root aphid	HOMOPTERA: Aphididae
Pemphigus populiramulorum Riley	poplar twig gall aphid	HOMOPTERA: Aphididae
Pemphigus populitransversus Riley	poplar petiolegall aphid	HOMOPTERA: Aphididae
Pemphigus populivenae Fitch	sugarbeet root aphid	HOMOPTERA: Aphididae
Penestrangania robusta (Uhler)	robust leafhopper	HOMOPTERA: Cicadellidae
Penicillaria jocosatrix Guenée	mango shoot caterpillar	LEPIDOPTERA: Noctuidae
Pennisetia marginata (Harris)	raspberry crown borer	LEPIDOPTERA: Sesiidae
Pentalonia nigronervosa Coquerel	banana aphid	HOMOPTERA: Aphididae
Penthaleus major (Dugès)	winter grain mite	ACARI: Eupodidae
Peranabrus scabricollis (Thomas)	coulee cricket	ORTHOPTERA: Tettigoniidae
Peregrinus maidis (Ashmead)	corn delphacid	HOMOPTERA: Delphacidae
Pericyma cruegeri (Butler)	poinciana looper	LEPIDOPTERA: Noctuidae
Peridroma saucia (Hübner)	variegated cutworm	LEPIDOPTERA: Noctuidae
Perillus bioculatus (Fabricius)	twospotted stink bug	HETEROPTERA: Pentatomidae
Periphyllus lyropictus (Kessler)	Norway maple aphid	HOMOPTERA: Aphididae
Periphyllus negundinis (Thomas)	boxelder aphid	HOMOPTERA: Aphididae
Periplaneta americana (Linnaeus)	American cockroach	BLATTODEA: Blattidae
Periplaneta australasiae (Fabricius)	Australian cockroach	BLATTODEA: Blattidae
Periplaneta brunnea Burmeister	brown cockroach	BLATTODEA: Blattidae
Periplaneta fuliginosa (Serville)	smokybrown cockroach	BLATTODEA: Blattidae
Perkinsiella saccharicida Kirkaldy	sugarcane delphacid	HOMOPTERA: Delphacidae
Petrobia latens (Müller)	brown wheat mite	ACARI: Tetranychidae
Petrova albicapitana (Busck)	northern pitch twig moth	LEPIDOPTERA: Tortricidae
Petrova comstockiana (Fernald)	pitch twig moth	LEPIDOPTERA: Tortricidae

Phaedon viridus (Melsheimer)	watercress leaf beetle	COLEOPTERA: Chrysomelidae
Phalacrus politus Melsheimer	smut beetle	COLEOPTERA: Phalacridae
Phanacis taraxaci (Ashmead)	dandelion gall wasp	HYMENOPTERA: Cynipidae
Phaneroptera furcifera Stål	Philippine katydid	ORTHOPTERA: Tettigoniidae
Pheidole megacephala (Fabricius)	bigheaded ant	HYMENOPTERA: Formicidae
Phenacoccus aceris (Signoret)	apple mealybug	HOMOPTERA: Pseudococcidae
Phenacoccus gossypii Townsend & Cockerell	Mexican mealybug	HOMOPTERA: Pseudococcidae
Phereoeca uterella Walsingham	household casebearer	LEPIDOPTERA: Tineidae
Philaenus spumarius (Linnaeus)	meadow spittlebug	HOMOPTERA: Cercopidae
Philodoria hauicola (Swezey)	hau leafminer	LEPIDOPTERA: Gracillariidae
Philodoria hibiscella (Swezey)	hibiscus leafminer	LEPIDOPTERA: Gracillariidae
Philodoria marginestrigata (Walsingham)	ilima leafminer	LEPIDOPTERA: Gracillariidae
Phloeosinus punctatus LeConte	western cedar bark beetle	COLEOPTERA: Scolytidae
Phloeotribus liminaris (Harris)	peach bark beetle	COLEOPTERA: Scolytidae
Phobetron pithecium (J.E. Smith)	hag moth	LEPIDOPTERA: Limacodidae
Phoenicococcus marlatti Cockerell	red date scale	HOMOPTERA: Phoenicococcidae
Phoracantha semipunctata (Fabricius)	eucalyptus longhorned borer	COLEOPTERA: Cerambycidae
Phormia regina (Meigen)	black blow fly	DIPTERA: Calliphoridae
Phorodon humuli (Schrank)	hop aphid	HOMOPTERA: Aphididae
Phryganidia californica Packard	California oakworm	LEPIDOPTERA: Dioptidae
Phthorimaea operculella (Zeller)	potato tuberworm	LEPIDOPTERA: Gelechiidae
Phyllobius intrusus Kôno	arborvitae weevil	COLEOPTERA: Curculionidae
Phyllocnistis meliacella Becker	mahogany leafminer	LEPIDOPTERA: Gracillariidae
Phyllocolpa bozemani (Cooley)	poplar leaffolding sawfly	HYMENOPTERA: Tenthredinidae
Phyllocoptes gracilis (Nalepa)	dryberry mite	ACARI: Eriophyidae
Phyllocoptruta oleivora (Ashmead)	citrus rust mite	ACARI: Eriophyidae
Phyllodesma americana (Harris)	lappet moth	LEPIDOPTERA: Lasiocampidae
Phyllonorycter blancardella (Fabricius)	spotted tentiform leafminer	LEPIDOPTERA: Gracillariidae
Phyllonorycter crataegella (Clemens)	apple blotch leafminer	LEPIDOPTERA: Gracillariidae
Phyllonorycter tremuloidiella (Braun)	aspen blotchminer	LEPIDOPTERA: Gracillariidae
Phyllotreta armoraciae (Koch)	horseradish flea beetle	COLEOPTERA: Chrysomelidae
Phyllotreta pusilla Horn	western black flea beetle	COLEOPTERA: Chrysomelidae
Phyllotreta ramosa (Crotch)	western striped flea beetle	COLEOPTERA: Chrysomelidae
Phyllotreta striolata (Fabricius)	striped flea beetle	COLEOPTERA: Chrysomelidae
Phylloxera devastatrix Pergande	pecan phylloxera	HOMOPTERA: Phylloxeridae
Phylloxera notabilis Pergande	pecan leaf phylloxera	HOMOPTERA: Phylloxeridae
Physokermes piceae (Schrank)	spruce bud scale	HOMOPTERA: Coccidae
Phytocoptella avellanae (Nalepa)	filbert bud mite	ACARI: Nalepellidae

Phytomyza ilicicola Loew	native holly leafminer	DIPTERA: Agromyzidae
Phytomyza ilicis Curtis	holly leafminer	DIPTERA: Agromyzidae
Phytomyza spp.	columbine leafminer complex[40]	DIPTERA: Agromyzidae
Phytomyza spp.	larkspur leafminer complex[41]	DIPTERA: Agromyzidae
Phytonemus pallidus (Banks)	cyclamen mite	ACARI: Tarsonemidae
Phytoptus pyri Pagenstecher	pearleaf blister mite	ACARI: Eriophyidae
Pieris rapae (Linnaeus)	imported cabbageworm	LEPIDOPTERA: Pieridae
Pikonema alaskensis (Rohwer)	yellowheaded spruce sawfly	HYMENOPTERA: Tenthredinidae
Pikonema dimmockii (Cresson)	greenheaded spruce sawfly	HYMENOPTERA: Tenthredinidae
Pilocrocis tripunctata (Fabricius)	sweetpotato leafroller	LEPIDOPTERA: Pyralidae
Pineus pini (Macquart)	Eurasian pine adelgid	HOMOPTERA: Adelgidae
Pineus pinifoliae (Fitch)	pine leaf adelgid	HOMOPTERA: Adelgidae
Pineus strobi (Hartig)	pine bark adelgid	HOMOPTERA: Adelgidae
Pinnaspis aspidistrae (Signoret)	fern scale	HOMOPTERA: Diaspididae
Piophila casei (Linnaeus)	cheese skipper	DIPTERA: Piophilidae
Pissodes nemorensis Germar	eastern pine weevil	COLEOPTERA: Curculionidae
Pissodes radiatae Hopkins	Monterey pine weevil	COLEOPTERA: Curculionidae
Pissodes schwarzi Hopkins	Yosemite bark weevil	COLEOPTERA: Curculionidae
Pissodes strobi (Peck)	Engelmann spruce weevil[42]	COLEOPTERA: Curculionidae
Pissodes terminalis Hopping	lodgepole terminal weevil	COLEOPTERA: Curculionidae
Placosternus crinicornis (Chevrolat)	kiawe roundheaded borer	COLEOPTERA: Cerambycidae
Plagiodera versicolora (Laicharting)	imported willow leaf beetle	COLEOPTERA: Chrysomelidae
Plagiohammus spinipennis Thomson	lantana cerambycid	COLEOPTERA: Cerambycidae
Plagiolepis alluaudi Emery	little yellow ant	HYMENOPTERA: Formicidae
Planococcus citri (Risso)	citrus mealybug	HOMOPTERA: Pseudococcidae
Plathypena scabra (Fabricius)	green cloverworm	LEPIDOPTERA: Noctuidae
Platyedra subcinerea (Haworth)	cotton stem moth	LEPIDOPTERA: Gelechiidae
Platylyus luridus (Reuter)	pine conelet bug	HETEROPTERA: Miridae
Platynota idaeusalis (Walker)	tufted apple bud moth	LEPIDOPTERA: Tortricidae
Platyptilia carduidactyla (Riley)	artichoke plume moth	LEPIDOPTERA: Pterophoridae
Platytetranychus multidigitali (Ewing)	honeylocust spider mite	ACARI: Tetranychidae
Plautia stali Scott	oriental stink bug	HETEROPTERA: Pentatomidae
Plectrodera scalator (Fabricius)	cottonwood borer	COLEOPTERA: Cerambycidae

---

[40]Includes *Phytomyza aquilegiana* Frost, *P. aquilegivora* Spencer, and *P. columbinae* Sehgal.
[41]Includes *Phytomza aconti* Hendel, *P. delphiniae* Frost, and *P. delphinivora* Spencer.
[42]Also called Sitka spruce weevil and white pine weevil.

Pleocoma spp.	rain beetles	COLEOPTERA: Scarabaeidae
Pleroneura brunneicornis Rohwer	balsam shootboring sawfly	HYMENOPTERA: Xyelidae
Plodia interpunctella (Hübner)	Indianmeal moth	LEPIDOPTERA: Pyralidae
Plutella xylostella (Linnaeus)	diamondback moth	LEPIDOPTERA: Plutellidae
Pnyxia scabiei (Hopkins)	potato scab gnat	DIPTERA: Sciaridae
Podapion gallicola Riley	pine gall weevil	COLEOPTERA: Curculionidae
Podisus maculiventris (Say)	spined soldier bug	HETEROPTERA: Pentatomidae
Podosesia aureocincta Purrington & Nielsen	banded ash clearwing	LEPIDOPTERA: Sesiidae
Podosesia syringae (Harris)	ash borer[43]	LEPIDOPTERA: Sesiidae
Poecilocapsus lineatus (Fabricius)	fourlined plant bug	HETEROPTERA: Miridae
Pogonomyrmex badius (Latreille)	Florida harvester ant	HYMENOPTERA: Formicidae
Pogonomyrmex barbatus (F. Smith)	red harvester ant	HYMENOPTERA: Formicidae
Pogonomyrmex californicus (Buckley)	California harvester ant	HYMENOPTERA: Formicidae
Pogonomyrmex maricopa Wheeler	Maricopa harvester ant	HYMENOPTERA: Formicidae
Pogonomyrmex occidentalis (Cresson)	western harvester ant	HYMENOPTERA: Formicidae
Pogonomyrmex rugosus Emery	rough harvester ant	HYMENOPTERA: Formicidae
Polididus armatissimus Stål	spiny assassin bug	HETEROPTERA: Reduviidae
Polistes fuscatus aurifer Saussure	golden paper wasp	HYMENOPTERA: Vespidae
Polistes macaensis (Fabricius)	Macao paper wasp	HYMENOPTERA: Vespidae
Pollenia rudis (Fabricius)	cluster fly	DIPTERA: Calliphoridae
Polydesma umbricola Boisduval	monkeypod moth	LEPIDOPTERA: Noctuidae
Polyphagotarsonemus latus (Banks)	broad mite	ACARI: Tarsonemidae
Polyphylla decemlineata (Say)	tenlined June beetle	COLEOPTERA: Scarabaeidae
Polyplax spinulosa (Burmeister)	spined rat louse	ANOPLURA: Hoplopleuridae
Pontania promixa (Lepeletier)	willow redgall sawfly	HYMENOPTERA: Tenthredinidae
Pontia protodice (Boisduval & LeConte)	southern cabbageworm	LEPIDOPTERA: Pieridae
Popillia japonica Newman	Japanese beetle	COLEOPTERA: Scarabaeidae
Prionoxystus macmurtrei (Guérin)	little carpenterworm	LEPIDOPTERA: Cossidae
Prionoxystus robiniae (Peck)	carpenterworm	LEPIDOPTERA: Cossidae
Prionus californicus Motschulsky	California prionus	COLEOPTERA: Cerambycidae
Prionus imbricornis (Linnaeus)	tilehorned prionus	COLEOPTERA: Cerambycidae
Prionus laticollis (Drury)	broadnecked root borer	COLEOPTERA: Cerambycidae
Pristiphora abbreviata (Hartig)	California pear sawfly	HYMENOPTERA: Tenthredinidae
Pristiphora erichsonii (Hartig)	larch sawfly	HYMENOPTERA: Tenthredinidae
Pristiphora geniculata (Hartig)	mountain-ash sawfly	HYMENOPTERA: Tenthredinidae

[43]Also called lilac borer.

Procambarus clarkii (Girard)	Louisiana red crayfish	DECAPODA: Cambaridae
Procecidochares utilis Stone	eupatorium gall fly	DIPTERA: Tephritidae
Prodiplosis citrulli (Felt)	cucurbit midge	DIPTERA: Cecidomyiidae
Prodiplosis vaccinii (Felt)	blueberry tip midge	DIPTERA: Cecidomyiidae
Prosapia bicincta (Say)	twolined spittlebug	HOMOPTERA: Cercopidae
Prostephanus truncatus (Horn)	larger grain borer	COLEOPTERA: Bostrichidae
Protaetia fusca (Herbst)	mango flower beetle	COLEOPTERA: Scarabaeidae
Protalebrella brasiliensis (Baker)	Brasilian leafhopper	HOMOPTERA: Cicadellidae
Proteoteras willingana (Kearfott)	boxelder twig borer	LEPIDOPTERA: Tortricidae
Protopulvinaria pyriformis (Cockerell)	pyriform scale	HOMOPTERA: Coccidae
Psedobryobia drummondi (Ewing)	creosotebush spider mite	ACARI: Tetranychidae
Pseudaletia unipuncta (Haworth)	armyworm	LEPIDOPTERA: Noctuidae
Pseudanthonomus validus Dietz	currant fruit weevil	COLEOPTERA: Curculionidae
Pseudaonidia duplex (Cockerell)	camphor scale	HOMOPTERA: Diaspididae
Pseudatomoscelis seriatus (Reuter)	cotton fleahopper	HETEROPTERA: Miridae
Pseudaulacaspis pentagona (Targioni-Tozzetti)	white peach scale	HOMOPTERA: Diaspididae
Pseudexentera mali Freeman	pale apple leafroller	LEPIDOPTERA: Tortricidae
Pseudococcus affinis (Maskell)	obscure mealybug	HOMOPTERA: Pseudococcidae
Pseudococcus calceolariae (Maskell)	citrophilus mealybug	HOMOPTERA: Pseudococcidae
Pseudococcus comstocki (Kuwana)	Comstock mealybug	HOMOPTERA: Pseudococcidae
Pseudococcus longispinus (Targioni-Tozzetti)	longtailed mealybug	HOMOPTERA: Pseudococcidae
Pseudococcus maritimus (Ehrhorn)	grape mealybug	HOMOPTERA: Pseudococcidae
Pseudogonatopus hospes Perkins	Chinese dryinid	HYMENOPTERA: Dryinidae
Pseudolynchia canariensis (Macquart)	pigeon fly	DIPTERA: Hippoboscidae
Pseudoplusia includens (Walker)	soybean looper	LEPIDOPTERA: Noctuidae
Psila rosae (Fabricius)	carrot rust fly	DIPTERA: Psilidae
Psoroptes equi (Raspail)	scab mite	ACARI: Psoroptidae
Psoroptes ovis (Hering)	sheep scab mite	ACARI: Psoroptidae
Psorosina hammondi (Riley)	appleleaf skeletonizer	LEPIDOPTERA: Pyralidae
Psylliodes punctulata Melsheimer	hop flea beetle	COLEOPTERA: Chrysomelidae
Pterophorus periscelidactylus Fitch	grape plume moth	LEPIDOPTERA: Pterophoridae
Pthirus pubis (Linnaeus)	crab louse	ANOPLURA: Pediculidae
Ptinus clavipes Panzer	brown spider beetle	COLEOPTERA: Ptinidae
Ptinus fur (Linnaeus)	whitemarked spider beetle	COLEOPTERA: Ptinidae
Ptinus ocellus Brown	Australian spider beetle	COLEOPTERA: Ptinidae
Ptinus villiger (Reitter)	hairy spider beetle	COLEOPTERA: Ptinidae
Pulex irritans (Linnaeus)	human flea	SIPHONAPTERA: Pulicidae
Pulvinaria amygdali Cockerell	cottony peach scale	HOMOPTERA: Coccidae

Pulvinaria innumerabilis (Rathvon)	cottony maple scale	HOMOPTERA: Coccidae
Pulvinaria mammeae Maskell	large cottony scale	HOMOPTERA: Coccidae
Pulvinaria psidii Maskell	green shield scale	HOMOPTERA: Coccidae
Puto sandini Washburn	spruce mealybug	HOMOPTERA: Pseudococcidae
Pycnoderes quadrimaculatus Guérin-Méneville	bean capsid	HETEROPTERA: Miridae
Pycnoscelus surinamensis (Linnaeus)	Surinam cockroach	BLATTODEA: Blaberidae
Pyemotes tritici (Lagrèze-Fossat & Montané)	straw itch mite	ACARI: Pyemotidae
Pyralis farinalis Linnaeus	meal moth	LEPIDOPTERA: Pyralidae
Pyroderces rileyi (Walsingham)	pink scavenger caterpillar	LEPIDOPTERA: Cosmopterigidae
Pyrrhalta cavicollis (LeConte)	cherry leaf beetle	COLEOPTERA: Chrysomelidae
Pyrrhalta decora carbo (LeConte)	Pacific willow leaf beetle	COLEOPTERA: Chrysomelidae
Pyrrhalta decora decora (Say)	gray willow leaf beetle	COLEOPTERA: Chrysomelidae
Pyrrhalta luteola (Müller)	elm leaf beetle	COLEOPTERA: Chrysomelidae
Pyrrharctia isabella (J.E. Smith)	banded woollybear	LEPIDOPTERA: Arctiidae

Q

Quadraspidiotus forbesi (Johnson)	Forbes scale	HOMOPTERA: Diaspididae
Quadraspidiotus juglandsregiae (Comstock)	walnut scale	HOMOPTERA: Diaspididae
Quadraspidiotus ostreaeformis (Curtis)	European fruit scale	HOMOPTERA: Diaspididae
Quadraspidiotus perniciosus (Comstock)	San Jose scale	HOMOPTERA: Diaspididae

R

Rabdophaga rigidae (Osten Sacken)	willow beaked-gall midge	DIPTERA: Cecidomyiidae
Recurvaria nanella (Denis & Schiffermüller)	lesser bud moth	LEPIDOPTERA: Gelechiidae
Reduvius personatus (Linnaeus)	masked hunter	HETEROPTERA: Reduviidae
Resseliella clavula (Beutenmüller)	dogwood clubgall midge	DIPTERA: Cecidomyiidae
Reticulitermes flavipes (Kollar)	eastern subterranean termite	ISOPTERA: Rhinotermitidae
Reticulitermes hesperus Banks	western subterranean termite	ISOPTERA: Rhinotermitidae
Rhabdopterus picipes (Olivier)	cranberry rootworm	COLEOPTERA: Chrysomelidae

Rhabdoscelus obscurus (Boisduval)	New Guinea sugarcane weevil	COLEOPTERA: Curculionidae
Rhagoletis cingulata (Loew)	cherry fruit fly[44]	DIPTERA: Tephritidae
Rhagoletis completa Cresson	walnut husk fly	DIPTERA: Tephritidae
Rhagoletis fausta (Osten Sacken)	black cherry fruit fly	DIPTERA: Tephritidae
Rhagoletis indifferens Curran	western cherry fruit fly	DIPTERA: Tephritidae
Rhagoletis mendax Curran	blueberry maggot	DIPTERA: Tephritidae
Rhagoletis pomonella (Walsh)	apple maggot	DIPTERA: Tephritidae
Rhinacloa forticornis Reuter	western plant bug	HETEROPTERA: Miridae
Rhinocapsus vanduzeei Uhler	azalea plant bug	HETEROPTERA: Miridae
Rhipicephalus sanguineus (Latreille)	brown dog tick	ACARI: Ixodidae
Rhizoecus falcifer Künckel d'Herculais	ground mealybug	HOMOPTERA: Pseudococcidae
Rhizoglyphus echinopus (Fumouze & Robin)	bulb mite	ACARI: Acaridae
Rhizotrogus (Amphimallon) majalis (Razoumowsky)	European chafer	COLEOPTERA: Scarabaeidae
Rhodobaenus quinquedecimpunctatus (Say)	cocklebur weevil	COLEOPTERA: Curculionidae
Rhopalomyia chrysanthemi (Ahlberg)	chrysanthemum gall midge	DIPTERA: Cecidomyiidae
Rhopalosiphum fitchii (Sanderson)	apple grain aphid	HOMOPTERA: Aphididae
Rhopalosiphum maidis (Fitch)	corn leaf aphid	HOMOPTERA: Aphididae
Rhopalosiphum nymphaeae (Linnaeus)	waterlily aphid	HOMOPTERA: Aphididae
Rhopalosiphum padi (Linnaeus)	bird cherry-oat aphid	HOMOPTERA: Aphididae
Rhopalosiphum rufiabdominalis (Sasaki)	rice root aphid	HOMOPTERA: Aphididae
Rhopobota naevana (Hübner)	blackheaded fireworm	LEPIDOPTERA: Tortricidae
Rhyacionia buoliana (Denis & Schiffermüller)	European pine shoot moth	LEPIDOPTERA: Tortricidae
Rhyacionia frustrana (Comstock)	Nantucket pine tip moth	LEPIDOPTERA: Tortricidae
Rhyacionia neomexicana (Dyar)	southwestern pine tip moth	LEPIDOPTERA: Tortricidae
Rhyacionia rigidana (Fernald)	pitch pine tip moth	LEPIDOPTERA: Tortricidae
Rhyacionia subtropica Miller	subtropical pine tip moth	LEPIDOPTERA: Tortricidae
Rhynchaenus pallicornis (Say)	apple flea weevil	COLEOPTERA: Curculionidae
Rhynchaenus rufipes (LeConte)	willow flea weevil	COLEOPTERA: Curculionidae
Rhyzobius ventralis (Erichson)	black lady beetle	COLEOPTERA: Coccinellidae
Rhyzopertha dominica (Fabricius)	lesser grain borer	COLEOPTERA: Bostrichidae
Ribautiana tenerrima (Herrich-Schäffer)	bramble leafhopper	HOMOPTERA: Cicadellidae
Rivellia quadrifasciata (Macquart)	soybean nodule fly	DIPTERA: Platystomatidae
Rodolia cardinalis (Mulsant)	vedalia	COLEOPTERA: Coccinellidae
Romalea guttata (Houttuyn)	eastern lubber grasshopper	ORTHOPTERA: Acrididae
Rosalia funebris Motschulsky	banded alder borer	COLEOPTERA: Cerambycidae

---

[44]Immature called cherry maggot.

Sabulodes aegrotata (Guenée)	omnivorous looper	LEPIDOPTERA: Geometridae
Saccharicoccus sacchari (Cockerell)	pink sugarcane mealybug	HOMOPTERA: Pseudococcidae
Saissetia coffeae (Walker)	hemispherical scale	HOMOPTERA: Coccidae
Saissetia miranda (Cockerell & Parrott)	Mexican black scale	HOMOPTERA: Coccidae
Saissetia neglecta De Lotto	Caribbean black scale	HOMOPTERA: Coccidae
Saissetia oleae (Olivier)	black scale	HOMOPTERA: Coccidae
Salbia haemorrhoidalis Guenée	lantana leaftier	LEPIDOPTERA: Pyralidae
Samia cynthia (Drury)	cynthia moth	LEPIDOPTERA: Saturniidae
Sannina uroceriformis Walker	persimmon borer	LEPIDOPTERA: Sesiidae
Saperda calcarata Say	poplar borer	COLEOPTERA: Cerambycidae
Saperda candida Fabricius	roundheaded appletree borer	COLEOPTERA: Cerambycidae
Saperda candida bipunctata Hopping	Saskatoon borer	COLEOPTERA: Cerambycidae
Saperda tridentata Olivier	elm borer	COLEOPTERA: Cerambycidae
Saperda vestita Say	linden borer	COLEOPTERA: Cerambycidae
Sarcoptes bovis Robin	cattle itch mite	ACARI: Sarcoptidae
Sarcoptes scabiei (De Geer)	itch mite	ACARI: Sarcoptidae
Scadra rufidens Stål	redmargined assassin bug	HETEROPTERA: Reduviidae
Scaphoideus luteolus Van Duzee	whitebanded elm leafhopper	HOMOPTERA: Cicadellidae
Scaphytopius loricatus (Van Duzee)	yellowfaced leafhopper	HOMOPTERA: Cicadellidae
Scapteriscus abbreviatus Scudder	shortwinged mole cricket	ORTHOPTERA: Gryllotalpidae
Scapteriscus acletus Rehn & Hebard	southern mole cricket	ORTHOPTERA: Gryllotalpidae
Scapteriscus didactylus (Latreille)	changa	ORTHOPTERA: Gryllotalpidae
Scapteriscus vicinus Scudder	tawny mole cricket	ORTHOPTERA: Gryllotalpidae
Schistocerca americana (Drury)	American grasshopper	ORTHOPTERA: Acrididae
Schistocerca nitens nitens (Thunberg)	vagrant grasshopper	ORTHOPTERA: Acrididae
Schizaphis graminum (Rondani)	greenbug	HOMOPTERA: Aphididae
Schizotetranychus asparagi (Oudemans)	asparagus spider mite	ACARI: Tetranychidae
Schizotetranychus celarius (Banks)	bamboo spider mite	ACARI: Tetranychidae
Schizura concinna (J.E. Smith)	redhumped caterpillar	LEPIDOPTERA: Notodontidae
Schizura unicornis (J.E. Smith)	unicorn caterpillar	LEPIDOPTERA: Notodontidae
Schreckensteinia festaliella (Hübner)	blackberry skeletonizer	LEPIDOPTERA: Heliodinidae
Sciopithes obscurus Horn	obscure root weevil	COLEOPTERA: Curculionidae
Scirtothrips citri (Moulton)	citrus thrips	THYSANOPTERA: Thripidae
Scleroracus vaccinii (Van Duzee)	bluntnosed cranberry leafhopper	HOMOPTERA: Cicadellidae
Scobicia declivis (LeConte)	leadcable borer	COLEOPTERA: Bostrichidae

Scolothrips sexmaculatus (Pergande)	sixspotted thrips	THYSANOPTERA: Thripidae
Scolytus mali (Bechstein)	larger shothole borer	COLEOPTERA: Scolytidae
Scolytus multistriatus (Marsham)	smaller European elm bark beetle	COLEOPTERA: Scolytidae
Scolytus muticus Say	hackberry engraver	COLEOPTERA: Scolytidae
Scolytus quadrispinosus Say	hickory bark beetle	COLEOPTERA: Scolytidae
Scolytus rugulosus (Müller)	shothole borer	COLEOPTERA: Scolytidae
Scolytus unispinosus LeConte	Douglas-fir engraver	COLEOPTERA: Scolytidae
Scolytus ventralis LeConte	fir engraver	COLEOPTERA: Scolytidae
Scotorythra paludicola (Butler)	koa moth	LEPIDOPTERA: Geometridae
Scudderia furcata Brunner von Wattenwyl	forktailed bush katydid	ORTHOPTERA: Tettigoniidae
Scutigera coleoptrata (Linnaeus)	house centipede	SCUTIGEROMORPHA: Scutigeridae
Scutigerella immaculata (Newport)	garden symphylan	SYMPHYLA: Scutigerellidae
Scymnodes lividigaster (Mulsant)	yellowshouldered lady beetle	COLEOPTERA: Coccinellidae
Selca brunella (Hampson)	melastoma borer	LEPIDOPTERA: Noctuidae
Selenothrips rubrocinctus (Giard)	redbanded thrips	THYSANOPTERA: Thripidae
Semanotus ligneus (Fabricius)	cedartree borer	COLEOPTERA: Cerambycidae
Semanotus litigiosus (Casey)	firtree borer	COLEOPTERA: Cerambycidae
Sericothrips variabilis (Beach)	soybean thrips	THYSANOPTERA: Thripidae
Sesia apiformis (Clerck)	hornet moth	LEPIDOPTERA: Sesiidae
Sesia tibialis (Harris)	American hornet moth	LEPIDOPTERA: Sesiidae
Sibine stimulea (Clemens)	saddleback caterpillar	LEPIDOPTERA: Limacodidae
Simulium meridionale Riley	turkey gnat	DIPTERA: Simuliidae
Sinea diadema (Fabricius)	spined assassin bug	HETEROPTERA: Reduviidae
Singhius hibisci (Kotinsky)	hibiscus whitefly	HOMOPTERA: Aleyrodidae
Sipha flava (Forbes)	yellow sugarcane aphid	HOMOPTERA: Aphididae
Sirex cyaneus Fabricius	blue horntail	HYMENOPTERA: Siricidae
Siteroptes graminum (Reuter)	grass mite	ACARI: Siteroptidae
Sitobion avenae (Fabricius)	English grain aphid	HOMOPTERA: Aphididae
Sitodiplosis mosellana (Géhin)	wheat midge	DIPTERA: Cecidomyiidae
Sitona cylindricollis Fåhraeus	sweetclover weevil	COLEOPTERA: Curculionidae
Sitona hispidulus (Fabricius)	clover root curculio	COLEOPTERA: Curculionidae
Sitona lineatus (Linnaeus)	pea leaf weevil	COLEOPTERA: Curculionidae
Sitophilus granarius (Linnaeus)	granary weevil	COLEOPTERA: Curculionidae
Sitophilus linearis (Herbst)	tamarind weevil	COLEOPTERA: Curculionidae
Sitophilus oryzae (Linnaeus)	rice weevil	COLEOPTERA: Curculionidae
Sitophilus zeamais Motschulsky	maize weevil	COLEOPTERA: Curculionidae
Sitotroga cerealella (Olivier)	Angoumois grain moth	LEPIDOPTERA: Gelechiidae
Smicronyx fulvus LeConte	red sunflower seed weevil	COLEOPTERA: Curculionidae

Smicronyx sculpticollis Casey	dodder gall weevil	COLEOPTERA: Curculionidae
Smicronyx sordidus LeConte	gray sunflower seed weevil	COLEOPTERA: Curculionidae
Sogatodes orizicola (Muir)	rice delphacid	HOMOPTERA: Delphacidae
Solenopsis geminata (Fabricius)	fire ant	HYMENOPTERA: Formicidae
Solenopsis invicta Buren	red imported fire ant	HYMENOPTERA: Formicidae
Solenopsis molesta (Say)	thief ant	HYMENOPTERA: Formicidae
Solenopsis richteri Forel	black imported fire ant	HYMENOPTERA: Formicidae
Solenopsis xyloni McCook	southern fire ant	HYMENOPTERA: Formicidae
Spaelotis clandestina (Harris)	w-marked cutworm	LEPIDOPTERA: Noctuidae
Spaelotis havilae (Grote)	western w-marked cutworm	LEPIDOPTERA: Noctuidae
Spanagonicus albofasciatus (Reuter)	whitemarked fleahopper	HETEROPTERA: Miridae
Sparganothis directana (Walker)	chokecherry leafroller	LEPIDOPTERA: Tortricidae
Sphaerolecanium prunastri (Boyer de Fonscolombe)	globose scale	HOMOPTERA: Coccidae
Sphecius speciosus (Drury)	cicada killer	HYMENOPTERA: Sphecidae
Sphenophorus aequalis aequalis Gyllenhal	claycolored billbug	COLEOPTERA: Curculionidae
Sphenophorus callosus (Olivier)	southern corn billbug	COLEOPTERA: Curculionidae
Sphenophorus cariosus (Olivier)	nutgrass billbug	COLEOPTERA: Curculionidae
Sphenophorus maidis Chittenden	maize billbug	COLEOPTERA: Curculionidae
Sphenophorus parvulus Gyllenhal	bluegrass billbug	COLEOPTERA: Curculionidae
Sphenophorus venatus vestitus Chittenden	hunting billbug	COLEOPTERA: Curculionidae
Sphinx chersis (Hübner)	great ash sphinx	LEPIDOPTERA: Sphingidae
Spilonota ocellana (Denis & Schiffermüller)	eyespotted bud moth	LEPIDOPTERA: Tortricidae
Spilosoma virginica (Fabricius)	yellow woollybear	LEPIDOPTERA: Arctiidae
Spissistilus festinus (Say)	threecornered alfalfa hopper	HOMOPTERA: Membracidae
Spodoptera eridania (Cramer)	southern armyworm	LEPIDOPTERA: Noctuidae
Spodoptera exempta (Walker)	nutgrass armyworm	LEPIDOPTERA: Noctuidae
Spodoptera exigua (Hübner)	beet armyworm	LEPIDOPTERA: Noctuidae
Spodoptera frugiperda (J.E. Smith)	fall armyworm	LEPIDOPTERA: Noctuidae
Spodoptera mauritia (Boisduval)	lawn armyworm	LEPIDOPTERA: Noctuidae
Spodoptera ornithogalli (Guenée)	yellowstriped armyworm	LEPIDOPTERA: Noctuidae
Spodoptera praefica (Grote)	western yellowstriped armyworm	LEPIDOPTERA: Noctuidae
Spoladea recurvalis (Fabricius)	Hawaiian beet webworm	LEPIDOPTERA: Pyralidae
Stagmomantis carolina (Johannson)	Carolina mantid	MANTODEA: Mantidae
Stator pruininus (Horn)	pruinose bean weevil	COLEOPTERA: Bruchidae
Stegasta bosqueella (Chambers)	rednecked peanutworm	LEPIDOPTERA: Gelechiidae
Stegobium paniceum (Linnaeus)	drugstore beetle	COLEOPTERA: Anobiidae
Stelidota geminata (Say)	strawberry sap beetle	COLEOPTERA: Nitidulidae
Steneotarsonemus bancrofti (Michael)	sugarcane stalk mite	ACARI: Tarsonemidae

Steneotarsonemus laticeps (Halbert)	bulb scale mite	ACARI: Tarsonemidae
Steneotarsoneumu ananas (Tryon)	pineapple tarsonemid	ACARI: Tarsonemidae
Stenolophus lecontei (Chaudoir)	seedcorn beetle	COLEOPTERA: Carabidae
Stenopelmatus fuscus Haldeman	Jerusalem cricket	ORTHOPTERA: Stenopelmatidae
Stephanitis pyriodes (Scott)	azalea lace bug	HETEROPTERA: Tingidae
Stephanitis rhododendri Horvath	rhododendron lace bug	HETEROPTERA: Tingidae
Sternechus paludatus (Casey)	bean stalk weevil	COLEOPTERA: Curculionidae
Stethorus picipes Casey	spider mite destroyer	COLEOPTERA: Coccinellidae
Stictocephala bisonia Kopp & Yonke	buffalo treehopper	HOMOPTERA: Membracidae
Stigmella gossypii (Forbes & Leonard)	cotton leafminer	LEPIDOPTERA: Nepticulidae
Stigmella juglandifoliella (Clemens)	pecan serpentine leafminer	LEPIDOPTERA: Nepticulidae
Stomoxys calcitrans (Linnaeus)	stable fly	DIPTERA: Muscidae
Strauzia longipennis (Wiedemann)	sunflower maggot	DIPTERA: Tephritidae
Strymon bazochii gundlachianus (Bates)	smaller lantana butterfly	LEPIDOPTERA: Lycaenidae
Strymon echion (Linnaeus)	larger lantana butterfly	LEPIDOPTERA: Lycaenidae
Strymon melinus Hübner	cotton square borer	LEPIDOPTERA: Lycaenidae
Subulina octona (Bruguiere)	subulina snail	STYLOMMATOPHORA: Subulinidae
Suidasia nesbitti Hughes	scaly grain mite	ACARI: Acaridae
Suleima helianthana (Riley)	sunflower bud moth	LEPIDOPTERA: Tortricidae
Supella longipalpa (Fabricius)	brownbanded cockroach	BLATTODEA: Blattellidae
Surattha indentella Kearfott	buffalograss webworm	LEPIDOPTERA: Pyralidae
Swezeyula lonicerae Zimmerman & Bradley	honeysuckle leafminer	LEPIDOPTERA: Elachistidae
Syagrius fulvitarsis Pascoe	Australian fern weevil	COLEOPTERA: Curculionidae
Symmerista leucitys Franclemont	orangehumped mapleworm	LEPIDOPTERA: Notodontidae
Sympherobius barberi (Banks)	Barber brown lacewing	NEUROPTERA: Hemerobiidae
Synanthedon acerni (Clemens)	maple callus borer	LEPIDOPTERA: Sesiidae
Synanthedon bibionipennis (Boisduval)	strawberry crown moth	LEPIDOPTERA: Sesiidae
Synanthedon exitiosa (Say)	peachtree borer	LEPIDOPTERA: Sesiidae
Synanthedon novaroensis (Hy. Edwards)	Douglas-fir pitch moth	LEPIDOPTERA: Sesiidae
Synanthedon pictipes (Grote & Robinson)	lesser peachtree borer	LEPIDOPTERA: Sesiidae
Synanthedon pini (Kellicott)	pitch mass borer	LEPIDOPTERA: Sesiidae
Synanthedon pyri (Harris)	apple bark borer	LEPIDOPTERA: Sesiidae
Synanthedon rhododendri (Beutenmüller)	rhododendron borer	LEPIDOPTERA: Sesiidae
Synanthedon scitula (Harris)	dogwood borer	LEPIDOPTERA: Sesiidae
Synanthedon sequoiae (Hy. Edwards)	sequoia pitch moth	LEPIDOPTERA: Sesiidae
Synanthedon tipuliformis (Clerck)	currant borer	LEPIDOPTERA: Sesiidae
Synclita obliteralis (Walker)	waterlily leafcutter	LEPIDOPTERA: Pyralidae
Syntexis libocedrii Rohwer	incense-cedar wasp	HYMENOPTERA: Anaxyelidae

Systena blanda Melsheimer	palestriped flea beetle	COLEOPTERA: Chrysomelidae
Systena elongata (Fabricius)	elongate flea beetle	COLEOPTERA: Chrysomelidae
Systoechus vulgaris Loew	grasshopper bee fly	DIPTERA: Bombyliidae
Szepligetella sericea (Cameron)	lesser ensign wasp	HYMENOPTERA: Evaniidae

T

Tabanus atratus Fabricius	black horse fly	DIPTERA: Tabanidae
Tabanus lineola Fabricius	striped horse fly	DIPTERA: Tabanidae
Tachycines asynamorus Adelung	greenhouse stone cricket	ORTHOPTERA: Gryllacrididae
Tachypompilus analis (Fabricius)	redtailed spider wasp	HYMENOPTERA: Pompilidae
Tachypterellus quadrigibbus (Say)	apple curculio	COLEOPTERA: Curculionidae
Taedia hawleyi (Knight)	hop plant bug	HETEROPTERA: Miridae
Taeniothrips inconsequens (Uzel)	pear thrips	THYSANOPTERA: Thripidae
Tanystoma maculicolle (Dejean)	tule beetle	COLEOPTERA: Carabidae
Tapinoma sessile (Say)	odorous house ant	HYMENOPTERA: Formicidae
Targalla delatrix Guenée	eugenia caterpillar	LEPIDOPTERA: Noctuidae
Tegeticula yuccasella (Riley)	yucca moth	LEPIDOPTERA: Incurvariidae
Tehama bonifatella (Hulst)	western lawn moth	LEPIDOPTERA: Pyralidae
Teleogryllus oceanicus (Le Guillou)	oceanic field cricket	ORTHOPTERA: Gryllidae
Teleonemia scrupulosa Stål	lantana lace bug	HETEROPTERA: Tingidae
Tenebrio molitor Linnaeus	yellow mealworm	COLEOPTERA: Tenebrionidae
Tenebrio obscurus Fabricius	dark mealworm	COLEOPTERA: Tenebrionidae
Tenebroides mauritanicus (Linnaeus)	cadelle	COLEOPTERA: Trogositidae
Tenodera aridifolia sinensis Saussure	Chinese mantid	MANTODEA: Mantidae
Tenodera augustipennis Saussure	narrowwinged mantid	MANTODEA: Mantidae
Tenodera australasiae (Leach)	Australian mantid	MANTODEA: Mantidae
Tetanops myopaeformis (Rder)	sugarbeet root maggot	DIPTERA: Otitidae
Tethida barda (Say)	blackheaded ash sawfly	HYMENOPTERA: Tenthredinidae
Tetraleurodes mori (Quaintance)	mulberry whitefly	HOMOPTERA: Aleyrodidae
Tetralopha robustella Zeller	pine webworm	LEPIDOPTERA: Pyralidae
Tetralopha scortealis (Lederer)	lespedeza webworm	LEPIDOPTERA: Pyralidae
Tetramesa grandis (Riley)	wheat strawworm	HYMENOPTERA: Eurytomidae
Tetramesa hordei (Harris)	barley jointworm	HYMENOPTERA: Eurytomidae
Tetramesa tritici (Fitch)	wheat jointworm	HYMENOPTERA: Eurytomidae
Tetramorium bicarinatum (Nylander)	Guinea ant	HYMENOPTERA: Formicidae

Tetramorium caespitum (Linnaeus)	pavement ant	HYMENOPTERA: Formicidae
Tetranychina harti (Ewing)	oxalis spider mite	ACARI: Tetranychidae
Tetranychus canadensis (McGregor)	fourspotted spider mite	ACARI: Tetranychidae
Tetranychus cinnabarinus (Boisduval)	carmine spider mite	ACARI: Tetranychidae
Tetranychus desertorum Banks	desert spider mite	ACARI: Tetranychidae
Tetranychus mcdanieli McGregor	McDaniel spider mite	ACARI: Tetranychidae
Tetranychus pacificus McGregor	Pacific spider mite	ACARI: Tetranychidae
Tetranychus schoenei McGregor	Schoene spider mite	ACARI: Tetranychidae
Tetranychus tumidus Banks	tumid spider mite	ACARI: Tetranychidae
Tetranychus turkestani Ugarov & Nikolski	strawberry spider mite	ACARI: Tetranychidae
Tetranychus urticae Koch	twospotted spider mite	ACARI: Tetranychidae
Tetraopes tetrophthalmus (Forster)	red milkweed beetle	COLEOPTERA: Cerambycidae
Tetropium abietis Fall	roundheaded fir borer	COLEOPTERA: Cerambycidae
Tetyra bipunctata (Herrich-Schäffer)	shieldbacked pine seed bug	HETEROPTERA: Pentatomidae
Theba pisana (Müller)	white garden snail	STYLOMMATOPHORA: Helicidae
Therioaphis maculata (Buckton)	spotted alfalfa aphid	HOMOPTERA: Aphididae
Therioaphis riehmi (Brner)	sweetclover aphid	HOMOPTERA: Aphididae
Therioaphis trifolii (Monell)	yellow clover aphid	HOMOPTERA: Aphididae
Thermobia domestica (Packard)	firebrat	THYSANURA: Lepismatidae
Thes bergrothi (Reitter)	ridgewinged fungus beetle	COLEOPTERA: Lathridiidae
Thoracaphis fici (Takahashi)	banyan aphid	HOMOPTERA: Aphididae
Thrips hawaiiensis (Morgan)	Hawaiian flower thrips	THYSANOPTERA: Thripidae
Thrips nigropilosus Uzel	chrysanthemum thrips	THYSANOPTERA: Thripidae
Thrips orientalis (Bagnall)	star jasmine thrips	THYSANOPTERA: Thripidae
Thrips simplex (Morison)	gladiolus thrips	THYSANOPTERA: Thripidae
Thrips tabaci Lindeman	onion thrips	THYSANOPTERA: Thripidae
Thyanta accerra McAtee	redshouldered stink bug	HETEROPTERA: Pentatomidae
Thylodrias contractus Motschulsky	odd beetle	COLEOPTERA: Dermestidae
Thyridopteryx ephemeraeformis (Haworth)	bagworm	LEPIDOPTERA: Psychidae
Tildenia inconspicuella (Murtfeldt)	eggplant leafminer	LEPIDOPTERA: Gelechiidae
Tinea pellionella Linnaeus	casemaking clothes moth	LEPIDOPTERA: Tineidae
Tineola bisselliella (Hummel)	webbing clothes moth	LEPIDOPTERA: Tineidae
Tinocallis kahawaluokalani (Kirkaldy)	crapemyrtle aphid	HOMOPTERA: Aphididae
Tinocallis ulmifolii (Monell)	elm leaf aphid	HOMOPTERA: Aphididae
Tinostoma smaragditis (Meyrick)	green sphinx	LEPIDOPTERA: Sphingidae
Tipula paludosa Meigen	European crane fly	DIPTERA: Tipulidae
Tipula simplex Doane	range crane fly	DIPTERA: Tipulidae
Tischeria malifoliella Clemens	appleleaf trumpet miner	LEPIDOPTERA: Tischeriidae

Tomostethus multicinctus (Rohwer)	brownheaded ash sawfly	HYMENOPTERA: Tenthredinidae
Torymus varians (Walker)	apple seed chalcid	HYMENOPTERA: Torymidae
Toumeyella liriodendri (Gmelin)	tuliptree scale	HOMOPTERA: Coccidae
Toumeyella parvicornis (Cockerell)	pine tortoise scale	HOMOPTERA: Coccidae
Toxoptera aurantii (Boyer de Fonscolombe)	black citrus aphid	HOMOPTERA: Aphididae
Toxoptera citricida (Kirkaldy)	brown citrus aphid	HOMOPTERA: Aphididae
Toxotrypana curvicauda Gerstaecker	papaya fruit fly	DIPTERA: Tephritidae
Trachelus tabidus (Fabricius)	black grain stem sawfly	HYMENOPTERA: Cephidae
Trachykele blondeli Marseul	western cedar borer	COLEOPTERA: Buprestidae
Tremex columba (Linnaeus)	pigeon tremex	HYMENOPTERA: Siricidae
Trialeurodes abutilonea (Haldeman)	bandedwinged whitefly	HOMOPTERA: Aleyrodidae
Trialeurodes floridensis (Quaintance)	avocado whitefly	HOMOPTERA: Aleyrodidae
Trialeurodes packardi (Morrill)	strawberry whitefly	HOMOPTERA: Aleyrodidae
Trialeurodes vaporariorum (Westwood)	greenhouse whitefly	HOMOPTERA: Aleyrodidae
Trialeurodes vittata (Quaintance)	grape whitefly	HOMOPTERA: Aleyrodidae
Triatoma protracta (Uhler)	western bloodsucking conenose	HETEROPTERA: Reduviidae
Triatoma rubrofasciata (De Geer)	large kissing bug	HETEROPTERA: Reduviidae
Triatoma sanguisuga (LeConte)	bloodsucking conenose	HETEROPTERA: Reduviidae
Tribolium audax Halstead	American black flour beetle	COLEOPTERA: Tenebrionidae
Tribolium castaneum (Herbst)	red flour beetle	COLEOPTERA: Tenebrionidae
Tribolium confusum Jacquelin du Val	confused flour beetle	COLEOPTERA: Tenebrionidae
Tricentrus albomaculatus Distant	whitemarked treehopper	HOMOPTERA: Membracidae
Trichobaris mucorea (LeConte)	tobacco stalk borer	COLEOPTERA: Curculionidae
Trichobaris trinotata (Say)	potato stalk borer	COLEOPTERA: Curculionidae
Trichodectes canis (De Geer)	dog biting louse	MALLOPHAGA: Trichodectidae
Trichogramma minutum Riley	minute egg parasite	HYMENOPTERA: Trichogrammatidae
Trichophaga tapetzella (Linnaeus)	carpet moth	LEPIDOPTERA: Tineidae
Trichoplusia ni (Hübner)	cabbage looper	LEPIDOPTERA: Noctuidae
Trichordestra legitima (Grote)	striped garden caterpillar	LEPIDOPTERA: Noctuidae
Trigoniulus lumbricinus (Gerst)	rusty millipede	SPIROBOLIDA: Pachybolidae
Trigonogenius globulum Solier	globular spider beetle	COLEOPTERA: Ptinidae
Trinoton anserinum (Fabricius)	goose body louse	MALLOPHAGA: Menoponidae
Trinoton querquedulae (Linnaeus)	large duck louse	MALLOPHAGA: Menoponidae
Trioza diospyri (Ashmead)	persimmon psylla	HOMOPTERA: Psyllidae
Trisetacus gemmavitians Styer	pine rosette mite	ACARI: Nalepellidae
Trisetacus pini (Nalepa)	pine bud mite	ACARI: Nalepellidae
Trogium pulsatorium (Linnaeus)	larger pale trogiid	PSOCOPTERA: Trogiidae
Trogoderma granarium Everts	khapra beetle	COLEOPTERA: Dermestidae

Trogoderma variabile Ballion	warehouse beetle	COLEOPTERA: Dermestidae
Tropidosteptes amoenus Reuter	ash plant bug	HETEROPTERA: Miridae
Trypodendron lineatum (Olivier)	striped ambrosia beetle	COLEOPTERA: Scolytidae
Tunga penetrans (Linnaeus)	chigoe	SIPHONAPTERA: Tungidae
Tychius picirostris (Fabricius)	clover seed weevil	COLEOPTERA: Curculionidae
Tychius stephensi Schnherr	red clover seed weevil	COLEOPTERA: Curculionidae
Tyloderma fragariae (Riley)	strawberry crown borer	COLEOPTERA: Curculionidae
Typhaea stercorea (Linnaeus)	hairy fungus beetle	COLEOPTERA: Mycetophagidae
Typhlocyba pomaria McAtee	white apple leafhopper	HOMOPTERA: Cicadellidae
Typophorus nigritus viridicyaneus (Crotch)	sweetpotato leaf beetle	COLEOPTERA: Chrysomelidae
Tyria jacobaeae (Linnaeus)	cinnabar moth	LEPIDOPTERA: Arctiidae
Tyrolichus casei Oudemans	cheese mite	ACARI: Acaridae
Tyrophagus putrescentiae (Schrank)	mold mite	ACARI: Acaridae

U

Udea profundalis (Packard)	false celery leaftier	LEPIDOPTERA: Pyralidae
Udea rubigalis (Guenée)	celery leaftier[45]	LEPIDOPTERA: Pyralidae
Ulochaetes leoninus LeConte	lion beetle	COLEOPTERA: Cerambycidae
Unaspis citri (Comstock)	citrus snow scale	HOMOPTERA: Diaspididae
Unaspis euonymi (Comstock)	euonymus scale	HOMOPTERA: Diaspididae
Urbanus proteus (Linnaeus)	bean leafroller	LEPIDOPTERA: Hesperiidae
Uresiphita reversalis (Guenée)	genista caterpillar	LEPIDOPTERA: Pyralidae
Uroplata girardi Pic	lantana hispid	COLEOPTERA: Chrysomelidae
Utetheisa bella (Linnaeus)	bella moth	LEPIDOPTERA: Arctiidae

V

Vaga blackburni (Tuely)	Blackburn butterfly	LEPIDOPTERA: Lycaenidae
Vanduzea segmentata (Fowler)	Van Duzee treehopper	HOMOPTERA: Membracidae

---

[45]Also called greenhouse leaftier.

Vanessa atalanta rubria (Fruhstorfer)	red admiral	LEPIDOPTERA: Nymphalidae
Vanessa cardui (Linnaeus)	painted lady	LEPIDOPTERA: Nymphalidae
Vanessa tameamea Eschscholtz	Kamehameha butterfly	LEPIDOPTERA: Nymphalidae
Vanessa virginiensis (Drury)	painted beauty	LEPIDOPTERA: Nymphalidae
Vasates quadripedes Shimer	maple bladdergall mite	ACARI: Eriophyidae
Vespa crabro Linnaeus	European hornet	HYMENOPTERA: Vespidae
Vespula consobrina (Saussure)	blackjacket	HYMENOPTERA: Vespidae
Vespula maculifrons (Buysson)	eastern yellowjacket	HYMENOPTERA: Vespidae
Vespula pensylvanica (Saussure)	western yellowjacket	HYMENOPTERA: Vespidae
Vitacea polistiformis (Harris)	grape root borer	LEPIDOPTERA: Sesiidae
Vitula edmandsae serratilineella Ragonot	driedfruit moth	LEPIDOPTERA: Pyralidae

W

Walshia miscecolorella (Chambers)	sweetclover root borer	LEPIDOPTERA: Cosmopterigidae
Winthemia quadripustulata (Fabricius)	redtailed tachina	DIPTERA: Tachinidae
Wyeomyia smithii (Coquillett)	pitcherplant mosquito	DIPTERA: Culicidae

X

Xenopsylla cheopis (Rothschild)	oriental rat flea	SIPHONAPTERA: Pulicidae
Xenopsylla vexabilis (Jordan)	Australian rat flea	SIPHONAPTERA: Pulicidae
Xestia spp.	spotted cutworm	LEPIDOPTERA: Noctuidae
Xylocopa virginica (Linnaeus)	carpenter bee	HYMENOPTERA: Anthophoridae
Xylocoris flavipes (Reuter)	warehouse pirate bug	HETEROPTERA: Anthocoridae
Xyloryctes jamaicensis (Drury)	rhinoceros beetle	COLEOPTERA: Scarabaeidae
Xylosandrus compactus (Eichhoff)	black twig borer	COLEOPTERA: Scolytidae
Xylotrechus aceris Fisher	gallmaking maple borer	COLEOPTERA: Cerambycidae
Xylotrechus colonus (Fabricius)	rustic borer	COLEOPTERA: Cerambycidae
Xyphon flaviceps (Riley)	yellowheaded leafhopper	HOMOPTERA: Cicadellidae
Xystrocera globosa (Olivier)	monkeypod roundheaded borer	COLEOPTERA: Cerambycidae

Y

Yponomeuta padella (Linnaeus)	ermine moth	LEPIDOPTERA: Yponomeutidae
Ypsolophus dentella (Fabricius)	European honeysuckle leafroller	LEPIDOPTERA: Plutellidae

Z

Zabrotes subfasciatus (Boheman)	Mexican bean weevil	COLEOPTERA: Bruchidae
Zaraea inflata Norton	honeysuckle sawfly	HYMENOPTERA: Cimbicidae
Zeiraphera canadensis Mutuura & Freeman	spruce bud moth	LEPIDOPTERA: Tortricidae
Zelleria haimbachi Busck	pine needle sheathminer	LEPIDOPTERA: Yponomeutidae
Zelus renardii Kolenati	leafhopper assassin bug	HETEROPTERA: Reduviidae
Zeuzera pyrina (Linnaeus)	leopard moth	LEPIDOPTERA: Cossidae
Zonosemata electa (Say)	pepper maggot	DIPTERA: Tephritidae
Zootermopsis angusticollis (Hagen)	Pacific dampwood termite	ISOPTERA: Termopsidae
Zophodia convolutella (Hübner)	gooseberry fruitworm	LEPIDOPTERA: Pyralidae
Zygogramma exclamationis (Fabricius)	sunflower beetle	COLEOPTERA: Chrysomelidae

Section III. Insects and Related Organisms Listed by Higher Taxonomic Category

A

ACARI: Acaridae	*Acarus siro* Linnaeus	grain mite
ACARI: Acaridae	*Aleuroglyphus ovatus* (Troupeau)	brownlegged grain mite
ACARI: Acaridae	*Rhizoglyphus echinopus* (Fumouze & Robin)	bulb mite
ACARI: Acaridae	*Suidasia nesbitti* Hughes	scaly grain mite
ACARI: Acaridae	*Tyrolichus casei* Oudemans	cheese mite
ACARI: Acaridae	*Tyrophagus putrescentiae* (Schrank)	mold mite
ACARI: Analgidae	*Megninia cubitalis* (Mégnin)	feather mite
ACARI: Argasidae	*Argas persicus* (Oken)	fowl tick
ACARI: Argasidae	*Ornithodoros turicata* (Dugès)	relapsing fever tick
ACARI: Argasidae	*Otobius megnini* (Dugès)	ear tick
ACARI: Carpoglyphidae	*Carpoglyphus lactis* (Linnaeus)	driedfruit mite
ACARI: Demodicidae	*Demodex bovis* Stiles	cattle follicle mite
ACARI: Demodicidae	*Demodex brevis* Bulanova	lesser follicle mite
ACARI: Demodicidae	*Demodex canis* Leydig	dog follicle mite
ACARI: Demodicidae	*Demodex caprae* Railliet	goat follicle mite
ACARI: Demodicidae	*Demodex cati* Mégnin	cat follicle mite
ACARI: Demodicidae	*Demodex equi* Railliet	horse follicle mite
ACARI: Demodicidae	*Demodex folliculorum* (Simon)	follicle mite
ACARI: Demodicidae	*Demodex ovis* Railliet	sheep follicle mite
ACARI: Demodicidae	*Demodex phylloides* Csokor	hog follicle mite
ACARI: Dermanyssidae	*Dermanyssus gallinae* (De Geer)	chicken mite
ACARI: Epidermoptidae	*Dermatophagoides farinae* Hughes	American house dust mite
ACARI: Epidermoptidae	*Dermatophagoides pteronyssinus* (Trouessart)	European house dust mite
ACARI: Eriophyidae	*Abacarus hystrix* (Nalepa)	grain rust mite
ACARI: Eriophyidae	*Acalitus essigi* (Hassan)	redberry mite
ACARI: Eriophyidae	*Acalitus gossypii* (Banks)	cotton blister mite
ACARI: Eriophyidae	*Acalitus vaccinii* (Keifer)	blueberry bud mite
ACARI: Eriophyidae	*Aculops lycopersici* (Massee)	tomato russet mite
ACARI: Eriophyidae	*Aculus cornutus* (Banks)	peach silver mite
ACARI: Eriophyidae	*Aculus fockeui* (Nalepa & Trouessart)	plum rust mite
ACARI: Eriophyidae	*Aculus schlechtendali* (Nalepa)	apple rust mite

ACARI: Eriophyidae	*Calepiterimerus thujae* (Garman)	tipdwarf mite
ACARI: Eriophyidae	*Cecidophyopsis ribis* (Westwood)	currant bud mite
ACARI: Eriophyidae	*Colomerus gardeniella* (Keifer)	gardenia bud mite
ACARI: Eriophyidae	*Colomerus vitis* (Pagenstecher)	grape erineum mite
ACARI: Eriophyidae	*Epitrimerus pyri* (Nalepa)	pear rust mite
ACARI: Eriophyidae	*Eriophyes aloinis* Keifer	aloe mite
ACARI: Eriophyidae	*Eriophyes caryae* Keifer	pecan leafroll mite
ACARI: Eriophyidae	*Eriophyes cynodoniensis* Sayed	Bermudagrass mite
ACARI: Eriophyidae	*Eriophyes erinea* (Nalepa)	walnut blister mite
ACARI: Eriophyidae	*Eriophyes ficus* Cotte	fig mite
ACARI: Eriophyidae	*Eriophyes litchii* Keifer	litchi mite
ACARI: Eriophyidae	*Eriophyes mangiferae* (Sayed)	mango bud mite
ACARI: Eriophyidae	*Eriophyes sheldoni* Ewing	citrus bud mite
ACARI: Eriophyidae	*Eriophyes tulipae* Keifer	wheat curl mite
ACARI: Eriophyidae	*Phyllocoptes gracilis* (Nalepa)	dryberry mite
ACARI: Eriophyidae	*Phyllocoptruta oleivora* (Ashmead)	citrus rust mite
ACARI: Eriophyidae	*Phytoptus pyri* Pagenstecher	pearleaf blister mite
ACARI: Eriophyidae	*Vasates quadripedes* Shimer	maple bladdergall mite
ACARI: Eupodidae	*Penthaleus major* (Dugès)	winter grain mite
ACARI: Glycyphagidae	*Aeroglyphus robustus* (Banks)	warty grain mite
ACARI: Glycyphagidae	*Glycyphagus domesticus* (De Geer)	house mite
ACARI: Glycyphagidae	*Gohieria fusca* (Oudemans)	brown flour mite
ACARI: Ixodidae	*Amblyomma americanum* (Linnaeus)	lone star tick
ACARI: Ixodidae	*Amblyomma cajennense* (Fabricius)	Cayenne tick
ACARI: Ixodidae	*Amblyomma maculatum* Koch	Gulf Coast tick
ACARI: Ixodidae	*Amblyomma tuberculatum* Marx	gophertortoise tick
ACARI: Ixodidae	*Anocentor nitens* (Neumann)	tropical horse tick
ACARI: Ixodidae	*Boophilus annulatus* (Say)	cattle tick
ACARI: Ixodidae	*Boophilus microplus* (Canestrini)	southern cattle tick
ACARI: Ixodidae	*Dermacentor albipictus* (Packard)	winter tick
ACARI: Ixodidae	*Dermacentor andersoni* Stiles	Rocky Mountain wood tick
ACARI: Ixodidae	*Dermacentor occidentalis* Marx	Pacific Coast tick
ACARI: Ixodidae	*Dermacentor variabilis* (Say)	American dog tick
ACARI: Ixodidae	*Haemaphysalis chordeilis* (Packard)	bird tick
ACARI: Ixodidae	*Haemaphysalis leporispalustris* (Packard)	rabbit tick
ACARI: Ixodidae	*Ixodes kingi* Bishopp	rotund tick
ACARI: Ixodidae	*Ixodes scapularis* Say	blacklegged tick
ACARI: Ixodidae	*Rhipicephalus sanguineus* (Latreille)	brown dog tick

ACARI: Macronyssidae	*Liponyssoides sanguineus* (Hirst)	house mouse mite
ACARI: Macronyssidae	*Ornithonyssus bacoti* (Hirst)	tropical rat mite
ACARI: Macronyssidae	*Ornithonyssus bursa* (Berlese)	tropical fowl mite
ACARI: Macronyssidae	*Ornithonyssus sylviarum* (Canestrini & Fanzago)	northern fowl mite
ACARI: Nalepellidae	*Phytocoptella avellanae* (Nalepa)	filbert bud mite
ACARI: Nalepellidae	*Trisetacus gemmavitians* Styer	pine rosette mite
ACARI: Nalepellidae	*Trisetacus pini* (Nalepa)	pine bud mite
ACARI: Phytoseiidae	*Galandromus occidentalis* (Nesbitt)	western predatory mite
ACARI: Psoroptidae	*Psoroptes equi* (Raspail)	scab mite
ACARI: Psoroptidae	*Psoroptes ovis* (Hering)	sheep scab mite
ACARI: Pyemotidae	*Pyemotes tritici* (Lagrèze-Fossat & Montané)	straw itch mite
ACARI: Sarcoptidae	*Knemidokoptes gallinae* (Railliet)	depluming mite
ACARI: Sarcoptidae	*Knemidokoptes mutans* (Robin & Lanquetin)	scalyleg mite
ACARI: Sarcoptidae	*Sarcoptes bovis* Robin	cattle itch mite
ACARI: Sarcoptidae	*Sarcoptes scabiei* (De Geer)	itch mite
ACARI: Siteroptidae	*Siteroptes graminum* (Reuter)	grass mite
ACARI: Tarsonemidae	*Acarapis woodi* (Rennie)	honey bee mite
ACARI: Tarsonemidae	*Phytonemus pallidus* (Banks)	cyclamen mite
ACARI: Tarsonemidae	*Polyphagotarsonemus latus* (Banks)	broad mite
ACARI: Tarsonemidae	*Steneotarsonemus bancrofti* (Michael)	sugarcane stalk mite
ACARI: Tarsonemidae	*Steneotarsonemus laticeps* (Halbert)	bulb scale mite
ACARI: Tarsonemidae	*Steneotarsoneumu ananas* (Tryon)	pineapple tarsonemid
ACARI: Tenuipalpidae	*Brevipalpus lewisi* McGregor	citrus flat mite
ACARI: Tenuipalpidae	*Brevipalpus obovatus* Donnadieu	privet mite
ACARI: Tenuipalpidae	*Brevipalpus phoenicis* (Geijskes)	red and black flat mite
ACARI: Tenuipalpidae	*Dolichotetranychus floridanus* (Banks)	pineapple false spider mite
ACARI: Tetranychidae	*Bryobia praetiosa* Koch	clover mite
ACARI: Tetranychidae	*Bryobia rubrioculus* (Scheuten)	brown mite
ACARI: Tetranychidae	*Eotetranychus carpini borealis* (Ewing)	yellow spider mite
ACARI: Tetranychidae	*Eotetranychus clitus* Pritchard & Baker	azalea white mite
ACARI: Tetranychidae	*Eotetranychus hicoriae* (McGregor)	pecan leaf scorch mite
ACARI: Tetranychidae	*Eotetranychus sexmaculatus* (Riley)	sixspotted mite
ACARI: Tetranychidae	*Eotetranychus yumensis* (McGregor)	Yuma spider mite
ACARI: Tetranychidae	*Eutetranychus banksi* (McGregor)	Texas citrus mite
ACARI: Tetranychidae	*Oligonychus coniferarum* (McGregor)	conifer spider mite
ACARI: Tetranychidae	*Oligonychus ilicis* (McGregor)	southern red mite
ACARI: Tetranychidae	*Oligonychus indicus* (Hirst)	sugarcane leaf mite
ACARI: Tetranychidae	*Oligonychus mangiferus* (Rahman & Sapra)	mango spider mite

ACARI: Tetranychidae	*Oligonychus pratensis* (Banks)	Banks grass mite
ACARI: Tetranychidae	*Oligonychus punicae* (Hirst)	avocado brown mite
ACARI: Tetranychidae	*Oligonychus ununguis* (Jacobi)	spruce spider mite
ACARI: Tetranychidae	*Oligonychus yothersi* (McGregor)	avocado red mite
ACARI: Tetranychidae	*Panonychus citri* (McGregor)	citrus red mite
ACARI: Tetranychidae	*Panonychus ulmi* (Koch)	European red mite
ACARI: Tetranychidae	*Petrobia latens* (Müller)	brown wheat mite
ACARI: Tetranychidae	*Platytetranychus multidigitali* (Ewing)	honeylocust spider mite
ACARI: Tetranychidae	*Psedobryobia drummondi* (Ewing)	creosotebush spider mite
ACARI: Tetranychidae	*Schizotetranychus asparagi* (Oudemans)	asparagus spider mite
ACARI: Tetranychidae	*Schizotetranychus celarius* (Banks)	bamboo spider mite
ACARI: Tetranychidae	*Tetranychina harti* (Ewing)	oxalis spider mite
ACARI: Tetranychidae	*Tetranychus canadensis* (McGregor)	fourspotted spider mite
ACARI: Tetranychidae	*Tetranychus cinnabarinus* (Boisduval)	carmine spider mite
ACARI: Tetranychidae	*Tetranychus desertorum* Banks	desert spider mite
ACARI: Tetranychidae	*Tetranychus mcdanieli* McGregor	McDaniel spider mite
ACARI: Tetranychidae	*Tetranychus pacificus* McGregor	Pacific spider mite
ACARI: Tetranychidae	*Tetranychus schoenei* McGregor	Schoene spider mite
ACARI: Tetranychidae	*Tetranychus tumidus* Banks	tumid spider mite
ACARI: Tetranychidae	*Tetranychus turkestani* Ugarov & Nikolski	strawberry spider mite
ACARI: Tetranychidae	*Tetranychus urticae* Koch	twospotted spider mite
ACARI: Trombiculidae	*Neoschoengastia americana* (Hirst)	turkey chigger
ACARI: Trombidiidae	*Eutrombidium trigonum* (Hermann)	red grasshopper mite
ACARI: Tydeidae	*Lorryia reticulata* (Oudemans)	reticulate mite
ANOPLURA: Haematopinidae	*Haematopinus asini* (Linnaeus)	horse sucking louse
ANOPLURA: Haematopinidae	*Haematopinus eurysternus* (Nitzsch)	shortnosed cattle louse
ANOPLURA: Haematopinidae	*Haematopinus quadripertusus* Fahrenholz	cattle tail louse
ANOPLURA: Haematopinidae	*Haematopinus suis* (Linnaeus)	hog louse
ANOPLURA: Hoplopleuridae	*Haemodipsus ventricosus* (Denny)	rabbit louse
ANOPLURA: Hoplopleuridae	*Hoplopleura pacifica* Ewing	tropical rat louse
ANOPLURA: Hoplopleuridae	*Polyplax spinulosa* (Burmeister)	spined rat louse
ANOPLURA: Linognathidae	*Linognathus setosus* (Olfers)	dog sucking louse
ANOPLURA: Linognathidae	*Linognathus stenopsis* (Burmeister)	goat sucking louse
ANOPLURA: Linognathidae	*Linognathus vituli* (Linnaeus)	longnosed cattle louse
ANOPLURA: Pediculidae	*Pediculus humanus capitis* De Geer	head louse
ANOPLURA: Pediculidae	*Pediculus humanus humanus* Linnaeus	body louse
ANOPLURA: Pediculidae	*Pthirus pubis* (Linnaeus)	crab louse
ARANEAE: Araneidae	*Argiope aurantia* Lucas	yellow garden spider

ARANEAE: Araneidae	*Argiope trifasciata* (Forskal)	whitebacked garden spider
ARANEAE: Araneidae	*Gasteracantha cancriformis* (Linnaeus)	spinybacked spider
ARANEAE: Clubionidae	*Chiracanthium mordax* Koch	pale leaf spider
ARANEAE: Loxoscelidae	*Loxosceles reclusa* Gertsch & Mulaik	brown recluse spider
ARANEAE: Oxyopidae	*Oxyopes salticus* Hentz	striped lynx spider
ARANEAE: Sparassidae	*Heteropoda venatoria* (Linnaeus)	large brown spider
ARANEAE: Theridiidae	*Latrodectus geometricus* (Fabricius)	brown widow spider
ARANEAE: Theridiidae	*Latrodectus mactans* (Fabricius)	black widow spider

---

B

BLATTODEA: Blaberidae	*Diploptera punctata* (Eschscholtz)	Pacific beetle cockroach
BLATTODEA: Blaberidae	*Leucophaea maderae* (Fabricius)	Madeira cockroach
BLATTODEA: Blaberidae	*Nauphoeta cinerea* (Olivier)	cinereous cockroach
BLATTODEA: Blaberidae	*Panchlora nivea* (Linnaeus)	Cuban cockroach
BLATTODEA: Blaberidae	*Pycnoscelus surinamensis* (Linnaeus)	Surinam cockroach
BLATTODEA: Blattellidae	*Blattella asahinai* Mizukubo	Asian cockroach
BLATTODEA: Blattellidae	*Blattella germanica* (Linnaeus)	German cockroach
BLATTODEA: Blattellidae	*Blattella lituricollis* (Walker)	false German cockroach
BLATTODEA: Blattellidae	*Ectobius pallidus* (Olivier)	spotted Mediterranean cockroach
BLATTODEA: Blattellidae	*Supella longipalpa* (Fabricius)	brownbanded cockroach
BLATTODEA: Blattidae	*Blatta (Shelfordella) lateralis* (Walker)	Turkestan cockroach
BLATTODEA: Blattidae	*Blatta orientalis* Linnaeus	oriental cockroach
BLATTODEA: Blattidae	*Melanozosteria soror* (Brunner)	whitemargined cockroach
BLATTODEA: Blattidae	*Neostylopyga rhombifolia* (Stoll)	harlequin cockroach
BLATTODEA: Blattidae	*Periplaneta americana* (Linnaeus)	American cockroach
BLATTODEA: Blattidae	*Periplaneta australasiae* (Fabricius)	Australian cockroach
BLATTODEA: Blattidae	*Periplaneta brunnea* Burmeister	brown cockroach
BLATTODEA: Blattidae	*Periplaneta fuliginosa* (Serville)	smokybrown cockroach
BLATTODEA: Polyphagidae	*Euthyrrhapha pacifica* (Coquebert)	Pacific cockroach

COLEOPTERA: Anobiidae	*Anobium punctatum* (De Geer)	furniture beetle
COLEOPTERA: Anobiidae	*Lasioderma serricorne* (Fabricius)	cigarette beetle
COLEOPTERA: Anobiidae	*Stegobium paniceum* (Linnaeus)	drugstore beetle
COLEOPTERA: Anthicidae	*Anthicus floralis* (Linnaeus)	narrownecked grain beetle
COLEOPTERA: Anthribidae	*Araecerus fasciculatus* (De Geer)	coffee bean weevil
COLEOPTERA: Anthribidae	*Araecerus levipennis* Jordan	koa haole seed weevil
COLEOPTERA: Anthribidae	*Araeocorynus cumingi* Jekel	mauna loa bean beetle
COLEOPTERA: Bostrichidae	*Amphicerus bicaudatus* (Say)	apple twig borer
COLEOPTERA: Bostrichidae	*Amphicerus cornutus* (Pallas)	powderpost bostrichid
COLEOPTERA: Bostrichidae	*Dinoderus minutus* (Fabricius)	bamboo powderpost beetle
COLEOPTERA: Bostrichidae	*Prostephanus truncatus* (Horn)	larger grain borer
COLEOPTERA: Bostrichidae	*Rhyzopertha dominica* (Fabricius)	lesser grain borer
COLEOPTERA: Bostrichidae	*Scobicia declivis* (LeConte)	leadcable borer
COLEOPTERA: Brentidae	*Arrhenodes minutus* (Drury)	oak timberworm
COLEOPTERA: Bruchidae	*Acanthoscelides obtectus* (Say)	bean weevil
COLEOPTERA: Bruchidae	*Algarobius bottimeri* Kingsolver	kiawe bean weevil
COLEOPTERA: Bruchidae	*Bruchus brachialis* Fåhraeus	vetch bruchid
COLEOPTERA: Bruchidae	*Bruchus pisorum* (Linnaeus)	pea weevil
COLEOPTERA: Bruchidae	*Bruchus rufimanus* Boheman	broadbean weevil
COLEOPTERA: Bruchidae	*Callosobruchus maculatus* (Fabricius)	cowpea weevil
COLEOPTERA: Bruchidae	*Stator pruininus* (Horn)	pruinose bean weevil
COLEOPTERA: Bruchidae	*Zabrotes subfasciatus* (Boheman)	Mexican bean weevil
COLEOPTERA: Buprestidae	*Agrilus anxius* Gory	bronze birch borer
COLEOPTERA: Buprestidae	*Agrilus aurichalceus* Redtenbacher	rose stem girdler
COLEOPTERA: Buprestidae	*Agrilus bilineatus* (Weber)	twolined chestnut borer
COLEOPTERA: Buprestidae	*Agrilus liragus* Barter & Brown	bronze poplar borer
COLEOPTERA: Buprestidae	*Agrilus ruficollis* (Fabricius)	rednecked cane borer
COLEOPTERA: Buprestidae	*Agrilus sinuatus* (Olivier)	sinuate peartree borer
COLEOPTERA: Buprestidae	*Buprestis apricans* Herbst	turpentine borer
COLEOPTERA: Buprestidae	*Buprestis aurulenta* Linnaeus	golden buprestid
COLEOPTERA: Buprestidae	*Chalcophora angulicollis* (LeConte)	sculptured pine borer
COLEOPTERA: Buprestidae	*Chrysobothris femorata* (Olivier)	flatheaded appletree borer
COLEOPTERA: Buprestidae	*Chrysobothris mali* Horn	Pacific flatheaded borer
COLEOPTERA: Buprestidae	*Chrysobothris tranquebarica* (Gmelin)	Australianpine borer
COLEOPTERA: Buprestidae	*Chrysophana placida conicola* Van Dyke	flatheaded cone borer

COLEOPTERA: Buprestidae	*Melanophila californica* Van Dyke	California flatheaded borer
COLEOPTERA: Buprestidae	*Melanophila consputa* LeConte	charcoal beetle
COLEOPTERA: Buprestidae	*Melanophila drummondi* (Kirby)	flatheaded fir borer
COLEOPTERA: Buprestidae	*Melanophila fulvoguttata* (Harris)	hemlock borer
COLEOPTERA: Buprestidae	*Trachykele blondeli* Marseul	western cedar borer
COLEOPTERA: Byturidae	*Byturus unicolor* Say	raspberry fruitworm
COLEOPTERA: Carabidae	*Calosoma calidum* (Fabricius)	fiery hunter
COLEOPTERA: Carabidae	*Clivina impressifrons* LeConte	slender seedcorn beetle
COLEOPTERA: Carabidae	*Nomius pygameus* (Dejean)	stink beetle
COLEOPTERA: Carabidae	*Stenolophus lecontei* (Chaudoir)	seedcorn beetle
COLEOPTERA: Carabidae	*Tanystoma maculicolle* (Dejean)	tule beetle
COLEOPTERA: Cerambycidae	*Apomecyna saltator* (Fabricius)	cucurbit longicorn
COLEOPTERA: Cerambycidae	*Arhopalus productus* (LeConte)	new house borer
COLEOPTERA: Cerambycidae	*Callidium antennatum hesperum* Casey	blackhorned pine borer
COLEOPTERA: Cerambycidae	*Canonura princeps* (Walker)	ponderosa pine bark borer
COLEOPTERA: Cerambycidae	*Chlorophorus annularis* (Fabricius)	bamboo borer
COLEOPTERA: Cerambycidae	*Clytoleptus albofasciatus* (Laporte & Gory)	grape trunk borer
COLEOPTERA: Cerambycidae	*Elaphidionoides villosus* (Fabricius)	twig pruner
COLEOPTERA: Cerambycidae	*Enaphalodes rufulus* (Haldeman)	red oak borer
COLEOPTERA: Cerambycidae	*Glycobius speciosus* (Say)	sugar maple borer
COLEOPTERA: Cerambycidae	*Goes tesselatus* (Haldeman)	oak sapling borer
COLEOPTERA: Cerambycidae	*Goes tigrinus* (De Geer)	white oak borer
COLEOPTERA: Cerambycidae	*Hylotrupes bajulus* (Linnaeus)	old house borer
COLEOPTERA: Cerambycidae	*Knulliana cincta* (Drury)	banded hickory borer
COLEOPTERA: Cerambycidae	*Lagocheirus undatus* (Voet)	plumeria borer
COLEOPTERA: Cerambycidae	*Megacyllene caryae* (Gahan)	painted hickory borer
COLEOPTERA: Cerambycidae	*Megacyllene robiniae* (Forster)	locust borer
COLEOPTERA: Cerambycidae	*Monochamus marmorator* Kirby	balsam fir sawyer
COLEOPTERA: Cerambycidae	*Monochamus mutator* LeConte	spotted pine sawyer
COLEOPTERA: Cerambycidae	*Monochamus notatus* (Drury)	northeastern sawyer
COLEOPTERA: Cerambycidae	*Monochamus scutellatus* (Say)	whitespotted sawyer
COLEOPTERA: Cerambycidae	*Monochamus scutellatus oregonensis* (LeConte)	Oregon fir sawyer
COLEOPTERA: Cerambycidae	*Monochamus titillator* (Fabricius)	southern pine sawyer
COLEOPTERA: Cerambycidae	*Neoclytus acuminatus* (Fabricius)	redheaded ash borer
COLEOPTERA: Cerambycidae	*Oberea bimaculata* (Olivier)	raspberry cane borer
COLEOPTERA: Cerambycidae	*Oberea tripunctata* (Swederus)	dogwood twig borer
COLEOPTERA: Cerambycidae	*Oncideres cingulata* (Say)	twig girdler
COLEOPTERA: Cerambycidae	*Paratimia conicola* Fisher	roundheaded cone borer

COLEOPTERA: Cerambycidae	*Phoracantha semipunctata* (Fabricius)	eucalyptus longhorned borer
COLEOPTERA: Cerambycidae	*Placosternus crinicornis* (Chevrolat)	kiawe roundheaded borer
COLEOPTERA: Cerambycidae	*Plagiohammus spinipennis* Thomson	lantana cerambycid
COLEOPTERA: Cerambycidae	*Plectrodera scalator* (Fabricius)	cottonwood borer
COLEOPTERA: Cerambycidae	*Prionus californicus* Motschulsky	California prionus
COLEOPTERA: Cerambycidae	*Prionus imbricornis* (Linnaeus)	tilehorned prionus
COLEOPTERA: Cerambycidae	*Prionus laticollis* (Drury)	broadnecked root borer
COLEOPTERA: Cerambycidae	*Rosalia funebris* Motschulsky	banded alder borer
COLEOPTERA: Cerambycidae	*Saperda calcarata* Say	poplar borer
COLEOPTERA: Cerambycidae	*Saperda candida* Fabricius	roundheaded appletree borer
COLEOPTERA: Cerambycidae	*Saperda candida bipunctata* Hopping	Saskatoon borer
COLEOPTERA: Cerambycidae	*Saperda tridentata* Olivier	elm borer
COLEOPTERA: Cerambycidae	*Saperda vestita* Say	linden borer
COLEOPTERA: Cerambycidae	*Semanotus ligneus* (Fabricius)	cedartree borer
COLEOPTERA: Cerambycidae	*Semanotus litigiosus* (Casey)	firtree borer
COLEOPTERA: Cerambycidae	*Tetraopes tetrophthalmus* (Forster)	red milkweed beetle
COLEOPTERA: Cerambycidae	*Tetropium abietis* Fall	roundheaded fir borer
COLEOPTERA: Cerambycidae	*Ulochaetes leoninus* LeConte	lion beetle
COLEOPTERA: Cerambycidae	*Xylotrechus aceris* Fisher	gallmaking maple borer
COLEOPTERA: Cerambycidae	*Xylotrechus colonus* (Fabricius)	rustic borer
COLEOPTERA: Cerambycidae	*Xystrocera globosa* (Olivier)	monkeypod roundheaded borer
COLEOPTERA: Chrysomelidae	*Acalymma trivittatum* (Mannerheim)	western striped cucumber beetle
COLEOPTERA: Chrysomelidae	*Acalymma vittatum* (Fabricius)	striped cucumber beetle
COLEOPTERA: Chrysomelidae	*Altica canadensis* Gentner	prairie flea beetle
COLEOPTERA: Chrysomelidae	*Altica carinata* Germar	elm flea beetle
COLEOPTERA: Chrysomelidae	*Altica chalybea* Illiger	grape flea beetle
COLEOPTERA: Chrysomelidae	*Altica sylvia* Malloch	blueberry flea beetle
COLEOPTERA: Chrysomelidae	*Anomoea laticlavia* (Forster)	claycolored leaf beetle
COLEOPTERA: Chrysomelidae	*Baliosus nervosus* (Panzer)	basswood leafminer
COLEOPTERA: Chrysomelidae	*Bromius obscurus* (Linnaeus)	western grape rootworm
COLEOPTERA: Chrysomelidae	*Calligrapha scalaris* (LeConte)	elm calligrapha
COLEOPTERA: Chrysomelidae	*Cerotoma trifurcata* (Forster)	bean leaf beetle
COLEOPTERA: Chrysomelidae	*Chaetocnema confinis* Crotch	sweetpotato flea beetle
COLEOPTERA: Chrysomelidae	*Chaetocnema denticulata* (Illiger)	toothed flea beetle
COLEOPTERA: Chrysomelidae	*Chaetocnema ectypa* Horn	desert corn flea beetle
COLEOPTERA: Chrysomelidae	*Chaetocnema pulicaria* Melsheimer	corn flea beetle
COLEOPTERA: Chrysomelidae	*Chelymorpha cassidea* (Fabricius)	argus tortoise beetle
COLEOPTERA: Chrysomelidae	*Chrysolina quadrigemina* (Suffrian)	Klamathweed beetle

COLEOPTERA: Chrysomelidae	*Chrysomela crotchi* Brown	aspen leaf beetle
COLEOPTERA: Chrysomelidae	*Chrysomela scripta* Fabricius	cottonwood leaf beetle
COLEOPTERA: Chrysomelidae	*Colaspis brunnea* (Fabricius)	grape colaspis
COLEOPTERA: Chrysomelidae	*Colaspis pini* Barber	pine colaspis
COLEOPTERA: Chrysomelidae	*Crioceris asparagi* (Linnaeus)	asparagus beetle
COLEOPTERA: Chrysomelidae	*Crioceris duodecimpunctata* (Linnaeus)	spotted asparagus beetle
COLEOPTERA: Chrysomelidae	*Deloyala guttata* (Olivier)	mottled tortoise beetle
COLEOPTERA: Chrysomelidae	*Derocrepis erythropus* (Melsheimer)	redlegged flea beetle
COLEOPTERA: Chrysomelidae	*Diabrotica balteata* LeConte	banded cucumber beetle
COLEOPTERA: Chrysomelidae	*Diabrotica barberi* Smith & Lawrence	northern corn rootworm
COLEOPTERA: Chrysomelidae	*Diabrotica undecimpunctata howardi* Barber	spotted cucumber beetle[46]
COLEOPTERA: Chrysomelidae	*Diabrotica undecimpunctata undecimpunctata* Mannerheim	western spotted cucumber beetle
COLEOPTERA: Chrysomelidae	*Diabrotica virgifera virgifera* LeConte	western corn rootworm
COLEOPTERA: Chrysomelidae	*Diabrotica virgifera zeae* Krysan & Smith	Mexican corn rootworm
COLEOPTERA: Chrysomelidae	*Diachus auratus* (Fabricius)	bronze leaf beetle
COLEOPTERA: Chrysomelidae	*Disonycha triangularis* (Say)	threespotted flea beetle
COLEOPTERA: Chrysomelidae	*Disonycha xanthomelas* (Dalman)	spinach flea beetle
COLEOPTERA: Chrysomelidae	*Entomoscelis americana* Brown	red turnip beetle
COLEOPTERA: Chrysomelidae	*Epitrix cucumeris* (Harris)	potato flea beetle
COLEOPTERA: Chrysomelidae	*Epitrix fuscula* Crotch	eggplant flea beetle
COLEOPTERA: Chrysomelidae	*Epitrix hirtipennis* (Melsheimer)	tobacco flea beetle
COLEOPTERA: Chrysomelidae	*Epitrix subcrinita* LeConte	western potato flea beetle
COLEOPTERA: Chrysomelidae	*Epitrix tuberis* Gentner	tuber flea beetle
COLEOPTERA: Chrysomelidae	*Erynephala puncticollis* (Say)	beet leaf beetle
COLEOPTERA: Chrysomelidae	*Fidia viticida* Walsh	grape rootworm
COLEOPTERA: Chrysomelidae	*Galeruca browni* Blake	peppergrass beetle
COLEOPTERA: Chrysomelidae	*Galerucella nymphaeae* (Linnaeus)	waterlily leaf beetle
COLEOPTERA: Chrysomelidae	*Gonioctena americana* (Schaeffer)	American aspen beetle
COLEOPTERA: Chrysomelidae	*Jonthonota nigripes* (Olivier)	blacklegged tortoise beetle
COLEOPTERA: Chrysomelidae	*Lema trilinea* White	threelined potato beetle
COLEOPTERA: Chrysomelidae	*Leptinotarsa decemlineata* (Say)	Colorado potato beetle
COLEOPTERA: Chrysomelidae	*Leptinotarsa juncta* (Germar)	false potato beetle
COLEOPTERA: Chrysomelidae	*Lilioceris lilii* (Scopoli)	lily leaf beetle
COLEOPTERA: Chrysomelidae	*Macrohaltica ambiens* (LeConte)	alder flea beetle

---

[46]Immature called southern corn rootworm.

COLEOPTERA: Chrysomelidae	*Metrioidea brunneus* (Crotch)	corn silk beetle
COLEOPTERA: Chrysomelidae	*Metriona bicolor* (Fabricius)	golden tortoise beetle
COLEOPTERA: Chrysomelidae	*Microtheca ochroloma* Stål	yellowmargined leaf beetle
COLEOPTERA: Chrysomelidae	*Monocesta coryli* (Say)	larger elm leaf beetle
COLEOPTERA: Chrysomelidae	*Neochlamisus cribripennis* (LeConte)	blueberry case beetle
COLEOPTERA: Chrysomelidae	*Nodonota puncticollis* (Say)	rose leaf beetle
COLEOPTERA: Chrysomelidae	*Octotoma scabripennis* Guérin-Méneville	lantana leaf beetle
COLEOPTERA: Chrysomelidae	*Odontota dorsalis* (Thunberg)	locust leafminer
COLEOPTERA: Chrysomelidae	*Oulema melanopus* (Linnaeus)	cereal leaf beetle
COLEOPTERA: Chrysomelidae	*Paria fragariae* Wilcox	strawberry rootworm
COLEOPTERA: Chrysomelidae	*Phaedon viridus* (Melsheimer)	watercress leaf beetle
COLEOPTERA: Chrysomelidae	*Phyllotreta armoraciae* (Koch)	horseradish flea beetle
COLEOPTERA: Chrysomelidae	*Phyllotreta pusilla* Horn	western black flea beetle
COLEOPTERA: Chrysomelidae	*Phyllotreta ramosa* (Crotch)	western striped flea beetle
COLEOPTERA: Chrysomelidae	*Phyllotreta striolata* (Fabricius)	striped flea beetle
COLEOPTERA: Chrysomelidae	*Plagiodera versicolora* (Laicharting)	imported willow leaf beetle
COLEOPTERA: Chrysomelidae	*Psylliodes punctulata* Melsheimer	hop flea beetle
COLEOPTERA: Chrysomelidae	*Pyrrhalta cavicollis* (LeConte)	cherry leaf beetle
COLEOPTERA: Chrysomelidae	*Pyrrhalta decora carbo* (LeConte)	Pacific willow leaf beetle
COLEOPTERA: Chrysomelidae	*Pyrrhalta decora decora* (Say)	gray willow leaf beetle
COLEOPTERA: Chrysomelidae	*Pyrrhalta luteola* (Müller)	elm leaf beetle
COLEOPTERA: Chrysomelidae	*Rhabdopterus picipes* (Olivier)	cranberry rootworm
COLEOPTERA: Chrysomelidae	*Systena blanda* Melsheimer	palestriped flea beetle
COLEOPTERA: Chrysomelidae	*Systena elongata* (Fabricius)	elongate flea beetle
COLEOPTERA: Chrysomelidae	*Typophorus nigritus viridicyaneus* (Crotch)	sweetpotato leaf beetle
COLEOPTERA: Chrysomelidae	*Uroplata girardi* Pic	lantana hispid
COLEOPTERA: Chrysomelidae	*Zygogramma exclamationis* (Fabricius)	sunflower beetle
COLEOPTERA: Cleridae	*Enoclerus lecontei* (Wolcott)	blackbellied clerid
COLEOPTERA: Cleridae	*Necrobia ruficollis* (Fabricius)	redshouldered ham beetle
COLEOPTERA: Cleridae	*Necrobia rufipes* (De Geer)	redlegged ham beetle
COLEOPTERA: Coccinellidae	*Adalia bipunctata* (Linnaeus)	twospotted lady beetle
COLEOPTERA: Coccinellidae	*Brumoides suturalis* (Fabricius)	threestriped lady beetle
COLEOPTERA: Coccinellidae	*Chilocorus stigma* (Say)	twicestabbed lady beetle
COLEOPTERA: Coccinellidae	*Coccinella septempunctata* Linnaeus	sevenspotted lady beetle
COLEOPTERA: Coccinellidae	*Coccinella transversoguttata richardsoni* Brown	transverse lady beetle
COLEOPTERA: Coccinellidae	*Coelophora inaequalis* (Fabricius)	common Australian lady beetle
COLEOPTERA: Coccinellidae	*Coelophora pupillata* (Swartz)	tenspotted lady beetle
COLEOPTERA: Coccinellidae	*Cryptolaemus montrouzieri* Mulsant	mealybug destroyer

COLEOPTERA: Coccinellidae	*Epilachna borealis* (Fabricius)	squash beetle
COLEOPTERA: Coccinellidae	*Epilachna varivestis* Mulsant	Mexican bean beetle
COLEOPTERA: Coccinellidae	*Hippodamia convergens* Guérin-Méneville	convergent lady beetle
COLEOPTERA: Coccinellidae	*Hippodamia sinuata* Mulsant	sinuate lady beetle
COLEOPTERA: Coccinellidae	*Hippodamia tredecimpunctata tibialis* (Say)	thirteenspotted lady beetle
COLEOPTERA: Coccinellidae	*Hyperaspis jocosa* (Mulsant)	orthezia lady beetle
COLEOPTERA: Coccinellidae	*Orcus chalybeus* (Boisduval)	steelblue lady beetle
COLEOPTERA: Coccinellidae	*Rhyzobius ventralis* (Erichson)	black lady beetle
COLEOPTERA: Coccinellidae	*Rodolia cardinalis* (Mulsant)	vedalia
COLEOPTERA: Coccinellidae	*Scymnodes lividigaster* (Mulsant)	yellowshouldered lady beetle
COLEOPTERA: Coccinellidae	*Stethorus picipes* Casey	spider mite destroyer
COLEOPTERA: Cryptophagidae	*Cryptophagus acutangulus* Gyllenhal	acute-angled fungus beetle
COLEOPTERA: Cryptophagidae	*Cryptophagus varus* Woodroffe & Coombs	Sigmoid fungus beetle
COLEOPTERA: Cucujidae	*Ahasverus advena* (Waltl)	foreign grain beetle
COLEOPTERA: Cucujidae	*Cathartus quadricollis* (Guérin-Méneville)	squarenecked grain beetle
COLEOPTERA: Cucujidae	*Cryptolestes ferrugineus* (Stephens)	rusty grain beetle
COLEOPTERA: Cucujidae	*Cryptolestes pusillus* (Schnherr)	flat grain beetle
COLEOPTERA: Cucujidae	*Oryzaephilus mercator* (Fauvel)	merchant grain beetle
COLEOPTERA: Cucujidae	*Oryzaephilus surinamensis* (Linnaeus)	sawtoothed grain beetle
COLEOPTERA: Curculionidae	*Agasphaerops nigra* Horn	lily weevil
COLEOPTERA: Curculionidae	*Ampeloglypter sesostris* (LeConte)	grape cane gallmaker
COLEOPTERA: Curculionidae	*Anthonomus eugenii* Cano	pepper weevil
COLEOPTERA: Curculionidae	*Anthonomus grandis grandis* Boheman	boll weevil
COLEOPTERA: Curculionidae	*Anthonomus grandis thurberiae* Pierce	thurberia weevil
COLEOPTERA: Curculionidae	*Anthonomus musculus* Say	cranberry weevil
COLEOPTERA: Curculionidae	*Anthonomus signatus* Say	strawberry bud weevil
COLEOPTERA: Curculionidae	*Apion (Fallapion) occidentale* Fall	black sunflower stem weevil
COLEOPTERA: Curculionidae	*Apion antiquum* Gyllenhal	South African emex weevil
COLEOPTERA: Curculionidae	*Apion longirostre* Olivier	hollyhock weevil
COLEOPTERA: Curculionidae	*Apion ulicis* (Frster)	gorse seed weevil
COLEOPTERA: Curculionidae	*Asynonychus godmani* Crotch	Fuller rose beetle
COLEOPTERA: Curculionidae	*Athesapeuta cyperi* Marshall	nutgrass weevil
COLEOPTERA: Curculionidae	*Baris lepidii* Germar	imported crucifer weevil
COLEOPTERA: Curculionidae	*Baris strenua* (LeConte)	sunflower root weevil
COLEOPTERA: Curculionidae	*Callirhopalus bifasciatus* (Roelofs)	twobanded Japanese weevil
COLEOPTERA: Curculionidae	*Calomycterus setarius* Roelofs	imported longhorned weevil
COLEOPTERA: Curculionidae	*Caulophilus oryzae* (Gyllenhal)	broadnosed grain weevil
COLEOPTERA: Curculionidae	*Ceutorhynchus assimilis* (Paykull)	cabbage seedpod weevil

COLEOPTERA: Curculionidae	*Ceutorhynchus quadridens* (Panzer)	cabbage seedstalk curculio
COLEOPTERA: Curculionidae	*Ceutorhynchus rapae* Gyllenhal	cabbage curculio
COLEOPTERA: Curculionidae	*Chalcodermus aeneus* Boheman	cowpea curculio
COLEOPTERA: Curculionidae	*Coccotorus hirsutus* Bruner	sandcherry weevil
COLEOPTERA: Curculionidae	*Coccotorus scutellaris* (LeConte)	plum gouger
COLEOPTERA: Curculionidae	*Conotrachelus crataegi* Walsh	quince curculio
COLEOPTERA: Curculionidae	*Conotrachelus juglandis* LeConte	butternut curculio
COLEOPTERA: Curculionidae	*Conotrachelus nenuphar* (Herbst)	plum curculio
COLEOPTERA: Curculionidae	*Conotrachelus retentus* (Say)	black walnut curculio
COLEOPTERA: Curculionidae	*Cosmopolites sordidus* (Germar)	banana root borer
COLEOPTERA: Curculionidae	*Craponius inaequalis* (Say)	grape curculio
COLEOPTERA: Curculionidae	*Cryptorhynchus lapathi* (Linnaeus)	poplar-and-willow borer
COLEOPTERA: Curculionidae	*Cryptorhynchus mangiferae* (Fabricius)	mango weevil
COLEOPTERA: Curculionidae	*Curculio caryae* (Horn)	pecan weevil
COLEOPTERA: Curculionidae	*Curculio caryatrypes* (Boheman)	large chestnut weevil
COLEOPTERA: Curculionidae	*Curculio obtusus* (Blanchard)	hazelnut weevil
COLEOPTERA: Curculionidae	*Curculio occidentis* (Casey)	filbert weevil
COLEOPTERA: Curculionidae	*Curculio sayi* (Gyllenhal)	small chestnut weevil
COLEOPTERA: Curculionidae	*Cylas formicarius elegantulus* (Summers)	sweetpotato weevil
COLEOPTERA: Curculionidae	*Cylindrocopturus adspersus* (LeConte)	sunflower stem weevil
COLEOPTERA: Curculionidae	*Cylindrocopturus furnissi* Buchanan	Douglas-fir twig weevil
COLEOPTERA: Curculionidae	*Cyrtepistomus castaneus* (Roelofs)	Asiatic oak weevil
COLEOPTERA: Curculionidae	*Diocalandra taitensis* (Guérin-Méneville)	Tahitian coconut weevil
COLEOPTERA: Curculionidae	*Elytroteinus subtruncatus* (Fairmaire)	Fijian ginger weevil
COLEOPTERA: Curculionidae	*Epicaerus imbricatus* (Say)	imbricated snout beetle
COLEOPTERA: Curculionidae	*Euscepes postfaciatus* (Fairmaire)	West Indian sweetpotato weevil
COLEOPTERA: Curculionidae	*Graphognathus* spp.	whitefringed beetles
COLEOPTERA: Curculionidae	*Haplorhynchites aeneus* (Boheman)	sunflower headclipping weevil
COLEOPTERA: Curculionidae	*Hylobius aliradicis* Warner	southern pine root weevil
COLEOPTERA: Curculionidae	*Hylobius assimilis* Boheman	pine root tip weevil
COLEOPTERA: Curculionidae	*Hylobius pales* (Herbst)	pales weevil
COLEOPTERA: Curculionidae	*Hylobius radicis* Buchanan	pine root collar weevil
COLEOPTERA: Curculionidae	*Hypera brunnipennis* (Boheman)	Egyptian alfalfa weevil
COLEOPTERA: Curculionidae	*Hypera meles* (Fabricius)	clover head weevil
COLEOPTERA: Curculionidae	*Hypera nigrirostris* (Fabricius)	lesser clover leaf weevil
COLEOPTERA: Curculionidae	*Hypera postica* (Gyllenhal)	alfalfa weevil
COLEOPTERA: Curculionidae	*Hypera punctata* (Fabricius)	clover leaf weevil
COLEOPTERA: Curculionidae	*Hypurus bertrandi* Perris	portulaca leafmining weevil

COLEOPTERA: Curculionidae	*Ithycerus noveboracensis* (Forster)	New York weevil
COLEOPTERA: Curculionidae	*Lissorhoptrus oryzophilus* Kuschel	rice water weevil
COLEOPTERA: Curculionidae	*Listroderes difficilis* Germar	vegetable weevil
COLEOPTERA: Curculionidae	*Listronotus oregonensis* (LeConte)	carrot weevil
COLEOPTERA: Curculionidae	*Lixus concavus* Say	rhubarb curculio
COLEOPTERA: Curculionidae	*Macrocopturus floridanus* (Fall)	mahogany bark weevil
COLEOPTERA: Curculionidae	*Magdalis aenescens* LeConte	bronze appletree weevil
COLEOPTERA: Curculionidae	*Magdalis armicollis* (Say)	red elm bark weevil
COLEOPTERA: Curculionidae	*Magdalis barbita* (Say)	black elm bark weevil
COLEOPTERA: Curculionidae	*Merhynchites bicolor* (Fabricius)	rose curculio
COLEOPTERA: Curculionidae	*Metamasius hemipterus hemipterus* (Linnaeus)	West Indian cane weevil
COLEOPTERA: Curculionidae	*Metamasius hemipterus sericeus* (Olivier)	silky cane weevil
COLEOPTERA: Curculionidae	*Metamasius ritchiei* Marshall	pineapple weevil
COLEOPTERA: Curculionidae	*Microlarinus lareynii* (Jacquelin du Val)	puncturevine seed weevil
COLEOPTERA: Curculionidae	*Microlarinus lypriformis* (Wollaston)	puncturevine stem weevil
COLEOPTERA: Curculionidae	*Mononychus vulpeculus* (Fabricius)	iris weevil
COLEOPTERA: Curculionidae	*Nemocestes incomptus* (Horn)	woods weevil
COLEOPTERA: Curculionidae	*Orchidophilus peregrinator* Buchanan	lesser orchid weevil
COLEOPTERA: Curculionidae	*Orthorhinus klugi* Boheman	immigrant acacia weevil
COLEOPTERA: Curculionidae	*Otiorhynchus cribricollis* Gyllenhal	cribrate weevil
COLEOPTERA: Curculionidae	*Otiorhynchus ligustici* (Linnaeus)	alfalfa snout beetle
COLEOPTERA: Curculionidae	*Otiorhynchus ovatus* (Linnaeus)	strawberry root weevil
COLEOPTERA: Curculionidae	*Otiorhynchus sulcatus* (Fabricius)	black vine weevil
COLEOPTERA: Curculionidae	*Pachnaeus litus* (Germar)	citrus root weevil
COLEOPTERA: Curculionidae	*Pachylobius picivorus* (Germar)	pitch-eating weevil
COLEOPTERA: Curculionidae	*Phyllobius intrusus* Kôno	arborvitae weevil
COLEOPTERA: Curculionidae	*Pissodes nemorensis* Germar	eastern pine weevil
COLEOPTERA: Curculionidae	*Pissodes radiatae* Hopkins	Monterey pine weevil
COLEOPTERA: Curculionidae	*Pissodes schwarzi* Hopkins	Yosemite bark weevil
COLEOPTERA: Curculionidae	*Pissodes strobi* (Peck)	Engelmann spruce weevil[47]
COLEOPTERA: Curculionidae	*Pissodes terminalis* Hopping	lodgepole terminal weevil
COLEOPTERA: Curculionidae	*Podapion gallicola* Riley	pine gall weevil
COLEOPTERA: Curculionidae	*Pseudanthonomus validus* Dietz	currant fruit weevil
COLEOPTERA: Curculionidae	*Rhabdoscelus obscurus* (Boisduval)	New Guinea sugarcane weevil
COLEOPTERA: Curculionidae	*Rhodobaenus quinquedecimpunctatus* (Say)	cocklebur weevil

---

[47]Also called Sitka spruce weevil and white pine weevil.

COLEOPTERA: Curculionidae	*Rhynchaenus pallicornis* (Say)	apple flea weevil
COLEOPTERA: Curculionidae	*Rhynchaenus rufipes* (LeConte)	willow flea weevil
COLEOPTERA: Curculionidae	*Sciopithes obscurus* Horn	obscure root weevil
COLEOPTERA: Curculionidae	*Sitona cylindricollis* Fåhraeus	sweetclover weevil
COLEOPTERA: Curculionidae	*Sitona hispidulus* (Fabricius)	clover root curculio
COLEOPTERA: Curculionidae	*Sitona lineatus* (Linnaeus)	pea leaf weevil
COLEOPTERA: Curculionidae	*Sitophilus granarius* (Linnaeus)	granary weevil
COLEOPTERA: Curculionidae	*Sitophilus linearis* (Herbst)	tamarind weevil
COLEOPTERA: Curculionidae	*Sitophilus oryzae* (Linnaeus)	rice weevil
COLEOPTERA: Curculionidae	*Sitophilus zeamais* Motschulsky	maize weevil
COLEOPTERA: Curculionidae	*Smicronyx fulvus* LeConte	red sunflower seed weevil
COLEOPTERA: Curculionidae	*Smicronyx sculpticollis* Casey	dodder gall weevil
COLEOPTERA: Curculionidae	*Smicronyx sordidus* LeConte	gray sunflower seed weevil
COLEOPTERA: Curculionidae	*Sphenophorus aequalis aequalis* Gyllenhal	claycolored billbug
COLEOPTERA: Curculionidae	*Sphenophorus callosus* (Olivier)	southern corn billbug
COLEOPTERA: Curculionidae	*Sphenophorus cariosus* (Olivier)	nutgrass billbug
COLEOPTERA: Curculionidae	*Sphenophorus maidis* Chittenden	maize billbug
COLEOPTERA: Curculionidae	*Sphenophorus parvulus* Gyllenhal	bluegrass billbug
COLEOPTERA: Curculionidae	*Sphenophorus venatus vestitus* Chittenden	hunting billbug
COLEOPTERA: Curculionidae	*Sternechus paludatus* (Casey)	bean stalk weevil
COLEOPTERA: Curculionidae	*Syagrius fulvitarsis* Pascoe	Australian fern weevil
COLEOPTERA: Curculionidae	*Tachypterellus quadrigibbus* (Say)	apple curculio
COLEOPTERA: Curculionidae	*Trichobaris mucorea* (LeConte)	tobacco stalk borer
COLEOPTERA: Curculionidae	*Trichobaris trinotata* (Say)	potato stalk borer
COLEOPTERA: Curculionidae	*Tychius picirostris* (Fabricius)	clover seed weevil
COLEOPTERA: Curculionidae	*Tychius stephensi* Schnherr	red clover seed weevil
COLEOPTERA: Curculionidae	*Tyloderma fragariae* (Riley)	strawberry crown borer
COLEOPTERA: Dermestidae	*Anthrenus flavipes* LeConte	furniture carpet beetle
COLEOPTERA: Dermestidae	*Anthrenus scrophulariae* (Linnaeus)	carpet beetle
COLEOPTERA: Dermestidae	*Anthrenus verbasci* (Linnaeus)	varied carpet beetle
COLEOPTERA: Dermestidae	*Attagenus fasciatus* (Thunberg)	wardrobe beetle
COLEOPTERA: Dermestidae	*Attagenus unicolor* (Brahm)	black carpet beetle
COLEOPTERA: Dermestidae	*Dermestes ater* De Geer	black larder beetle
COLEOPTERA: Dermestidae	*Dermestes lardarius* Linnaeus	larder beetle
COLEOPTERA: Dermestidae	*Dermestes maculatus* De Geer	hide beetle
COLEOPTERA: Dermestidae	*Thylodrias contractus* Motschulsky	odd beetle
COLEOPTERA: Dermestidae	*Trogoderma granarium* Everts	khapra beetle
COLEOPTERA: Dermestidae	*Trogoderma variabile* Ballion	warehouse beetle

COLEOPTERA: Elateridae	*Agriotes lineatus* (Linnaeus)	lined click beetle
COLEOPTERA: Elateridae	*Agriotes mancus* (Say)	wheat wireworm
COLEOPTERA: Elateridae	*Alaus oculatus* (Linnaeus)	eyed click beetle
COLEOPTERA: Elateridae	*Conoderus amplicollis* (Gyllenhal)	Gulf wireworm
COLEOPTERA: Elateridae	*Conoderus falli* Lane	southern potato wireworm
COLEOPTERA: Elateridae	*Conoderus vespertinus* (Fabricius)	tobacco wireworm
COLEOPTERA: Elateridae	*Ctenicera aeripennis aeripennis* (Kirby)	Puget Sound wireworm
COLEOPTERA: Elateridae	*Ctenicera aeripennis destructor* (Brown)	prairie grain wireworm
COLEOPTERA: Elateridae	*Ctenicera glauca* (Germar)	dryland wireworm
COLEOPTERA: Elateridae	*Ctenicera pruinina* (Horn)	Great Basin wireworm
COLEOPTERA: Elateridae	*Horistonotus uhlerii* Horn	sand wireworm
COLEOPTERA: Elateridae	*Hypolithus abbreviatus* (Say)	abbreviated wireworm
COLEOPTERA: Elateridae	*Limonius agonus* (Say)	eastern field wireworm
COLEOPTERA: Elateridae	*Limonius californicus* (Mannerheim)	sugarbeet wireworm
COLEOPTERA: Elateridae	*Limonius canus* LeConte	Pacific Coast wireworm
COLEOPTERA: Elateridae	*Limonius infuscatus* Motschulsky	western field wireworm
COLEOPTERA: Elateridae	*Limonius subauratus* LeConte	Columbia Basin wireworm
COLEOPTERA: Elateridae	*Melanotus longulus oregonensis* (LeConte)	Oregon wireworm
COLEOPTERA: Languriidae	*Languria mozardi* Latreille	clover stem borer
COLEOPTERA: Lathridiidae	*Cartodere constricta* (Gyllenhal)	plaster beetle
COLEOPTERA: Lathridiidae	*Lathridius minutus* (Linnaeus)	squarenosed fungus beetle
COLEOPTERA: Lathridiidae	*Thes bergrothi* (Reitter)	ridgewinged fungus beetle
COLEOPTERA: Lucanidae	*Lucanus elaphus* Fabricius	giant stag beetle
COLEOPTERA: Lyctidae	*Lyctus planicollis* LeConte	southern lyctus beetle
COLEOPTERA: Lymexylidae	*Hylecoetus lugubris* Say	sapwood timberworm
COLEOPTERA: Lymexylidae	*Melittomma sericeum* (Harris)	chestnut timberworm
COLEOPTERA: Meloidae	*Epicauta cinerea* (Forster)	clematis blister beetle
COLEOPTERA: Meloidae	*Epicauta fabricii* (LeConte)	ashgray blister beetle
COLEOPTERA: Meloidae	*Epicauta lemniscata* (Fabricius)	threestriped blister beetle
COLEOPTERA: Meloidae	*Epicauta maculata* (Say)	spotted blister beetle
COLEOPTERA: Meloidae	*Epicauta pennsylvanica* (De Geer)	black blister beetle
COLEOPTERA: Meloidae	*Epicauta pestifera* Werner	margined blister beetle
COLEOPTERA: Meloidae	*Epicauta subglabra* (Fall)	caragana blister beetle
COLEOPTERA: Meloidae	*Epicauta vittata* (Fabricius)	striped blister beetle
COLEOPTERA: Meloidae	*Lytta (Pomphopoea) sayi* (LeConte)	Say blister beetle
COLEOPTERA: Meloidae	*Lytta nuttalli* Say	Nuttall blister beetle
COLEOPTERA: Meloidae	*Lytta vesicatoria* (Linnaeus)	Spanishfly
COLEOPTERA: Mycetophagidae	*Mycetophagus quadriguttatus* P. Müller	spotted hairy fungus beetle

COLEOPTERA: Mycetophagidae	*Typhaea stercorea* (Linnaeus)	hairy fungus beetle
COLEOPTERA: Nitidulidae	*Carpophilus dimidiatus* (Fabricius)	corn sap beetle
COLEOPTERA: Nitidulidae	*Carpophilus hemipterus* (Linnaeus)	driedfruit beetle
COLEOPTERA: Nitidulidae	*Carpophilus lugubris* Murray	dusky sap beetle
COLEOPTERA: Nitidulidae	*Stelidota geminata* (Say)	strawberry sap beetle
COLEOPTERA: Oedemeridae	*Eobia bicolor* (Fairmaire)	redblack oedemerid
COLEOPTERA: Oedemeridae	*Nacerdes melanura* (Linnaeus)	wharf borer
COLEOPTERA: Passalidae	*Odontotaenius disjunctus* (Illiger)	horned passalus
COLEOPTERA: Phalacridae	*Phalacrus politus* Melsheimer	smut beetle
COLEOPTERA: Ptinidae	*Mezium americanum* (Laporte)	American spider beetle
COLEOPTERA: Ptinidae	*Niptus hololeucus* (Faldermann)	golden spider beetle
COLEOPTERA: Ptinidae	*Ptinus clavipes* Panzer	brown spider beetle
COLEOPTERA: Ptinidae	*Ptinus fur* (Linnaeus)	whitemarked spider beetle
COLEOPTERA: Ptinidae	*Ptinus ocellus* Brown	Australian spider beetle
COLEOPTERA: Ptinidae	*Ptinus villiger* (Reitter)	hairy spider beetle
COLEOPTERA: Ptinidae	*Trigonogenius globulum* Solier	globular spider beetle
COLEOPTERA: Scarabaeidae	*Adoretus sinicus* Burmeister	Chinese rose beetle
COLEOPTERA: Scarabaeidae	*Anomala oblivia* Horn	pine chafer
COLEOPTERA: Scarabaeidae	*Anomala orientalis* Waterhouse	oriental beetle
COLEOPTERA: Scarabaeidae	*Ataenius spretulus* (Haldeman)	black turfgrass ataenius
COLEOPTERA: Scarabaeidae	*Copris incertus prociduus* (Say)	black dung beetle
COLEOPTERA: Scarabaeidae	*Cotinis nitida* (Linnaeus)	green June beetle
COLEOPTERA: Scarabaeidae	*Cyclocephala borealis* Arrow	northern masked chafer
COLEOPTERA: Scarabaeidae	*Cyclocephala immaculata* (Olivier)	southern masked chafer
COLEOPTERA: Scarabaeidae	*Dichelonyx backi* (Kirby)	green rose chafer
COLEOPTERA: Scarabaeidae	*Dynastes granti* Horn	southwestern Hercules beetle
COLEOPTERA: Scarabaeidae	*Dynastes tityus* (Linnaeus)	eastern Hercules beetle
COLEOPTERA: Scarabaeidae	*Euetheola humilis rugiceps* (LeConte)	sugarcane beetle
COLEOPTERA: Scarabaeidae	*Euphoria inda* (Linnaeus)	bumble flower beetle
COLEOPTERA: Scarabaeidae	*Ligyrus gibbosus* (De Geer)	carrot beetle
COLEOPTERA: Scarabaeidae	*Macrodactylus subspinosus* (Fabricius)	rose chafer
COLEOPTERA: Scarabaeidae	*Maladera castanea* (Arrow)	Asiatic garden beetle
COLEOPTERA: Scarabaeidae	*Onthophagus gazella* Fabricius	brown dung beetle
COLEOPTERA: Scarabaeidae	*Pleocoma* spp.	rain beetles
COLEOPTERA: Scarabaeidae	*Polyphylla decemlineata* (Say)	tenlined June beetle
COLEOPTERA: Scarabaeidae	*Popillia japonica* Newman	Japanese beetle
COLEOPTERA: Scarabaeidae	*Protaetia fusca* (Herbst)	mango flower beetle
COLEOPTERA: Scarabaeidae	*Rhizotrogus (Amphimallon) majalis* (Razoumowsky)	European chafer

Order: Family	Species	Common name
COLEOPTERA: Scarabaeidae	*Xyloryctes jamaicensis* (Drury)	rhinoceros beetle
COLEOPTERA: Scolytidae	*Alniphagus aspericollis* (LeConte)	alder bark beetle
COLEOPTERA: Scolytidae	*Conophthorus banksianae* McPherson	jack pine tip beetle
COLEOPTERA: Scolytidae	*Conophthorus coniperda* (Schwarz)	white pine cone beetle
COLEOPTERA: Scolytidae	*Conophthorus edulis* Hopkins	pinon cone beetle
COLEOPTERA: Scolytidae	*Conophthorus lambertianae* Hopkins	sugar pine cone beetle
COLEOPTERA: Scolytidae	*Conophthorus ponderosae* Hopkins	ponderosa pine cone beetle[48]
COLEOPTERA: Scolytidae	*Conophthorus radiatae* Hopkins	Monterey pine cone beetle
COLEOPTERA: Scolytidae	*Conophthorus resinosae* Hopkins	red pine cone beetle
COLEOPTERA: Scolytidae	*Corthylus columbianus* Hopkins	Columbian timber beetle
COLEOPTERA: Scolytidae	*Dendroctonus adjunctus* Blandford	roundheaded pine beetle
COLEOPTERA: Scolytidae	*Dendroctonus approximatus* Dietz	Mexican pine beetle
COLEOPTERA: Scolytidae	*Dendroctonus brevicomis* LeConte	western pine beetle
COLEOPTERA: Scolytidae	*Dendroctonus frontalis* Zimmermann	southern pine beetle
COLEOPTERA: Scolytidae	*Dendroctonus jeffreyi* Hopkins	Jeffrey pine beetle
COLEOPTERA: Scolytidae	*Dendroctonus micans* (Kugelann)	European spruce beetle
COLEOPTERA: Scolytidae	*Dendroctonus murrayanae* Hopkins	lodgepole pine beetle
COLEOPTERA: Scolytidae	*Dendroctonus ponderosae* Hopkins	mountain pine beetle
COLEOPTERA: Scolytidae	*Dendroctonus pseudotsugae* Hopkins	Douglas-fir beetle
COLEOPTERA: Scolytidae	*Dendroctonus punctatus* LeConte	Allegheny spruce beetle
COLEOPTERA: Scolytidae	*Dendroctonus rufipennis* (Kirby)	spruce beetle
COLEOPTERA: Scolytidae	*Dendroctonus simplex* LeConte	eastern larch beetle
COLEOPTERA: Scolytidae	*Dendroctonus terebrans* (Olivier)	black turpentine beetle
COLEOPTERA: Scolytidae	*Dendroctonus valens* LeConte	red turpentine beetle
COLEOPTERA: Scolytidae	*Dryocoetes betulae* Hopkins	birch bark beetle
COLEOPTERA: Scolytidae	*Dryocoetes confusus* Swaine	western balsam bark beetle
COLEOPTERA: Scolytidae	*Hylastinus obscurus* (Marsham)	clover root borer
COLEOPTERA: Scolytidae	*Hylurgopinus rufipes* (Eichhoff)	native elm bark beetle
COLEOPTERA: Scolytidae	*Hypocryphalus mangiferae* (Stebbing)	mango bark beetle
COLEOPTERA: Scolytidae	*Hypothenemus birmanus* (Eichhoff)	kiawe scolytid
COLEOPTERA: Scolytidae	*Hypothenemus obscurus* (Fabricius)	apple twig beetle
COLEOPTERA: Scolytidae	*Hypothenemus pubescens* Hopkins	grass scolytid
COLEOPTERA: Scolytidae	*Ips avulsus* (Eichhoff)	small southern pine engraver
COLEOPTERA: Scolytidae	*Ips calligraphus* (Germar)	sixspined ips
COLEOPTERA: Scolytidae	*Ips grandicollis* (Eichhoff)	eastern fivespined ips

[48]Also called lodgepole cone weevil.

COLEOPTERA: Scolytidae	*Ips paraconfusus* Lanier	California fivespined ips
COLEOPTERA: Scolytidae	*Ips pini* (Say)	pine engraver
COLEOPTERA: Scolytidae	*Phloeosinus punctatus* LeConte	western cedar bark beetle
COLEOPTERA: Scolytidae	*Phloeotribus liminaris* (Harris)	peach bark beetle
COLEOPTERA: Scolytidae	*Scolytus mali* (Bechstein)	larger shothole borer
COLEOPTERA: Scolytidae	*Scolytus multistriatus* (Marsham)	smaller European elm bark beetle
COLEOPTERA: Scolytidae	*Scolytus muticus* Say	hackberry engraver
COLEOPTERA: Scolytidae	*Scolytus quadrispinosus* Say	hickory bark beetle
COLEOPTERA: Scolytidae	*Scolytus rugulosus* (Müller)	shothole borer
COLEOPTERA: Scolytidae	*Scolytus unispinosus* LeConte	Douglas-fir engraver
COLEOPTERA: Scolytidae	*Scolytus ventralis* LeConte	fir engraver
COLEOPTERA: Scolytidae	*Trypodendron lineatum* (Olivier)	striped ambrosia beetle
COLEOPTERA: Scolytidae	*Xylosandrus compactus* (Eichhoff)	black twig borer
COLEOPTERA: Staphylinidae	*Creophilus maxillosus* (Linnaeus)	hairy rove beetle
COLEOPTERA: Tenebrionidae	*Alphitobius diaperinus* (Panzer)	lesser mealworm
COLEOPTERA: Tenebrionidae	*Alphitobius laevigatus* (Fabricius)	black fungus beetle
COLEOPTERA: Tenebrionidae	*Alphitophagus bifasciatus* (Say)	twobanded fungus beetle
COLEOPTERA: Tenebrionidae	*Cynaeus angustus* (LeConte)	larger black flour beetle
COLEOPTERA: Tenebrionidae	*Eleodes opacus* (Say)	plains false wireworm
COLEOPTERA: Tenebrionidae	*Gnatocerus cornutus* (Fabricius)	broadhorned flour beetle
COLEOPTERA: Tenebrionidae	*Gnatocerus maxillosus* (Fabricius)	slenderhorned flour beetle
COLEOPTERA: Tenebrionidae	*Latheticus oryzae* Waterhouse	longheaded flour beetle
COLEOPTERA: Tenebrionidae	*Palorus ratzeburgi* (Wissmann)	smalleyed flour beetle
COLEOPTERA: Tenebrionidae	*Palorus subdepressus* (Wollaston)	depressed flour beetle
COLEOPTERA: Tenebrionidae	*Tenebrio molitor* Linnaeus	yellow mealworm
COLEOPTERA: Tenebrionidae	*Tenebrio obscurus* Fabricius	dark mealworm
COLEOPTERA: Tenebrionidae	*Tribolium audax* Halstead	American black flour beetle
COLEOPTERA: Tenebrionidae	*Tribolium castaneum* (Herbst)	red flour beetle
COLEOPTERA: Tenebrionidae	*Tribolium confusum* Jacquelin du Val	confused flour beetle
COLEOPTERA: Trogositidae	*Tenebroides mauritanicus* (Linnaeus)	cadelle
COLLEMBOLA: Bourletiellidae	*Bourletiella hortensis* (Fitch)	garden springtail

---

D

DECAPODA: Cambaridae	*Procambarus clarkii* (Girard)	Louisiana red crayfish
DERMAPTERA: Chelisochidae	*Chelisoches morio* (Fabricius)	black earwig

DERMAPTERA: Forficulidae	*Forficula auricularia* Linnaeus	European earwig
DERMAPTERA: Labiduridae	*Euborellia annulipes* (Lucas)	ringlegged earwig
DERMAPTERA: Labiduridae	*Labidura riparia* Pallas	striped earwig
DIPTERA: Agromyzldae	*Agromyza frontella* (Rondani)	alfalfa blotch leafminer
DIPTERA: Agromyzidae	*Agromyza parvicornis* Loew	corn blotch leafminer
DIPTERA: Agromyzidae	*Calycomyza humeralis* (Roser)	aster leafminer
DIPTERA: Agromyzidae	*Cerodontha dorsalis* (Loew)	grass sheathminer
DIPTERA: Agromyzidae	*Chromatomyia syngenesiae* Hardy	chrysanthemum leafminer
DIPTERA: Agromyzidae	*Liriomyza brassicae* (Riley)	serpentine leafminer
DIPTERA: Agromyzidae	*Liriomyza huidobrensis* (Blanchard)	pea leafminer
DIPTERA: Agromyzidae	*Liriomyza sativae* Blanchard	vegetable leafminer
DIPTERA: Agromyzidae	*Ophiomyia lantanae* (Froggatt)	lantana seed fly
DIPTERA: Agromyzidae	*Ophiomyia phaseoli* (Tryon)	bean fly
DIPTERA: Agromyzidae	*Ophiomyia simplex* (Loew)	asparagus miner
DIPTERA: Agromyzidae	*Phytomyza ilicicola* Loew	native holly leafminer
DIPTERA: Agromyzidae	*Phytomyza ilicis* Curtis	holly leafminer
DIPTERA: Agromyzidae	*Phytomyza* spp.	columbine leafminer complex[49]
DIPTERA: Agromyzidae	*Phytomyza* spp.	larkspur leafminer complex[50]
DIPTERA: Anthomyiidae	*Delia antiqua* (Meigen)	onion maggot
DIPTERA: Anthomyiidae	*Delia brunnescens* (Zetterstedt)	carnation maggot
DIPTERA: Anthomyiidae	*Delia echinata* (Séguy)	carnation tip maggot
DIPTERA: Anthomyiidae	*Delia floralis* (Fallén)	turnip maggot
DIPTERA: Anthomyiidae	*Delia florilega* (Zetterstedt)	bean seed maggot
DIPTERA: Anthomyiidae	*Delia platura* (Meigen)	seedcorn maggot
DIPTERA: Anthomyiidae	*Delia radicum* (Linnaeus)	cabbage maggot
DIPTERA: Anthomyiidae	*Pegomya betae* Curtis	beet leafminer
DIPTERA: Anthomyiidae	*Pegomya hyoscyami* (Panzer)	spinach leafminer
DIPTERA: Anthomyiidae	*Pegomya rubivora* (Coquillett)	raspberry cane maggot
DIPTERA: Bombyliidae	*Systoechus vulgaris* Loew	grasshopper bee fly
DIPTERA: Calliphoridae	*Chrysomya rufifacies* (Macquart)	hairy maggot blow fly
DIPTERA: Calliphoridae	*Cochliomyia hominivorax* (Coquerel)	screwworm
DIPTERA: Calliphoridae	*Cochliomyia macellaria* (Fabricius)	secondary screwworm
DIPTERA: Calliphoridae	*Phormia regina* (Meigen)	black blow fly
DIPTERA: Calliphoridae	*Pollenia rudis* (Fabricius)	cluster fly

[49]Includes *Phytomyza aquilegiana* Frost, *P. aquilegivora* Spencer, and *P. columbinae* Sehgal.
[50]Includes *Phytomyza aconti* Hendel, *P. delphiniae* Frost, and *P. delphinivora* Spencer.

DIPTERA: Cecidomyiidae	*Asphondylia websteri* Felt	alfalfa gall midge
DIPTERA: Cecidomyiidae	*Cecidomyia resinicoloides* Williams	Monterey pine resin midge
DIPTERA: Cecidomyiidae	*Clinodiplosis rhododendri* (Felt)	rhododendron gall midge
DIPTERA: Cecidomyiidae	*Contarinia bromicola* (Marikovskij & Agafonova)	bromegrass seed midge
DIPTERA: Cecidomyiidae	*Contarinia catalpae* (Comstock)	catalpa midge
DIPTERA: Cecidomyiidae	*Contarinia johnsoni* Felt	grape blossom midge
DIPTERA: Cecidomyiidae	*Contarinia juniperina* Felt	juniper midge
DIPTERA: Cecidomyiidae	*Contarinia pyrivora* (Riley)	pear midge
DIPTERA: Cecidomyiidae	*Contarinia schulzi* Gagné	sunflower midge
DIPTERA: Cecidomyiidae	*Contarinia sorghicola* (Coquillett)	sorghum midge
DIPTERA: Cecidomyiidae	*Contarinia texana* (Felt)	guar midge
DIPTERA: Cecidomyiidae	*Dasineura leguminicola* (Lintner)	clover seed midge
DIPTERA: Cecidomyiidae	*Dasineura rhodophaga* (Coquillett)	rose midge
DIPTERA: Cecidomyiidae	*Dasineura swainei* (Felt)	spruce bud midge
DIPTERA: Cecidomyiidae	*Dasineura trifolii* (Loew)	clover leaf midge
DIPTERA: Cecidomyiidae	*Mayetiola destructor* (Say)	Hessian fly
DIPTERA: Cecidomyiidae	*Monarthropalpus flavus* (Schrank)	boxwood leafminer
DIPTERA: Cecidomyiidae	*Neolasioptera murtfeldtiana* (Felt)	sunflower seed midge
DIPTERA: Cecidomyiidae	*Oligotrophus betheli* Felt	juniper tip midge
DIPTERA: Cecidomyiidae	*Paradiplosis tumifex* Gagné	balsam gall midge
DIPTERA: Cecidomyiidae	*Prodiplosis citrulli* (Felt)	cucurbit midge
DIPTERA: Cecidomyiidae	*Prodiplosis vaccinii* (Felt)	blueberry tip midge
DIPTERA: Cecidomyiidae	*Rabdophaga rigidae* (Osten Sacken)	willow beaked-gall midge
DIPTERA: Cecidomyiidae	*Resseliella clavula* (Beutenmüller)	dogwood clubgall midge
DIPTERA: Cecidomyiidae	*Rhopalomyia chrysanthemi* (Ahlberg)	chrysanthemum gall midge
DIPTERA: Cecidomyiidae	*Sitodiplosis mosellana* (Géhin)	wheat midge
DIPTERA: Chaoboridae	*Chaoborus astictopus* Dyar & Shannon	Clear Lake gnat
DIPTERA: Chloropidae	*Meromyza americana* Fitch	wheat stem maggot
DIPTERA: Chloropidae	*Oscinella frit* (Linnaeus)	frit fly
DIPTERA: Culicidae	*Aedes aboriginis* Dyar	northwest coast mosquito
DIPTERA: Culicidae	*Aedes aegypti* (Linnaeus)	yellowfever mosquito
DIPTERA: Culicidae	*Aedes albopictus* (Skuse)	forest day mosquito
DIPTERA: Culicidae	*Aedes cantator* (Coquillett)	brown saltmarsh mosquito
DIPTERA: Culicidae	*Aedes sierrensis* (Ludlow)	western treehole mosquito
DIPTERA: Culicidae	*Aedes sollicitans* (Walker)	saltmarsh mosquito
DIPTERA: Culicidae	*Aedes squamiger* (Coquillett)	California saltmarsh mosquito
DIPTERA: Culicidae	*Aedes sticticus* (Meigen)	floodwater mosquito
DIPTERA: Culicidae	*Aedes vexans* (Meigen)	vexans mosquito

DIPTERA: Culicidae	*Anopheles quadrimaculatus* Say	common malaria mosquito
DIPTERA: Culicidae	*Culex pipiens* Linnaeus	northern house mosquito
DIPTERA: Culicidae	*Culex quinquefasciatus* Say	southern house mosquito
DIPTERA: Culicidae	*Deinocerites cancer* Theobald	crabhole mosquito
DIPTERA: Culicidae	*Wyeomyia smithii* (Coquillett)	pitcherplant mosquito
DIPTERA: Hippoboscidae	*Melophagus ovinus* (Linnaeus)	sheep ked
DIPTERA: Hippoboscidae	*Olfersia spinifera* (Leach)	frigate bird fly
DIPTERA: Hippoboscidae	*Pseudolynchia canariensis* (Macquart)	pigeon fly
DIPTERA: Muscidae	*Fannia canicularis* (Linnaeus)	little house fly
DIPTERA: Muscidae	*Fannia pusio* (Wiedemann)	chicken dung fly
DIPTERA: Muscidae	*Fannia scalaris* (Fabricius)	latrine fly
DIPTERA: Muscidae	*Haematobia irritans* (Linnaeus)	horn fly
DIPTERA: Muscidae	*Musca autumnalis* De Geer	face fly
DIPTERA: Muscidae	*Musca domestica* Linnaeus	house fly
DIPTERA: Muscidae	*Musca domestica vicina* Macquart	oriental house fly
DIPTERA: Muscidae	*Muscina stabulans* (Fallén)	false stable fly
DIPTERA: Muscidae	*Stomoxys calcitrans* (Linnaeus)	stable fly
DIPTERA: Oestridae	*Dermatobia hominis* (Linnaeus, Jr.)	torsalo
DIPTERA: Oestridae	*Gasterophilus haemorrhoidalis* (Linnaeus)	nose bot fly
DIPTERA: Oestridae	*Gasterophilus intestinalis* (De Geer)	horse bot fly
DIPTERA: Oestridae	*Gasterophilus nasalis* (Linnaeus)	throat bot fly
DIPTERA: Oestridae	*Hypoderma bovis* (Linnaeus)	northern cattle grub
DIPTERA: Oestridae	*Hypoderma lineatum* (Villers)	common cattle grub
DIPTERA: Oestridae	*Oestrus ovis* Linnaeus	sheep bot fly
DIPTERA: Otitidae	*Tetanops myopaeformis* (Rder)	sugarbeet root maggot
DIPTERA: Piophilidae	*Piophila casei* (Linnaeus)	cheese skipper
DIPTERA: Platystomatidae	*Rivellia quadrifasciata* (Macquart)	soybean nodule fly
DIPTERA: Psilidae	*Psila rosae* (Fabricius)	carrot rust fly
DIPTERA: Sarcophagidae	*Blaesoxipha* spp.	grasshopper maggots
DIPTERA: Sciaridae	*Pnyxia scabiei* (Hopkins)	potato scab gnat
DIPTERA: Simuliidae	*Cnephia pecuarum* (Riley)	southern buffalo gnat
DIPTERA: Simuliidae	*Simulium meridionale* Riley	turkey gnat
DIPTERA: Stratiomyidae	*Exaireta spiniqera* (Wiedemann)	blue soldier fly
DIPTERA: Stratiomyidae	*Hermetia illucens* (Linnaeus)	black soldier fly
DIPTERA: Syrphidae	*Eristalis tenax* (Linnaeus)	drone fly
DIPTERA: Syrphidae	*Eumerus figurans* Walker	ginger maggot
DIPTERA: Syrphidae	*Eumerus strigatus* (Fallén)	onion bulb fly
DIPTERA: Syrphidae	*Eumerus tuberculatus* Rondani	lesser bulb fly

DIPTERA: Syrphidae	*Merodon equestris* (Fabricius)	narcissus bulb fly
DIPTERA: Tabanidae	*Tabanus atratus* Fabricius	black horse fly
DIPTERA: Tabanidae	*Tabanus lineola* Fabricius	striped horse fly
DIPTERA: Tachinidae	*Winthemia quadripustulata* (Fabricius)	redtailed tachina
DIPTERA: Tephritidae	*Acinia picturata* (Snow)	sourbush seed fly
DIPTERA: Tephritidae	*Anastrepha ludens* (Loew)	Mexican fruit fly
DIPTERA: Tephritidae	*Anastrepha obliqua* (Macquart)	West Indian fruit fly
DIPTERA: Tephritidae	*Anastrepha pallens* Coquillett	bumelia fruit fly
DIPTERA: Tephritidae	*Anastrepha suspensa* (Loew)	Caribbean fruit fly
DIPTERA: Tephritidae	*Ceratitis capitata* (Wiedemann)	Mediterranean fruit fly
DIPTERA: Tephritidae	*Dacus cucurbitae* Coquillett	melon fly
DIPTERA: Tephritidae	*Dacus dorsalis* Hendel	oriental fruit fly
DIPTERA: Tephritidae	*Dacus oleae* (Gmelin)	olive fruit fly
DIPTERA: Tephritidae	*Ensina sonchi* (Linnaeus)	sonchus fly
DIPTERA: Tephritidae	*Epochra canadensis* (Loew)	currant fruit fly
DIPTERA: Tephritidae	*Eutreta xanthochaeta* Aldrich	lantana gall fly
DIPTERA: Tephritidae	*Procecidochares utilis* Stone	eupatorium gall fly
DIPTERA: Tephritidae	*Rhagoletis cingulata* (Loew)	cherry fruit fly[51]
DIPTERA: Tephritidae	*Rhagoletis completa* Cresson	walnut husk fly
DIPTERA: Tephritidae	*Rhagoletis fausta* (Osten Sacken)	black cherry fruit fly
DIPTERA: Tephritidae	*Rhagoletis indifferens* Curran	western cherry fruit fly
DIPTERA: Tephritidae	*Rhagoletis mendax* Curran	blueberry maggot
DIPTERA: Tephritidae	*Rhagoletis pomonella* (Walsh)	apple maggot
DIPTERA: Tephritidae	*Strauzia longipennis* (Wiedemann)	sunflower maggot
DIPTERA: Tephritidae	*Toxotrypana curvicauda* Gerstaecker	papaya fruit fly
DIPTERA: Tephritidae	*Zonosemata electa* (Say)	pepper maggot
DIPTERA: Tipulidae	*Tipula paludosa* Meigen	European crane fly
DIPTERA: Tipulidae	*Tipula simplex* Doane	range crane fly

E

EMBIIDINA: Oligotomidae	*Aposthonia oceania* (Ross)	oceanic embiid
EMBIIDINA: Oligotomidae	*Oligotoma saundersii* (Westwood)	Saunders embiid

---

[51]Immature called cherry maggot.

HETEROPTERA: Anthocoridae	*Orius insidiosus* (Say)	insidious flower bug
HETEROPTERA: Anthocoridae	*Orius tristicolor* (White)	minute pirate bug
HETEROPTERA: Anthocoridae	*Xylocoris flavipes* (Reuter)	warehouse pirate bug
HETEROPTERA: Belostomatidae	*Lethocerus americanus* (Leidy)	giant water bug
HETEROPTERA: Berytidae	*Jalysus wickhami* Van Duzee	spined stilt bug
HETEROPTERA: Cimicidae	*Cimex lectularius* Linnaeus	bed bug
HETEROPTERA: Cimicidae	*Haematosiphon inodorus* (Dugès)	poultry bug
HETEROPTERA: Cimicidae	*Oeciacus vicarius* Horvath	swallow bug
HETEROPTERA: Coreidae	*Anasa armigera* (Say)	horned squash bug
HETEROPTERA: Coreidae	*Anasa tristis* (De Geer)	squash bug
HETEROPTERA: Coreidae	*Leptoglossus corculus* (Say)	leaffooted pine seed bug
HETEROPTERA: Coreidae	*Leptoglossus phyllopus* (Linnaeus)	leaffooted bug
HETEROPTERA: Cydnidae	*Geotomus pygmaeus* (Dallas)	oceanic burrower bug
HETEROPTERA: Gelastocoridae	*Gelastocoris oculatus* (Fabricius)	toad bug
HETEROPTERA: Gerridae	*Halobates hawaiiensis* Usinger	Hawaiian pelagic water strider
HETEROPTERA: Gerridae	*Halobates sericeus* Eschscholtz	Pacific pelagic water strider
HETEROPTERA: Lygaeidae	*Blissus insularis* Barber	southern chinch bug
HETEROPTERA: Lygaeidae	*Blissus leucopterus hirtus* Montandon	hairy chinch bug
HETEROPTERA: Lygaeidae	*Blissus leucopterus leucopterus* (Say)	chinch bug
HETEROPTERA: Lygaeidae	*Blissus occiduus* Barber	western chinch bug
HETEROPTERA: Lygaeidae	*Geocoris bullatus* (Say)	large bigeyed bug
HETEROPTERA: Lygaeidae	*Geocoris pallens* Stål	western bigeyed bug
HETEROPTERA: Lygaeidae	*Graptostethus manillensis* (Stål)	woodrose bug
HETEROPTERA: Lygaeidae	*Lygaeus kalmii* Stål	small milkweed bug
HETEROPTERA: Lygaeidae	*Neacoryphus bicrucis* (Say)	whitecrossed seed bug
HETEROPTERA: Lygaeidae	*Nysius caledoniae* Distant	Caledonia seed bug
HETEROPTERA: Lygaeidae	*Nysius raphanus* Howard	false chinch bug
HETEROPTERA: Lygaeidae	*Nysius* spp.	seed bugs
HETEROPTERA: Lygaeidae	*Oncopeltus fasciatus* (Dallas)	large milkweed bug
HETEROPTERA: Miridae	*Adelphocoris lineolatus* (Goeze)	alfalfa plant bug
HETEROPTERA: Miridae	*Adelphocoris rapidus* (Say)	rapid plant bug
HETEROPTERA: Miridae	*Adelphocoris superbus* (Uhler)	superb plant bug
HETEROPTERA: Miridae	*Brooksetta althaeae* (Hussey)	hollyhock plant bug
HETEROPTERA: Miridae	*Chlamydatus associatus* (Uhler)	ragweed plant bug
HETEROPTERA: Miridae	*Cyrtopeltis modesta* (Distant)	tomato bug

HETEROPTERA: Miridae	*Cyrtopeltis notata* (Distant)	suckfly
HETEROPTERA: Miridae	*Diaphnocoris chlorionis* (Say)	honeylocust plant bug
HETEROPTERA: Miridae	*Halticotoma valida* Townsend	yucca plant bug
HETEROPTERA: Miridae	*Halticus bractatus* (Say)	garden fleahopper
HETEROPTERA: Miridae	*Halticus chrysolepis* Kirkaldy	grass fleahopper
HETEROPTERA: Miridae	*Hyalopeplus pellucidus* (Stål)	transparentwinged plant bug
HETEROPTERA: Miridae	*Leptopterna dolabrata* (Linnaeus)	meadow plant bug
HETEROPTERA: Miridae	*Lindbergocapsus allii* (Knight)	onion plant bug
HETEROPTERA: Miridae	*Lopidea dakota* Knight	caragana plant bug
HETEROPTERA: Miridae	*Lopidea davisi* Knight	phlox plant bug
HETEROPTERA: Miridae	*Lygidea mendax* Reuter	apple red bug
HETEROPTERA: Miridae	*Lygocoris caryae* (Knight)	hickory plant bug
HETEROPTERA: Miridae	*Lygocoris communis* (Knight)	pear plant bug
HETEROPTERA: Miridae	*Lygus elisus* Van Duzee	pale legume bug
HETEROPTERA: Miridae	*Lygus lineolaris* (Palisot de Beauvois)	tarnished plant bug
HETEROPTERA: Miridae	*Neurocolpus nubilus* (Say)	clouded plant bug
HETEROPTERA: Miridae	*Platylyus luridus* (Reuter)	pine conelet bug
HETEROPTERA: Miridae	*Poecilocapsus lineatus* (Fabricius)	fourlined plant bug
HETEROPTERA: Miridae	*Pseudatomoscelis seriatus* (Reuter)	cotton fleahopper
HETEROPTERA: Miridae	*Pycnoderes quadrimaculatus* Guérin-Méneville	bean capsid
HETEROPTERA: Miridae	*Rhinacloa forticornis* Reuter	western plant bug
HETEROPTERA: Miridae	*Rhinocapsus vanduzeei* Uhler	azalea plant bug
HETEROPTERA: Miridae	*Spanagonicus albofasciatus* (Reuter)	whitemarked fleahopper
HETEROPTERA: Miridae	*Taedia hawleyi* (Knight)	hop plant bug
HETEROPTERA: Miridae	*Tropidosteptes amoenus* Reuter	ash plant bug
HETEROPTERA: Nabidae	*Nabis alternatus* Parshley	western damsel bug
HETEROPTERA: Nabidae	*Nabis americoferus* Carayon	common damsel bug
HETEROPTERA: Nabidae	*Nabis blackburni* White	Blackburn damsel bug
HETEROPTERA: Nabidae	*Nabis capsiformis* Germar	pale damsel bug
HETEROPTERA: Pentatomidae	*Acrosternum hilare* (Say)	green stink bug
HETEROPTERA: Pentatomidae	*Brochymena quadripustulata* (Fabricius)	rough stink bug
HETEROPTERA: Pentatomidae	*Chlorochroa ligata* (Say)	conchuela
HETEROPTERA: Pentatomidae	*Chlorochroa sayi* (Stål)	Say stink bug
HETEROPTERA: Pentatomidae	*Coleotichus blackburniae* White	koa bug
HETEROPTERA: Pentatomidae	*Euschistus servus* (Say)	brown stink bug
HETEROPTERA: Pentatomidae	*Euschistus tristigmus* (Say)	dusky stink bug
HETEROPTERA: Pentatomidae	*Euschistus variolarius* (Palisot de Beauvois)	onespotted stink bug
HETEROPTERA: Pentatomidae	*Murgantia histrionica* (Hahn)	harlequin bug

HETEROPTERA: Pentatomidae	*Nezara viridula* (Linnaeus)	southern green stink bug
HETEROPTERA: Pentatomidae	*Oebalus pugnax* (Fabricius)	rice stink bug
HETEROPTERA: Pentatomidae	*Perillus bioculatus* (Fabricius)	twospotted stink bug
HETEROPTERA: Pcntatomidae	*Plautia stali* Scott	oriental stink bug
HETEROPTERA: Pentatomidae	*Podisus maculiventris* (Say)	spined soldier bug
HETEROPTERA: Pentatomidae	*Tetyra bipunctata* (Herrich-Schäffer)	shieldbacked pine seed bug
HETEROPTERA: Pentatomidae	*Thyanta accerra* McAtee	redshouldered stink bug
HETEROPTERA: Plataspidae	*Coptosoma xanthogramma* (White)	black stink bug
HETEROPTERA: Pyrrhocoridae	*Dysdercus suturellus* (Herrich-Schäffer)	cotton stainer
HETEROPTERA: Reduviidae	*Arilus cristatus* (Linnaeus)	wheel bug
HETEROPTERA: Reduviidae	*Empicoris rubromaculatus* (Blackburn)	thread bug
HETEROPTERA: Reduviidae	*Haematoloecha rubescens* Distant	red assassin bug
HETEROPTERA: Reduviidae	*Oncocephalus pacificus* (Kirkaldy)	Pacific kissing bug
HETEROPTERA: Reduviidae	*Polididus armatissimus* Stål	spiny assassin bug
HETEROPTERA: Reduviidae	*Reduvius personatus* (Linnaeus)	masked hunter
HETEROPTERA: Reduviidae	*Scadra rufidens* Stål	redmargined assassin bug
HETEROPTERA: Reduviidae	*Sinea diadema* (Fabricius)	spined assassin bug
HETEROPTERA: Reduviidae	*Triatoma protracta* (Uhler)	western bloodsucking conenose
HETEROPTERA: Reduviidae	*Triatoma rubrofasciata* (De Geer)	large kissing bug
HETEROPTERA: Reduviidae	*Triatoma sanguisuga* (LeConte)	bloodsucking conenose
HETEROPTERA: Reduviidae	*Zelus renardii* Kolenati	leafhopper assassin bug
HETEROPTERA: Rhopalidae	*Boisea rubrolineata* Barber	western boxelder bug
HETEROPTERA: Rhopalidae	*Boisea trivittata* (Say)	boxelder bug
HETEROPTERA: Rhopalidae	*Liorhyssus hyalinus* (Fabricius)	hyaline grass bug
HETEROPTERA: Thyreocoridae	*Corimelaena pulicaria* (Germar)	black bug
HETEROPTERA: Tingidae	*Corythucha arcuata* (Say)	oak lace bug
HETEROPTERA: Tingidae	*Corythucha celtidis* Osborn & Drake	hackberry lace bug
HETEROPTERA: Tingidae	*Corythucha ciliata* (Say)	sycamore lace bug
HETEROPTERA: Tingidae	*Corythucha cydoniae* (Fitch)	hawthorn lace bug
HETEROPTERA: Tingidae	*Corythucha gossypii* (Fabricius)	cotton lace bug
HETEROPTERA: Tingidae	*Corythucha marmorata* (Uhler)	chrysanthemum lace bug
HETEROPTERA: Tingidae	*Corythucha morrilli* Osborn & Drake	Morrill lace bug
HETEROPTERA: Tingidae	*Corythucha ulmi* Osborn & Drake	elm lace bug
HETEROPTERA: Tingidae	*Gargaphia solani* Heidemann	eggplant lace bug
HETEROPTERA: Tingidae	*Gargaphia tiliae* (Walsh)	basswood lace bug
HETEROPTERA: Tingidae	*Stephanitis pyriodes* (Scott)	azalea lace bug
HETEROPTERA: Tingidae	*Stephanitis rhododendri* Horvath	rhododendron lace bug
HETEROPTERA: Tingidae	*Teleonemia scrupulosa* Stål	lantana lace bug

HOMOPTERA: Adelgidae	*Adelges abietis* (Linnaeus)	eastern spruce gall adelgid
HOMOPTERA: Adelgidae	*Adelges cooleyi* (Gillette)	Cooley spruce gall adelgid
HOMOPTERA: Adelgidae	*Adelges piceae* (Ratzeburg)	balsam woolly adelgid
HOMOPTERA: Adelgidae	*Adelges tsugae* Annand	hemlock woolly adelgid
HOMOPTERA: Adelgidae	*Pineus pini* (Macquart)	Eurasian pine adelgid
HOMOPTERA: Adelgidae	*Pineus pinifoliae* (Fitch)	pine leaf adelgid
HOMOPTERA: Adelgidae	*Pineus strobi* (Hartig)	pine bark adelgid
HOMOPTERA: Aleyrodidae	*Aleurocanthus spiniferus* (Quaintance)	orange spiny whitefly
HOMOPTERA: Aleyrodidae	*Aleurocanthus woglumi* Ashby	citrus blackfly
HOMOPTERA: Aleyrodidae	*Aleurothrixus floccosus* (Maskell)	woolly whitefly
HOMOPTERA: Aleyrodidae	*Aleyrodes shizuokensis* Kuwana	oxalis whitefly
HOMOPTERA: Aleyrodidae	*Bemisia giffardi* (Kotinsky)	Giffard whitefly
HOMOPTERA: Aleyrodidae	*Bemisia tabaci* (Gennadius)	sweetpotato whitefly
HOMOPTERA: Aleyrodidae	*Dialeurodes chittendeni* Laing	rhododendron whitefly
HOMOPTERA: Aleyrodidae	*Dialeurodes citri* (Ashmead)	citrus whitefly
HOMOPTERA: Aleyrodidae	*Dialeurodes citrifolii* (Morgan)	cloudywinged whitefly
HOMOPTERA: Aleyrodidae	*Dialeurodes kirkaldyi* (Kotinsky)	Kirkaldy whitefly
HOMOPTERA: Aleyrodidae	*Paraleyrodes perseae* (Quaintance)	plumeria whitefly
HOMOPTERA: Aleyrodidae	*Pealius azaleae* (Baker & Moles)	azalea whitefly
HOMOPTERA: Aleyrodidae	*Singhius hibisci* (Kotinsky)	hibiscus whitefly
HOMOPTERA: Aleyrodidae	*Tetraleurodes mori* (Quaintance)	mulberry whitefly
HOMOPTERA: Aleyrodidae	*Trialeurodes abutilonea* (Haldeman)	bandedwinged whitefly
HOMOPTERA: Aleyrodidae	*Trialeurodes floridensis* (Quaintance)	avocado whitefly
HOMOPTERA: Aleyrodidae	*Trialeurodes packardi* (Morrill)	strawberry whitefly
HOMOPTERA: Aleyrodidae	*Trialeurodes vaporariorum* (Westwood)	greenhouse whitefly
HOMOPTERA: Aleyrodidae	*Trialeurodes vittata* (Quaintance)	grape whitefly
HOMOPTERA: Aphididae	*Acyrthosiphon (Rhodobium) porosum* (Sanderson)	yellow rose aphid
HOMOPTERA: Aphididae	*Acyrthosiphon caraganae* (Cholodkovsky)	caragana aphid
HOMOPTERA: Aphididae	*Acyrthosiphon pisum* (Harris)	pea aphid
HOMOPTERA: Aphididae	*Anuraphis maidiradicis* (Forbes)	corn root aphid
HOMOPTERA: Aphididae	*Aphis craccivora* Koch	cowpea aphid
HOMOPTERA: Aphididae	*Aphis fabae* Scopoli	bean aphid
HOMOPTERA: Aphididae	*Aphis forbesi* Weed	strawberry root aphid
HOMOPTERA: Aphididae	*Aphis gossypii* Glover	cotton aphid[52]
HOMOPTERA: Aphididae	*Aphis hederae* Kaltenbach	ivy aphid

---

[52]Also called melon ahpid.

HOMOPTERA: Aphididae	*Aphis illinoisensis* Shimer	grapevine aphid
HOMOPTERA: Aphididae	*Aphis middletonii* (Thomas)	erigeron root aphid
HOMOPTERA: Aphididae	*Aphis nasturtii* Kaltenbach	buckthorn aphid
HOMOPTERA: Aphididae	*Aphis ncrii* Boyer de Fonscolombe	oleander aphid
HOMOPTERA: Aphididae	*Aphis pomi* De Geer	apple aphid
HOMOPTERA: Aphididae	*Aphis spiraecola* Patch	spirea aphid
HOMOPTERA: Aphididae	*Aphis viburniphila* Patch	viburnum aphid
HOMOPTERA: Aphididae	*Aulacorthum solani* (Kaltenbach)	foxglove aphid
HOMOPTERA: Aphididae	*Brachycaudus cardui* (Linnaeus)	thistle aphid
HOMOPTERA: Aphididae	*Brachycaudus persicae* (Passerini)	black peach aphid
HOMOPTERA: Aphididae	*Brachycolus heraclei* Takahashi	celery aphid
HOMOPTERA: Aphididae	*Brachycorynella asparagi* (Mordvilko)	asparagus aphid
HOMOPTERA: Aphididae	*Brevicoryne brassicae* (Linnaeus)	cabbage aphid
HOMOPTERA: Aphididae	*Cerataphis orchidearum* (Westwood)	fringed orchid aphid
HOMOPTERA: Aphididae	*Chaetosiphon fragaefolii* (Cockerell)	strawberry aphid
HOMOPTERA: Aphididae	*Chromaphis juglandicola* (Kaltenbach)	walnut aphid
HOMOPTERA: Aphididae	*Cinara atlantica* (Wilson)	Carolina conifer aphid
HOMOPTERA: Aphididae	*Cinara fornacula* Hottes	green spruce aphid
HOMOPTERA: Aphididae	*Cinara laricis* (Walker)	larch aphid
HOMOPTERA: Aphididae	*Cinara strobi* (Fitch)	white pine aphid
HOMOPTERA: Aphididae	*Colopha ulmicola* (Fitch)	elm cockscombgall aphid
HOMOPTERA: Aphididae	*Cryptomyzus ribis* (Linnaeus)	currant aphid
HOMOPTERA: Aphididae	*Dactynotus rudbeckiae* (Fitch)	goldenglow aphid
HOMOPTERA: Aphididae	*Diuraphis (Holcaphis) tritici* (Gillette)	western wheat aphid
HOMOPTERA: Aphididae	*Diuraphis noxia* (Mordvilko)	Russian wheat aphid
HOMOPTERA: Aphididae	*Drepanaphis acerifoliae* (Thomas)	painted maple aphid
HOMOPTERA: Aphididae	*Dysaphis apiifolia* (Theobald)	rusty banded aphid
HOMOPTERA: Aphididae	*Dysaphis plantaginea* (Passerini)	rosy apple aphid
HOMOPTERA: Aphididae	*Dysaphis tulipae* (Boyer de Fonscolombe)	tulip bulb aphid
HOMOPTERA: Aphididae	*Elatobium abietinum* (Walker)	spruce aphid
HOMOPTERA: Aphididae	*Eriosoma americanum* (Riley)	woolly elm aphid
HOMOPTERA: Aphididae	*Eriosoma lanigerum* (Hausmann)	woolly apple aphid
HOMOPTERA: Aphididae	*Eriosoma pyricola* Baker & Davidson	woolly pear aphid
HOMOPTERA: Aphididae	*Fagiphagus imbricator* (Fitch)	beech blight aphid
HOMOPTERA: Aphididae	*Hyalopterus pruni* (Geoffroy)	mealy plum aphid
HOMOPTERA: Aphididae	*Hysteroneura setariae* (Thomas)	rusty plum aphid
HOMOPTERA: Aphididae	*Idiopterus nephrelepidis* Davis	fern aphid
HOMOPTERA: Aphididae	*Kakimia houghtonensis* (Troop)	gooseberry witchbroom aphid

HOMOPTERA: Aphididae	*Lipaphis erysimi* (Kaltenbach)	turnip aphid
HOMOPTERA: Aphididae	*Longistigma caryae* (Harris)	giant bark aphid
HOMOPTERA: Aphididae	*Macrosiphoniella sanborni* (Gillette)	chrysanthemum aphid
HOMOPTERA: Aphididae	*Macrosiphum euphorbiae* (Thomas)	potato aphid
HOMOPTERA: Aphididae	*Macrosiphum lilii* (Monell)	purplespotted lily aphid
HOMOPTERA: Aphididae	*Macrosiphum liriodendri* (Monell)	tuliptree aphid
HOMOPTERA: Aphididae	*Macrosiphum luteum* (Buckton)	orchid aphid
HOMOPTERA: Aphididae	*Macrosiphum rosae* (Linnaeus)	rose aphid
HOMOPTERA: Aphididae	*Macrosiphum scoliopi* Essig	western lily aphid
HOMOPTERA: Aphididae	*Melanaphis sacchari* (Zehntner)	sugarcane aphid
HOMOPTERA: Aphididae	*Melanocallis caryaefoliae* (Davis)	black pecan aphid
HOMOPTERA: Aphididae	*Micromyzus violae* (Pergande)	violet aphid
HOMOPTERA: Aphididae	*Mindarus abietinus* Koch	balsam twig aphid
HOMOPTERA: Aphididae	*Monellia caryella* (Fitch)	blackmargined aphid
HOMOPTERA: Aphididae	*Monelliopsis pecanis* Bissell	yellow pecan aphid
HOMOPTERA: Aphididae	*Mordvilkoja vagabunda* (Walsh)	poplar vagabond apid
HOMOPTERA: Aphididae	*Myzocallis coryli* (Goetze)	filbert aphid
HOMOPTERA: Aphididae	*Myzus ascalonicus* Doncaster	shallot aphid
HOMOPTERA: Aphididae	*Myzus cerasi* (Fabricius)	black cherry aphid
HOMOPTERA: Aphididae	*Myzus ligustri* (Mosley)	privet aphid
HOMOPTERA: Aphididae	*Myzus nicotianae* Blackman	tobacco aphid
HOMOPTERA: Aphididae	*Myzus ornatus* Laing	ornate aphid
HOMOPTERA: Aphididae	*Myzus persicae* (Sulzer)	green peach aphid
HOMOPTERA: Aphididae	*Nasonovia lactucae* (Linnaeus)	sow thistle aphid
HOMOPTERA: Aphididae	*Nearctaphis bakeri* (Cowen)	clover aphid
HOMOPTERA: Aphididae	*Neoceruraphis viburnicola* (Gillette)	snowball aphid
HOMOPTERA: Aphididae	*Neomyzus circumflexus* (Buckton)	crescentmarked lily aphid
HOMOPTERA: Aphididae	*Neophyllaphis araucariae* Takahashi	araucaria aphid
HOMOPTERA: Aphididae	*Neotoxoptera formosana* (Takahashi)	onion aphid
HOMOPTERA: Aphididae	*Ovatus crataegarius* (Walker)	mint aphid
HOMOPTERA: Aphididae	*Paraprociphilus tessellatus* (Fitch)	woolly alder aphid
HOMOPTERA: Aphididae	*Pemphigus bursarius* (Linnaeus)	lettuce root aphid
HOMOPTERA: Aphididae	*Pemphigus populiramulorum* Riley	poplar twig gall aphid
HOMOPTERA: Aphididae	*Pemphigus populitransversus* Riley	poplar petiolegall aphid
HOMOPTERA: Aphididae	*Pemphigus populivenae* Fitch	sugarbeet root aphid
HOMOPTERA: Aphididae	*Pentalonia nigronervosa* Coquerel	banana aphid
HOMOPTERA: Aphididae	*Periphyllus lyropictus* (Kessler)	Norway maple aphid
HOMOPTERA: Aphididae	*Periphyllus negundinis* (Thomas)	boxelder aphid

HOMOPTERA: Aphididae	*Phorodon humuli* (Schrank)	hop aphid
HOMOPTERA: Aphididae	*Rhopalosiphum fitchii* (Sanderson)	apple grain aphid
HOMOPTERA: Aphididae	*Rhopalosiphum maidis* (Fitch)	corn leaf aphid
HOMOPTERA: Aphididae	*Rhopalosiphum nymphaeae* (Linnaeus)	waterlily aphid
HOMOPTERA: Aphididae	*Rhopalosiphum padi* (Linnaeus)	bird cherry-oat aphid
HOMOPTERA: Aphididae	*Rhopalosiphum rufiabdominalis* (Sasaki)	rice root aphid
HOMOPTERA: Aphididae	*Schizaphis graminum* (Rondani)	greenbug
HOMOPTERA: Aphididae	*Sipha flava* (Forbes)	yellow sugarcane aphid
HOMOPTERA: Aphididae	*Sitobion avenae* (Fabricius)	English grain aphid
HOMOPTERA: Aphididae	*Therioaphis maculata* (Buckton)	spotted alfalfa aphid
HOMOPTERA: Aphididae	*Therioaphis riehmi* (Brner)	sweetclover aphid
HOMOPTERA: Aphididae	*Therioaphis trifolii* (Monell)	yellow clover aphid
HOMOPTERA: Aphididae	*Thoracaphis fici* (Takahashi)	banyan aphid
HOMOPTERA: Aphididae	*Tinocallis kahawaluokalani* (Kirkaldy)	crapemyrtle aphid
HOMOPTERA: Aphididae	*Tinocallis ulmifolii* (Monell)	elm leaf aphid
HOMOPTERA: Aphididae	*Toxoptera aurantii* (Boyer de Fonscolombe)	black citrus aphid
HOMOPTERA: Aphididae	*Toxoptera citricida* (Kirkaldy)	brown citrus aphid
HOMOPTERA: Asterolecaniidae	*Asterolecanium pustulans* (Cockerell)	oleander pit scale
HOMOPTERA: Asterolecaniidae	*Asterolecanium variolosum* (Ratzeburg)	golden oak scale
HOMOPTERA: Cercopidae	*Aphrophora parallela* (Say)	pine spittlebug
HOMOPTERA: Cercopidae	*Aphrophora saratogensis* (Fitch)	Saratoga spittlebug
HOMOPTERA: Cercopidae	*Clastoptera achatina* Germar	pecan spittlebug
HOMOPTERA: Cercopidae	*Clastoptera obtusa* (Say)	alder spittlebug
HOMOPTERA: Cercopidae	*Clastoptera proteus* Fitch	dogwood spittlebug
HOMOPTERA: Cercopidae	*Clastoptera saintcyri* Provancher	heath spittlebug
HOMOPTERA: Cercopidae	*Clastoptera xanthocephala* Germar	sunflower spittlebug
HOMOPTERA: Cercopidae	*Lepyronia quadrangularis* (Say)	diamondbacked spittlebug
HOMOPTERA: Cercopidae	*Neophilaenus lineatus* (Linnaeus)	lined spittlebug
HOMOPTERA: Cercopidae	*Philaenus spumarius* (Linnaeus)	meadow spittlebug
HOMOPTERA: Cercopidae	*Prosapia bicincta* (Say)	twolined spittlebug
HOMOPTERA: Cicadellidae	*Aceratagallia sanguinolenta* (Provancher)	clover leafhopper
HOMOPTERA: Cicadellidae	*Acinopterus angulatus* Lawson	angulate leafhopper
HOMOPTERA: Cicadellidae	*Balclutha incisa hospes* (Kirkaldy)	little green leafhopper
HOMOPTERA: Cicadellidae	*Balclutha saltuella* (Kirschbaum)	Beardsley leafhopper
HOMOPTERA: Cicadellidae	*Circulifer tenellus* (Baker)	beet leafhopper
HOMOPTERA: Cicadellidae	*Colladonus clitellarius* (Say)	saddled leafhopper
HOMOPTERA: Cicadellidae	*Colladonus montanus* (Van Duzee)	mountain leafhopper
HOMOPTERA: Cicadellidae	*Dalbulus maidis* (DeLong & Wolcott)	corn leafhopper

HOMOPTERA: Cicadellidae	*Deltocephalus hospes* Kirkaldy	lawn leafhopper
HOMOPTERA: Cicadellidae	*Draeculacephala minerva* Ball	grass sharpshooter
HOMOPTERA: Cicadellidae	*Draeculacephala mollipes* (Say)	watercress sharpshooter
HOMOPTERA: Cicadellidae	*Edwardsiana prunicola* (Edwards)	prune leafhopper
HOMOPTERA: Cicadellidae	*Edwardsiana rosae* (Linnaeus)	rose leafhopper
HOMOPTERA: Cicadellidae	*Empoasca abrupta* DeLong	western potato leafhopper
HOMOPTERA: Cicadellidae	*Empoasca fabae* (Harris)	potato leafhopper
HOMOPTERA: Cicadellidae	*Empoasca maligna* (Walsh)	apple leafhopper
HOMOPTERA: Cicadellidae	*Empoasca solana* DeLong	southern garden leafhopper
HOMOPTERA: Cicadellidae	*Empoasca stevensi* Young	Stevens leafhopper
HOMOPTERA: Cicadellidae	*Endria inimica* (Say)	painted leafhopper
HOMOPTERA: Cicadellidae	*Erythroneura comes* (Say)	eastern grape leafhopper
HOMOPTERA: Cicadellidae	*Erythroneura elegantula* Osborn	western grape leafhopper
HOMOPTERA: Cicadellidae	*Erythroneura tricincta* Fitch	threebanded leafhopper
HOMOPTERA: Cicadellidae	*Erythroneura ziczac* Walsh	Virginiacreeper leafhopper
HOMOPTERA: Cicadellidae	*Exitianus exitiosus* (Uhler)	gray lawn leafhopper
HOMOPTERA: Cicadellidae	*Graminella nigrifrons* (Forbes)	blackfaced leafhopper
HOMOPTERA: Cicadellidae	*Graminella sonora* (Ball)	lesser lawn leafhopper
HOMOPTERA: Cicadellidae	*Macropsis trimaculata* (Fitch)	plum leafhopper
HOMOPTERA: Cicadellidae	*Macrosteles quadrilineatus* Forbes	aster leafhopper
HOMOPTERA: Cicadellidae	*Nephotettix nigropictus* (Stål)	rice leafhopper
HOMOPTERA: Cicadellidae	*Opsius stactogalus* Fieber	tamarix leafhopper
HOMOPTERA: Cicadellidae	*Paraphlepsius irroratus* (Say)	brown speckled leafhopper
HOMOPTERA: Cicadellidae	*Penestrangania robusta* (Uhler)	robust leafhopper
HOMOPTERA: Cicadellidae	*Protalebrella brasiliensis* (Baker)	Brasilian leafhopper
HOMOPTERA: Cicadellidae	*Ribautiana tenerrima* (Herrich-Schäffer)	bramble leafhopper
HOMOPTERA: Cicadellidae	*Scaphoideus luteolus* Van Duzee	whitebanded elm leafhopper
HOMOPTERA: Cicadellidae	*Scaphytopius loricatus* (Van Duzee)	yellowfaced leafhopper
HOMOPTERA: Cicadellidae	*Scleroracus vaccinii* (Van Duzee)	bluntnosed cranberry leafhopper
HOMOPTERA: Cicadellidae	*Typhlocyba pomaria* McAtee	white apple leafhopper
HOMOPTERA: Cicadellidae	*Xyphon flaviceps* (Riley)	yellowheaded leafhopper
HOMOPTERA: Cicadidae	*Magicicada septendecim* (Linnaeus)	periodical cicada
HOMOPTERA: Cixiidae	*Myndus crudus* Van Duzee	American palm cixiid
HOMOPTERA: Coccidae	*Ceroplastes cirripediformis* Comstock	barnacle scale
HOMOPTERA: Coccidae	*Ceroplastes floridensis* Comstock	Florida wax scale
HOMOPTERA: Coccidae	*Ceroplastes rubens* Maskell	red wax scale
HOMOPTERA: Coccidae	*Coccus hesperidum* Linnaeus	brown soft scale
HOMOPTERA: Coccidae	*Coccus longulus* (Douglas)	long brown scale

156

HOMOPTERA: Coccidae	*Coccus pseudomagnoliarum* (Kuwana)	citricola scale
HOMOPTERA: Coccidae	*Coccus viridis* (Green)	green scale
HOMOPTERA: Coccidae	*Eucalymnatus tessellatus* (Signoret)	tessellated scale
HOMOPTERA: Coccidae	*Eulecanium cerasorum* (Cockerell)	calico scale
HOMOPTERA: Coccidae	*Kilifia acuminata* (Signoret)	acuminate scale
HOMOPTERA: Coccidae	*Mesolecanium nigrofasciatum* (Pergande)	terrapin scale
HOMOPTERA: Coccidae	*Neolecanium cornuparvum* (Thro)	magnolia scale
HOMOPTERA: Coccidae	*Parasaissetra nigra* (Nietner)	nigra scale
HOMOPTERA: Coccidae	*Parthenolecanium corni* (Bouché)	European fruit lecanium
HOMOPTERA: Coccidae	*Parthenolecanium fletcheri* (Cockerell)	Fletcher scale
HOMOPTERA: Coccidae	*Parthenolecanium persicae* (Fabricius)	European peach scale
HOMOPTERA: Coccidae	*Parthenolecanium quercifex* (Fitch)	oak lecanium
HOMOPTERA: Coccidae	*Physokermes piceae* (Schrank)	spruce bud scale
HOMOPTERA: Coccidae	*Protopulvinaria pyriformis* (Cockerell)	pyriform scale
HOMOPTERA: Coccidae	*Pulvinaria amygdali* Cockerell	cottony peach scale
HOMOPTERA: Coccidae	*Pulvinaria innumerabilis* (Rathvon)	cottony maple scale
HOMOPTERA: Coccidae	*Pulvinaria mammeae* Maskell	large cottony scale
HOMOPTERA: Coccidae	*Pulvinaria psidii* Maskell	green shield scale
HOMOPTERA: Coccidae	*Saissetia coffeae* (Walker)	hemispherical scale
HOMOPTERA: Coccidae	*Saissetia miranda* (Cockerell & Parrott)	Mexican black scale
HOMOPTERA: Coccidae	*Saissetia neglecta* De Lotto	Caribbean black scale
HOMOPTERA: Coccidae	*Saissetia oleae* (Olivier)	black scale
HOMOPTERA: Coccidae	*Sphaerolecanium prunastri* (Boyer de Fonscolombe)	globose scale
HOMOPTERA: Coccidae	*Toumeyella liriodendri* (Gmelin)	tuliptree scale
HOMOPTERA: Coccidae	*Toumeyella parvicornis* (Cockerell)	pine tortoise scale
HOMOPTERA: Dactylopiidae	*Dactylopius coccus* Costa	cochineal insect
HOMOPTERA: Delphacidae	*Peregrinus maidis* (Ashmead)	corn delphacid
HOMOPTERA: Delphacidae	*Perkinsiella saccharicida* Kirkaldy	sugarcane delphacid
HOMOPTERA: Delphacidae	*Sogatodes orizicola* (Muir)	rice delphacid
HOMOPTERA: Diaspididae	*Abgrallaspis ithacae* (Ferris)	hemlock scale
HOMOPTERA: Diaspididae	*Aonidiella aurantii* (Maskell)	California red scale
HOMOPTERA: Diaspididae	*Aonidiella citrina* (Coquillett)	yellow scale
HOMOPTERA: Diaspididae	*Aonidiella inornata* McKenzie	inornate scale
HOMOPTERA: Diaspididae	*Aspidiotus destructor* Signoret	coconut scale
HOMOPTERA: Diaspididae	*Aspidiotus nerii* Bouché	oleander scale
HOMOPTERA: Diaspididae	*Aulacaspis rosae* (Bouché)	rose scale
HOMOPTERA: Diaspididae	*Aulacaspis rosarum* Borchsenius	Asiatic rose scale
HOMOPTERA: Diaspididae	*Carulaspis juniperi* (Bouché)	juniper scale

HOMOPTERA: Diaspididae	*Chionaspis americana* Johnson	elm scurfy scale
HOMOPTERA: Diaspididae	*Chionaspis corni* Cooley	dogwood scale
HOMOPTERA: Diaspididae	*Chionaspis furfura* (Fitch)	scurfy scale
HOMOPTERA: Diaspididae	*Chionaspis pinifoliae* (Fitch)	pine needle scale
HOMOPTERA: Diaspididae	*Chrysomphalus aonidum* (Linnaeus)	Florida red scale
HOMOPTERA: Diaspididae	*Chrysomphalus dictyospermi* (Morgan)	dictyospermum scale
HOMOPTERA: Diaspididae	*Diaspidiotus ancylus* (Putnam)	Putnam scale
HOMOPTERA: Diaspididae	*Diaspidiotus uvae* (Comstock)	grape scale
HOMOPTERA: Diaspididae	*Diaspis boisduvalii* Signoret	Boisduval scale
HOMOPTERA: Diaspididae	*Diaspis bromeliae* (Kerner)	pineapple scale
HOMOPTERA: Diaspididae	*Diaspis echinocacti* (Bouché)	cactus scale
HOMOPTERA: Diaspididae	*Dynaspidiotus britannicus* (Newstead)	holly scale
HOMOPTERA: Diaspididae	*Epidiaspis leperii* (Signoret)	Italian pear scale
HOMOPTERA: Diaspididae	*Fiorinia externa* Ferris	elongate hemlock scale
HOMOPTERA: Diaspididae	*Fiorinia theae* Green	tea scale
HOMOPTERA: Diaspididae	*Furcaspis biformis* (Cockerell)	red orchid scale
HOMOPTERA: Diaspididae	*Hemiberlesia lataniae* (Signoret)	latania scale
HOMOPTERA: Diaspididae	*Hemiberlesia rapax* (Comstock)	greedy scale
HOMOPTERA: Diaspididae	*Howardia biclavis* (Comstock)	mining scale
HOMOPTERA: Diaspididae	*Ischnaspis longirostris* (Signoret)	black thread scale
HOMOPTERA: Diaspididae	*Lepidosaphes beckii* (Newman)	purple scale
HOMOPTERA: Diaspididae	*Lepidosaphes camelliae* Hoke	camellia scale
HOMOPTERA: Diaspididae	*Lepidosaphes conchiformis* (Gmelin)	fig scale
HOMOPTERA: Diaspididae	*Lepidosaphes gloveri* (Packard)	Glover scale
HOMOPTERA: Diaspididae	*Lepidosaphes tokionis* (Kuwana)	croton mussel scale
HOMOPTERA: Diaspididae	*Lepidosaphes ulmi* (Linnaeus)	oystershell scale
HOMOPTERA: Diaspididae	*Melanaspis bromiliae* (Leonardi)	brown pineapple scale
HOMOPTERA: Diaspididae	*Melanaspis obscura* (Comstock)	obscure scale
HOMOPTERA: Diaspididae	*Melanaspis tenebricosa* (Comstock)	gloomy scale
HOMOPTERA: Diaspididae	*Nilotaspis halli* (Green)	Hall scale
HOMOPTERA: Diaspididae	*Nuculaspis californica* (Coleman)	black pineleaf scale
HOMOPTERA: Diaspididae	*Parlatoreopsis chinensis* (Marlatt)	Chinese obscure scale
HOMOPTERA: Diaspididae	*Parlatoria blanchardi* (Targioni-Tozzetti)	parlatoria date scale
HOMOPTERA: Diaspididae	*Parlatoria oleae* (Colvée)	olive scale
HOMOPTERA: Diaspididae	*Parlatoria pergandii* Comstock	chaff scale
HOMOPTERA: Diaspididae	*Pinnaspis aspidistrae* (Signoret)	fern scale
HOMOPTERA: Diaspididae	*Pseudaonidia duplex* (Cockerell)	camphor scale
HOMOPTERA: Diaspididae	*Pseudaulacaspis pentagona* (Targioni-Tozzetti)	white peach scale

HOMOPTERA: Diaspididae	*Quadraspidiotus forbesi* (Johnson)	Forbes scale
HOMOPTERA: Diaspididae	*Quadraspidiotus juglandsregiae* (Comstock)	walnut scale
HOMOPTERA: Diaspididae	*Quadraspidiotus ostreaeformis* (Curtis)	European fruit scale
HOMOPTERA: Diaspididae	*Quadraspidiotus perniciosus* (Comstock)	San Jose scale
HOMOPTERA: Diaspididae	*Unaspis citri* (Comstock)	citrus snow scale
HOMOPTERA: Diaspididae	*Unaspis euonymi* (Comstock)	euonymus scale
HOMOPTERA: Eriococcidae	*Cryptococcus fagisuga* Lindinger	beech scale
HOMOPTERA: Eriococcidae	*Eriococcus azaleae* Comstock	azalea bark scale
HOMOPTERA: Eriococcidae	*Eriococcus carolinae* Williams	beachgrass scale
HOMOPTERA: Eriococcidae	*Gossyparia spuria* (Modeer)	European elm scale
HOMOPTERA: Flatidae	*Anormenis antillarum* (Kirkaldy)	West Indian flatid
HOMOPTERA: Issidae	*Asarcopus palmarum* Horvath	datebug
HOMOPTERA: Margarodidae	*Icerya purchasi* Maskell	cottonycushion scale
HOMOPTERA: Margarodidae	*Matsucoccus resinosae* Bean & Godwin	red pine scale
HOMOPTERA: Membracidae	*Antianthe expansa* (Germar)	solanaceous treehopper
HOMOPTERA: Membracidae	*Enchenopa binotata* (Say)	twomarked treehopper
HOMOPTERA: Membracidae	*Glossonotus crataegi* (Fitch)	quince treehopper
HOMOPTERA: Membracidae	*Spissistilus festinus* (Say)	threecornered alfalfa hopper
HOMOPTERA: Membracidae	*Stictocephala bisonia* Kopp & Yonke	buffalo treehopper
HOMOPTERA: Membracidae	*Tricentrus albomaculatus* Distant	whitemarked treehopper
HOMOPTERA: Membracidae	*Vanduzea segmentata* (Fowler)	Van Duzee treehopper
HOMOPTERA: Ortheziidae	*Orthezia insignis* Browne	greenhouse orthezia
HOMOPTERA: Phoenicococcidae	*Phoenicococcus marlatti* Cockerell	red date scale
HOMOPTERA: Phylloxeridae	*Daktulosphaira vitifoliae* (Fitch)	grape phylloxera
HOMOPTERA: Phylloxeridae	*Phylloxera devastatrix* Pergande	pecan phylloxera
HOMOPTERA: Phylloxeridae	*Phylloxera notabilis* Pergande	pecan leaf phylloxera
HOMOPTERA: Pseudococcidae	*Antonina graminis* (Maskell)	Rhodesgrass mealybug
HOMOPTERA: Pseudococcidae	*Chaetococcus bambusae* (Maskell)	bamboo mealybug
HOMOPTERA: Pseudococcidae	*Dysmicoccus boninsis* (Kuwana)	gray sugarcane mealybug
HOMOPTERA: Pseudococcidae	*Dysmicoccus brevipes* (Cockerell)	pineapple mealybug
HOMOPTERA: Pseudococcidae	*Dysmicoccus neobrevipes* Beardsley	gray pineapple mealybug
HOMOPTERA: Pseudococcidae	*Ferrisia virgata* (Cockerell)	striped mealybug
HOMOPTERA: Pseudococcidae	*Laminicoccus pandani* (Cockerell)	pandanus mealybug
HOMOPTERA: Pseudococcidae	*Nipaecoccus nipae* (Maskell)	coconut mealybug
HOMOPTERA: Pseudococcidae	*Nipaecoccus viridis* (Newstead)	hibiscus mealybug
HOMOPTERA: Pseudococcidae	*Palmicultor palmarum* (Ehrhorn)	palm mealybug
HOMOPTERA: Pseudococcidae	*Phenacoccus aceris* (Signoret)	apple mealybug
HOMOPTERA: Pseudococcidae	*Phenacoccus gossypii* Townsend & Cockerell	Mexican mealybug

HOMOPTERA: Pseudococcidae	*Planococcus citri* (Risso)	citrus mealybug
HOMOPTERA: Pseudococcidae	*Pseudococcus affinis* (Maskell)	obscure mealybug
HOMOPTERA: Pseudococcidae	*Pseudococcus calceolariae* (Maskell)	citrophilus mealybug
HOMOPTERA: Pseudococcidae	*Pseudococcus comstocki* (Kuwana)	Comstock mealybug
HOMOPTERA: Pseudococcidae	*Pseudococcus longispinus* (Targioni-Tozzetti)	longtailed mealybug
HOMOPTERA: Pseudococcidae	*Pseudococcus maritimus* (Ehrhorn)	grape mealybug
HOMOPTERA: Pseudococcidae	*Puto sandini* Washburn	spruce mealybug
HOMOPTERA: Pseudococcidae	*Rhizoecus falcifer* Künckel d'Herculais	ground mealybug
HOMOPTERA: Pseudococcidae	*Saccharicoccus sacchari* (Cockerell)	pink sugarcane mealybug
HOMOPTERA: Psyllidae	*Acizzia uncatoides* (Ferris & Klyver)	acacia psyllid
HOMOPTERA: Psyllidae	*Cacopsylla buxi* (Linnaeus)	boxwood psyllid
HOMOPTERA: Psyllidae	*Cacopsylla mali* (Schmidberger)	apple sucker
HOMOPTERA: Psyllidae	*Cacopsylla negundinis* Mally	boxelder psyllid
HOMOPTERA: Psyllidae	*Cacopsylla pyricola* Foerster	pear psylla
HOMOPTERA: Psyllidae	*Pachypsylla celtidismamma* (Fletcher)	hackberry nipplegall maker
HOMOPTERA: Psyllidae	*Paratrioza cockerelli* (Sulc)	potato psyllid[53]
HOMOPTERA: Psyllidae	*Trioza diospyri* (Ashmead)	persimmon psylla
HYMENOPTERA: Agaonidae	*Blastophaga psenes* (Linnaeus)	fig wasp
HYMENOPTERA: Anaxyelidae	*Syntexis libocedrii* Rohwer	incense-cedar wasp
HYMENOPTERA: Anthophoridae	*Habropoda laboriosa* (Fabricius)	southeastern blueberry bee
HYMENOPTERA: Anthophoridae	*Xylocopa virginica* (Linnaeus)	carpenter bee
HYMENOPTERA: Apidae	*Apis mellifera* Linnaeus	honey bee
HYMENOPTERA: Argidae	*Arge pectoralis* (Leach)	birch sawfly
HYMENOPTERA: Bethylidae	*Cephalonomia waterstoni* Gahan	parasitic grain wasp
HYMENOPTERA: Braconidae	*Opius longicaudatus* Ashmead	longtailed fruit fly parasite
HYMENOPTERA: Cephidae	*Cephus cinctus* Norton	wheat stem sawfly
HYMENOPTERA: Cephidae	*Cephus pygmaeus* (Linnaeus)	European wheat stem sawfly
HYMENOPTERA: Cephidae	*Janus abbreviatus* (Say)	willow shoot sawfly
HYMENOPTERA: Cephidae	*Janus integer* (Norton)	currant stem girdler
HYMENOPTERA: Cephidae	*Trachelus tabidus* (Fabricius)	black grain stem sawfly
HYMENOPTERA: Cimbicidae	*Cimbex americana* Leach	elm sawfly
HYMENOPTERA: Cimbicidae	*Zaraea inflata* Norton	honeysuckle sawfly
HYMENOPTERA: Cynipidae	*Diplolepis radicum* (Osten Sacken)	roseroot gall wasp
HYMENOPTERA: Cynipidae	*Diplolepis rosae* (Linnaeus)	mossyrose gall wasp
HYMENOPTERA: Cynipidae	*Phanacis taraxaci* (Ashmead)	dandelion gall wasp

---

[53]Also called tomato psyllid.

HYMENOPTERA: Diprionidae	*Diprion similis* (Hartig)	introduced pine sawfly
HYMENOPTERA: Diprionidae	*Gilpinia hercyniae* (Hartig)	European spruce sawfly
HYMENOPTERA: Diprionidae	*Neodiprion abietis* (Harris)	balsam fir sawfly
HYMENOPTERA: Dlprlonidae	*Neodiprion burkei* Middleton	lodgepole sawfly
HYMENOPTERA: Diprionidae	*Neodiprion dubiosus* Schedl	brownheaded jack pine sawfly
HYMENOPTERA: Diprionidae	*Neodiprion excitans* Rohwer	blackheaded pine sawfly
HYMENOPTERA: Diprionidae	*Neodiprion lecontei* (Fitch)	redheaded pine sawfly
HYMENOPTERA: Diprionidae	*Neodiprion merkeli* Ross	slash pine sawfly
HYMENOPTERA: Diprionidae	*Neodiprion nanulus nanulus* Schedl	red pine sawfly
HYMENOPTERA: Diprionidae	*Neodiprion pinetum* (Norton)	white pine sawfly
HYMENOPTERA: Diprionidae	*Neodiprion pratti banksianae* Rohwer	jack pine sawfly
HYMENOPTERA: Diprionidae	*Neodiprion pratti pratti* (Dyar)	Virginia pine sawfly
HYMENOPTERA: Diprionidae	*Neodiprion rugifrons* Middleton	redheaded jack pine sawfly
HYMENOPTERA: Diprionidae	*Neodiprion sertifer* (Geoffroy)	European pine sawfly
HYMENOPTERA: Diprionidae	*Neodiprion swainei* Middleton	Swaine jack pine sawfly
HYMENOPTERA: Diprionidae	*Neodiprion taedae linearis* Ross	loblolly pine sawfly
HYMENOPTERA: Diprionidae	*Neodiprion taedae taedae* Ross	spotted loblolly pine sawfly
HYMENOPTERA: Diprionidae	*Neodiprion tsugae* Middleton	hemlock sawfly
HYMENOPTERA: Dryinidae	*Pseudogonatopus hospes* Perkins	Chinese dryinid
HYMENOPTERA: Encyrtidae	*Aphelinus lapisliqni* Howard	clover aphid parasite
HYMENOPTERA: Eurytomidae	*Bruchophagus platyptera* (Walker)	clover seed chalcid
HYMENOPTERA: Eurytomidae	*Bruchophagus roddi* (Gussakovsky)	alfalfa seed chalcid
HYMENOPTERA: Eurytomidae	*Eurytoma orchidearum* (Westwood)	orchidfly
HYMENOPTERA: Eurytomidae	*Evoxysoma vitis* (Saunders)	grape seed chalcid
HYMENOPTERA: Eurytomidae	*Tetramesa grandis* (Riley)	wheat strawworm
HYMENOPTERA: Eurytomidae	*Tetramesa hordei* (Harris)	barley jointworm
HYMENOPTERA: Eurytomidae	*Tetramesa tritici* (Fitch)	wheat jointworm
HYMENOPTERA: Evaniidae	*Szepligetella sericea* (Cameron)	lesser ensign wasp
HYMENOPTERA: Formicidae	*Acanthomyops claviger* (Roger)	smaller yellow ant
HYMENOPTERA: Formicidae	*Acanthomyops interjectus* (Mayr)	larger yellow ant
HYMENOPTERA: Formicidae	*Anoplolepis longipes* (Jerdon)	longlegged ant
HYMENOPTERA: Formicidae	*Atta texana* (Buckley)	Texas leafcutting ant
HYMENOPTERA: Formicidae	*Camponotus abdominalis* (Fabricius)	Florida carpenter ant
HYMENOPTERA: Formicidae	*Camponotus ferrugineus* (Fabricius)	red carpenter ant
HYMENOPTERA: Formicidae	*Camponotus pennsylvanicus* (De Geer)	black carpenter ant
HYMENOPTERA: Formicidae	*Camponotus variegatus* (F. Smith)	Hawaiian carpenter ant
HYMENOPTERA: Formicidae	*Conomyrma insana* (Buckley)	pyramid ant
HYMENOPTERA: Formicidae	*Formica exsectoides* Forel	Allegheny mound ant

HYMENOPTERA: Formicidae	*Formica fusca* Linnaeus	silky ant
HYMENOPTERA: Formicidae	*Formica obscuripes* Forel	western thatching ant
HYMENOPTERA: Formicidae	*Iridomyrmex humilis* (Mayr)	Argentine ant
HYMENOPTERA: Formicidae	*Lasius alienus* (Foerster)	cornfield ant
HYMENOPTERA: Formicidae	*Monomorium minimum* (Buckley)	little black ant
HYMENOPTERA: Formicidae	*Monomorium pharaonis* (Linnaeus)	Pharaoh ant
HYMENOPTERA: Formicidae	*Ochetomyrmex auropunctatus* (Roger)	little fire ant
HYMENOPTERA: Formicidae	*Paratrechina longicornis* (Latreille)	crazy ant
HYMENOPTERA: Formicidae	*Pheidole megacephala* (Fabricius)	bigheaded ant
HYMENOPTERA: Formicidae	*Plagiolepis alluaudi* Emery	little yellow ant
HYMENOPTERA: Formicidae	*Pogonomyrmex badius* (Latreille)	Florida harvester ant
HYMENOPTERA: Formicidae	*Pogonomyrmex barbatus* (F. Smith)	red harvester ant
HYMENOPTERA: Formicidae	*Pogonomyrmex californicus* (Buckley)	California harvester ant
HYMENOPTERA: Formicidae	*Pogonomyrmex maricopa* Wheeler	Maricopa harvester ant
HYMENOPTERA: Formicidae	*Pogonomyrmex occidentalis* (Cresson)	western harvester ant
HYMENOPTERA: Formicidae	*Pogonomyrmex rugosus* Emery	rough harvester ant
HYMENOPTERA: Formicidae	*Solenopsis geminata* (Fabricius)	fire ant
HYMENOPTERA: Formicidae	*Solenopsis invicta* Buren	red imported fire ant
HYMENOPTERA: Formicidae	*Solenopsis molesta* (Say)	thief ant
HYMENOPTERA: Formicidae	*Solenopsis richteri* Forel	black imported fire ant
HYMENOPTERA: Formicidae	*Solenopsis xyloni* McCook	southern fire ant
HYMENOPTERA: Formicidae	*Tapinoma sessile* (Say)	odorous house ant
HYMENOPTERA: Formicidae	*Tetramorium bicarinatum* (Nylander)	Guinea ant
HYMENOPTERA: Formicidae	*Tetramorium caespitum* (Linnaeus)	pavement ant
HYMENOPTERA: Halictidae	*Nomia melanderi* Cockerell	alkali bee
HYMENOPTERA: Megachilidae	*Megachile concinna* Smith	pale leafcutting bee
HYMENOPTERA: Megachilidae	*Megachile rotundata* (Fabricius)	alfalfa leafcutting bee
HYMENOPTERA: Pamphiliidae	*Acantholyda erythrocephala* (Linnaeus)	pine false webworm
HYMENOPTERA: Pamphiliidae	*Neurotoma inconspicua* (Norton)	plum webspinning sawfly
HYMENOPTERA: Pompilidae	*Tachypompilus analis* (Fabricius)	redtailed spider wasp
HYMENOPTERA: Siricidae	*Sirex cyaneus* Fabricius	blue horntail
HYMENOPTERA: Siricidae	*Tremex columba* (Linnaeus)	pigeon tremex
HYMENOPTERA: Sphecidae	*Ampulex compressa* (Fabricius)	emerald cockroach wasp
HYMENOPTERA: Sphecidae	*Dolichurus stantoni* (Ashmead)	black cockroach wasp
HYMENOPTERA: Sphecidae	*Liris aurulentus* (Fabricius)	golden cricket wasp
HYMENOPTERA: Sphecidae	*Sphecius speciosus* (Drury)	cicada killer
HYMENOPTERA: Tenthredinidae	*Allantus cinctus* (Linnaeus)	curled rose sawfly
HYMENOPTERA: Tenthredinidae	*Ametastegia glabrata* (Fallén)	dock sawfly

HYMENOPTERA: Tenthredinidae	*Ametastegia pallipes* (Spinola)	violet sawfly
HYMENOPTERA: Tenthredinidae	*Caliroa cerasi* (Linnaeus)	pear sawfly
HYMENOPTERA: Tenthredinidae	*Caliroa quercuscoccineae* (Dyar)	scarlet oak sawfly
HYMENOPTERA: Tenthredinidae	*Caulocampus acericaulis* (MacGillivray)	maple petiole borer
HYMENOPTERA: Tenthredinidae	*Cladius difformis* (Panzer)	bristly roseslug
HYMENOPTERA: Tenthredinidae	*Croesus latitarsus* Norton	dusky birch sawfly
HYMENOPTERA: Tenthredinidae	*Endelomyia aethiops* (Fabricius)	roseslug
HYMENOPTERA: Tenthredinidae	*Erythraspides vitis* (Harris)	grape sawfly
HYMENOPTERA: Tenthredinidae	*Fenusa dohrnii* (Tischbein)	European alder leafminer
HYMENOPTERA: Tenthredinidae	*Fenusa pusilla* (Lepeletier)	birch leafminer
HYMENOPTERA: Tenthredinidae	*Fenusa ulmi* Sundevall	elm leafminer
HYMENOPTERA: Tenthredinidae	*Hemichroa crocea* (Geoffroy)	striped alder sawfly
HYMENOPTERA: Tenthredinidae	*Hoplocampa cookei* (Clarke)	cherry fruit sawfly
HYMENOPTERA: Tenthredinidae	*Hoplocampa testudinea* (Klug)	European apple sawfly
HYMENOPTERA: Tenthredinidae	*Monophadnoides geniculatus* (Hartig)	raspberry sawfly
HYMENOPTERA: Tenthredinidae	*Nematus ribesii* (Scopoli)	imported currantworm
HYMENOPTERA: Tenthredinidae	*Nematus ventralis* Say	willow sawfly
HYMENOPTERA: Tenthredinidae	*Pachynematus extensicornis* (Norton)	grass sawfly
HYMENOPTERA: Tenthredinidae	*Phyllocolpa bozemani* (Cooley)	poplar leaffolding sawfly
HYMENOPTERA: Tenthredinidae	*Pikonema alaskensis* (Rohwer)	yellowheaded spruce sawfly
HYMENOPTERA: Tenthredinidae	*Pikonema dimmockii* (Cresson)	greenheaded spruce sawfly
HYMENOPTERA: Tenthredinidae	*Pontania promixa* (Lepeletier)	willow redgall sawfly
HYMENOPTERA: Tenthredinidae	*Pristiphora abbreviata* (Hartig)	California pear sawfly
HYMENOPTERA: Tenthredinidae	*Pristiphora erichsonii* (Hartig)	larch sawfly
HYMENOPTERA: Tenthredinidae	*Pristiphora geniculata* (Hartig)	mountain-ash sawfly
HYMENOPTERA: Tenthredinidae	*Tethida barda* (Say)	blackheaded ash sawfly
HYMENOPTERA: Tenthredinidae	*Tomostethus multicinctus* (Rohwer)	brownheaded ash sawfly
HYMENOPTERA: Torymidae	*Torymus varians* (Walker)	apple seed chalcid
HYMENOPTERA: Trichogrammatidae	*Trichogramma minutum* Riley	minute egg parasite
HYMENOPTERA: Vespidae	*Delta campaniformis campaniformis* (Fabricius)	yellow and black potter wasp
HYMENOPTERA: Vespidae	*Delta latreillei petiolaris* (Schulz)	orangetailed potter wasp
HYMENOPTERA: Vespidae	*Delta pyriformis philippinensis* (Bequaert)	black potter wasp
HYMENOPTERA: Vespidae	*Dolichovespula arenaria* (Fabricius)	aerial yellowjacket
HYMENOPTERA: Vespidae	*Dolichovespula maculata* (Linnaeus)	baldfaced hornet
HYMENOPTERA: Vespidae	*Pachodynerus nasidens* (Latreille)	keyhole wasp
HYMENOPTERA: Vespidae	*Paravespula germanica* (Linnaeus)	German yellowjacket
HYMENOPTERA: Vespidae	*Polistes fuscatus aurifer* Saussure	golden paper wasp
HYMENOPTERA: Vespidae	*Polistes macaensis* (Fabricius)	Macao paper wasp

HYMENOPTERA: Vespidae	*Vespa crabro* Linnaeus	European hornet
HYMENOPTERA: Vespidae	*Vespula consobrina* (Saussure)	blackjacket
HYMENOPTERA: Vespidae	*Vespula maculifrons* (Buysson)	eastern yellowjacket
HYMENOPTERA: Vespidae	*Vespula pensylvanica* (Saussure)	western yellowjacket
HYMENOPTERA: Xyelidae	*Pleroneura brunneicornis* Rohwer	balsam shootboring sawfly

I

ISOPODA: Asellidae	*Lirceus brachyurus* (Harger)	watercress sowbug
ISOPTERA: Kalotermitidae	*Incisitermes immigrans* (Snyder)	lowland tree termite
ISOPTERA: Kalotermitidae	*Incisitermes minor* (Hagen)	western drywood termite
ISOPTERA: Kalotermitidae	*Neotermes connexus* Snyder	forest tree termite
ISOPTERA: Rhinotermitidae	*Coptotermes formosanus* Shiraki	Formosan subterranean termite
ISOPTERA: Rhinotermitidae	*Reticulitermes flavipes* (Kollar)	eastern subterranean termite
ISOPTERA: Rhinotermitidae	*Reticulitermes hesperus* Banks	western subterranean termite
ISOPTERA: Termopsidae	*Zootermopsis angusticollis* (Hagen)	Pacific dampwood termite

L

LEPIDOPTERA: Acrolepiidae	*Acrolepiopsis assectella* (Zeller)	leek moth
LEPIDOPTERA: Agonoxenidae	*Agonoxena argaula* Meyrick	coconut leafminer
LEPIDOPTERA: Arctiidae	*Estigmene acrea* (Drury)	saltmarsh caterpillar
LEPIDOPTERA: Arctiidae	*Halysidota harrisii* Walsh	sycamore tussock moth
LEPIDOPTERA: Arctiidae	*Halysidota tessellaris* (J.E. Smith)	pale tussock moth
LEPIDOPTERA: Arctiidae	*Hyphantria cunea* (Drury)	fall webworm
LEPIDOPTERA: Arctiidae	*Lophocampa argentata* (Packard)	silverspotted tiger moth
LEPIDOPTERA: Arctiidae	*Lophocampa caryae* (Harris)	hickory tussock moth
LEPIDOPTERA: Arctiidae	*Lophocampa maculata* Harris	spotted tussock moth
LEPIDOPTERA: Arctiidae	*Pyrrharctia isabella* (J.E. Smith)	banded woollybear
LEPIDOPTERA: Arctiidae	*Spilosoma virginica* (Fabricius)	yellow woollybear
LEPIDOPTERA: Arctiidae	*Tyria jacobaeae* (Linnaeus)	cinnabar moth
LEPIDOPTERA: Arctiidae	*Utetheisa bella* (Linnaeus)	bella moth
LEPIDOPTERA: Argyresthiidae	*Argyresthia conjugella* Zeller	apple fruit moth

LEPIDOPTERA: Argyresthiidae	*Argyresthia thuiella* (Packard)	arborvitae leafminer
LEPIDOPTERA: Bombycidae	*Bombyx mori* (Linnaeus)	silkworm
LEPIDOPTERA: Choreutidae	*Choreutis pariana* (Clerck)	apple-and-thorn skeletonizer
LEPIDOPTERA: Cochylidae	*Aethes rutilana* (Hübner)	pale juniper webworm
LEPIDOPTERA: Cochylidae	*Cochylis hospes* Walsingham	banded sunflower moth
LEPIDOPTERA: Cochylidae	*Lorita abornana* Busck	chrysanthemum flower borer
LEPIDOPTERA: Coleophoridae	*Coleophora laricella* (Hübner)	larch casebearer
LEPIDOPTERA: Coleophoridae	*Coleophora laticornella* Clemens	pecan cigar casebearer
LEPIDOPTERA: Coleophoridae	*Coleophora malivorella* Riley	pistol casebearer
LEPIDOPTERA: Coleophoridae	*Coleophora pruniella* Clemens	cherry casebearer
LEPIDOPTERA: Coleophoridae	*Coleophora serratella* (Linnaeus)	birch casebearer[54]
LEPIDOPTERA: Coleophoridae	*Coleophora ulmifoliella* McDunnough	elm casebearer
LEPIDOPTERA: Coleophoridae	*Homaledra sabalella* (Chambers)	palm leafskeletonizer
LEPIDOPTERA: Cosmopterigidae	*Ithome concolorella* (Chambers)	kiawe flower moth
LEPIDOPTERA: Cosmopterigidae	*Pyroderces rileyi* (Walsingham)	pink scavenger caterpillar
LEPIDOPTERA: Cosmopterigidae	*Walshia miscecolorella* (Chambers)	sweetclover root borer
LEPIDOPTERA: Cossidae	*Cossula magnifica* (Strecker)	pecan carpenterworm
LEPIDOPTERA: Cossidae	*Prionoxystus macmurtrei* (Guérin)	little carpenterworm
LEPIDOPTERA: Cossidae	*Prionoxystus robiniae* (Peck)	carpenterworm
LEPIDOPTERA: Cossidae	*Zeuzera pyrina* (Linnaeus)	leopard moth
LEPIDOPTERA: Danaidae	*Danaus plexippus* (Linnaeus)	monarch butterfly
LEPIDOPTERA: Dioptidae	*Phryganidia californica* Packard	California oakworm
LEPIDOPTERA: Elachistidae	*Swezeyula lonicerae* Zimmerman & Bradley	honeysuckle leafminer
LEPIDOPTERA: Gelechiidae	*Anarsia lineatella* Zeller	peach twig borer
LEPIDOPTERA: Gelechiidae	*Aroga websteri* Clarke	sagebrush defoliator
LEPIDOPTERA: Gelechiidae	*Coleotechnites milleri* (Busck)	lodgepole needleminer
LEPIDOPTERA: Gelechiidae	*Dichomeris acuminata* (Standinger)	alfalfa leaftier
LEPIDOPTERA: Gelechiidae	*Dichomeris ligulella* Hübner	palmerworm
LEPIDOPTERA: Gelechiidae	*Dichomeris marginella* (Fabricius)	juniper webworm
LEPIDOPTERA: Gelechiidae	*Exoteleia nepheos* Freeman	pine candle moth
LEPIDOPTERA: Gelechiidae	*Exoteleia pinifoliella* (Chambers)	pine needleminer
LEPIDOPTERA: Gelechiidae	*Fascista cercerisella* (Chambers)	redbud leaffolder
LEPIDOPTERA: Gelechiidae	*Keiferia lycopersicella* (Walsingham)	tomato pinworm
LEPIDOPTERA: Gelechiidae	*Monochroa fragariae* (Busck)	strawberry crownminer
LEPIDOPTERA: Gelechiidae	*Pectinophora gossypiella* (Saunders)	pink bollworm

[54]Also called cigar casebearer.

LEPIDOPTERA: Gelechiidae	*Phthorimaea operculella* (Zeller)	potato tuberworm
LEPIDOPTERA: Gelechiidae	*Platyedra subcinerea* (Haworth)	cotton stem moth
LEPIDOPTERA: Gelechiidae	*Recurvaria nanella* (Denis & Schiffermüller)	lesser bud moth
LEPIDOPTERA: Gelechiidae	*Sitotroga cerealella* (Olivier)	Angoumois grain moth
LEPIDOPTERA: Gelechiidae	*Stegasta bosqueella* (Chambers)	rednecked peanutworm
LEPIDOPTERA: Gelechiidae	*Tildenia inconspicuella* (Murtfeldt)	eggplant leafminer
LEPIDOPTERA: Geometridae	*Alsophila pometaria* (Harris)	fall cankerworm
LEPIDOPTERA: Geometridae	*Biston betularia cognataria* (Guenée)	pepper-and-salt moth
LEPIDOPTERA: Geometridae	*Cingilia catenaria* (Drury)	chainspotted geometer
LEPIDOPTERA: Geometridae	*Ennomos subsignaria* (Hübner)	elm spanworm
LEPIDOPTERA: Geometridae	*Erannis tiliaria* (Harris)	linden looper
LEPIDOPTERA: Geometridae	*Eulithis diversilineata* (Hübner)	grapevine looper
LEPIDOPTERA: Geometridae	*Eupithecia spermaphaga* (Dyar)	fir cone looper
LEPIDOPTERA: Geometridae	*Itame ribearia* (Fitch)	currant spanworm
LEPIDOPTERA: Geometridae	*Lambdina fiscellaria fiscellaria* (Guenée)	hemlock looper
LEPIDOPTERA: Geometridae	*Lambdina fiscellaria lugubrosa* (Hulst)	western hemlock looper
LEPIDOPTERA: Geometridae	*Lambdina fiscellaria somniaria* (Hulst)	western oak looper
LEPIDOPTERA: Geometridae	*Lambdina pellucidaria* (Grote & Robinson)	eastern pine looper
LEPIDOPTERA: Geometridae	*Nematocampa limbata* (Haworth)	filament bearer
LEPIDOPTERA: Geometridae	*Nepytia canosaria* (Walker)	false hemlock looper
LEPIDOPTERA: Geometridae	*Nepytia phantasmaria* (Strecker)	phantom hemlock looper
LEPIDOPTERA: Geometridae	*Nepytia semiclusaria* (Walker)	pine conelet looper
LEPIDOPTERA: Geometridae	*Operophtera bruceata* (Hulst)	Bruce spanworm
LEPIDOPTERA: Geometridae	*Operophtera brumata* (Linnaeus)	winter moth
LEPIDOPTERA: Geometridae	*Paleacrita vernata* (Peck)	spring cankerworm
LEPIDOPTERA: Geometridae	*Sabulodes aegrotata* (Guenée)	omnivorous looper
LEPIDOPTERA: Geometridae	*Scotorythra paludicola* (Butler)	koa moth
LEPIDOPTERA: Gracillariidae	*Caloptilia azaleella* (Brants)	azalea leafminer
LEPIDOPTERA: Gracillariidae	*Caloptilia cuculipennella* (Hübner)	privet leafminer
LEPIDOPTERA: Gracillariidae	*Caloptilia negundella* (Chambers)	boxelder leafroller
LEPIDOPTERA: Gracillariidae	*Caloptilia syringella* (Fabricius)	lilac leafminer
LEPIDOPTERA: Gracillariidae	*Cameraria cincinnatiella* (Chambers)	gregarious oak leafminer
LEPIDOPTERA: Gracillariidae	*Cameraria hamadryadella* (Clemens)	solitary oak leafminer
LEPIDOPTERA: Gracillariidae	*Cremastobombycia lantanella* (Schrank)	lantana leafminer
LEPIDOPTERA: Gracillariidae	*Marmara elotella* (Busck)	apple barkminer
LEPIDOPTERA: Gracillariidae	*Marmara pomonella* Busck	apple fruitminer
LEPIDOPTERA: Gracillariidae	*Philodoria hauicola* (Swezey)	hau leafminer
LEPIDOPTERA: Gracillariidae	*Philodoria hibiscella* (Swezey)	hibiscus leafminer

LEPIDOPTERA: Gracillariidae	*Philodoria marginestrigata* (Walsingham)	ilima leafminer
LEPIDOPTERA: Gracillariidae	*Phyllocnistis meliacella* Becker	mahogany leafminer
LEPIDOPTERA: Gracillariidae	*Phyllonorycter blancardella* (Fabricius)	spotted tentiform leafminer
LEPIDOPTERA: Gracillariidae	*Phyllonorycter crataegella* (Clemens)	apple blotch leafminer
LEPIDOPTERA: Gracillariidae	*Phyllonorycter tremuloidiella* (Braun)	aspen blotchminer
LEPIDOPTERA: Heliodinidae	*Schreckensteinia festaliella* (Hübner)	blackberry skeletonizer
LEPIDOPTERA: Heliozelidae	*Antispila nysaefoliella* Clemens	tupelo leafminer
LEPIDOPTERA: Heliozelidae	*Coptodisca splendoriferella* (Clemens)	resplendent shield bearer
LEPIDOPTERA: Hesperiidae	*Calpodes ethlius* (Stoll)	larger canna leafroller
LEPIDOPTERA: Hesperiidae	*Epargyreus clarus* (Cramer)	silverspotted skipper
LEPIDOPTERA: Hesperiidae	*Erionota thrax* (Linnaeus)	banana skipper
LEPIDOPTERA: Hesperiidae	*Hylephila phyleus* (Drury)	fiery skipper
LEPIDOPTERA: Hesperiidae	*Lerodea eufala* (Edwards)	rice leaffolder
LEPIDOPTERA: Hesperiidae	*Urbanus proteus* (Linnaeus)	bean leafroller
LEPIDOPTERA: Incurvariidae	*Lampronia rubiella* (Bjerkander)	raspberry bud moth
LEPIDOPTERA: Incurvariidae	*Paraclemensia acerifoliella* (Fitch)	maple leafcutter
LEPIDOPTERA: Incurvariidae	*Tegeticula yuccasella* (Riley)	yucca moth
LEPIDOPTERA: Lasiocampidae	*Malacosoma americanum* (Fabricius)	eastern tent caterpillar
LEPIDOPTERA: Lasiocampidae	*Malacosoma californicum* (Packard)	western tent caterpillar
LEPIDOPTERA: Lasiocampidae	*Malacosoma constrictum* (Hy. Edwards)	Pacific tent caterpillar
LEPIDOPTERA: Lasiocampidae	*Malacosoma disstria* Hübner	forest tent caterpillar
LEPIDOPTERA: Lasiocampidae	*Malacosoma incurvum* (Hy. Edwards)	southwestern tent caterpillar
LEPIDOPTERA: Lasiocampidae	*Malacosoma tigris* (Dyar)	Sonoran tent caterpillar
LEPIDOPTERA: Lasiocampidae	*Phyllodesma americana* (Harris)	lappet moth
LEPIDOPTERA: Limacodidae	*Cnidocampa flavescens* (Walker)	oriental moth
LEPIDOPTERA: Limacodidae	*Parasa indetermina* (Boisduval)	stinging rose caterpillar
LEPIDOPTERA: Limacodidae	*Phobetron pithecium* (J.E. Smith)	hag moth
LEPIDOPTERA: Limacodidae	*Sibine stimulea* (Clemens)	saddleback caterpillar
LEPIDOPTERA: Lycaenidae	*Euphilotes battoides allyni* (Shields)	El Segundo blue
LEPIDOPTERA: Lycaenidae	*Euphilotes enoptes smithi* (Mattoni)	Smith blue
LEPIDOPTERA: Lycaenidae	*Icaricia icarioides missionensis* (Hovanitz)	mission blue
LEPIDOPTERA: Lycaenidae	*Incisalia fotis bayensis* (R.M. Brown)	San Bruno elfin
LEPIDOPTERA: Lycaenidae	*Lampides boeticus* (Linnaeus)	bean butterfly
LEPIDOPTERA: Lycaenidae	*Lycaeides argyrognomon lotis* (Lintner)	lotis blue
LEPIDOPTERA: Lycaenidae	*Strymon bazochii gundlachianus* (Bates)	smaller lantana butterfly
LEPIDOPTERA: Lycaenidae	*Strymon echion* (Linnaeus)	larger lantana butterfly
LEPIDOPTERA: Lycaenidae	*Strymon melinus* Hübner	cotton square borer
LEPIDOPTERA: Lycaenidae	*Vaga blackburni* (Tuely)	Blackburn butterfly

LEPIDOPTERA: Lymantriidae	*Dasychira pinicola* (Dyar)	pine tussock moth
LEPIDOPTERA: Lymantriidae	*Euproctis chrysorrhoea* (Linnaeus)	browntail moth
LEPIDOPTERA: Lymantriidae	*Leucoma salicis* (Linnaeus)	satin moth
LEPIDOPTERA: Lymantriidae	*Lymantria dispar* (Linnaeus)	gypsy moth
LEPIDOPTERA: Lymantriidae	*Orgyia antiqua* (Linnaeus)	rusty tussock moth
LEPIDOPTERA: Lymantriidae	*Orgyia leucostigma* (J.E. Smith)	whitemarked tussock moth
LEPIDOPTERA: Lymantriidae	*Orgyia pseudotsugata* (McDunnough)	Douglas-fir tussock moth
LEPIDOPTERA: Lymantriidae	*Orgyia vetusta* (Boisduval)	western tussock moth
LEPIDOPTERA: Lyonetiidae	*Bedellia orchilella* Walsingham	sweetpotato leafminer
LEPIDOPTERA: Lyonetiidae	*Bedellia somnulentella* (Zeller)	morningglory leafminer
LEPIDOPTERA: Lyonetiidae	*Bucculatrix ainsliella* Murtfeldt	oak skeletonizer
LEPIDOPTERA: Lyonetiidae	*Bucculatrix canadensisella* Chambers	birch skeletonizer
LEPIDOPTERA: Lyonetiidae	*Bucculatrix thurberiella* Busck	cotton leafperforator
LEPIDOPTERA: Megalopygidae	*Lagoa crispata* (Packard)	crinkled flannel moth
LEPIDOPTERA: Megalopygidae	*Megalopyge opercularis* (J.E. Smith)	puss caterpillar
LEPIDOPTERA: Nepticulidae	*Obrussa ochrefasciella* (Chambers)	hard maple budminer
LEPIDOPTERA: Nepticulidae	*Stigmella gossypii* (Forbes & Leonard)	cotton leafminer
LEPIDOPTERA: Nepticulidae	*Stigmella juglandifoliella* (Clemens)	pecan serpentine leafminer
LEPIDOPTERA: Noctuidae	*Achaea janata* (Linnaeus)	croton caterpillar
LEPIDOPTERA: Noctuidae	*Achatodes zeae* (Harris)	elder shoot borer
LEPIDOPTERA: Noctuidae	*Acontia dacia* Druce	brown cotton leafworm
LEPIDOPTERA: Noctuidae	*Acronicta americana* (Harris)	American dagger moth
LEPIDOPTERA: Noctuidae	*Acronicta lepusculina* Guenée	cottonwood dagger moth
LEPIDOPTERA: Noctuidae	*Acronicta oblinita* (J.E. Smith)	smeared dagger moth
LEPIDOPTERA: Noctuidae	*Actebia fennica* (Tauscher)	black army cutworm
LEPIDOPTERA: Noctuidae	*Agrotis crinigera* (Butler)	larger Hawaiian cutworm
LEPIDOPTERA: Noctuidae	*Agrotis dislocata* (Walker)	smaller Hawaiian cutworm
LEPIDOPTERA: Noctuidae	*Agrotis gladiaria* Morrison	claybacked cutworm
LEPIDOPTERA: Noctuidae	*Agrotis ipsilon* (Hufnagel)	black cutworm
LEPIDOPTERA: Noctuidae	*Agrotis malefida* Guenée	palesided cutworm
LEPIDOPTERA: Noctuidae	*Agrotis orthogonia* Morrison	pale western cutworm
LEPIDOPTERA: Noctuidae	*Agrotis subterranea* (Fabricius)	granulate cutworm
LEPIDOPTERA: Noctuidae	*Alabama argillacea* (Hübner)	cotton leafworm
LEPIDOPTERA: Noctuidae	*Alypia octomaculata* (Fabricius)	eightspotted forester
LEPIDOPTERA: Noctuidae	*Amyna natalis* (Walker)	ilima moth
LEPIDOPTERA: Noctuidae	*Anagrapha falcifera* (Kirby)	celery looper
LEPIDOPTERA: Noctuidae	*Anticarsia gemmatalis* Hübner	velvetbean caterpillar
LEPIDOPTERA: Noctuidae	*Apamea amputatrix* (Fitch)	yellowheaded cutworm

LEPIDOPTERA: Noctuidae	*Apamea devastator* (Brace)	glassy cutworm
LEPIDOPTERA: Noctuidae	*Ascalapha odorata* (Linnaeus)	black witch
LEPIDOPTERA: Noctuidae	*Athetis mindara* (Barnes & McDunnough)	roughskinned cutworm
LEPIDOPTERA: Noctuidae	*Autographa californica* (Speyer)	alfalfa looper
LEPIDOPTERA: Noctuidae	*Autoplusia egena* (Guenée)	bean leafskeletonizer
LEPIDOPTERA: Noctuidae	*Bellura densa* (Walker)	pickerelweed borer
LEPIDOPTERA: Noctuidae	*Caenurgina crassiuscula* (Haworth)	clover looper
LEPIDOPTERA: Noctuidae	*Caenurgina erechtea* (Cramer)	forage looper
LEPIDOPTERA: Noctuidae	*Callopistria floridensis* (Guenée)	Florida fern caterpillar
LEPIDOPTERA: Noctuidae	*Chrysodeixis eriosoma* (Doubleday)	green garden looper
LEPIDOPTERA: Noctuidae	*Discestra trifolii* (Hufnagel)	clover cutworm
LEPIDOPTERA: Noctuidae	*Euxoa auxiliaris* (Grote)	army cutworm
LEPIDOPTERA: Noctuidae	*Euxoa messoria* (Harris)	darksided cutworm
LEPIDOPTERA: Noctuidae	*Euxoa ochrogaster* (Guenée)	redbacked cutworm
LEPIDOPTERA: Noctuidae	*Euxoa scandens* (Riley)	white cutworm
LEPIDOPTERA: Noctuidae	*Euxoa tessellata* (Harris)	striped cutworm
LEPIDOPTERA: Noctuidae	*Faronta diffusa* (Walker)	wheat head armyworm
LEPIDOPTERA: Noctuidae	*Feltia ducens* Walker	dingy cutworm
LEPIDOPTERA: Noctuidae	*Helicoverpa hawaiiensis* (Quaintance & Brues)	Hawaiian bud moth
LEPIDOPTERA: Noctuidae	*Helicoverpa virescens* (Fabricius)	tobacco budworm
LEPIDOPTERA: Noctuidae	*Helicoverpa zea* (Boddie)	bollworm[55]
LEPIDOPTERA: Noctuidae	*Heliothis ononis* (Denis & Schiffermüller)	flax bollworm
LEPIDOPTERA: Noctuidae	*Hydraecia micacea* (Esper)	potato stem borer
LEPIDOPTERA: Noctuidae	*Hypena humuli* (Harris)	hop looper
LEPIDOPTERA: Noctuidae	*Hypena strigata* (Fabricius)	lantana defoliator caterpillar
LEPIDOPTERA: Noctuidae	*Lacinipolia renigera* (Stephens)	bristly cutworm
LEPIDOPTERA: Noctuidae	*Lithophane antennata* (Walker)	green fruitworm
LEPIDOPTERA: Noctuidae	*Loxagrotis albicosta* (Smith)	western bean cutworm
LEPIDOPTERA: Noctuidae	*Macronoctua onusta* Grote	iris borer
LEPIDOPTERA: Noctuidae	*Mamestra configurata* Walker	bertha armyworm
LEPIDOPTERA: Noctuidae	*Melanchra picta* (Harris)	zebra caterpillar
LEPIDOPTERA: Noctuidae	*Neogalea sunia* (Guenée)	lantana stick caterpillar
LEPIDOPTERA: Noctuidae	*Nephelodes minians* Guenée	bronzed cutworm
LEPIDOPTERA: Noctuidae	*Nola sorghiella* Riley	sorghum webworm
LEPIDOPTERA: Noctuidae	*Oligia fractilinea* (Grote)	lined stalk borer

---

[55]Also called corn earworm and tomato fruitworm.

LEPIDOPTERA: Noctuidae	*Papaipema cataphracta* (Grote)	burdock borer
LEPIDOPTERA: Noctuidae	*Papaipema nebris* (Guenée)	stalk borer
LEPIDOPTERA: Noctuidae	*Papaipema purpurifascia* (Grote & Robinson)	columbine borer
LEPIDOPTERA: Noctuidae	*Penicillaria jocosatrix* Guenée	mango shoot caterpillar
LEPIDOPTERA: Noctuidae	*Pericyma cruegeri* (Butler)	poinciana looper
LEPIDOPTERA: Noctuidae	*Peridroma saucia* (Hübner)	variegated cutworm
LEPIDOPTERA: Noctuidae	*Plathypena scabra* (Fabricius)	green cloverworm
LEPIDOPTERA: Noctuidae	*Polydesma umbricola* Boisduval	monkeypod moth
LEPIDOPTERA: Noctuidae	*Pseudaletia unipuncta* (Haworth)	armyworm
LEPIDOPTERA: Noctuidae	*Pseudoplusia includens* (Walker)	soybean looper
LEPIDOPTERA: Noctuidae	*Selca brunella* (Hampson)	melastoma borer
LEPIDOPTERA: Noctuidae	*Spaelotis clandestina* (Harris)	w-marked cutworm
LEPIDOPTERA: Noctuidae	*Spaelotis havilae* (Grote)	western w-marked cutworm
LEPIDOPTERA: Noctuidae	*Spodoptera eridania* (Cramer)	southern armyworm
LEPIDOPTERA: Noctuidae	*Spodoptera exempta* (Walker)	nutgrass armyworm
LEPIDOPTERA: Noctuidae	*Spodoptera exigua* (Hübner)	beet armyworm
LEPIDOPTERA: Noctuidae	*Spodoptera frugiperda* (J.E. Smith)	fall armyworm
LEPIDOPTERA: Noctuidae	*Spodoptera mauritia* (Boisduval)	lawn armyworm
LEPIDOPTERA: Noctuidae	*Spodoptera ornithogalli* (Guenée)	yellowstriped armyworm
LEPIDOPTERA: Noctuidae	*Spodoptera praefica* (Grote)	western yellowstriped armyworm
LEPIDOPTERA: Noctuidae	*Targalla delatrix* Guenée	eugenia caterpillar
LEPIDOPTERA: Noctuidae	*Trichoplusia ni* (Hübner)	cabbage looper
LEPIDOPTERA: Noctuidae	*Trichordestra legitima* (Grote)	striped garden caterpillar
LEPIDOPTERA: Noctuidae	*Xestia* spp.	spotted cutworm
LEPIDOPTERA: Notodontidae	*Datana integerrima* Grote & Robinson	walnut caterpillar
LEPIDOPTERA: Notodontidae	*Datana major* Grote & Robinson	azalea caterpillar
LEPIDOPTERA: Notodontidae	*Datana ministra* (Drury)	yellownecked caterpillar
LEPIDOPTERA: Notodontidae	*Heterocampa guttivitta* (Walker)	saddled prominent
LEPIDOPTERA: Notodontidae	*Heterocampa manteo* (Doubleday)	variable oakleaf caterpillar
LEPIDOPTERA: Notodontidae	*Ichthyura inclusa* (Hübner)	poplar tentmaker
LEPIDOPTERA: Notodontidae	*Schizura concinna* (J.E. Smith)	redhumped caterpillar
LEPIDOPTERA: Notodontidae	*Schizura unicornis* (J.E. Smith)	unicorn caterpillar
LEPIDOPTERA: Notodontidae	*Symmerista leucitys* Franclemont	orangehumped mapleworm
LEPIDOPTERA: Nymphalidae	*Basilarchia archippus* (Cramer)	viceroy
LEPIDOPTERA: Nymphalidae	*Nymphalis antiopa* (Linnaeus)	mourningcloak butterfly
LEPIDOPTERA: Nymphalidae	*Nymphalis californica* (Boisduval)	California tortoiseshell
LEPIDOPTERA: Nymphalidae	*Vanessa atalanta rubria* (Fruhstorfer)	red admiral
LEPIDOPTERA: Nymphalidae	*Vanessa cardui* (Linnaeus)	painted lady

LEPIDOPTERA: Nymphalidae	*Vanessa tameamea* Eschscholtz	Kamehameha butterfly
LEPIDOPTERA: Nymphalidae	*Vanessa virginiensis* (Drury)	painted beauty
LEPIDOPTERA: Oecophoridae	*Depressaria pastinacella* (Duponchel)	parsnip webworm
LEPIDOPTERA: Oecophoridae	*Endrosis sarcitrella* (Linnaeus)	whiteshouldered house moth
LEPIDOPTERA: Oecophoridae	*Ethmia nigroapicella* (Saalmüller)	kou leafworm
LEPIDOPTERA: Oecophoridae	*Hofmannophila pseudospretella* (Stainton)	brown house moth
LEPIDOPTERA: Papilionidae	*Battus philenor* (Linnaeus)	pipevine swallowtail
LEPIDOPTERA: Papilionidae	*Papilio andraemon bonhotei* Sharpe	Bahaman swallowtail
LEPIDOPTERA: Papilionidae	*Papilio aristodemus ponceanus* Schaus	Schaus swallowtail
LEPIDOPTERA: Papilionidae	*Papilio cresphontes* Cramer	orangedog
LEPIDOPTERA: Papilionidae	*Papilio glaucus* Linnaeus	tiger swallowtail
LEPIDOPTERA: Papilionidae	*Papilio polyxenes asterius* Stoll	black swallowtail[56]
LEPIDOPTERA: Papilionidae	*Papilio troilus* Linnaeus	spicebush swallowtail
LEPIDOPTERA: Papilionidae	*Papilio xuthus* Linnaeus	citrus swallowtail
LEPIDOPTERA: Pieridae	*Colias eurytheme* Boisduval	alfalfa caterpillar
LEPIDOPTERA: Pieridae	*Colias philodice* Godart	clouded sulfur
LEPIDOPTERA: Pieridae	*Neophasia menapia* (Felder & Felder)	pine butterfly
LEPIDOPTERA: Pieridae	*Pieris rapae* (Linnaeus)	imported cabbageworm
LEPIDOPTERA: Pieridae	*Pontia protodice* (Boisduval & LeConte)	southern cabbageworm
LEPIDOPTERA: Plutellidae	*Homadaula anisocentra* Meyrick	mimosa webworm
LEPIDOPTERA: Plutellidae	*Plutella xylostella* (Linnaeus)	diamondback moth
LEPIDOPTERA: Plutellidae	*Ypsolophus dentella* (Fabricius)	European honeysuckle leafroller
LEPIDOPTERA: Psychidae	*Thyridopteryx ephemeraeformis* (Haworth)	bagworm
LEPIDOPTERA: Pterophoridae	*Lantanophaga pusillidactyla* (Walker)	lantana plume moth
LEPIDOPTERA: Pterophoridae	*Platyptilia carduidactyla* (Riley)	artichoke plume moth
LEPIDOPTERA: Pterophoridae	*Pterophorus periscelidactylus* Fitch	grape plume moth
LEPIDOPTERA: Pyralidae	*Achroia grisella* (Fabricius)	lesser wax moth
LEPIDOPTERA: Pyralidae	*Achyra rantalis* (Guenée)	garden webworm
LEPIDOPTERA: Pyralidae	*Acrobasis betulella* Hulst	birch tubemaker
LEPIDOPTERA: Pyralidae	*Acrobasis comptoniella* Hulst	sweetfern leaf casebearer
LEPIDOPTERA: Pyralidae	*Acrobasis demotella* Grote	walnut shoot moth
LEPIDOPTERA: Pyralidae	*Acrobasis indigenella* (Zeller)	leaf crumpler
LEPIDOPTERA: Pyralidae	*Acrobasis juglandis* (LeBaron)	pecan leaf casebearer
LEPIDOPTERA: Pyralidae	*Acrobasis nuxvorella* Neunzig	pecan nut casebearer
LEPIDOPTERA: Pyralidae	*Acrobasis vaccinii* Riley	cranberry fruitworm

---

[56]Immature called parsleyworm.

LEPIDOPTERA: Pyralidae	*Agriphila vulgivagella* (Clemens)	vagabond crambus
LEPIDOPTERA: Pyralidae	*Amyelois transitella* (Walker)	navel orangeworm
LEPIDOPTERA: Pyralidae	*Anagasta kuehniella* (Zeller)	Mediterranean flour moth
LEPIDOPTERA: Pyralidae	*Aphomia gularis* (Zeller)	stored nut moth
LEPIDOPTERA: Pyralidae	*Blepharomastix ebulealis* (Guenée)	clidemia leafroller
LEPIDOPTERA: Pyralidae	*Cactoblastis cactorum* (Berg)	cactus moth
LEPIDOPTERA: Pyralidae	*Cadra cautella* (Walker)	almond moth
LEPIDOPTERA: Pyralidae	*Cadra figulilella* (Gregson)	raisin moth
LEPIDOPTERA: Pyralidae	*Chilo plejadellus* Zincken	rice stalk borer
LEPIDOPTERA: Pyralidae	*Chilo suppressalis* (Walker)	Asiatic rice borer
LEPIDOPTERA: Pyralidae	*Chrysoteuchia topiaria* (Zeller)	cranberry girdler
LEPIDOPTERA: Pyralidae	*Corcyra cephalonica* (Stainton)	rice moth
LEPIDOPTERA: Pyralidae	*Crambus caliginosellus* Clemens	corn root webworm
LEPIDOPTERA: Pyralidae	*Cryptoblabes gnidiella* (Millière)	Christmas berry webworm
LEPIDOPTERA: Pyralidae	*Desmia funeralis* (Hübner)	grape leaffolder
LEPIDOPTERA: Pyralidae	*Diaphania hyalinata* (Linnaeus)	melonworm
LEPIDOPTERA: Pyralidae	*Diaphania nitidalis* (Stoll)	pickleworm
LEPIDOPTERA: Pyralidae	*Diatraea crambidoides* (Grote)	southern cornstalk borer
LEPIDOPTERA: Pyralidae	*Diatraea grandiosella* Dyar	southwestern corn borer
LEPIDOPTERA: Pyralidae	*Diatraea saccharalis* (Fabricius)	sugarcane borer
LEPIDOPTERA: Pyralidae	*Dioryctria amatella* (Hulst)	southern pine coneworm
LEPIDOPTERA: Pyralidae	*Dioryctria clarioralis* (Walker)	blister coneworm
LEPIDOPTERA: Pyralidae	*Dioryctria disclusa* Heinrich	webbing coneworm
LEPIDOPTERA: Pyralidae	*Dioryctria ebeli* Mutuura & Munroe	south coastal coneworm
LEPIDOPTERA: Pyralidae	*Dioryctria pygmaeella* Ragonot	baldcypress coneworm
LEPIDOPTERA: Pyralidae	*Dioryctria reniculelloides* Mutuura & Munroe	spruce coneworm
LEPIDOPTERA: Pyralidae	*Dioryctria resinosella* Mutuura	red pine shoot moth
LEPIDOPTERA: Pyralidae	*Dioryctria yatesi* Mutuura & Munroe	mountain pine coneworm
LEPIDOPTERA: Pyralidae	*Dioryctria zimmermani* (Grote)	Zimmerman pine moth
LEPIDOPTERA: Pyralidae	*Elasmopalpus lignosellus* (Zeller)	lesser cornstalk borer
LEPIDOPTERA: Pyralidae	*Eoreuma loftini* (Dyar)	Mexican rice borer
LEPIDOPTERA: Pyralidae	*Ephestia elutella* (Hübner)	tobacco moth
LEPIDOPTERA: Pyralidae	*Etiella zinckenella* (Treitschke)	limabean pod borer
LEPIDOPTERA: Pyralidae	*Euzophera semifuneralis* (Walker)	American plum borer
LEPIDOPTERA: Pyralidae	*Evergestis pallidata* (Hufnagel)	purplebacked cabbageworm
LEPIDOPTERA: Pyralidae	*Evergestis rimosalis* (Guenée)	cross-striped cabbageworm
LEPIDOPTERA: Pyralidae	*Fundella pellucens* Zeller	Caribbean pod borer
LEPIDOPTERA: Pyralidae	*Galleria mellonella* (Linnaeus)	greater wax moth

LEPIDOPTERA: Pyralidae	*Geshna cannalis* (Quaintance)	lesser canna leafroller
LEPIDOPTERA: Pyralidae	*Hedylepta accepta* (Butler)	sugarcane leafroller
LEPIDOPTERA: Pyralidae	*Hedylepta blackburni* (Butler)	coconut leafroller
LEPIDOPTERA: Pyralidae	*Hellula rogatalis* (Hulst)	cabbage webworm
LEPIDOPTERA: Pyralidae	*Herpetogramma bipunctalis* (Fabricius)	southern beet webworm
LEPIDOPTERA: Pyralidae	*Herpetogramma licarsisalis* (Walker)	grass webworm
LEPIDOPTERA: Pyralidae	*Herpetogramma phaeopteralis* Guenée	tropical sod webworm
LEPIDOPTERA: Pyralidae	*Homoeosoma electellum* (Hulst)	sunflower moth
LEPIDOPTERA: Pyralidae	*Hulstia undulatella* (Clemens)	sugarbeet crown borer
LEPIDOPTERA: Pyralidae	*Hymenia perspectalis* (Hübner)	spotted beet webworm
LEPIDOPTERA: Pyralidae	*Hypsopygia costalis* (Fabricius)	clover hayworm
LEPIDOPTERA: Pyralidae	*Loxostege cerealis* (Zeller)	alfalfa webworm
LEPIDOPTERA: Pyralidae	*Loxostege sticticalis* (Linnaeus)	beet webworm
LEPIDOPTERA: Pyralidae	*Macalla thyrsisalis* Walker	mahogany webworm
LEPIDOPTERA: Pyralidae	*Maruca testulalis* (Geyer)	bean pod borer
LEPIDOPTERA: Pyralidae	*Melitara dentata* (Grote)	blue cactus borer
LEPIDOPTERA: Pyralidae	*Mimoschinia rufofascialis* (Stephens)	barberpole caterpillar
LEPIDOPTERA: Pyralidae	*Monoptilota pergratialis* (Hulst)	limabean vine borer
LEPIDOPTERA: Pyralidae	*Nephopterix subcaesiella* (Clemens)	locust leafroller
LEPIDOPTERA: Pyralidae	*Omphisa anastomosalis* (Guenée)	sweetpotato vine borer
LEPIDOPTERA: Pyralidae	*Ostrinia nubilalis* (Hübner)	European corn borer
LEPIDOPTERA: Pyralidae	*Ostrinia obumbratalis* (Lederer)	smartweed borer
LEPIDOPTERA: Pyralidae	*Pantographa limata* Grote & Robinson	basswood leafroller
LEPIDOPTERA: Pyralidae	*Parapediasia teterrella* (Zincken)	bluegrass webworm
LEPIDOPTERA: Pyralidae	*Pilocrocis tripunctata* (Fabricius)	sweetpotato leafroller
LEPIDOPTERA: Pyralidae	*Plodia interpunctella* (Hübner)	Indianmeal moth
LEPIDOPTERA: Pyralidae	*Psorosina hammondi* (Riley)	appleleaf skeletonizer
LEPIDOPTERA: Pyralidae	*Pyralis farinalis* Linnaeus	meal moth
LEPIDOPTERA: Pyralidae	*Salbia haemorrhoidalis* Guenée	lantana leaftier
LEPIDOPTERA: Pyralidae	*Spoladea recurvalis* (Fabricius)	Hawaiian beet webworm
LEPIDOPTERA: Pyralidae	*Surattha indentella* Kearfott	buffalograss webworm
LEPIDOPTERA: Pyralidae	*Synclita obliteralis* (Walker)	waterlily leafcutter
LEPIDOPTERA: Pyralidae	*Tehama bonifatella* (Hulst)	western lawn moth
LEPIDOPTERA: Pyralidae	*Tetralopha robustella* Zeller	pine webworm
LEPIDOPTERA: Pyralidae	*Tetralopha scortealis* (Lederer)	lespedeza webworm

LEPIDOPTERA: Pyralidae	*Udea profundalis* (Packard)	false celery leaftier
LEPIDOPTERA: Pyralidae	*Udea rubigalis* (Guenée)	celery leaftier[57]
LEPIDOPTERA: Pyralidae	*Uresiphita reversalis* (Guenée)	genista caterpillar
LEPIDOPTERA: Pyralidae	*Vitula edmandsae serratilineella* Ragonot	driedfruit moth
LEPIDOPTERA: Pyralidae	*Zophodia convolutella* (Hübner)	gooseberry fruitworm
LEPIDOPTERA: Riodinidae	*Apodemia mormo langei* Comstock	Lange metalmark
LEPIDOPTERA: Saturniidae	*Actias luna* (Linnaeus)	luna moth
LEPIDOPTERA: Saturniidae	*Anisota senatoria* (J.E. Smith)	orangestriped oakworm
LEPIDOPTERA: Saturniidae	*Anisota stigma* (Fabricius)	spiny oakworm
LEPIDOPTERA: Saturniidae	*Anisota virginiensis* (Drury)	pinkstriped oakworm
LEPIDOPTERA: Saturniidae	*Antheraea polyphemus* (Cramer)	polyphemus moth
LEPIDOPTERA: Saturniidae	*Automeris io* (Fabricius)	io moth
LEPIDOPTERA: Saturniidae	*Callosamia promethea* (Drury)	promethea moth
LEPIDOPTERA: Saturniidae	*Citheronia regalis* (Fabricius)	regal moth[58]
LEPIDOPTERA: Saturniidae	*Coloradia pandora* Blake	pandora moth
LEPIDOPTERA: Saturniidae	*Dryocampa rubicunda* (Fabricius)	greenstriped mapleworm
LEPIDOPTERA: Saturniidae	*Eacles imperialis* (Drury)	imperial moth
LEPIDOPTERA: Saturniidae	*Hemileuca maia* (Drury)	buck moth
LEPIDOPTERA: Saturniidae	*Hemileuca oliviae* Cockerell	range caterpillar
LEPIDOPTERA: Saturniidae	*Hyalophora cecropia* (Linnaeus)	cecropia moth
LEPIDOPTERA: Saturniidae	*Hyalophora euryalus* (Boisduval)	ceanothus silk moth
LEPIDOPTERA: Saturniidae	*Samia cynthia* (Drury)	cynthia moth
LEPIDOPTERA: Sesiidae	*Melittia calabaza* Duckworth & Eichlin	southwestern squash vine borer
LEPIDOPTERA: Sesiidae	*Melittia cucurbitae* (Harris)	squash vine borer
LEPIDOPTERA: Sesiidae	*Paranthrene asilipennis* (Boisduval)	oak clearwing moth
LEPIDOPTERA: Sesiidae	*Paranthrene robiniae* (Hy. Edwards)	western poplar clearwing
LEPIDOPTERA: Sesiidae	*Pennisetia marginata* (Harris)	raspberry crown borer
LEPIDOPTERA: Sesiidae	*Podosesia aureocincta* Purrington & Nielsen	banded ash clearwing
LEPIDOPTERA: Sesiidae	*Podosesia syringae* (Harris)	ash borer[59]
LEPIDOPTERA: Sesiidae	*Sannina uroceriformis* Walker	persimmon borer
LEPIDOPTERA: Sesiidae	*Sesia apiformis* (Clerck)	hornet moth
LEPIDOPTERA: Sesiidae	*Sesia tibialis* (Harris)	American hornet moth
LEPIDOPTERA: Sesiidae	*Synanthedon acerni* (Clemens)	maple callus borer

---

[57]Also called greenhouse leaftier.
[58]Immature called hickory horned devil.
[59]Also called lilac borer.

Order: Family	Species	Common name
LEPIDOPTERA: Sesiidae	*Synanthedon bibionipennis* (Boisduval)	strawberry crown moth
LEPIDOPTERA: Sesiidae	*Synanthedon exitiosa* (Say)	peachtree borer
LEPIDOPTERA: Sesiidae	*Synanthedon novaroensis* (Hy. Edwards)	Douglas-fir pitch moth
LEPIDOPTERA: Sesiidae	*Synanthedon pictipes* (Grote & Robinson)	lesser peachtree borer
LEPIDOPTERA: Sesiidae	*Synanthedon pini* (Kellicott)	pitch mass borer
LEPIDOPTERA: Sesiidae	*Synanthedon pyri* (Harris)	apple bark borer
LEPIDOPTERA: Sesiidae	*Synanthedon rhododendri* (Beutenmüller)	rhododendron borer
LEPIDOPTERA: Sesiidae	*Synanthedon scitula* (Harris)	dogwood borer
LEPIDOPTERA: Sesiidae	*Synanthedon sequoiae* (Hy. Edwards)	sequoia pitch moth
LEPIDOPTERA: Sesiidae	*Synanthedon tipuliformis* (Clerck)	currant borer
LEPIDOPTERA: Sesiidae	*Vitacea polistiformis* (Harris)	grape root borer
LEPIDOPTERA: Sphingidae	*Agrius cingulata* (Fabricius)	sweetpotato hornworm
LEPIDOPTERA: Sphingidae	*Ceratomia amyntor* (Geyer)	elm sphinx
LEPIDOPTERA: Sphingidae	*Ceratomia catalpae* (Boisduval)	catalpa sphinx
LEPIDOPTERA: Sphingidae	*Daphnis nerii* (Linnaeus)	oleander hawk moth
LEPIDOPTERA: Sphingidae	*Darapsa myron* (Cramer)	Virginiacreeper sphinx
LEPIDOPTERA: Sphingidae	*Eumorpha achemon* (Drury)	achemon sphinx
LEPIDOPTERA: Sphingidae	*Hyles calida* (Butler)	Hawaiian sphinx
LEPIDOPTERA: Sphingidae	*Hyles lineata* (Fabricius)	whitelined sphinx
LEPIDOPTERA: Sphingidae	*Hyles wilsoni* (Rothschild)	Wilson sphinx
LEPIDOPTERA: Sphingidae	*Laothoe juglandis* (J.E. Smith)	walnut sphinx
LEPIDOPTERA: Sphingidae	*Manduca quinquemaculata* (Haworth)	tomato hornworm
LEPIDOPTERA: Sphingidae	*Manduca sexta* (Linnaeus)	tobacco hornworm
LEPIDOPTERA: Sphingidae	*Sphinx chersis* (Hübner)	great ash sphinx
LEPIDOPTERA: Sphingidae	*Tinostoma smaragditis* (Meyrick)	green sphinx
LEPIDOPTERA: Tineidae	*Nemapogon granella* (Linnaeus)	European grain moth
LEPIDOPTERA: Tineidae	*Neodecadarachis flavistriata* (Walsingham)	sugarcane bud moth
LEPIDOPTERA: Tineidae	*Niditinea spretella* (Dennis & Schiffermüller)	poultry house moth
LEPIDOPTERA: Tineidae	*Phereoeca uterella* Walsingham	household casebearer
LEPIDOPTERA: Tineidae	*Tinea pellionella* Linnaeus	casemaking clothes moth
LEPIDOPTERA: Tineidae	*Tineola bisselliella* (Hummel)	webbing clothes moth
LEPIDOPTERA: Tineidae	*Trichophaga tapetzella* (Linnaeus)	carpet moth
LEPIDOPTERA: Tischeriidae	*Tischeria malifoliella* Clemens	appleleaf trumpet miner
LEPIDOPTERA: Tortricidae	*Acleris gloverana* (Walsingham)	western blackheaded budworm
LEPIDOPTERA: Tortricidae	*Acleris minuta* (Robinson)	yellowheaded fireworm
LEPIDOPTERA: Tortricidae	*Acleris variana* (Fernald)	eastern blackheaded budworm
LEPIDOPTERA: Tortricidae	*Amorbia emigratella* Busck	Mexican leafroller
LEPIDOPTERA: Tortricidae	*Ancylis comptana* (Froelich)	strawberry leafroller

LEPIDOPTERA: Tortricidae	*Archips argyrospila* (Walker)	fruittree leafroller
LEPIDOPTERA: Tortricidae	*Archips cerasivorana* (Fitch)	uglynest caterpillar
LEPIDOPTERA: Tortricidae	*Archips fervidana* (Clemens)	oak webworm
LEPIDOPTERA: Tortricidae	*Archips mortuana* Kearfott	duskyback leafroller
LEPIDOPTERA: Tortricidae	*Archips semiferana* (Walker)	oak leafroller
LEPIDOPTERA: Tortricidae	*Argyrotaenia citrana* (Fernald)	orange tortrix
LEPIDOPTERA: Tortricidae	*Argyrotaenia juglandana* (Fernald)	hickory leafroller
LEPIDOPTERA: Tortricidae	*Argyrotaenia mariana* (Fernald)	graybanded leafroller
LEPIDOPTERA: Tortricidae	*Argyrotaenia pinatubana* (Kearfott)	pine tube moth
LEPIDOPTERA: Tortricidae	*Argyrotaenia quadrifasciana* (Fernald)	fourbanded leafroller
LEPIDOPTERA: Tortricidae	*Argyrotaenia velutinana* (Walker)	redbanded leafroller
LEPIDOPTERA: Tortricidae	*Bactra venosana* (Zeller)	nutgrass borer moth
LEPIDOPTERA: Tortricidae	*Barbara colfaxiana* (Kearfott)	Douglas-fir cone moth
LEPIDOPTERA: Tortricidae	*Choristoneura conflictana* (Walker)	large aspen tortrix
LEPIDOPTERA: Tortricidae	*Choristoneura fumiferana* (Clemens)	spruce budworm
LEPIDOPTERA: Tortricidae	*Choristoneura occidentalis* Freeman	western spruce budworm
LEPIDOPTERA: Tortricidae	*Choristoneura pinus* Freeman	jack pine budworm
LEPIDOPTERA: Tortricidae	*Choristoneura rosaceana* (Harris)	obliquebanded leafroller
LEPIDOPTERA: Tortricidae	*Cnephasia longana* (Haworth)	omnivorous leaftier
LEPIDOPTERA: Tortricidae	*Croesia semipurpurana* (Kearfott)	oak leaftier
LEPIDOPTERA: Tortricidae	*Cryptophlebia illepida* (Butler)	koa seedworm
LEPIDOPTERA: Tortricidae	*Cryptophlebia ombrodelta* (Lower)	litchi fruit moth
LEPIDOPTERA: Tortricidae	*Cydia anaranjada* (Miller)	slash pine seedworm
LEPIDOPTERA: Tortricidae	*Cydia bracteatana* (Fernald)	fir seed moth
LEPIDOPTERA: Tortricidae	*Cydia caryana* (Fitch)	hickory shuckworm
LEPIDOPTERA: Tortricidae	*Cydia ingens* (Heinrich)	longleaf pine seedworm
LEPIDOPTERA: Tortricidae	*Cydia latiferreana* (Walsingham)	filbertworm
LEPIDOPTERA: Tortricidae	*Cydia nigricana* (Fabricius)	pea moth
LEPIDOPTERA: Tortricidae	*Cydia pomonella* (Linnaeus)	codling moth
LEPIDOPTERA: Tortricidae	*Cydia strobilella* (Linnaeus)	spruce seed moth
LEPIDOPTERA: Tortricidae	*Cydia toreuta* (Grote)	eastern pine seedworm
LEPIDOPTERA: Tortricidae	*Ecdytolopha insiticiana* Zeller	locust twig borer
LEPIDOPTERA: Tortricidae	*Endopiza viteana* Clemens	grape berry moth
LEPIDOPTERA: Tortricidae	*Endothenia albolineana* (Kearfott)	spruce needleminer
LEPIDOPTERA: Tortricidae	*Endothenia hebesana* (Walker)	verbena bud moth
LEPIDOPTERA: Tortricidae	*Epiblema otiosana* (Clemens)	bidens borer
LEPIDOPTERA: Tortricidae	*Epiblema strenuana* (Walker)	ragweed borer
LEPIDOPTERA: Tortricidae	*Epinotia aceriella* (Clemens)	maple trumpet skeletonizer

LEPIDOPTERA: Tortricidae	*Epinotia meritana* Heinrich	white fir needleminer
LEPIDOPTERA: Tortricidae	*Epiphyas postvittana* (Walker)	light brown apple moth
LEPIDOPTERA: Tortricidae	*Eucosma cocana* Kearfott	shortleaf pine cone borer
LEPIDOPTERA: Tortricidae	*Eucosma gloriola* Heinrich	eastern pine shoot borer
LEPIDOPTERA: Tortricidae	*Eucosma sonomana* Kearfott	western pine shoot borer
LEPIDOPTERA: Tortricidae	*Eucosma tocullionana* Heinrich	white pine cone borer
LEPIDOPTERA: Tortricidae	*Grapholita interstinctana* (Clemens)	clover head caterpillar
LEPIDOPTERA: Tortricidae	*Grapholita molesta* (Busck)	oriental fruit moth
LEPIDOPTERA: Tortricidae	*Grapholita packardi* Zeller	cherry fruitworm
LEPIDOPTERA: Tortricidae	*Grapholita prunivora* (Walsh)	lesser appleworm
LEPIDOPTERA: Tortricidae	*Gretchena bolliana* (Slingerland)	pecan bud moth
LEPIDOPTERA: Tortricidae	*Gypsonoma haimbachiana* (Kearfott)	cottonwood twig borer
LEPIDOPTERA: Tortricidae	*Hedya chionosema* (Zeller)	twinspotted budworm
LEPIDOPTERA: Tortricidae	*Hedya nubiferana* (Haworth)	green budworm
LEPIDOPTERA: Tortricidae	*Olethreutes permundana* (Clemens)	raspberry leafroller
LEPIDOPTERA: Tortricidae	*Pandemis limitata* (Robinson)	threelined leafroller
LEPIDOPTERA: Tortricidae	*Petrova albicapitana* (Busck)	northern pitch twig moth
LEPIDOPTERA: Tortricidae	*Petrova comstockiana* (Fernald)	pitch twig moth
LEPIDOPTERA: Tortricidae	*Platynota idaeusalis* (Walker)	tufted apple bud moth
LEPIDOPTERA: Tortricidae	*Proteoteras willingana* (Kearfott)	boxelder twig borer
LEPIDOPTERA: Tortricidae	*Pseudexentera mali* Freeman	pale apple leafroller
LEPIDOPTERA: Tortricidae	*Rhopobota naevana* (Hübner)	blackheaded fireworm
LEPIDOPTERA: Tortricidae	*Rhyacionia buoliana* (Denis & Schiffermüller)	European pine shoot moth
LEPIDOPTERA: Tortricidae	*Rhyacionia frustrana* (Comstock)	Nantucket pine tip moth
LEPIDOPTERA: Tortricidae	*Rhyacionia neomexicana* (Dyar)	southwestern pine tip moth
LEPIDOPTERA: Tortricidae	*Rhyacionia rigidana* (Fernald)	pitch pine tip moth
LEPIDOPTERA: Tortricidae	*Rhyacionia subtropica* Miller	subtropical pine tip moth
LEPIDOPTERA: Tortricidae	*Sparganothis directana* (Walker)	chokecherry leafroller
LEPIDOPTERA: Tortricidae	*Spilonota ocellana* (Denis & Schiffermüller)	eyespotted bud moth
LEPIDOPTERA: Tortricidae	*Suleima helianthana* (Riley)	sunflower bud moth
LEPIDOPTERA: Tortricidae	*Zeiraphera canadensis* Mutuura & Freeman	spruce bud moth
LEPIDOPTERA: Yponomeutidae	*Atteva punctella* (Cramer)	ailanthus webworm
LEPIDOPTERA: Yponomeutidae	*Yponomeuta padella* (Linnaeus)	ermine moth
LEPIDOPTERA: Yponomeutidae	*Zelleria haimbachi* Busck	pine needle sheathminer
LEPIDOPTERA: Zygaenidae	*Harrisina americana* (Guérin)	grapeleaf skeletonizer
LEPIDOPTERA: Zygaenidae	*Harrisina brillians* Barnes & McDunnough	western grapeleaf skeletonizer

MALLOPHAGA: Gyropidae	*Gliricola porcelli* (Schrank)	slender guineapig louse
MALLOPHAGA: Gyropidae	*Gyropus ovalis* Burmeister	oval guineapig louse
MALLOPHAGA: Menoponidae	*Menacanthus stramineus* (Nitzsch)	chicken body louse
MALLOPHAGA: Menoponidae	*Menopon gallinae* (Linnaeus)	shaft louse
MALLOPHAGA: Menoponidae	*Trinoton anserinum* (Fabricius)	goose body louse
MALLOPHAGA: Menoponidae	*Trinoton querquedulae* (Linnaeus)	large duck louse
MALLOPHAGA: Philopteridae	*Anaticola anseris* (Linnaeus)	slender goose louse
MALLOPHAGA: Philopteridae	*Anaticola crassicornis* (Scopoli)	slender duck louse
MALLOPHAGA: Philopteridae	*Campanulotes bidentatus compar* (Burmeister)	small pigeon louse
MALLOPHAGA: Philopteridae	*Chelopistes meleagridis* (Linnaeus)	large turkey louse
MALLOPHAGA: Philopteridae	*Columbicola columbae* (Linnaeus)	slender pigeon louse
MALLOPHAGA: Philopteridae	*Cuclotogaster heterographus* (Nitzsch)	chicken head louse
MALLOPHAGA: Philopteridae	*Goniocotes gallinae* (De Geer)	fluff louse
MALLOPHAGA: Philopteridae	*Goniodes dissimilis* Denny	brown chicken louse
MALLOPHAGA: Philopteridae	*Goniodes gigas* (Taschenberg)	large chicken louse
MALLOPHAGA: Philopteridae	*Goniodes numidae* Mjberg	Guinea feather louse
MALLOPHAGA: Philopteridae	*Liperus caponis* (Linnaeus)	wing louse
MALLOPHAGA: Philopteridae	*Lipeurus numidae* (Denny)	slender guinea louse
MALLOPHAGA: Philopteridae	*Oxylipeurus polytrapezius* (Burmeister)	slender turkey louse
MALLOPHAGA: Trichodectidae	*Bovicola bovis* (Linnaeus)	cattle biting louse
MALLOPHAGA: Trichodectidae	*Bovicola caprae* (Gurlt)	goat biting louse
MALLOPHAGA: Trichodectidae	*Bovicola crassipes* (Rudow)	Angora goat biting louse
MALLOPHAGA: Trichodectidae	*Bovicola equi* (Denny)	horse biting louse
MALLOPHAGA: Trichodectidae	*Bovicola ovis* (Schrank)	sheep biting louse
MALLOPHAGA: Trichodectidae	*Felicola subrostratus* (Burmeister)	cat louse
MALLOPHAGA: Trichodectidae	*Trichodectes canis* (De Geer)	dog biting louse
MANTODEA: Mantidae	*Mantis religiosa* Linnaeus	European mantid
MANTODEA: Mantidae	*Orthodera burmeisteri* Wood-Mason	Burmeister mantid
MANTODEA: Mantidae	*Stagmomantis carolina* (Johannson)	Carolina mantid
MANTODEA: Mantidae	*Tenodera aridifolia sinensis* Saussure	Chinese mantid
MANTODEA: Mantidae	*Tenodera augustipennis* Saussure	narrowwinged mantid
MANTODEA: Mantidae	*Tenodera australasiae* (Leach)	Australian mantid

N

NEUROPTERA: Chrysopidae	*Chrysopa carnea* Stephens	common green lacewing
NEUROPTERA: Chrysopidae	*Chrysopa comanche* Banks	comanche lacewing
NEUROPTERA: Chrysopidae	*Chrysopa oculata* Say	goldeneyed lacewing
NEUROPTERA: Corydalidae	*Corydalus cornutus* (Linnaeus)	dobsonfly[60]
NEUROPTERA: Hemerobiidae	*Sympherobius barberi* (Banks)	Barber brown lacewing
NEUROPTERA: Myrmeleontidae	*Dendroleon obsoletus* (Say)	spottedwinged antlion
NEUROPTERA: Myrmeleontidae	*Eidoleon wilsoni* (McLachlan)	Hawaiian antlion

O

ODONATA: Aeschnidae	*Anax junius* (Drury)	common green darner
ODONATA: Aeschnidae	*Anax strenuus* Hagen	giant Hawaiian dragonfly
ODONATA: Libellulidae	*Nesogonia blackburni* (McLachlan)	Blackburn dragonfly
ORTHOPTERA: Acrididae	*Aulocara elliotti* (Thomas)	bigheaded grasshopper
ORTHOPTERA: Acrididae	*Brachystola magna* (Girard)	lubber grasshopper
ORTHOPTERA: Acrididae	*Camnula pellucida* (Scudder)	clearwinged grasshopper
ORTHOPTERA: Acrididae	*Chortophaga viridifasciata* (De Geer)	greenstriped grasshopper
ORTHOPTERA: Acrididae	*Dissosteira carolina* (Linnaeus)	Carolina grasshopper
ORTHOPTERA: Acrididae	*Dissosteira longipennis* (Thomas)	high plains grasshopper
ORTHOPTERA: Acrididae	*Melanoplus bivittatus* (Say)	twostriped grasshopper
ORTHOPTERA: Acrididae	*Melanoplus devastator* Scudder	devastating grasshopper
ORTHOPTERA: Acrididae	*Melanoplus differentialis* (Thomas)	differential grasshopper
ORTHOPTERA: Acrididae	*Melanoplus femurrubrum* (De Geer)	redlegged grasshopper
ORTHOPTERA: Acrididae	*Melanoplus packardii* Scudder	Packard grasshopper
ORTHOPTERA: Acrididae	*Melanoplus rugglesi* Gurney	Nevada sage grasshopper
ORTHOPTERA: Acrididae	*Melanoplus sanguinipes* (Fabricius)	migratory grasshopper
ORTHOPTERA: Acrididae	*Melanoplus spretus* (Walsh)	Rocky Mountain grasshopper
ORTHOPTERA: Acrididae	*Oxya japonica* (Thunberg)	Japanese grasshopper
ORTHOPTERA: Acrididae	*Romalea guttata* (Houttuyn)	eastern lubber grasshopper

[60]Immature called hellgrammite.

ORTHOPTERA: Acrididae	*Schistocerca americana* (Drury)	American grasshopper
ORTHOPTERA: Acrididae	*Schistocerca nitens nitens* (Thunberg)	vagrant grasshopper
ORTHOPTERA: Gryllacrididae	*Tachycines asynamorus* Adelung	greenhouse stone cricket
ORTHOPTERA: Gryllidae	*Acheta domesticus* (Linnaeus)	house cricket
ORTHOPTERA: Gryllidae	*Oecanthus fultoni* Walker	snowy tree cricket
ORTHOPTERA: Gryllidae	*Oecanthus nigricornis* Walker	blackhorned tree cricket
ORTHOPTERA: Gryllidae	*Oecanthus quadripunctatus* Beutenmüller	fourspotted tree cricket
ORTHOPTERA: Gryllidae	*Teleogryllus oceanicus* (Le Guillou)	oceanic field cricket
ORTHOPTERA: Gryllotalpidae	*Gryllotalpa africana* Palisot de Beauvois	African mole cricket
ORTHOPTERA: Gryllotalpidae	*Neocurtilla hexadactyla* (Perty)	northern mole cricket
ORTHOPTERA: Gryllotalpidae	*Scapteriscus abbreviatus* Scudder	shortwinged mole cricket
ORTHOPTERA: Gryllotalpidae	*Scapteriscus acletus* Rehn & Hebard	southern mole cricket
ORTHOPTERA: Gryllotalpidae	*Scapteriscus didactylus* (Latreille)	changa
ORTHOPTERA: Gryllotalpidae	*Scapteriscus vicinus* Scudder	tawny mole cricket
ORTHOPTERA: Pyrgomorphidae	*Atractomorpha sinensis* Bolivar	pinkwinged grasshopper
ORTHOPTERA: Stenopelmatidae	*Stenopelmatus fuscus* Haldeman	Jerusalem cricket
ORTHOPTERA: Tettigoniidae	*Anabrus simplex* Haldeman	Mormon cricket
ORTHOPTERA: Tettigoniidae	*Holochlora japonica* Brunner von Wattenwyl	Japanese broadwinged katydid
ORTHOPTERA: Tettigoniidae	*Microcentrum retinerve* (Burmeister)	angularwinged katydid
ORTHOPTERA: Tettigoniidae	*Microcentrum rhombifolium* (Saussure)	broadwinged katydid
ORTHOPTERA: Tettigoniidae	*Peranabrus scabricollis* (Thomas)	coulee cricket
ORTHOPTERA: Tettigoniidae	*Phaneroptera furcifera* Stål	Philippine katydid
ORTHOPTERA: Tettigoniidae	*Scudderia furcata* Brunner von Wattenwyl	forktailed bush katydid

P

PHASMATODEA: Heteronemiidae	*Diapheromera femorata* (Say)	walkingstick
PHASMATODEA: Pseudophasmatidae	*Anisomorpha buprestoides* (Stoll)	twostriped walkingstick
POLYDESMIDA: Paradoxoxomatidae	*Oxidus gracilis* Koch	garden millipede
PSOCOPTERA: Lachesillidae	*Lachesilla pedicularia* (Linnaeus)	cosmopolitan grain psocid
PSOCOPTERA: Liposcelidae	*Liposcelis corrodens* Heymons	booklouse
PSOCOPTERA: Trogiidae	*Lepinotus reticulatus* Enderlein	reticulatewinged trogiid
PSOCOPTERA: Trogiidae	*Trogium pulsatorium* (Linnaeus)	larger pale trogiid

S

SCORPIONES: Buthidae	*Isometrus maculatus* De Geer	lesser brown scorpion
SCUTIGEROMORPHA: Scutigeridae	*Scutigera coleoptrata* (Linnaeus)	house centipede
SIPHONAPTERA: Ceratophyllidae	*Ceratophyllus gallinae* (Schrank)	European chicken flea
SIPHONAPTERA: Ceratophyllidae	*Ceratophyllus niger* (Fox)	western chicken flea
SIPHONAPTERA: Ceratophyllidae	*Nosopsyllus fasciatus* (Bosc)	northern rat flea
SIPHONAPTERA: Leptopsyllidae	*Leptopsylla segnis* (Schnherr)	European mouse flea
SIPHONAPTERA: Pulicidae	*Ctenocephalides canis* (Curtis)	dog flea
SIPHONAPTERA: Pulicidae	*Ctenocephalides felis* (Bouché)	cat flea
SIPHONAPTERA: Pulicidae	*Echicnophaga gallinacea* (Westwood)	sticktight flea
SIPHONAPTERA: Pulicidae	*Pulex irritans* (Linnaeus)	human flea
SIPHONAPTERA: Pulicidae	*Xenopsylla cheopis* (Rothschild)	oriental rat flea
SIPHONAPTERA: Pulicidae	*Xenopsylla vexabilis* (Jordan)	Australian rat flea
SIPHONAPTERA: Tungidae	*Tunga penetrans* (Linnaeus)	chigoe
SPIROBOLIDA: Pachybolidae	*Trigoniulus lumbricinus* (Gerst)	rusty millipede
STYLOMMATOPHORA: Achatinidae	*Achatina fulica* Bowdich	giant African snail
STYLOMMATOPHORA: Arionidae	*Arion ater rufus* (Linnaeus)	large red slug
STYLOMMATOPHORA: Helicidae	*Cepaea nemoralis* (Linnaeus)	banded wood snail
STYLOMMATOPHORA: Helicidae	*Helix aspersa* Müller	brown garden snail
STYLOMMATOPHORA: Helicidae	*Theba pisana* (Müller)	white garden snail
STYLOMMATOPHORA: Limacidae	*Agriolimax laevis* (Müller)	marsh slug
STYLOMMATOPHORA: Limacidae	*Agriolimax reticulatus* (Müller)	gray garden slug
STYLOMMATOPHORA: Limacidae	*Limax flavus* Linnaeus	tawny garden slug
STYLOMMATOPHORA: Limacidae	*Limax maximus* Linnaeus	spotted garden slug
STYLOMMATOPHORA: Limacidae	*Milax gagates* (Draparnaud)	greenhouse slug
STYLOMMATOPHORA: Oleacinidae	*Euglandina rosea* (Férussac)	rosy predator snail
STYLOMMATOPHORA: Subulinidae	*Subulina octona* (Bruguiere)	subulina snail
SYMPHYLA: Scutigerellidae	*Scutigerella immaculata* (Newport)	garden symphylan

T

THYSANOPTERA: Aeolothripidae	*Franklinothrips vespiformis* (D.L. Crawford)	vespiform thrips
THYSANOPTERA: Phlaeothripidae	*Gnophothrips fuscus* (Morgan)	slash pine flower thrips

THYSANOPTERA: Phlaeothripidae	*Gynaikothrips ficorum* (Marchal)	Cuban laurel thrips
THYSANOPTERA: Phlaeothripidae	*Haplothrips gowdeyi* (Franklin)	black flower thrips
THYSANOPTERA: Phlaeothripidae	*Haplothrips verbasci* (Osborn)	mullein thrips
THYSANOPTERA: Phlaeothripidae	*Leptothrips mali* (Fitch)	black hunter thrips
THYSANOPTERA: Phlaeothripidae	*Liothrips floridensis* (Watson)	camphor thrips
THYSANOPTERA: Phlaeothripidae	*Liothrips urichi* Karny	clidemia thrips
THYSANOPTERA: Phlaeothripidae	*Liothrips vaneeckei* Priesner	lily bulb thrips
THYSANOPTERA: Thripidae	*Anaphothrips obscurus* (Müller)	grass thrips
THYSANOPTERA: Thripidae	*Anaphothrips swezeyi* Moulton	Hawaiian grass thrips
THYSANOPTERA: Thripidae	*Baliothrips minutus* (van Deventer)	sugarcane thrips
THYSANOPTERA: Thripidae	*Caliothrips fasciatus* (Pergande)	bean thrips
THYSANOPTERA: Thripidae	*Dendrothrips ornatus* (Jablonowski)	privet thrips
THYSANOPTERA: Thripidae	*Dichromothrips corbetti* (Priesner)	vanda thrips
THYSANOPTERA: Thripidae	*Drepanothrips reuteri* Uzel	grape thrips
THYSANOPTERA: Thripidae	*Frankliniella fusca* (Hinds)	tobacco thrips
THYSANOPTERA: Thripidae	*Frankliniella occidentalis* (Pergande)	western flower thrips
THYSANOPTERA: Thripidae	*Frankliniella tritici* (Fitch)	flower thrips
THYSANOPTERA: Thripidae	*Frankliniella vaccinii* Morgan	blueberry thrips
THYSANOPTERA: Thripidae	*Heliothrips haemorrhoidalis* (Bouché)	greenhouse thrips
THYSANOPTERA: Thripidae	*Hercinothrips femoralis* (O.M. Reuter)	banded greenhouse thrips
THYSANOPTERA: Thripidae	*Iridothrips iridis* (Watson)	iris thrips
THYSANOPTERA: Thripidae	*Limothrips cerealium* (Haliday)	grain thrips
THYSANOPTERA: Thripidae	*Microcephalothrips abdominalis* (D.L. Crawford)	composite thrips
THYSANOPTERA: Thripidae	*Scirtothrips citri* (Moulton)	citrus thrips
THYSANOPTERA: Thripidae	*Scolothrips sexmaculatus* (Pergande)	sixspotted thrips
THYSANOPTERA: Thripidae	*Selenothrips rubrocinctus* (Giard)	redbanded thrips
THYSANOPTERA: Thripidae	*Sericothrips variabilis* (Beach)	soybean thrips
THYSANOPTERA: Thripidae	*Taeniothrips inconsequens* (Uzel)	pear thrips
THYSANOPTERA: Thripidae	*Thrips hawaiiensis* (Morgan)	Hawaiian flower thrips
THYSANOPTERA: Thripidae	*Thrips nigropilosus* Uzel	chrysanthemum thrips
THYSANOPTERA: Thripidae	*Thrips orientalis* (Bagnall)	star jasmine thrips
THYSANOPTERA: Thripidae	*Thrips simplex* (Morison)	gladiolus thrips
THYSANOPTERA: Thripidae	*Thrips tabaci* Lindeman	onion thrips
THYSANURA: Lepismatidae	*Lepisma saccharina* Linnaeus	silverfish
THYSANURA: Lepismatidae	*Thermobia domestica* (Packard)	firebrat

Section IV. Phylum, Class, Order, and Family Names

Phylum MOLLUSCA

Gastropoda (Subclass Pulmonata)
- A. Stylommatophora . . . . snails and slugs
  - 1. Achatinidae . . . . snails
  - 2. Arionidae . . . . slugs
  - 3. Helicidae . . . . snails
  - 4. Limacidae . . . . slugs
  - 5. Oleacinidae . . . . snails
  - 6. Subulinidae . . . . snails

Phylum ARTHROPODA

Crustacea . . . . crustaceans
- A. Decapoda . . . . crayfish
  - 1. Cambaridae . . . . crayfish
- B. Isopoda . . . . pillbugs and sowbugs
  - 1. Asellidae . . . . sowbugs

Diplopoda . . . . millipedes
- A. Polyxenida
  - 1. Polyxenidae
- B. Glomerida . . . . pill millipedes
- C. Polydesmida
  - 1. Paradoxosomatidae . . . . millipedes
  - 2. Platyrhacidae
  - 3. Polydesmidae
  - 4. Xystodesmidae
- D. Callipodida
  - 1. Schizopetalidae . . . . crested millipedes
- E. Chordeumatida
- F. Platydesmida
- G. Julida
  - 1. Blaniulidae
  - 2. Julidae
  - 3. Parajulidae

  H. Spirostreptida
      1. Cambalidae
      2. Spirostreptidae
  I.   Spirobolida . . . . millipedes
      1. Pachybolidae . . . . millipedes
      2. Rhinocricidae
      3. Spirobolidae
  J.   Polyzoniida
  K. Siphonophorida
Chilopoda . . . . centipedes
  A. Scutigeromorpha . . . . house centipedes
      1. Scutigeridae . . . . house centipedes
  B. Lithobiomorpha . . . . stone centipedes
      1. Henicopidae
      2. Lithobiidae
  C. Scolopendromorpha . . . . tropical centipedes
      1. Cryptopidae
      2. Scolopendridae
  D. Geophilomorpha . . . . snail centipedes
      1. Dignathodontidae
      2. Geophilidae
      3. Mecistocephalidae
Symphyla . . . . symphylans
  A. (Order name withheld pending further investigation)
      1. Scutigerellidae . . . . symphylans
Arachnida . . . . arachnids
  A. Scorpiones . . . . scorpions
      1. Buthidae . . . . scorpions
  B. Pseudoscorpiones . . . . pseudoscorpions
  C. Solifugae . . . . windscorpions
  D. Amblypygi . . . . tailless whipscorpions
  E. Uropygi . . . . whipscorpions
  F. Opiliones . . . . daddylonglegs or harvestmen

G. Araneae . . . . spiders
   1. Agelenidae . . . . grass spiders
   2. Araneidae . . . . orb spiders
   3. Clubionidac . . . . twoclawed hunting spiders
   4. Linyphiidae . . . . sheetweb spiders
   5. Loxoscelidae . . . . recluse spiders
   6. Lycosidae . . . . wolf spiders
   7. Oxyopidae . . . . lynx spiders
   8. Pisauridae . . . . nurseryweb spiders
   9. Salticidae . . . . jumping spiders
 10. Scytodidae . . . . spitting spiders
 11. Sparassidae . . . . giant crab spiders
 12. Theraphosidae . . . . tarantulas
 13. Theridiidae . . . . combfooted spiders
 14. Thomisidae . . . . crab spiders
H. Acari . . . . mites and ticks
   1. Acaridae . . . . acarid mites
   2. Analgidae . . . . feather mites
   3. Argasidae . . . . softbacked ticks
   4. Carpoglyphidae . . . . driedfruit mites
   5. Dermanyssidae . . . . dermanyssid mites
   6. Demodicidae . . . . follicle mites
   7. Epidermoptidae . . . . epidermoptid mites
   8. Eriophyidae . . . . eriophyid mites
   9. Eupodidae . . . . eupodid mites
 10. Glycyphagidae . . . . glycyphagid mites
 11. Ixodidae . . . . hardbacked ticks
 12. Macronyssidae . . . . macronyssid mites
 13. Nalepellidae . . . . nalepellid mites
 14. Nuttalliellidae . . . . (tick)
 15. Phytoseiidae . . . . phytoseiid mites
 16. Psoroptidae . . . . scab mites
 17. Pyemotidae . . . . pyemotid mites
 18. Sarcoptidae . . . . itch mites
 19. Siteroptidae . . . . siteroptid mites

F. Odonata . . . . damselflies and dragonflies
    1. Aeschnidae . . . . darners
    2. Calopterygidae . . . . broadwinged damselflies
    3. Coenagrionidae . . . . narrowwinged damselflies
    4. Cordulegastridae . . . . biddies
    5. Corduliidae . . . . greeneyed skimmers
    6. Gomphidae . . . . clubtails
    7. Lestidae . . . . spreadwinged damselflies
    8. Libellulidae . . . . common skimmers
    9. Petaluridae . . . . grayback
G. Plecoptera . . . . stoneflies
    1. Capniidae . . . . snowflies
    2. Chloroperlidae . . . . green stoneflies
    3. Leuctridae . . . . needleflies
    4. Nemouridae . . . . forestflies
    5. Peltoperlidae . . . . roachflies
    6. Perlidae . . . . common stoneflies
    7. Perloidae . . . . springflies and stripetails
    8. Pteronarcidae . . . . salmonflies
    9. Taeniopterygidae . . . . willowflies
H. Orthoptera . . . . crickets, grasshoppers, katydids, and allies
    1. Acrididae . . . . grasshoppers
    2. Eumastacidae . . . . monkey grasshoppers
    3. Gryllacrididae . . . . cave and camel crickets
    4. Gryllidae . . . . crickets
    5. Gryllotalpidae . . . . mole crickets
    6. Prophalangopsidae . . . . primitive katydids
    7. Pyrgomorphidae . . . . pyrgomorphids
    8. Stenopelmatidae . . . . Jerusalem crickets
    9. Tanaoceridae . . . . tanaocerids
    10. Tetrigidae . . . . pigmy grasshoppers or grouse locusts
    11. Tettigoniidae . . . . longhorned grasshoppers and katydids
    12. Tridactylidae . . . . pigmy mole crickets

I. Blattodea (= Blattaria; Dictyoptera in part) . . . . cockroaches
   1. Blaberidae . . . . giant cockroaches
   2. Blattellidae . . . . wood cockroaches
   3. Blattidae . . . . oriental and American cockroaches
   4. Cryptocercidae . . . . brown-hooded cockroaches
   5. Polyphagidae . . . . sand cockroaches
J. Mantodea (Dictyoptera in part) . . . . mantids
   1. Mantidae . . . . mantids
K. Grylloblattodea (= Notoptera) . . . . grylloblattids
   1. Grylloblattidae . . . . grylloblattids or rockcrawlers
L. Phasmatodea (= Phasmida) . . . . walkingsticks
   1. Heteronemiidae
   2. Phasmatidae
   3. Pseudophasmatidae
M. Dermaptera . . . . earwigs
   1. Chelisochidae . . . . black earwigs
   2. Forficulidae . . . . European earwigs
   3. Labiduridae . . . . striped earwigs
   4. Labiidae . . . . little earwigs
N. Embiidina (= Embioptera) . . . . embiids or webspinners
   1. Oligotomidae . . . . webspinners
   2. Teratembiidae . . . . webspinners
O. Isoptera . . . . termites
   1. Hodotermitidae . . . . dampwood termites
   2. Kalotermitidae . . . . dampwood, drywood, and powderpost termites
   3. Rhinotermitidae . . . . subterranean termites
   4. Termitidae . . . . nasutiform and soldierless termites
   5. Termopsidae . . . . dampwood termites
P. Psocoptera (= Corrodentia) . . . . booklice, psocids, and trogiids
   1. Lachesillidae . . . . psocids
   2. Liposcelidae . . . . booklice
   3. Psocidae . . . . psocids
   4. Trogiidae . . . . trogiids
Q. Zoraptera . . . . zorapterans
   1. Zorotypidae . . . . zorapterans

R. Mallophaga (Phthiraptera in part) . . . . chewing lice
   1. Gyropidae . . . . rodent chewing lice
   2. Menoponidae . . . . poultry body lice
   3. Philopteridae . . . . feather chewing lice
   4. Trichodectidae . . . . mammal chewing lice
S. Anoplura (Phthiraptera in part) . . . . sucking lice
   1. Haematopinidae . . . . wrinkled sucking lice
   2. Hoplopleuridae . . . . smallmammal sucking lice
   3. Linognathidae . . . . smooth sucking lice
   4. Pediculidae . . . . human lice
T. Thysanoptera . . . . thrips
   1. Aeolothripidae . . . . banded thrips
   2. Heterothripidae . . . . heterothripids
   3. Phlaeothripidae . . . . phlaeothripids
   4. Thripidae . . . . common thrips
U. Heteroptera . . . . true bugs
   1. Anthocoridae . . . . flower bugs and minute pirate bugs
   2. Aradidae . . . . flat bugs
   3. Belostomatidae . . . . giant water bugs
   4. Berytidae . . . . stilt bugs
   5. Cimicidae . . . . bat, bed, and bird bugs
   6. Coreidae . . . . coreid or leaffooted bugs
   7. Corixidae . . . . water boatmen
   8. Cydnidae . . . . cydnid bugs or burrower bugs
   9. Gelastocoridae . . . . toad bugs or gelastocorids
  10. Gerridae . . . . water striders
  11. Hydrometridae . . . . water treders
  12. Lygaeidae . . . . lygaeid or seed bugs
  13. Miridae . . . . plant bugs
  14. Nabidae . . . . damsel bugs
  15. Naucoridae . . . . creeping waterbugs
  16. Nepidae . . . . waterscorpions
  17. Notonectidae . . . . backswimmers
  18. Ochteridae . . . . velvety shore bugs
  19. Pentatomidae . . . . stink bugs
  20. Phymatidae . . . . ambush bugs

W. Neuroptera (includes Megaloptera, Sialodea, Planipennia, and
   Raphidiodea or Raphidioptera) . . . . lacewings and allies
   1. Ascalaphidae . . . . owlflies
   2. Berothidae . . . . beaded lacewings
   3. Chrysopidae . . . . green lacewings
   4. Coniopterygidae . . . . dustywings
   5. Corydalidae . . . . dobsonflies
   6. Hemerobiidae . . . . brown lacewings
   7. Inocelliidae . . . . snakeflies
   8. Mantispidae . . . . mantispids or mantidflies
   9. Myrmeleontidae . . . . antlions
   10. Raphidiidae . . . . snakeflies
   11. Sialidae . . . . alderflies
   12. Sisyridae . . . . spongillaflies
X. Mecoptera . . . . scorpionflies
   1. Bittacidae . . . . hanging scorpionflies
   2. Boreidae . . . . snow scorpionflies
   3. Panorpidae . . . . common scorpionflies
Y. Trichoptera . . . . caddisflies
   1. Heliocopsychidae . . . . snailcase caddisflies
   2. Hydropsychidae . . . . netspinning caddisflies
   3. Leptoceridae . . . . longhorned caddisflies
   4. Limnephilidae . . . . northern caddisflies
   5. Phryganeidae . . . . large caddisflies
   6. Psychomyiidae . . . . tubemaking and trumpetnet caddisflies
   7. Rhyacophilidae . . . . primitive caddisflies
Z. Lepidoptera . . . . butterflies, moths, and skippers
   1. Acrolepiidae . . . . acrolepiid moths
   2. Agonoxenidae . . . . nut and fruit borers
   3. Arctiidae . . . . tiger moths
   4. Argyresthiidae . . . . argyresthiid moths
   5. Bombycidae . . . . silkworm moths
   6. Choreutidae . . . . choreutid moths
   7. Cochylidae . . . . cochylid moths
   8. Coleophoridae . . . . casebearer moths

9. Cosmopterigidae . . . . leaf miner moths
10. Cossidae . . . . carpenterworm and leopard moths
11. Danaidae . . . . milkweed butterflies
12. Dioptidae . . . . oakworms
13. Elachistidae . . . . grass leafminer moths
14. Gelechiidae . . . . gelechiid moths
15. Geometridae . . . . geometrid moths and measuringworms
16. Glyphipterigidae . . . . glyphidteridid moths
17. Gracillariidae . . . . leafblotch miners
18. Heliodinidae . . . . heliodinid moths
19. Heliozelidae . . . . shield bearers
20. Hepialidae . . . . ghost moths and swifts
21. Hesperiidae . . . . skippers
22. Incurvariidae . . . . incurvariid moths
23. Lasiocampidae . . . . tent caterpillar moths
24. Limacodidae . . . . slug caterpillar moths
25. Lycaenidae . . . . blues, coppers, and hairstreaks
26. Lymantriidae . . . . tussock moths
27. Lyonetiidae . . . . lyonetiid moths
28. Megalopygidae . . . . flannel moths
29. Momphidae . . . . momphid moths
30. Nepticulidae . . . . nepticulid moths
31. Noctuidae . . . . owlet moths and underwings
32. Notodontidae . . . . notodontid moths
33. Nymphalidae . . . . brushfooted butterflies
34. Oecophoridae . . . . oecophorid moths
35. Papilionidae . . . . swallowtail butterflies
36. Pieridae . . . . whites and sulfur butterflies
37. Plutellidae . . . . diamondback moths
38. Psychidae . . . . bagworm moths
39. Pterophoridae . . . . plume moths
40. Pyralidae . . . . pyralid, grass, and wax moths
41. Riodinidae . . . . metalmarks
42. Saturniidae . . . . giant silkworm and royal moths

43.	Satyridae	satyr butterflies and wood nymphs
44.	Scythrididae	scythridid moths
45.	Sesiidae	clearwing moths
46.	Sphingidae	sphinx or hawk moths
47.	Tineidae	clothes moths
48.	Tischeriidae	tischeriid moths
49.	Tortricidae	leafroller and olethreutine moths
50.	Yponomeutidae	ermine moths
51.	Zygaenidae	leafskeletonizer moths
AA.	Coleoptera (includes Strepsiptera)	beetles
1.	Anobiidae	deathwatch and drugstore beetles
2.	Anthicidae	antlike flower beetles
3.	Anthribidae	fungus weevils
4.	Bostrichidae	false powderpost beetles
5.	Brentidae	brentid beetles
6.	Bruchidae	seed beetles
7.	Buprestidae	flatheaded or metallic wood borers
8.	Byturidae	fruitworm beetles
9.	Cantharidae	soldier beetles
10.	Carabidae	ground and tiger beetles
11.	Cerambycidae	longhorned beetles or roundheaded wood borers
12.	Chrysomelidae	leaf beetles
13.	Cleridae	checkered beetles
14.	Coccinellidae	lady beetles
15.	Cryptophagidae	silken fungus beetles
16.	Cucujidae	cucujid or flat bark beetles
17.	Curculionidae	snout beetles or weevils
18.	Dermestidae	dermestid beetles
19.	Dytiscidae	predaceous diving beetles
20.	Elateridae	click beetles or wireworms
21.	Elmidae	riffle beetles
22.	Gyrinidae	whirligig beetles
23.	Histeridae	hister beetles
24.	Hydrophilidae	water scavenger beetles
25.	Lampyridae	fireflies or lightningbugs

8. Braconidae . . . . braconid wasps
9. Cephidae . . . . stem sawflies
10. Chalcididae . . . . chalcidid wasps
11. Chrysididae . . . . cuckoo wasps
12. Cimbicidae . . . . cimbicid sawflies
13. Colletidae . . . . colletid bees
14. Cynipidae . . . . cynipids or cynipid gall wasps
15. Diprionidae . . . . conifer sawflies
16. Dryinidae . . . . dryinid wasps
17. Encyrtidae . . . . encyrtid wasps
18. Eulophidae . . . . eulophid wasps
19. Eurytomidae . . . . eurytomids, jointworms, and seed chalcids
20. Evaniidae . . . . ensign wasps
21. Formicidae . . . . ants
22. Halictidae . . . . halictid and sweat bees
23. Ichneumonidae . . . . ichneumons or ichneumon wasps
24. Magachilidae . . . . leafcutting bees
25. Mutillidae . . . . velvet ants
26. Pamphilidae . . . . webspinning and leafrolling sawflies
27. Pelecinidae . . . . pelecinid wasps
28. Pompilidae . . . . spider wasps
29. Pteromalidae . . . . pteromalid wasps
30. Scelionidae . . . . scelionid wasps
31. Siricidae . . . . horntails
32. Sphecidae . . . . cicadakillers, mud daubers, and sand wasps
33. Syntexidae . . . . syntexid wasps
34. Tenthredinidae . . . . tenthredinid sawflies
35. Tiphiidae . . . . tiphiid wasps
36. Torymidae . . . . torymid wasps
37. Trichogrammatidae . . . . trichogrammatid wasps
38. Vespidae . . . . hornets, yellowjackets, potter wasps, and paper wasps
39. Xyelidae . . . . xyelid sawflies

Entomological Society of America

Proposal Form for New Common Name or Change of ESA-Approved Common Name

The proposer is expected to be familiar with the rules, recommendations, and procedures outlined in the introduction to the current approved list of names and with the discussion by A. B. Gurney, 1953, J. Econ. Entomol. 46: 207–211.

The undersigned recommends to the ESA Standing Committee on Common Names of Insects the adoption of the following common name or name change:

1. Proposed new common name _____

2. Previously approved common name (if any) _____

3. Scientific name (genus species author)_____

   Order _____Family _____

Supporting Information

4. Economic or medical importance (include references):

5. Other reasons supporting the need for the proposed common name:

6. Stage or characteristic to which the proposed common name refers:

7. Distribution (include references):

8. Principal hosts (include references):

Proposal Form for New Common Name or Change of ESA-Approved Common Name

9. References containing previous use of the proposed common name:

10. References using common names (give names) other than that proposed:

11. Other insects or organisms to which the proposed common name might apply:

12. Steps you have taken to consult with other workers who are familiar with the insect or organism, as to suitability of and need for the proposed common name:

Proposed by Dr., Mr., Mrs., Miss, Ms. _____

Address _____   Telephone _____

_____

_____   Date _____

_____

Please send the original and, if possible, eight copies of the completed proposal form and all supporting material to the current committee chairman or to

Entomological Society of America
Attn: Standing Committee on Common Names of Insects
9301 Annapolis Road
Lanham, Maryland 20706   USA
(301) 731-4535